Global Power Shift

Ample empirical evidence points to recent power shifts in multiple areas of international relations taking place between industrialized countries and emerging powers, as well as between states and non-state actors. However, there is a dearth of theoretical interpretation and synthesis of these findings, and a growing need for coherent approaches to understand and measure the transformation. The central issues to be addressed include theoretical questions and empirical puzzles: How can studies of global power shift and the rise of 'emerging powers' benefit from existing theories, and which alternative aspects and theoretical approaches might be suitable? How can the meanings, perceptions, dynamics, and consequences of global power shift be determined and assessed? This edited series will include highly innovative research on these topics. It aims to bring together scholars from all major world regions as well as different disciplines, including political science, economics and human geography. The overall aim is to discuss and possibly blend their different approaches and provide new frameworks for understanding global affairs and the governance of global power shifts.

All titles in this series are peer-reviewed.

This book series is indexed in Scopus.

Gorden Moyo • Sabelo J. Ndlovu-Gatsheni
Editors

Global Storms and Africa in World Politics

Contemporary Challenges and Decolonial Responses

Springer

Editors
Gorden Moyo
Faculty of Humanities
University of the Free State
Qwaqwa, South Africa

Sabelo J. Ndlovu-Gatsheni
Faculty of Humanities and Social Science
University of Bayreuth
Bayreuth, Germany

ISSN 2198-7343 ISSN 2198-7351 (electronic)
Global Power Shift
ISBN 978-3-031-83867-5 ISBN 978-3-031-83868-2 (eBook)
https://doi.org/10.1007/978-3-031-83868-2

This Springer imprint is published by the registered company Springer Nature Switzerland AG
The registered company address is: Gewerbestrasse 11, 6330 Cham, Switzerland

About the Book

This book focuses on ecological, normative, ideological, systemic, institutional, structural, ethical, and epistemic storms that are haunting the Global South and Africa in particular. Africa is an ideal locus of enunciation to examine these global storms. There are many reasons that make thinking from Africa into the world very important. The *first* is how Africa is positioned within the modern world system. As a result of how it was subjected to the transcendental model of power called coloniality, which ensued from the fifteenth century, Africa continues to occupy a subaltern position. This positionality enables a consistent critique of the operations of the modern world system and it's shifting global orders. The *second* is that Africa continues to be a site of anti-racism, anti-enslavement, anti-colonialism, and anti-racial capitalism—these being motive forces for reworlding the world from the vantage point of the oppressed and exploited. The *third* is that Africa continues to be represented as a geographical frontier available for conquest, exploration, and handsome financial profit opportunities for investors. The *fourth* is that Africa continues to exhibit fragility and vulnerability to global storms within a context in which it has consistently been made into an object rather than agent of development. The *fifth* is that there is no African problem which is not simultaneously a global problem. By tackling the global storms from Africa's perspective, the book surfaces the historical asymmetries that stand on the way of resolving them, hence its quest for decolonial African agency that is capable of liberating the continent from global structures of dominance.

Contents

1 **Introduction: Reflections on Global Storms from African Locus of Enunciation** 1
Sabelo J. Ndlovu-Gatsheni and Gorden Moyo

Part I Global Financial Architecture and Debt Crisis

2 **Decolonising the Global Financial Architecture: Towards Financial Sovereignty in Africa** 17
Arthur Fidelis Chikerema and Vincent Chakunda

3 **Specters of Global Financial Apartheid in Africa** 39
Gorden Moyo

4 **Development Under Threat: The Return of the Debt Crisis in Africa** 59
Sizo Nkala

5 **Creditor Contributions, Benefits, and Solutions to Debt Crisis in Africa** 77
Janet Mudzviti-Zhou

Part II Global Climate Crisis

6 **Climate Colonialism in Africa** 101
Vincent Chenzi, Nyasha Trishia Murau, and Washington Mazorodze

7 **The Bane of Climate Colonialism in Africa: A Decolonial Approach** 119
Mufaro Dzingirai, Tatenda Leeroy Murombedzi, and Anesu Ndoro

8 **Capitalocene and Disaster Capitalism: Reflections on the Climate Crisis in Africa** 133
Vincent Chenzi, Nyasha Trishia Murau, and Admire Ndamba

9 **Implications of Climate Crisis in Southern Africa** 151
Gracsious Maviza, Divane Nzima, Siyaxola Enerst Gadu, and Ntobeko Ndlovu

Part III Global Health Crisis

10 **Vaccine Apartheid: An Indictment of Global Health System** 169
Ephraim Chifamba

11 **Vaccine Imperialism** 183
Chambiwa Elijah and Sakirai Gift

12 **External Funding for Small and Medium-Sized Enterprises in Post-COVID Africa** 199
Wehnam Peter Dabale

13 **COVID-19 and the Global South: An Integrative Review** 211
Idah Moyo and Benny Moyo

14 **Emergency Humanitarian Commodity Management Conundrum During the COVID-19 Pandemic Era: A Zimbabwean Experience** 223
Shepherd Gudyani

Part IV Russo-Ukraine War, Coups in Africa and African Agency

15 **The Impact of the Russia-Ukraine War on the Global South: The Case of Africa** 243
Charles Mutasa

16 **Russia's Search for International Recognition and Ontological Security in the Global South Post the Ukraine Conflict** 255
Dylan Yanano Mangani and Ntsikelelo Benjamin Breakfast

17 **Resurgence of Coups and Anti-French Sentiments in West Africa: A Review of the "Unconstitutional" Change of Governments in Burkina Faso and Niger** 271
Divane Nzima, Mubarak Aliyu, Herbert Mba Aki, and Gorden Moyo

18 **Global Politics and Recent Political Changes in West and Central Africa: A Decolonial Analysis** 289
Funa Moyo and Sihlanganiso Khumalo

19 **Coups d'etat and Democratic Backsliding in Africa: Legitimizing Unconstitutional Power Grabs and Implications for Continental Political Stability** 307
Aaron Rwodzi

20 **African Agency in the Context of a New World Dis(Order)** 327
Mbongeni Nhliziyo

About the Editors

Gorden Moyo, PhD is currently the Senior Research Fellow in the Department of Sociology, Faculty of Humanities at the University of the Free State (UFS) in South Africa; Senior Lecturer in the Faculty of Social Sciences and Humanities at Lupane State University (LSU) in Zimbabwe; Member of the Editorial Board of the Sabella Abidde Publishing House, University of Alabama (USA); Director of the Public Policy and Research Institute of Zimbabwe (PPRIZ); Associate Member of the International Society for Development and Sustainability (ISDS) in Japan; the President of the Development Studies Association of Zimbabwe (DeSAZ); Member of the Southern African Development Parliamentary Forum Technical Group on Public Financial Management; ex-Minister of State in the Prime Minister's Office, ex-Minister of State Enterprises and Parastatals, and ex-Member of Parliament of Zimbabwe (2009–2013); ex-British Council Facilitator of the Pan-African Leadership Interaction Programme in 19 countries across Africa including Botswana, Cameroon, Eritrea, Ethiopia, Eswatini, Ghana, Kenya, Lesotho, Liberia, Malawi, Mauritius, Namibia, Nigeria, South Africa, Tanzania, Uganda, Zambia, and Zimbabwe. He is a Chevening Scholar whose primary research interests are in global finance, international economic relations, developmental states, public leadership, military commercialism, Africa-China relations, and African Agency among others. He has published several articles in peer-reviewed journals and several book chapters. His most recent books include *African Agency, Finance, and Developmental States* (Palgrave McMillan, 2021); *Making Politics in Zimbabwe's Second Republic: The Formative Project by Emmerson Mnangagwa* (Springer, 2023) co-edited with Prof Kirk Helliker; and *Africa in the Global Economy: Capital Outflows, Enablers and Decolonial Responses* (Springer, 2024).

Sabelo J. Ndlovu-Gatsheni is currently Professor and Chair of Epistemologies of the Global South with Emphasis on Africa and Vice-Dean of Research in the Africa Multiple Cluster of Excellence at the University of Bayreuth in Germany; Professor Extraordinarius in the Department of Leadership and Transformation (DLT) in the Principal and Vice-Chancellor's Office at the University of South Africa (UNISA); Professor Extraordinarius at the Centre for Gender and African Studies at the University of Free State (UFS) in South Africa; Honorary Professor in the School of Education (Education & Development Studies) at the University of KwaZulu-Natal (UKZN) in South Africa; Research Associate at the Ali Mazrui Centre for Higher Education at the University of Johannesburg (UJ) in South Africa; Research Associate at the Department of Political Science at the University of Pretoria (UP) in South Africa; and Research Associate at The Ferguson Centre for African and Asian Studies at The Open University in the United Kingdom. Professor Ndlovu-Gatsheni is a prolific scholar with a hundred publications including more than 20 books to his name. His latest publications include *Epistemic Freedom in Africa: Deprovincialization and Decolonization* (Routledge, 2018); *Decolonization, Development and Knowledge in Africa: Turning Over A New Leaf* (Routledge, 2020); *Marxism and Decolonization in the 21st Century: Living Theories and True Ideas* (Routledge, 2022) co-edited with Morgan Ndlovu; and *Beyond the Coloniality of Internationalism: Reworlding the World from the Global South* (CODESRIA Book Series, 2024). The leading African historian Professor Toyin Falola has written a book-length study on his work entitled *Sabelo Ndlovu-Gatsheni and Decolonial African Studies* (Routledge, 2024).

List of Abbreviations and Acronyms

AfCFTA	African Continental Free Trade Area
ASEAN	Association of Southeast Asian Nations
AU	African Union
BASIC	Brazil, South Africa, India, and China
BIPOC	Black, Indigenous, and People of Color
BP	British Petroleum
BRICS	Brazil Russia India China South Africa
CAR	Central African Republic
CDD	Centre for Democracy and Development
CDM	Clean Development Mechanism
CIA	Central Intelligence Agency
CO_2	Carbon Dioxide
COMESA	Common Market for Eastern and Southern Africa
COP	Conference of Parties
COVID-19	Coronavirus disease, an infectious disease caused by the SARS-CoV-2 virus
CSB	Corn-Soya Blend Plus porridge
DRR	Disaster Risk Reduction
EAC	East African Community
ECOWAS	Economic Community of West African States
EGPS	Emergent Global Political Society
FDI	Foreign Direct Investment
FDP	Food Distribution Points
EU	European Union
GDP	Gross Domestic Product
GFA	Global Financial Architecture
GHG	Green House Gases
GWL	Global Warming Level
HDP	Humanitarian-Development-Peace
HSCs	Humanitarian Supply Chains

IBSA	India, Brazil, and South Africa
IFI	International Financial Institution
IFRC	International Federation of Red Cross
IKS	Indigenous Knowledge Systems
IMF	International Monetary Fund
IPC	Infection Prevention and Control
IPCC	Intergovernmental Panel on Climate Change
LICS	Low-Income Countries
LSA	Lean Season Assistance
MENA	Middle East and North Africa
MICS	Middle-Income Countries
MMC	Multihazard Mitigation Council
MSUs	Mobile Storage Units
MTAC	Microsoft Treat Analysis Centre
NATO	North Atlantic Treaty Organisation
NEPAD	New Partnership for Africa's Development
NGOs	Non-Governmental Organizations
NFIs	Non-Food Items
NIES	Newly Industrialized Economies
OCED	Organisation for Economic Co-operation and Development
ODA	Official Development Assistance
PIDA	Programme for Infrastructure Development in Africa
PPE	Personal Protective Equipment
REC	Regional Economic Community
RT	Russia Today
SADC	Southern African Development Community
SAPs	Structural Adjustment Programs
SDGs	Sustainable Development Goals
SDRs	Special Drawing Rights
SFDRR	Sendai Framework for Disaster Risk Reduction
SIU	Special Investigating Unit
TIKA	Turkish Co-Operation Agency
UN	United Nations
UNCCS	United Nations Climate Change Secretariat
UNDAC	United Nations Disaster Assessment and Coordination
UNDP	United Nations Development Program
UNDRR	United Nations Office for Disaster Risk Reduction
UNFCCC	United Nations Framework Convention on Climate Change
UNGA	United Nations General Assembly
UNSC	United Nations Security Council
UNWFP	United Nations World Food Programme
USA	United States of America
WB	World Bank

WFP	World Food Programme
WHO	World Health Organization
WHS	World Humanitarian Summit
WST	World Systems Theory

Chapter 1
Introduction: Reflections on Global Storms from African Locus of Enunciation

Sabelo J. Ndlovu-Gatsheni and Gorden Moyo

Abstract This introductory chapter is a gateway to the profound discussions about the global polycrisis and its implications for Africa and the rest of the Global South. The chapter locates Africa's experience within the discursive contexts, histories, geographies, biographies, and politics of crises. In this way, it serves a double purpose. On the one hand, it introduces the reader to the global storms ranging from ecological/climatic, normative, ideological, financial, health, unemployment, systemic, institutional, structural, and ethical to epistemic crises that are haunting the world today. On the other hand, it is an invitation to the reader to interact with the ideas, insights, reflections, paradigms, and philosophies that interpret the global polycrisis from decolonial and other heterodox perspectives. To this extent, the chapter is a prospectus of the book you are reading now.

Introduction

Africa is an ideal locus of enunciation to examine contemporary global storms. There are many reasons that make thinking from Africa into the world very important. The first is how Africa is positioned within the modern world system. As a result of how Africa was subjected to the transcendental model of power called coloniality, which ensued from the fifteenth century, it continues to occupy a subaltern position. This positionality enables a consistent critique of the operations of the modern world system and its shifting global orders. The second is that Africa continues to be a site of anti-racism, anti-enslavement, anti-colonialism, and anti-racial capitalism—these being motive forces for reworlding the world from the vantage point of the oppressed and exploited (see Ndlovu-Gatsheni, 2024). The third is that

S. J. Ndlovu-Gatsheni
Faculty of Humanities and Social Science, University of Bayreuth, Bayreuth, Germany

G. Moyo (✉)
Faculty of Humanities, University of the Free State, Qwaqwa, South Africa

G. Moyo, S. J. Ndlovu-Gatsheni (eds.), *Global Storms and Africa in World Politics*, Global Power Shift, https://doi.org/10.1007/978-3-031-83868-2_1

Africa continues to be represented as a geographical frontier available for conquest, exploration, and handsome financial profit opportunities for investors (Alami, 2020). The fourth is that Africa continues to exhibit fragility and vulnerability to global storms within a context in which it has consistently been made into an object rather than an agent of development. The fifth is that there is no African problem that is not simultaneously a global problem.

This is why this book provides well-thought-out critical reflections on contemporary global storms haunting the world. These global storms range from ecological/climatic, normative, ideological, financial, health, unemployment, systemic, institutional, structural, and ethical to epistemic crises (Ndlovu-Gatsheni, 2024). Taken together, the multifaceted and multidimensional crises reflect what Aime Cesaire (1955/2000) correctly termed a "civilizational" crisis. The Western civilization in place, dominant, and hegemonic since the fifteenth century is besieged by crises. Euro-modernity as a leitmotif of Western civilization, has produced a litany of modern problems of which it is dismally failing to offer modern solutions. Cesaire (1955/2000) warned the world about clinging to a decadent and dying civilization that generates numerous problems and then turns away and ignores them. By then, in 1955, Cesaire identified colonialism and the labor questions as the key problems generated by Western civilization, of which it was ignoring.

The problem of colonialism has not yet been resolved. The shift from empires to modern nation-states that was pre-maturely celebrated as decolonization was largely part of the modern world system rebooting and reorganizing itself. This happened within the context of the modern world system that was besieged by anti-colonial and anti-imperialist forces as well as under pressure from the two emerging superpowers (the Soviet Union and the United States of America), which were opposed to physical empires. Therefore, the dismantlement of the physical empires was meant to enable a reorganization of the modern world into modern nation-states. For the Soviet Union and the United States of America, their agenda was to break physical empires, which were dominated by Britain and France, who were monopolizing trade. The "capital of capital" was shifting from Europe to North America as Europe had been weakened by the two world wars (1914–1918 and 1939–1945). In this context, a new global order of modern nation-states was ideal for the march of American capital across the world and the spread of American political influence. The Soviet Union was also able to "paint some parts of the world red" ideologically, within the context of the Cold War.

In short, the post-1945 global dispensation was never an age of genuine decolonization. The architecture of the transcendental model of power that emerged in the fifteenth century remained hierarchical, with the United States of America at its apex and the Soviet Union contending with it. Racism, patriarchy, and sexism remained as underpinnings of the hierarchical modern power structure. The hierarchical power structure reproduced itself within the United Nations to the extent that the victorious powers in the Second World War occupied the center of the Security Council with veto powers, whereas the new nation-states from the Global South became a quantity, not quality, within the General Assembly. It was within this context that such African critical thinkers as Kwame Nkrumah of Ghana (1965) coined "neo-colonialism" to capture the continuation of colonialism after the dismantlement of the physical empires. It was also within this context that such scholars as Walter Rodney (1972) wrote about how Europe underdeveloped Africa. The conditions of Africa were enabling a critical reading and interpretation of the modern world system from the vantage point of those it dominated, exploited, and repressed.

Racial capitalism continued to make Africa the provider of cheap labor and cheap raw materials. The modern global division of labor still reflected racial, colonial, patriarchal, and sexist logics in which those people who were racialized became the most exploited. Lands that were expropriated *gratis* were never restored to their previous owners except in countries like Zimbabwe, where it had to be taken by force, two decades after independence. For daring to take land and distribute it to its rightful owners, Zimbabwe was accused of having violated property rights, human rights, and democracy. Sanctions were imposed on it. All these are signs of a world that is still underpinned by global colonial matrices of power supportive of a racially hierarchized and gendered modern world system.

Of course, the dominated peoples of the world confronted and fought against the hierarchical modern world system, and they used different grammars of liberation. These grammars of liberation ranged from abolition, decolonization, Africanization, deracialization, feminisms, indigenization, restitution, and reparations to epistemological decolonization (see Ndlovu-Gatsheni, 2018). The anti-systemic forces for liberation and freedom challenged what James Blaut (1993) termed the "colonizer's model of the world." The African anti-colonial nationalists of various ideological persuasions tried to create postcolonial nation-states with their own national economies that serviced the Africans rather than global capital in the 1960s and 1970s. The popular national projects of the 1960s and 1970s were characterized by attempts to turn the colonially created economies, which were outside-looking in the service of global imperial designs, into national economies that were inward-looking and of service to African people (also see Moyo, 2021; Ndlovu-Gatsheni, 2023).

Rigged Global Financial Architecture

By the mid-1970s, African national projects were failing, and economies in Africa were collapsing. It was within this context that agents of global imperial designs, namely the Bretton Woods financial institutions (International Monetary Fund and World Bank), prescribed structural adjustment programs to African governments. The central logic and message of structural adjustment programs was for African governments to abandon national projects and let economies in Africa continue looking outside and servicing global capital in lieu of economic growth (Moyo, 2024). Economic growth was sold to African governments as though it was development itself. Such conditionalities as deregulation, destatization, desubsidization, decontrol, downsizing, and privatization were meant to allow global capital to march unhindered across the continent and to reap profits. Consequently, Africa underwent a shift from economic development to economic growth.

The result was deep indebtedness of Africa to the bilateral creditors, including the Paris Club, global capital markets, and global financial institutions, in particular the duo of the IMF and the World Bank. The loan offers from these creditors and lenders became a key colonial matrix of power, sustaining a hierarchical model of the global financial system. Today, countries such as Burundi, Cameroon, Chad, Congo, Gambia, Ghana, Guinea, Sudan, Togo, Zambia, and Zimbabwe are, for all intents and purposes, debt states (Moyo, 2024). These countries have been trapped in a vicious cycle of debt distress where they borrow in order to borrow. Recently the IMF disbursed US$189 million to Zambia in order for the Southern African country to service its sovereign debt as part of its debt restructuring effort under the G-20 Common Framework on Debt Treatment. Just like the Highly Indebted Poor Countries (HIPC) programme of 1996, the Multilateral Debt Relief Initiative (MDRI) of 2005, and the Debt Service Suspension Initiative (DSSI) of 2020, the G-20 Common Framework for Debt Treatments is bound to fire blanks, and countries like Zambia, Ethiopia, and Chad that are fancying resolving their debt conundrum through this truncated global financial architecture will be disappointed like others before them. The fact is that the Bretton Woods Institutions (BWIs) have never confronted the structural factors that have continued to consign African countries to penury. As Kaboub (2023) noted, these institutions have no vision for de-imperializing finance or decolonizing African economies or addressing the aetiologies and root causes of external financial and economic ills on the African continent and the global South in general.

What is worrying is that African countries are losing more finance capital through a colonially designed global financial system that facilitates mispricing, profit shifting, profit transfers, and tax dodging, among many other modes of capital outflows from Africa and the other economically vulnerable global South economies (Christensen, 2009; UNCTAD, 2020; Inieke, 2021; Moyo, 2021). The money that is lost via capital outflows from Africa is far more than the funds the continent receives in the form of grants, aid, loans, and foreign direct investment. If the Euro-Western powers, as well as tax havens that act as sanctuaries for illicit funds, were to repatriate the stolen money back to Africa, then African countries would not need to borrow, nor would they need aid from their erstwhile ex-colonizers and their juridical institutions. To be clear, the negative net financial flows are the direct result of the role that was historically imposed on the African continent as the geography where the industrialized countries acquire cheap raw materials and where the industrial output from the global North and, more recently, also from the global East, is dumped in a large consumer market (Kaboub, 2023).

Neoliberal scholars such as Freidrich Hayek, Milton Friedman, Ludwig von Mises, and James Buchanan, and many more, present the global North countries and their financial and economic institutions as endowed with messianic qualities, which they generously use to support the poor African countries. Their logic is upside down. In fact, their views have lost theoretical purchase in Africa and the rest of the global South as it is dawning on more and more people that, in fact, Africa is a net creditor to the rest of the world (Ndikumana & Boyce, 2001). There is no harm in iterating that more funds leave Africa to the rest of the world than funds are received in Africa from the rest of the world per year. This confirms that Africa is a rich continent with poor people. No wonder why some scholars, building on paradigms of racial capitalism, have renovated a research agenda on the "color of money," "racism in finance," and "financial apartheid" (see Torkelson, 2020; Morgan, 2020; University of Missouri-Kansas, 2020; Moyo, 2024). What is emerging in this emerging body of literature is that global relations of race and coloniality are reproduced through the hegemony of the market that is sustained by the archetypical Northern financial, economic, and political institutions such as the World Trade Organization (WTO), World Bank, IMF, and North Atlantic Treaty Organization (NATO); international credit rating agencies, including the Big Three, namely, Fitch Investment, Moody's, and Standard and Poor's; and multinational corporations (MNCs), among others.

Global Racial Capitalism

The granite fact is that Africa and the rest of the global South are hostages to the coloniality of markets. This position has been perpetuated by structures, institutions, systems, and practices that were established at the time of colonial encounters, and these were not changed at independence. This is one of the reasons why a rupture with a colonial past is urgently required, especially during this era of global storms. Such scholars as Samir Amin (1990), who consistently studied global racial capitalism, suggested "delinking" as a strategy of economic liberation of Africa from global imperial designs. This strategy did not work mainly because the modern world system has devised methods of physical liquidation of those African leaders who were genuinely anti-systemic in their political practices. Examples of Patrice Lumumba of the Democratic Republic of Congo and Thomas Sankara of Burkina Faso come to mind. Others like Kwame Nkrumah suffered from sponsored military coups and were removed from power.

The period from 1973 became dominated by the neoliberal project. With its anti-statist philosophies and its projection of market fundamentalism, it wreaked havoc not only on economies but even on institutions of higher education. It enabled global financial capitalism with its particular capitalist epistemology of quantification of things, commercialization, and corporatization. Knowledge for life became knowledge for profits. Education for living became a commodity for sale. Students became customers who needed skills rather than knowledge. Nature became a natural resource available for extraction. Extractivism became the main instrument of making wealth. Money became used to make more money. Development became the "development-industrial-complex" (Murrey & Delay, 2023) with a flourishing "humanitarian industry" at its center. In pursuit of profits and strategic resources, the foreign policies of dominant countries like the United States of America embraced the paradigm of war to invade Africa (Libya in 2011), Latin America (interferences in Venezuela), the Middle East (Iraq), and other parts of the world (Ndlovu-Gatsheni, 2024).

The current conjuncture is characterized by a plethora of crises born out of inimical global politics and misbehaviors of the dominant powers. Besides Western civilization (1500–2023) being in deep crisis, there is the crisis of the neoliberal project (1973–2023) as well as the crisis of US liberal hegemony (1945–2023). The so-called "rules-based" internationalism is in tatters. There are increased disputations over the control of global colonial matrices of power, taking the form of contestations between "re-westernization" (led by the United States of America and its European Union partners) and "dewesternization" led by China and its "global East" partners (Ndlovu-Gatsheni, 2023, 2024; Moyo, 2024). At another level, the global South (made up of Global Africa and Global East) is also intensifying struggles for decolonization/decoloniality as an unfinished liberation project predicated on what Sabelo J. Ndlovu-Gatsheni (2024) termed "reworlding the world from the global South." Deep structural issues, including terms of trade, capital flight, and financial subordination, should form the major part of the reworlding project. These structures have served to reproduce the marginalization and dependence of the African continent on external economies, finance, and trade, as well as technology, among other things.

It is within this context that this book was conceived as a timely intervention from Africa that is predicated on critical reflections on the contemporary global storms haunting the contemporary world. The book was conceived before the current resurgence of war between Israel and Palestine; hence it is not covered in this book. But what is emerging poignantly from this book is how the present conjuncture is characterized by resurgences of violence, war, and genocides, with the United States supporting factions rather than working for peace. The Israel-Palestine conflict is not new. It dates back to 1948 when the state of Israel was established within a region where it was not recognized and was deemed as an act of colonialism, dispossession, and displacement. What is clear is the crisis of leadership capable of mediating the conflicts and delivering peace. The United Nations is paralyzed in the face of escalating wars in Ukraine, Gaza, the Democratic Republic of Congo, Syria, and other parts of the world. The United States of America is also failing to pull the rest of the world behind its claims to be a leader of the so-called "free world."

Russia's military invasion of Ukraine is a sign of the times just as the genocidal operations of Israeli forces are in Gaza. There are signs of a civilizational crisis within which the paradigm of war is deployed strangely as though it will deliver peace. Military-industrial complexes, as merchants of war, are making massive profits. Previously, weapons were used to fight wars, and today, wars are fomented to sell weapons. Wars are part of what this book terms global storms. As such, the book takes a global historical approach, theorizes about coercive integration of Africa into the modern global system, focuses on the global storms, and decouples technologies of subjectivation that underpin the subordinate position of Africa in the modern global system.

Organization of the Book

The book is divided into four broad parts covering issues of the global financial crisis, global climate crisis, global health crisis, and the Russia-Ukraine War, as well as the renewed spate of military coups in Africa. Part I of the book begins with Chakunda and Chikerema, who discuss how Africa navigates and circumvents some hurdles that affect the continent's quest to reconfigure the global financial system to achieve financial sovereignty. The authors raise a number of issues relating to Africa's marginalization in the global financial system, including the continent's weak global engagement strategy, dominance of Western-centric knowledge and expertise, debt burden, and unsustainable finance. The authors note that in the context of these wide-ranging issues, there is a notable expansion and growing influence of the BRICS (Brazil, Russia, India, China, and South Africa) and the associated institutions that purport to challenge the existing hegemony of Western supremacy. However, the authors do not explore the degree to which the BRICS bloc and its expanded members, namely Egypt, Ethiopia, Iran, Saudi Arabia, and Turkiye, can be said to be providing an alternative financial architecture that could possibly help Africa to recover its financial independence. Nonetheless, the authors conclude that the continent should prioritize reforms that promote collective action for a more just and inclusive financial system, thus reducing dependency on external financial institutions and creating a more equitable and impartial financial system that supports the continent's development agenda.

The following chapter by Gorden Moyo discusses the notion of global financial apartheid that is implicated in the project of sustaining Africa as a Lilliputian of the world. He argues that although the world has changed a lot since the colonial encounters over five centuries ago, the subordinate position of Africa in the global algebra of power, economy, and finance has hardly shifted. Moyo traces the colonial genealogies and biographies of the current financial apartheid regime in Africa back to the structural defects caused by colonialism and extractive dependence. He argues that the global financial system has consigned African countries and those of the economically vulnerable countries of the Global South to dependencies such that they now lurch in the morass of the vicious cycle of financial dependence, financial subordination, and subjugation. He concludes by canvassing for radical transformation in Africa, without which existing patterns of financial dependence, domination, and subjugation will likely continue defining the future of the continent.

Sizo Nkala's chapter delves deeper into Africa's debt crisis from a historical and political economy perspective. He argues that the current debt crisis in Africa has been exacerbated by the ongoing Russia-Ukraine conflict and the sluggish global economic recovery from COVID-19, the dominance of private lenders, and the emergence of nontraditional lenders like China. Like the other authors in Part I, Nkala calls for radical transformation of the global financial architecture that will give a breathing space for African economies. Part I is completed by Janet Zhou, a debt justice researcher and activist who also takes up the centered theme of debt sustainability in Africa as a pressing concern, with significant implications for the continent's economic development and social progress. She examines how creditors are contributing to and benefiting from Africa's debt while also exploring how their proposed solutions have exacerbated, rather than resolved, the underlying debt problem in the continent. The author also traces the origins of the crisis back to unsustainable lending practices by international financial institutions, especially the World Bank and the IMF. She argues that the exploitative nature of lending arrangements, such as the issuance of loans with high interest rates, conditionalities, and collateralization of strategic assets, has enabled creditors to extract substantial financial gains while exacerbating the financial vulnerability of African nations. Zhou is critical of the solutions put forward by creditors, such as austerity measures and structural adjustment programs, as conditions for debt relief. These have resulted in social hardships, weakened public services, and hindered long-term development prospects, perpetuating the cycle of debt, as African countries struggle to meet repayment obligations.

Part II is comprised of Chaps. 6–10 that discuss the climate crisis. In Chap. 6, Vincent Chenzi, Nyasha Trishia Murau, and Admire Ndamba examine the role of the western capitalist system on climate change. The authors argue that climate change and its global challenges are intricately linked to the global capitalist system, which is driven by profit, resource extraction, and exploitation. The chapter attempts to respond to the questions: What role has the western capitalist system contributed to the current climate crisis? How has the global capitalist system affected the emergence and management of disasters on the continent? And, in what way are the capitalist-driven solutions to climate change impacting the continent?

In Chap. 7, Mufaro Dzingirai, Tatenda Leeroy Murombedzi, and Anesu Ndoro review the effects of the climate colonialism on climate crisis in Africa. The authors conclude by recommending that governments in Africa should advocate for climate policies that do away with dominant knowledge systems from the global North as well as the power imbalances related to international climate platforms. While Vincent Chenzi, Nyasha Trishia Murau, and Washington Mazorodze in Chap. 8 argue that climate interventions in Africa by the rich countries are part of what some observers have termed climate colonialism. These interventions include neoliberal policies such as carbon offsetting, green policing, natural resource exploitation, and smart solutions to climate change. The authors conclude by canvassing for the decolonization of climate change discourse in order to address the existential threat of climate change in Africa and the other vulnerable global South countries.

Happy Mathew Tirivangasi and Louis Nyahunda's chapter focuses on climate communication. They argue that the entanglement between climate and language creates a difficult challenge for how different people perceive, understand, and respond to the climate crisis. The authors propose that climate change communication should be decolonized and repackaged in the languages of African indigenous communities. Part II is concluded by Gracsious Mavisa and Divane Nzima with a chapter arguing that the imperialist world system has perpetuated climate imperialism and climate colonialism that have in turn created a capitalist climate economy. The authors also note that the global powers have managed to keep those most affected by climate change in perpetual dependence on the global North with limited resources available either for mitigation or adaptation. In short, the authors provide a comprehensive analysis of the adverse effects of climate devastation and how these effects are connected to climate imperialism.

Part III of the book examines the health crisis. While Chaps. 11, 12, and 13 examine the broader issues of vaccine imperialism, Chaps. 14 and 15 offer some country studies of Nigeria and Zimbabwe. In Chap. 11, Ephraim Chifamba deploys Freire's Pedagogy of the Oppressed and the decolonial lens to examine the linkage between capitalism and the unequal access to Covid-19 vaccines. The author argues that the public health sector has been caught up in the global 'vaccine apartheid, which impedes inclusive delivery of health in the global South generally and Africa in particular. The author views decolonization and de-imperialization of the global health systems as viable options for addressing unequal access to drugs and vaccines between the global North and global South. Similarly, in Chap. 12, Elijah Chambiwa and Gift Sakirai also discuss the notion of vaccine imperialism. The authors note that the distribution of COVID-19 vaccines wrought into existence a highly polarized world that was split between the wealthy global North and the poor global South countries. This state of affairs accentuated a historical imbalance that has been in existence since the era of colonial encounters. The global South is interminably othered and systematically relegated to the periphery of the existential matrix. The authors also note that the Western companies solely focused on Western countries whilst the global South was condemned to a terrible fate of facing the deadly disease without the respite of a vaccine.

In Chap. 13, Wehnam Peter Dabale provides a case study of a global storm from a local perspective. He examines the factors that influence the acquisition of external capital and their correlation with the success of small and medium-sized enterprises (SMEs) in Nigeria following the COVID-19 pandemic. The author discusses a number of obstacles that small and medium-sized enterprises (SMEs) encounter when seeking external financing, including the issue of elevated interest rates and rigorous collateral prerequisites, among others. The author concludes by suggesting that customized financial strategies be put in place to make it easier for small and medium-sized businesses to get external funding in the post-COVID-19 era. On the other hand, in Chap. 14, Shepherd Gudyani argues that the COVID-19 outbreak exacerbated the need for humanitarian assistance in Africa and the rest of the world. The author argues that the global logistics management concerns made it difficult for humanitarian attempts to contain the COVID-19 catastrophe in Africa. This chapter provides a case study of the role that mobile storage units played in Zimbabwe's response to the COVID-19 epidemic.

The final chapter of this part of the book discusses the fragility of health systems in Africa (Chap. 13). Idah Moyo and Benny Moyo note that the global South is characterized by fragile health systems, underfunding, manpower constraints, medicine, and other consumable shortages. These challenges were glaring during the COVID-19 pandemic. The authors note that whilst a large number of people were vaccinated in the global North, only a small minority were fully vaccinated in Africa and the other countries of the global South. Like other authors in this section, Moyo and Moyo note that the western-owned pharmaceutical companies were selective in their distribution to the North; as such, the authors conclude by calling for Africa to work on developing its own pharmaceutical companies and vaccines to avoid similar vaccine imperialism in responding to future pandemics.

The last part of the book (Part IV) addresses the challenging issues of the Russo-Ukraine War as well as the recent spate of coups that is sweeping across Africa. In Chap. 16, Charles Mutasa discusses the impact of the Russian-Ukrainian war on Africa's major and smaller nations. The author takes a critical look at the policy of neutrality that has been adopted by countries such as South Africa. The biggest questions tackled are: Is this war widening the rift between the Global North and Global South? What should be done to keep global unity and cooperation, considering the current impact and aftermath of the Russian-Ukrainian war? The author concludes by looking at possible future international cooperation scenarios and recommendations. At the same time, Dylan Yanano Mangani and Ntsikelelo Benjamin Breakfast (in Chap. 17) attempt a futuring study of Russia's international choices towards the global South after its war in Ukraine. The authors note that various interpretations surround Russia's invasion of Ukraine, including NATO's unmitigated expansion towards Eastern Europe and the subsequent security dilemma this posed for Russia. The chapter contributes some insights into Russia's recalibration of its foreign policy in the global South in search of allies, hegemonic status, and ontological security by taking advantage of resources at its disposal, such as military and natural resources.

In Chap. 18, Divane Nzima, Mubarak Aliyu, Herbert Mba Aki, and Gorden Moyo discuss the growing anti-French sentiments in the West and Central Africa regions. The authors focus on the recent coups in West and Central Africa in the context of the emerging global geopolitical makeup since the Russia-Ukraine war, given the acceptance of Russian private military groups in Africa. The authors also decouple the anti-imperial stance taken by coup leaders and supported by masses against the position taken by regional bodies such as the Economic Community of West African States (ECOWAS). They conclude that while the political direction of military governments is controversial, the wind of revolutionary victory against neo-colonial forces in the Sahel region cannot be escaped. In the same vein, Funa Moyo and Sihlanganiso Khumalo in Chap. 19 discuss the naturalized, universalized, and conveniently abused Euro-modern concept of 'coup d'état. The authors conclude that although the main causes of coups are painted local, in reality they have qualities of a global war, with a heavy influence of the former colonizers. The authors recommend decoloniality of governance as a possible conversation towards free decolonial pluriversal genial futures.

In Chap. 20, Aaron Rwodzi provides a damning critique of the local conditions in Africa and the incessant role of Western and Eastern international actors in providing coup leaders and their executors a helping hand towards the finish line to consolidate putsches' power. The author addresses four key questions: What explains the sudden plethora of coups in West and Central Africa? Why have coups been sanitized as if they represent basic characteristics of goodwill towards the collective good of the nations where they take place? Can soldiers who successfully organize the putsch be regarded as saviors of the people against recalcitrant regimes that do not yield to election results? What is the future of democracy amidst recurrent coups in Africa? The author concludes that continental and international legitimation of coups in Africa points to the failure of western democracy and heralds new perceptions about the futility of elections, particularly when, as is generally the case, they retain unpopular incumbents through chicanery.

The last chapter of this book by Mbongeni Nhliziyo draws the attention of the reader towards the brewing storm of the US–China contestations and their impact on the global response to developmental challenges such as climate change, peace, security, and health emergencies (Chap. 21). The author concludes that Africa must develop its own policy maturity, diplomatic adeptness, political leadership, and policy capacity in order to effectively engage with the US and China.

What the book does is to connect the dots of what constitutes global storms from an African vantage point. It is a timely study of the present conjuncture. Whenever a civilization and its underpinning global order are in deep crisis, conflicts, violence, and wars become inevitable. The global North is resistant to the rise of the global East. The global South is rejecting a subaltern position and being pulled behind United States Atlanticism as a hegemonic project. One emerging debate is on a polycentric world with China as its *primus inter peres* its leader. The lingering question is, will China preside over a still hierarchical model of power, with problems of racism, patriarchy, and sexism still unresolved? How prepared is China to enable genuine decolonization, depatriarchization, de-Cold War, and de-imperialization? How will the new polycentric world deal with global financial crises and ecological problems? Will China just take control of the global colonial matrices of power and only shift the capital of capital from North America and Europe to Beijing?

Of major concern is that the voting powers of China, Brazil, Russia, and India in the IMF Board of Governors have been increased at the expense of those of Africa in general and South Africa and Nigeria in particular. For example, while China's voting power increased by 35%, Brazil, India, and Russia increased by 23, 11, and 8 percentage points, respectively, Nigeria and South Africa had theirs reduced by 41% and 21%, respectively (see Moyo, 2024). This is despite the fact that African countries campaigned together with their emergent and emerging global South friends (Brazil, Russia, India, and China) for the IMF reforms, but when Africa got nothing out of the resultant reforms, its powerful global South friends looked aside and walked away. Again, there are concerns that poor countries seeking to access more than 30% of their borrowing quota from the New Development Bank (BRICS Bank) are obliged to first sign up to an IMF structural adjustment program, thus amplifying neoliberalism rather than eroding it (Moyo, 2024).

More worryingly, African countries are now more indebted to China than to any other bilateral lenders, including the US, the EU, the UK, Germany, and France, leading some observers to argue that China and other emerging powers are merely seeking accommodation in the global house of capitalism rather than seeking a fairer global governance order. Lastly, there are also questions of Chinese and Euro-Western elites seating in each other's corporate boards and strengthening their mutual global capitalist interests, especially during their Davos annual meetings.

The contradictions presented by these geofinancial convergences of global East and global West business elites, on one hand, and the geopolitical divergences represented by global East and global West political actors, call for a more nuanced role of Africa in the emerging multipolar global system. These contradictions should be part of the ongoing debates about how Africa should increase its global agency in order to avoid what Olukoshi (2023) described as the danger of moving from one unhappy partnership to another.

References

Alami, I. (2020). *'Afro-pessimism' and Emerging Market Finance*. https://www.manchesterhive.com/configurable/content/9781526163455$002f9781526163455.00024.xml?t:ac=9781526163455%24002f9781526163455.00024.xml

Amin, S. (1990). *Delinking: Towards a polycentric world*. Zed Books.

Blaut, J. M. (1993). *The Colonizer's model of the world*. The Gilford Press.

Cesaire, A. (1955/2000). *Discourse of colonialism*. Monthly Review Press.

Christensen, J. (2009). Africa's bane: Tax havens, Capital flight and the corruption interface. *Elcano Newsletter, 52*, 24. http://biblioteca.ribei.org/id/eprint/1782/1/WP-1-2009.pdf

Inieke, O. (2021). *African Financial Independence is a threat to Imperialism, Hood Communist (07 June)*. https://www.blackagendareport.com/index.php/african-financial-independence-threat-imperialism

Kaboub, F. (2023). *Decolonising the Global Economic Architecture: The prerequisite for a just transition*. https://www.brettonwoodsproject.org/2023/12/decolonising-the-global-economic-architecture-the-prerequisite-for-a-just-transition/

Morgan, R. (2020). *Race in finance-making black lives matter in financial services*. Racial Justice, Investors, Financial Advisors. https://adasina.com/race-in-finance-making-black-lives-matter-in-financial-services-installment-4-is-your-financial-advisor-working-against-systemic-racism/

Moyo, G. (2021). *African agency, finance and developmental states*. Palgrave Macmillan.

Moyo, G. (2024). *Africa in the global economy: Capital flight, financial subordination and decolonial responses*. Palgrave Macmillan.

Murrey, A., & Delay, P. (2023). *Learning disobedience: Decolonizing development studies*. Pluto Press.

Ndikumana, L., & Boyce, J. J. (2001). Is Africa a net creditor? New estimates of capital flight from severely indebted Su-Saharan African countries, 1970–1996. *Journal of Development Studies, 38*(2), 27–56. https://www.econstor.eu/bitstream/10419/105716/1/2000-01.pdf

Ndlovu-Gatsheni, S. J. (2018). *Epistemic freedom in Africa: Deprovincialization and decolonization*. Routledge.

Ndlovu-Gatsheni, S. J. (2023). Beyond the Coloniser's model of the world: Towards reworlding from the Global South. *Third World Quarterly, 44*(10), 2246–2262. https://doi.org/10.1080/01436597.2023.2171389

Ndlovu-Gatsheni, S. J. (2024). *Beyond the coloniality internationalism: Reworlding the World in Global South*. CODESRIA Books Series.

Nkrumah, K. (1965). *Neo-colonialism: The last stage imperialism*. International Publishers.

Olukoshi, A. (2023). *From rule-taker to rule maker: Africa in the changing world order*, European Council on Foreign Relations.

Rodney, W. (1972). *How Europe underdeveloped Africa*. Tanzania Publishing House.

Torkelson, E. (2020). Sophia's choice: Debt, social welfare, and racial finance capitalism. *Society and Space, 39*(1), 67–84. https://doi.org/10.1177/023775820973680

UNCTAD. (2020). World investment report 2020: International production beyond the pandemic. *United Nations Conference on Trade and Development*, Geneva and New York, 2020, 247 pp. ISBN: 978-9211129854. https://unctad.org/en/PublicationsLibrary/wir2020_en.pdf

University of Missouri-Kansas. (2020). *The color of money: Racism in finance*. https://www.umkc.edu/news/posts/2020/september/the-color-of-money-racism-in-finance.html

Sabelo J. Ndlovu-Gatsheni is currently Professor and Chair of Epistemologies of the Global South with Emphasis on Africa and Vice-Dean of Research in the Africa Multiple Cluster of Excellence at the University of Bayreuth in Germany; Professor Extraordinarius in the Department of Leadership and Transformation (DLT) in the Principal & Vice-Chancellor's Office at the University of South Africa (UNISA); Professor Extraordinarius at the Centre for Gender and African Studies at the University of Free State (UFS) in South Africa; Honorary Professor in the School of Education (Education & Development Studies) at the University of KwaZulu-Natal (UKZN) in South Africa; Research Associate at the Ali Mazrui Centre for Higher Education at the University of Johannesburg (UJ) in South Africa; Research Associate at the Department of Political Science at the University of Pretoria (UP) in South Africa; and Research Associate at The Ferguson Centre for African and Asian Studies at The Open University in the United Kingdom. Professor Ndlovu-Gatsheni is a prolific scholar with a hundred publications including more than 20 books to his name. His latest publications include *Epistemic Freedom in Africa: Deprovincialization and Decolonization* (Routledge, 2018); *Decolonization, Development and Knowledge in Africa: Turning Over A New Leaf* (Routledge, 2020); *Marxism and Decolonization in the 21st Century: Living Theories and True Ideas* (Routledge, 2022) co-edited with Morgan Ndlovu; and *Beyond the Coloniality of Internationalism: Reworlding the World from the Global South* (CODESRIA Book Series, 2024). The leading African historian Professor Toyin Falola has written a book-length study on his work entitled *Sabelo Ndlovu-Gatsheni and Decolonial African Studies* (Routledge, 2024).

Gorden Moyo (PhD) is currently the Senior Research Fellow in the Department of Sociology, Faculty of Humanities at the University of the Free State (UFS) in South Africa; Senior Lecturer in the Faculty of Social Sciences and Humanities at Lupane State University (LSU) in Zimbabwe; Member of the Editorial Board of the Sabella Abidde Publishing House, University of Alabama (USA); Director of the Public Policy and Research Institute of Zimbabwe (PPRIZ); Associate Member of the International Society for Development and Sustainability (ISDS) in Japan; the President of the Development Studies Association of Zimbabwe (DeSAZ); Member of the Southern African Development Parliamentary Forum Technical Group on Public Financial Management; ex-Minister of State in the Prime Minister's Office, ex-Minister of State Enterprises and Parastatals, and ex-Member of Parliament of Zimbabwe (2009–2013); ex-British Council Facilitator of the Pan-African Leadership Interaction Programme in 19 countries across Africa including Botswana, Cameroon, Eritrea, Ethiopia, Eswatini, Ghana, Kenya, Lesotho, Liberia, Malawi, Mauritius, Namibia, Nigeria, South Africa, Tanzania, Uganda, Zambia, and Zimbabwe. He is a Chevening Scholar whose primary research interests are in global finance, international economic relations, developmental states, public leadership, military commercialism, Africa–China relations, and African Agency among others. He has published several articles in peer-reviewed journals and several book chapters. His most recent books include *African Agency, Finance, and Developmental States* (Palgrave McMillan, 2021); *Making Politics in Zimbabwe's Second Republic: The Formative Project by Emmerson Mnangagwa* (Springer, 2023) co-edited with Prof Kirk Helliker; and *Africa in the Global Economy: Capital Outflows, Enablers and Decolonial Responses* (Springer, 2024).

Part I
Global Financial Architecture and Debt Crisis

Chapter 2
Decolonising the Global Financial Architecture: Towards Financial Sovereignty in Africa

Arthur Fidelis Chikerema and Vincent Chakunda

Abstract The global financial architecture has been shaped by colonial legacies and power imbalances that have generally disadvantaged the Global South. The present international monetary system emerged from the Bretton Woods Conference in 1944. The Bretton Woods Institutions promoted the acceleration of globalization and the Global South's economic dependence. The existing global financial system perpetuates deeper fragmentation despite multipolarity and geopolitical competition. The expansion of the BRICS brings a critical dimension to global financial and decoloniality discourse. The block's economic strength, demographic weight, and geopolitical significance challenge the dominance of the Western hegemony in shaping global power dynamics. Guided by a desktop approach, the chapter is underpinned by the decoloniality paradigms. The major issues emerging from the analysis relate to the continent's weak global engagement strategy and the dominance of Western knowledge. The chapter recommends reforms that promote collective action for an inclusive financial system that supports Africa's development agenda.

Introduction

The global financial architecture has been dominated and defined by the global north, perpetuating historical legacies of colonialism and neo-colonial economic practices. Arguably, this global financial system is wired to promote Eurocentric epistemologies that seem to propagate economic disparities and hinder the global south's progression. The structure of the global financial system has been viewed as alien to the global south's developing aspirations, leading to a growing movement towards advocating for the decolonization of the system and promoting financial sovereignty in Africa. The emergence of what is known as Developing and Emerging

A. F. Chikerema (✉) · V. Chakunda
Governance and Public Management, Midlands State University, Gweru, Zimbabwe
e-mail: chikeremaaf@staff.msu.ac.zw; chakundav@staff.msu.ac.zw

G. Moyo, S. J. Ndlovu-Gatsheni (eds.), *Global Storms and Africa in World Politics*, Global Power Shift, https://doi.org/10.1007/978-3-031-83868-2_2

Economies (DEEs) has signified one of the most momentous transformations in the global fiscal landscape in contemporary eras (Alami, 2022). For instance, by 2010, China had assumed the position of the world's leading exporter, while by 2018, foreign direct investment (FDI) flowing into DEEs had exceeded that directed to developed nations (UNCTAD, 2019). Despite their increasing economic influence and prominence in the global economy, DEEs have not managed to alter their subordinate status within global fiscal markets. This is evidenced by recurring instances of abrupt exchange rate devaluations and financial instability, often influenced by conditions prevailing in international financial markets (Naqvi, 2019). Nevertheless, the financial subordination of DEEs extends well beyond sporadic crises, significantly shaping everyday economic interactions that carry extensive implications for the development prospects of the global south. These implications range from decision-making processes to industrial advancements, urban development patterns, spatial reorganization, class dynamics, distributional conflicts, and the movement of value transfer across borders (Rey, 2015). Although growth rates higher than those in the global north have been achieved in numerous DEEs for particular periods, very few have managed to sustain this process long enough to witness per capita wealth reach the levels of developed countries (Rey, 2015).

This chapter posits that financial subordination seems to be a structural impediment contributing to persistent global inequalities. Evidence echoes Rey's (2015) contention that DEEs are increasingly subjected to a global financial/liquidity cycle over which they have no control, and which renders many domestic policy levers irrelevant. Furthermore, for Reys, the decoloniality movement seeks to address the structural imbalances and power dynamics that have marginalized global south economies and empower the global north to determine their own economic policies and development conduits. During the colonial era, global South economies were primarily exploited for the benefit of colonial powers, leading to the extraction of resources and the establishment of economic structures that favored external interests (Nkrumah, 1965). Authors such as Walter Rodney have argued that the global north developed through plundering and exploiting resources from the global south, resulting in the skewed geopolitical arrangements of the core and the periphery. The geopolitical arrangement was couched and dominated by Western modes of economic, political, and epistemic productions, which universalized "European" values over other development paradigms. According to Nabudere (2013), the contradictions of capitalism in 'Europe have been transplanted to other parts of the world in an attempt to promote economic accumulation at the expense of cheap labor.

Following independence, most African nations inherited financial systems that were designed to serve the interests of the global north, perpetuating economic dependence and limiting their ability to pursue sovereign and indigenous development models hinged on the local context. The current global financial architecture, dominated by Eurocentric institutions—the International Monetary Fund (IMF) and the World Bank—has often imposed straitjacket approaches and uniform economic policies on African countries, without contextualizing their unique needs and circumstances (Nkrumah, 1965). The decoloniality movement calls for the global south to integrate, cooperate, and explore geopolitical and multipolar systems' comparative advantages to amplify their collective voice and influence in global financial governance. The major objective of the movement is for the global south to delink and reclaim financial sovereignty and have the power to redesign their economic policies and institutions, reducing reliance on the core. The chapter is divided into various sections. It explains the background of the global financial institutions to understand the dynamics of global monetary processes, debt policies, and the position of the Global South, Africa to be specific. The second aspect will deal with the explanation of the decolonial terms and paradigms that relate to international political economy. Finally, the paper will explain the contending issues that emerged from the review and analysis of international financial subordination and dependency literature and previous research.

Context of Global South's Financial Dependence

The theorization of colonialism and imperialism by Frantz Fanon (1967) in his book "Wretched of the Earth" led to the development of the decolonial theoretical praxis. Fanon described colonialism as the process of "mental demonization" or dispossession of the people of color by the colonial forms of cultures and knowledge production. For Fanon (1967), colonialism was more than physical; it reflected the mental discourse whereby the people of color are subjected to rages, referred to as damnes/wretched of the Earth. The section is hinged on two theories, namely, decolonial theory and theories of financial dependence. Decoloniality is a theoretical framework that emerged as a response to the ongoing legacies of colonialism and seeks to challenge and dismantle the structures of power, knowledge, and representation associated with colonialism. The decolonial theory originated from post-structural analysis of being, self, and society liberation. The theory emphasizes the disbandment of structures and institutions associated with the Enlightenment era, which was premised on the dominance of rationality, individualism, progress, and the pursuit of universal truths (Amin, 1974). Trans-modernity proposes an alternative framework that seeks to address pluralism and diversity of human experiences, cultures, and knowledge systems, emphasizing the acceptance and coexistence of multiple perspectives and rejecting the notion of a single universal truth or way of being (Maldonado-Torres, 2018). Evidence notes that the world needs to depict the hybrid nature of contemporary societies and the constant intermixing of cultures, identities, and ideas, promoting the idea of interculturality, where different cultures interact, exchange, and learn from each other, fostering dialogue and understanding. The theory underscores the importance of contextualizing and localizing funding and development policies, rejects the idea of universal solutions (SAPs), and calls for context-specific approaches that take into account local knowledge, histories, and conditions (Mignolo, 2013). Broader thinking (Anzaldua, 1983), delinking (Amin, 2009), and decoloniality (Mignolo, 2013) shape the trans-modernity methodological approach in dismantling the existing global coloniality of power, thought, and being. The theory defines the world as a Eurocentric construct depicting conditions that dehumanize, depersonalize, and epistemicide the non-Western world, which was facilitated through religion, trade, politics, and education (Maldonado-Torres, 2018). Mignolo (2013), one of the proponents of the decoloniality theory, due to what he viewed as a skewed global financial system, advocated for the global south to effect epistemic disobedience/de-linking as a decolonial option. Epistemic disobedience leads to the adoption of global south epistemologies of power, knowledge, being, and economics (Kapuya, 2019).

According to Duvisac (2022), decolonial theory offers a framework of tools and processes to realize decolonial futures. One of the tools is the analytical lens of coloniality to examine how colonialism continues to shape modern political, economic, cultural, social, and knowledge systems. Second is the call to de-link from coloniality; doing so means naming and continually unlearning, reimagining, and reshaping the structures, norms, and values that emerged from Western colonialism and continue to shape present-day economies, institutions, societies, and cultures. De-linking from coloniality occurs both at the societal and individual levels, and it requires individuals to interrogate how they may be reproducing systems of coloniality in daily life. The decolonial theory further advocates for individuals and institutions to center and cede power to the knowledge, voices, and experiences of people marginalized by colonialism and coloniality. Calls to decolonize should radically undo coloniality to create material changes. They must also be rooted in local histories and dynamics. Indigenous movements from the global south grouped under collective well-being should be formed and flourish (Duvisac, 2022). It is the conviction of the argument that the global south will radically reimagine concepts such as "development" by drawing on alternative knowledge systems and engaging in epistemic reconstitution and reparations. The global south needs to dismantle the core of mainstream Western developmental theory and advocate for a way of life that centers on justice for individuals within the context of community and environmental well-being. For example, this has meant advocating for property relations in which individuals do not own land and land resources but are rather stewards of them and have community permission to use associated resources, breaking from colonial frameworks of private property. For knowledge production systems, the theorists advocated for the development of education not as a mere tool to meet labor market needs but rather as one that enhances individuals' knowledge and relationship to the world they live in. The institutionalization of the reimagined knowledge production system will advocate for stronger community control and non-capitalist forms of market exchange and land use (Duvisac, 2022). The argument is also premised on the dependency theory, as it is relevant to understanding how IFS relates to structures of production. The factors driving IFS in dependency theory are traced back to the development of colonial systems of production and extraction that also impact the financial systems in the periphery. While financial subordination has been less theorized in the decoloniality literature than "real" subordination (Alami, 2022), significant contributions in the literature have delved into financial dependencies from two distinct perspectives. The first perspective links financial dependency to the real economy, where deficiencies in the latter drive the former. Nkrumah (1965) contended that despite formal decolonization in West

Africa, dependency endured due to foreign control within tightly consolidated banking sectors, structured to serve colonial interests by supporting production and extraction activities. The primary function of colonial banks was to finance the export of goods required by the colonizers and facilitate the repatriation of profits by metropolitan enterprises. Likewise, Amin (1974) highlighted that the monetary challenges faced by underdeveloped nations stemmed from their banking systems' emphasis on short-term financing rather than channelling savings into long-term investments. This extractive model has persisted across significant portions of the global periphery (Koddenbrock et al., 2022). Furthermore, Prebisch (1939) argued that dependent development led to peripheral economies' financial sector dependence on global liquidity and global business cycles. Prebisch (1939) emphasized that peripheral economies' subordination is also reflected in their inability to fine-tune monetary policies according to domestic needs, given that they are on the receiving end of financial cycles generated by core countries. In these analyses, the cause of subordination remains the structure of the productive economy. However, subordinate banking and monetary systems exacerbate the situation of dependence on the current global financial architecture.

The second important intervention in the dependency literature has come from theorists who see IFS as the primary driver of dependency. Tavares (1985) pioneered this line of reasoning, arguing that the fundamental obstacle to development was financial dependency, reflected in the inability of peripheral economies to borrow in their currencies. Within this view, it is intermittent access to finance (and especially foreign finance) that drives balance-of-payments constraints, ultimately leading to low growth (Vernengo, 2006). From the analysis, dependency theorists argue that the cause of IFS is due to peripherality in the global system and colonial legacies. In contrast, Marxist dependency theorists emphasized class analysis. For example, Marini (1973) viewed the working class in dependent nations as subjected to political domination and fiscal exploitation, akin to conditions in all capitalist societies, but highlighted that these class dynamics assume distinct configurations owing to international subjugation. According to Marini, to maintain an average profit rate, businesses in dependent economies enforce particularly severe forms of labor exploitation on their workers (referred to as "super-exploitation"). A contemporary interpretation of dependency theory by Musthaq (2021) extends Amin's notion of imperialist "labor arbitrage" to illustrate how hierarchical global monetary and financial relations create opportunities for imperial "financial arbitrage." Within a hierarchy favoring global reserve currencies, the increasing sensitivity of capital flows to monetary policies in developed nations exacerbates challenges for countries occupying subordinate monetary positions in the global economic framework (Sylla, 2021).

According to dependency theory, subordination impacts peripheral nations, corporations, financial sectors, and labor. The policy implications associated with the more radical branches of dependency theory often focus on the reformation of social dynamics by challenging the fundamental structures of the global capitalist system itself or by suggesting methods to rebalance power dynamics in favor of the peripheral working class within the international class framework. Conversely, less radical interpretations suggest ways to contest the hierarchical nature of the system within the capitalist framework, such as dismantling cartels in the core, allowing greater policy autonomy for peripheral nations, and devising strategies to shield peripheral actors from the recurring variations and shocks originating from the global fiscal arrangement. Both perspectives advocate for a form of epistemological confrontation to combat international fiscal subservience enforced by the current global financial framework.

Historicizing Global Financial Institutions

The history of global financial institutions can be traced back to the beginning of the twentieth century when the relations of states developed into financial exchanges for industrial development (Calomiris & Neal, 2020). The development and evolution of these institutions have been shaped by a multifaceted interplay of historical events, power dynamics, and economic ideologies. In 1944, the world experienced the transformation of an "international political economy" into a more capitalist one in an attempt to facilitate the processes of globalization (Williamson, 2008). In 1944, the Bretton Woods Conference discussed the potential of global financial institutions (Barrow & Lee, 2003) and passed a resolution of establishing financial institutions to assist the reconstruction of states affected by war based on non-interest loans. In 1945, the San Francisco Conference, as a post-war settlement, authorized the establishment of the World Bank (WB) and International Monetary Fund (IMF) to fund the reconstruction of "Europe" ((Williamson, 2008). The establishment of the Bretton Woods system marked a significant turning point in the history of global finance. However, from their inception, these institutions were dominated by Western powers, particularly the United States and European nations, reflecting the geopolitical realities of the time. Suggestions note that though the Bretton Woods system has occasionally been adjusted to reflect the acceleration of globalization and countries' deepening economic interdependence, it has amplified business-cycle fluctuations, impeded economic catch-up by poorer countries, and perpetuated the dichotomy of developed and developing countries.

The 1980s and 1990s also observed the escalation of neoliberal economic dogmas and the so-called "Washington Consensus" (Williamson, 2008). Neoliberalism emphasized free market principles, deregulation, and abridged state intervention in the economy. This ideology strongly influenced the policies advocated by global financial institutions, leading to an emphasis on market-oriented reforms and a reduced role for the state in economic affairs. More so, the Washington Consensus restructured the global financial institutions to meet the present global circumstances and also to counter the rapid development of communism in post-colonial states (Lienau, 2016). The IMF and World Bank began to provide loans to the Global South' to alleviate poverty, address economic crises, and promote democratization. The capitalists saw an opportunity in the "political economy" crisis experienced by the newly independent states due to the inexperienced bureaucrats, civil wars, and economic sabotage by the capitalists to adhere to their demands (Muhumed & Gaas, 2016). Therefore, loans with interest were issued by the bank to fund agrarian and industrial development in the Global South. The idea was founded on neoliberal discourses of promoting trade, development, and democracy to the struggling nations, yet behind the smoke screen, the idea was to promote a capitalist, globalized world.

During the 1980s and 1990s, the IMF and the World Bank implemented structural adjustment programs (SAPs) in developing countries, particularly in Africa, Latin America, and Asia. SAPs were designed to address economic crises and promote economic liberalization through measures such as austerity, privatization, and deregulation (Williamson, 2008). SAPs enhanced capitalist orientation to the Global South (Muhumed, 2016). However, these policies often led to social dislocation, increased inequality, and limited economic sovereignty for borrowing nations. The policy, however, affected the economies of the Global South in many respects; for instance, the privatization of industries, though aimed at promoting professionalism and production, resulted in massive retrenchment and the reduction of public service salaries (Makumbe, 2011). The prices of basic amenities skyrocketed and inflation began to take course. SAPs also led to the decline of domestic industries, whereby they failed to compete with foreign capitals in both domestic and international environments (Muhumed, 2016). Despite all these maneuvers, the global south remains stagnant in a subordinate position of emerging markets in the geographies of money and power. Furthermore, the Asian Financial Crisis (1997–1998) is important to note in the chronology and development of global finance. The crisis exposed the vulnerabilities of the global financial system and highlighted the limitations of prevailing policies. The crisis exposed the risks associated with stopgap capital flows, excessive financial liberalization, and scant financial regulation. It prompted a review of the policies advocated by the IMF and the World Bank, as well as a gratitude for the need for better consideration of local frameworks and systemic risks (Todaro, 2014).

The rise and expansion of the BRICS provided a turning point in taming the global influence of the Western-oriented international financial system. In recent years, the global financial landscape has witnessed the rise of emerging economies, particularly in Asia. Countries such as China, India, South Africa, Russia, and Brazil have gained economic influence and have sought to challenge the dominance of Western-led institutions. This has led to the establishment of alternative institutions, such as the Asian Infrastructure Investment Bank (AIIB), BRICS Bank, BRICS currency, and the New Development Bank (NDB), which aim to provide financing options outside the traditional Western-dominated institutions. Therefore, the current global financial systems seem to be predatory and premised on the "coloniality" of power, being, and knowledge. They hold the power to define poverty and development discourses, which shows that the economies of the Global South are entrapped and snared in global coloniality (Ndhlovu-Gatsheni, 2013), and the Bretton Woods system has long perpetuated and deepened inequalities between advanced economies and the global South. The historical legacy of global financial institutions and policies has been subject to increasing scrutiny and criticism in recent times. Evidence shows that these institutions have perpetuated global economic imbalances, reinforced power asymmetries, and failed to adequately address the needs and aspirations of emerging economies. Therefore, calls for reform for greater representation of the Global South in decision-making processes and a more inclusive approach to global financial governance have been made.

Decoloniality and the Global Financial System

The concept of decoloniality offers a critical lens through which to scrutinize the global financial system, highlighting the chronological legacies of colonialism and the enduring power imbalances embedded within it. Decoloniality seeks to test and transform the structures, practices, and ideologies that perpetuate colonial relations of power, and this perspective has important implications for understanding and reshaping the global financial system. According to Afolabi (2020), the global financial system is dominated by Eurocentric paradigms and platforms and is characterized by asymmetrical and superior-inferior relationships between the global North and the global South. For Hall and Tandon (2017), the current global financial system has deep roots in colonialism, as European powers established economic structures and institutions to exploit and extract resources from colonized regions. Furthermore, colonial economic systems were designed to serve the interests of the colonizers, facilitating the transfer of wealth from colonized territories to the colonial centers. Evidence shows that the prevailing global finance regime still perpetuates patterns of inequality and dependency. Ndhlovu-Gatsheni (2013) argues that decoloniality depicts the inherent power imbalances in the GFS, where a few dominant nations and institutions hold significant control over economic decision-making and resource allocation. The power dynamics reflect a continuation of colonial relationships, with former colonial powers and their financial institutions exerting influence over the economic policies and development trajectories of former colonies. This perpetuates a dependency on external actors and limits the agency and self-determination of nations in shaping their economic futures.

Ndhlovu-Gatsheni (2013) argues that the GFS is buttressed by Western epistemologies and knowledge frameworks, which often marginalize and devalue non-Western ways of understanding and organizing economies. Therefore, decoloniality seems to be the panacea that recognizes and values diverse knowledge systems, for instance, indigenous and local perspectives, in shaping economic theories, policies, and practices. The chapter notes that for the global south to develop, extractive financial practices that perpetuate economic disparities, for instance, debt burdens, exploitative lending conditions, and speculative financial flows that prioritize short-term gains over long-term sustainable development, need to be revoked. It is the objective of the chapter that decolonizing the GFS will foster financial sovereignty and self-determination by dismantling the structures that perpetuate external control over economic decision-making as peripheral nations determine their economic priorities to extend supporting efforts to develop regional financial institutions (BRICS

Bank), fostering alternative financing mechanisms, and promoting inclusive and participatory economic governance.

Africa is a strategic actor in international politics and development as it plays an important role in determining the development trajectory of the new multipolar world. The development of a strong bond between and among African states gives the continent leverage, assertiveness, and bargaining power to regain the lost luster due to the colonization of the means of production and state administration. The repositioning and involvement of Africa in the decoloniality narrative, especially of the existing global finance system, would promote the continent's economic development and address historical inequalities. Evidence shows that the African continent has realized its significance in a multipolar world as regional integration enhances economic cooperation, trade, and development. The chapter underscores the importance of integration as it fosters intra-African trade, investment, and collaboration, as these maneuvers strengthen the continent's collective bargaining power and reduce dependence on the Global North. According to Shiferaw (2023), Africa's growing global significance has largely been interpreted through the prism of geopolitical competition. The changing global geopolitical context, the need for alliances, and the rush for critical minerals have enhanced Africa's global significance. But Africa's recognition as a strategic partner is equally driven by endogenous factors such as economic growth, population growth, assertive political leadership, and a young digitized population that can challenge archaic narratives about the continent (Shiferaw, 2023).

Evidence shows that Western financial institutions' hegemony and influence are still entrenched in the tentacles of the existing global financial systems. Many African countries have historically relied on Western-dominated financial institutions, such as the IMF and World Bank, for loans, technical assistance, and policy advice. An example is the IMF's Staff Monitored Program for the Ministry of Finance and the RBZ staff. However, due to conditionalities that are disarticulated from Africa's long-term development goals, the continent needs to de-link and explore alternatives, such as seeking funding from emerging economies from the BRICS, establishing regional development banks, strengthening the capacity of the African Development Bank (the bank also needs to be decolonized as the USA holds significant shares), and strengthening member countries' domestic resources mobilization framework to reduce dependency on global north actors (Signe', 2022). It is important for Africa to de-link from the global north and diversify financial partnerships by engaging with non-traditional partners, including China, India, Russia, and other emerging economies. These partnerships offer opportunities for infrastructure development, investment, and trade diversification, but in all these engagements, African countries need to be cautious to negotiate fair and equitable agreements that prioritize mutual benefits, sustainability, and respect for local epistemologies.

According to Todaro (2014), development economics has a greater scope and is multi-dimensional. In addition to being concerned with the efficient allocation of existing scarce productive resources and their sustained growth over time, it must also deal with the economic, social, political, and institutional mechanisms, both public and private, necessary to bring about rapid (at least by historical standards) and large-scale improvements in levels of living for the peoples of the global south. For Todaro (2014), the existing financial system must be concerned with the economic, cultural, and political requirements for effecting rapid structural and institutional transformations of entire societies in a manner that will most efficiently bring the fruits of economic progress to the broadest segments of their populations. Furthermore, it must focus on the mechanisms that keep families, regions, and even entire nations in poverty traps, in which past poverty causes future poverty, and on the most effective strategies for breaking out of these traps. Africa is cognizant that the existing global financial system relies on metrics that prioritize economic growth over social and environmental well-being. The continent's development trajectory then needs to be couched and packaged to include measures of social progress, environmental sustainability, and human well-being (Todaro, 2014). From the preceding submission, the continent needs to challenge the dominance of Western knowledge production and promote African perspectives and expertise by investing in research and education to build local capacities, generate knowledge, and shape policy debates depicting local contexts. African leaders have been lethargic in developing robust South-South cooperation frameworks and development models that resonate with indigenous knowledge systems. For instance, in the area of knowledge production, where the former colonies believe that "*to be is to be like the former oppressor,*" and the Global Finance System (GFS) is also skewed in a way that punishes South-to-South cooperation. The continent's development models have to support African entrepreneurship through business incubators, access to finance programs, and skills development, thus fostering economic diversification, job creation, and sustainable development. To this end, the continent still needs to craft a comprehensive and multifaceted development approach that promotes regional integration, diversifies partnerships, mobilizes domestic resources, empowers local entrepreneurs, advocates for fair global financial reforms, and invests in knowledge and capacity building, thus diffusing Western hegemony.

On the BRICS, the continent or member states need to remain skeptical and worry about the block's benevolence. The major concern is whether there is going to be a comprehensive paradigm shift from the status quo (Global North hegemony). According to Moyo (2024), China and the BRICS are not offering something substantially new to Africa. Despite 20 years of their activities on the continent, they are still specializing in commodity imports and exporting manufactured goods to Africa and extracting raw minerals (chrome, iron ore, gold, and lithium) for their economies, just like the Western imperialists. Their institutions are following the precepts of the IMF in most respects; Africa has lost its voting powers in the IMF, and yet China, India, and Brazil gained. They did not help the continent in the spirit of South-South cooperation to fight this loss simply because they are the beneficiaries. Some members of the BRICS seem to seek accommodation in global governance and not radical transformation as they have developed as a result of the adoption of capitalism (Moyo, 2024). The preceding argument notes the importance of the continent in asserting greater agency, promoting inclusive development, and addressing historical imbalances in the global financial system as a collective continent.

BRICS and Global Financial Hegemony of the West

International politics is not static, but it is a dynamic space that promotes the development of new discourses, phenomena, and political realities. After the collapse of the Union of Soviet Socialist Republics (USSR), a new world order emerged (Fukuyama, 1992). Liberalism ideology triumphed against Marxism, and the capitalist world spread to the former communist states. The BRICS (Brazil, Russia, India, China, and South Africa) is a grouping of emerging economies that have gained prominence in recent years (Bonizzi et al., 2022).

Historically, Western countries, particularly the United States and Western European nations, have held significant influence over global financial institutions, the International Monetary Fund (IMF), the World Bank, and the global reserve currency, the U.S. dollar. This dominance has allowed the West to shape global financial rules, policies, and institutions in line with their interests (Apita & Maududa, 2023). The formation of BRICS was informed by the emphasis on creating South-South cooperation as the panacea to end the exploitative North-South relations (Ban & Blyth, 2013). The realization by the emerging economies of the limitations of the existing global financial architecture has led the global south to appeal for the regeneration of institutions that reflect the evolving global economic order (Powell, 2019). Evidence shows the need for the Global South to challenge Western-dominated global financial hegemony by establishing alternative financial institutions. It is a reality that the BRICS block collectively represents a significant share of global gross domestic product (GDP), trade, and investment and gives member states more leverage and bargaining power in global financial discussions (Ban & Blyth, 2013).

On the currency issues, there has been a suffocation of the diversification currency as the United States dollar has been entrenched as a global currency. The global south tends to be disturbed by the continued and robust entrenchment of the US currency as the common denominator or primary reserve in international business transactions (Vom Hau et al., 2012). The BRICS countries believe that the overreliance on a single currency poses risks and vulnerabilities for global economic stability, so the block is contemplating introducing its currency or promoting the use of alternative reserve currencies, such as the Chinese yuan or a basket of currencies (Stuenkel, 2020). BRICS provides an alternative to the Western attempts to promote financial hegemony in the international system. The BRICS bloc has been advocating for a multipolar system in global governance and the diversification of the global currency landscape. When the European powers conquered territories and asserted their political domination, they immediately sought to destroy the indigenous monetary practices and replace them with practices that met the requirements of capitalist accumulation (Guyer & Pallaver, 2018). This "monetary transition," according to Saul (2004 cited), was necessary, as the control of the production and exchange circuits required the control of money production and its circuits. The colonial governments began by banning the indigenous currencies and then sanctioning anyone who did not accept the colonial currency in market transactions and the payment of taxes (Pigeaud & Sylla, 2018). Given these excruciating limitations, the inception of the BRICS dismantled the unipolar hegemony of the Americans and their allies. Evidence abounds that these emerging and emergent economies are advocating for a multipolar system in global finance governance, challenging the dominance of Western powers. The BRICS need to strengthen their involvement in decision-making and representation in global institutions for a more balanced, evolving global economic order that shapes global rules, policies, and institutions to ensure their interests are adequately represented (Vom Hau et al., 2012). Most regional engagements, for instance, SADC, AU, and ECOWAS, failed to adopt their regional currencies for regional and international transactions (Chatterjee & Naka, 2022). BRICS realized the effects of not having a currency that entrapped the Global South in the snares of global coloniality and adopted the idea of establishing a currency for international trade.

The other major concern is the system of international payment, such as the Society for Worldwide Interbank Financial Telecommunication ("SWIFT"), which also favors the West and makes it easy for them to sanction other nations. In 2012, for example, the European Union passed a sanction against Iran that compelled SWIFT to disconnect sanctioned Iranian banks. In 2022, European Union Council Regulation (EU) 833/2014 prohibited SWIFT and other financial messaging providers from providing services to designated Russian entities and subsidiaries. Based in Belgium, SWIFT must comply with EU regulations. EU Council Regulation (EU) 765/2006 prohibited SWIFT from working with designated Belarusian entities and subsidiaries. As a result, both Russian and Belarusian entities were disconnected from SWIFT (Seth, 2023). This prompted Russia to adopt the Chinese system of international payments and transactions. SWIFT is a member-owned cooperative controlled by its shareholders (certain member financial institutions), representing some firms worldwide. SWIFT is overseen by the Group of Ten Countries' G-10 central banks. These countries are Belgium, Canada, France, Germany, Italy, Japan, the Netherlands, Sweden, Switzerland, the United Kingdom, and the United States. The European country of Belgium acts as the lead overseer alongside other members such as the United States. Federal Reserve (Seth, 2023). Evidence abounds that, outside the Bretton system, the global South needs to devise its international payment system since the over-reliance on the current regime of payment systems has compelled Zimbabwean banks to use corresponding banking arrangements; hence, payments take longer and attract huge premium charges.

It is worth noting that the position of the BRICS, premised on a "revolutionary worldview," acts as an important step towards decolonizing global financial institutions. However, the purpose of this endeavor is for the bloc to be able to overcome its internal challenges to dismantle the global financial hegemony of the West, as the existing global financial system is complex and multifaceted, and the influence and hegemony of the West are still deeply entrenched. While BRICS countries have made efforts to challenge this hegemony, evidence shows that epistemic disobedience or delinking is an ongoing process that involves navigating complex political, economic, and institutional dynamics.

Epistemologies of the South

The decoloniality discourse emphasizes the importance of recognizing and valuing diverse epistemologies and knowledge systems that have been historically marginalized or suppressed within the dominant Western-centric framework. This perspective acknowledges that knowledge production has been influenced by colonial legacies, and it calls for the decolonization of knowledge and the inclusion of Global South epistemologies in shaping understanding of the world. According to Afolabi (2020), concepts such as colonization, decolonization, and decoloniality reflect the lived and shared experiences of Africans. Afolabi (2020) conceptualizes colonialism as the forceful subjugation and occupation of a territory by another state or political power that imposes its will and administration on that territory. In the same vein of knowledge production, colonial authorities imposed their preferred method of education on the colonized territories, principally through Western missionaries and colonial administrators/paid educators. Decolonization then eradicated the effects of colonialization by doing away with alien vestiges of colonialization. However, for Ndhlovu-Gatsheni (2013), decoloniality goes beyond decolonization as it argues that coloniality still exists, must be understood in its modern form (coloniality), and must be dismantled for the global South to develop.

Associated with Mignolo (2013), the concept of decoloniality has come to be linked with various structures, forms, and vestiges of coloniality that continually shape African images of self, identity, and memory. Therefore, "decoloniality is born out of a realization that the Global South exists in an asymmetrical world order that is sustained not only by colonial matrices of power but also by pedagogies and epistemologies of equilibrium that continue to produce alienated Africans who are socialized into hating the Africa that produced them and liking the Europe and America that rejects them" (Ndhlovu-Gatsheni, 2013:11). The chapter notes that decoloniality is premised on three important narratives: power, being, and knowledge. The concept of the coloniality of power elucidates the formation of the current "global political" framework and the international power hierarchy. Another concept, the coloniality of knowledge, delves into epistemological concerns, the creation of knowledge, political implications, and the origins, foundations, and objectives of knowledge. Additionally, the notion of the coloniality of being underscores inquiries into individual identity, the contrast between partiality and impartiality, and the dichotomy of oppressed versus oppressor, particularly with unfavorable conclusions for Africans (Ndhlovu-Gatsheni, 2013). This negativity manifests in the commodification and objectification of Africans within the global knowledge production system, economies, and development structures. Decoloniality strives to "epistemologically surpass, decolonize the Western canon, and epistemology" (Grosfoguel, 2016:211). It serves as a platform and an African-centered initiative aiming to reshape diverse methodologies, teaching approaches, and socio-cultural impacts that relegate Africans to secondary status in a globalized society (Mignolo, 2013). The chapter highlights the need for the global south to leverage its rich diversity of knowledge systems, for instance, indigenous knowledge, local practices, and non-Western philosophies. These epistemologies promote knowing, understanding, and engaging with the world by encompassing holistic, relational, and context-specific development trajectories. Decoloniality should foster pluralism by challenging the hegemony of Western knowledge and advocating for the inclusion and validation of these diverse epistemologies (Afolabi, 2020). The global south needs to prioritize oral and communal traditions that emphasize the importance of collective wisdom, intergenerational knowledge transmission, and the interconnectedness of humans with their natural and social environments.

According to Afolabi (2020), every tribe, race, and nation has its epistemic foundation on which its values, ideas, and educational systems are founded. Whether called traditional or modern, value-free or value-laden, the reality is that each society is run based on the knowledge system to which it subscribes. In Africa, through formal colonialism and informal coloniality, Western knowledge system dominance has resulted in the debasement and near extinction of African knowledge systems. Indigenous knowledge systems in Africa have been relegated to second class because of Western pretensions about epistemic diversity and the insistence on its knowledge system as being scientific, universal, and monolithic (Musila, 2017). For Mbembe (2015:9), the Western knowledge system is encased in the Eurocentric canon that "attributes truth only to the Western way of knowledge production. It is a canon that disregards other knowledge traditions. The Western knowledge system views African knowledge production as primitive, barbaric, and descriptive. The effect of this has been to downgrade African epistemologies during the colonial era and, through what is referred to as the coloniality of knowledge, to actively create knowledge disarticulation in African knowledge systems. Disarticulation of knowledge, or knowledge disarticulation, occurs when the main activities of knowledge and its end products, such as enlightenment and development, are contradictory to and divorced from learners' social realities. In most cases, disarticulation of knowledge results in irrelevant knowledge that is disassociated from the needed trajectories of development in Africa. Endogenous and indigenous knowledge has been pushed to the margins of society. Africa is today saddled with irrelevant knowledge that disempowers rather than empowers individuals and communities (Ndhlovu-Gatsheni, 2013:11).

Afolabi (2020) highlights that the detrimental effects of dismantling African knowledge systems persist today, where African traditional philosophies are often regarded as inferior and met with suspicion and contempt by Africans influenced by colonial mentalities and by the Western world. This perspective underscores the significance of decoloniality in liberating Africa from its marginalized position in a globalized context. The economic dynamics of globalization have significantly contributed to upholding the suppression of African knowledge and its utility. Even attempts to challenge the epistemic dominance of Western scholars by initiating philosophical discussions on the value of all knowledge systems face resistance from local intellectuals unaware of the power dynamics in knowledge exchanges between the global North and South, as well as from Western academics who dismiss such endeavors as unscientific, lacking universality, and thus subpar

(Ndhlovu-Gatsheni, 2013:11). Therefore, the emphasis is on the inculcation of Global South epistemologies and knowledge production in their development matrix, thereby promoting the inclusion of diverse perspectives, the empowerment of marginalized communities, and the recognition of alternative ways of knowing, contributing to a more inclusive, equitable, and decolonized understanding of the world.

Loopholes of Africa's Engagement Strategy

It is important to note that for the global south to tender a genuine epistemological delinking and challenge the entrenched Western hegemony, there is a need for a strategic and robust engagement context to reform the global finance system to be inclusive. The continent seems to have a pathetic international engagement framework and strategy as compared to Asia, Latin America, Europe, and North America. Such a flaw affects the continent's diplomatic realities, practices, and relations at the global level. From the neo-realist perspective, the international system is a predatory space dominated by national interest and power struggles that motivate states to enter into diplomatic relations with other states. According to Shiferaw (2023), Africa needs to harness the expertise of an increasing number of African public servants serving and leading international organizations such as the World Health Organization or the World Trade Organization, thus normalizing the idea of Africa as a global player and Africans as global citizens. This kind of engagement by the continent contributes to a paradigm shift in Africa's global image from viewing African countries as spectators to active global participants with interests and contributions. The continent seems to have the arsenal to envision ways of shaping the very rules and politics behind global governance. This would allow for a more long-term and strategic engagement at the global level while incentivizing innovative thinking on how to create and not just seize opportunities.

Moreover, of importance in the fourth industrial revolution is to explore, exploit, and embrace technological advancement/digital technology for Africa's engagement and development. For Signé and Chris Heitzig (2022), technology offers the opportunity to reverse historical declines, putting emerging economies on an impressive growth trajectory. Artificial intelligence and emerging technologies are shaping every corner of the planet, from the economy to climate to health, and their deployment has only grown during the pandemic. Fourth Industrial Revolution (4IR) technologies such as artificial intelligence and machine learning, automated vehicles, 3D printing, the Internet of Things, big data, robotics and automation, blockchain, cloud and edge computing, and 5G networks have the potential to inspire rapid growth and reduce poverty if wielded responsibly. Such technologies have already led to improvements in financial inclusion and connectivity across the region (Signé & Chris Heitzig, 2022), as increased financial inclusion facilitates financial planning and expenditure. Harnessing the comparative advantages the continent possesses will enable member states to navigate disastrous relations with emergent economies; for instance, Russia and China have adopted resource-extractivist foreign policies in Africa, which is reflected by their presence in mineral resource extractions. Extractivism is defined as the extraction of resources by private players to maximize profits while the people's needs and the environment are ignored (Gudynas, 2021). Thus, mineral resources such as lithium, gold, diamonds, silver, emeralds, uranium, platinum, and cobalt are judiciously extracted and exploited by the Russians, Chinese, and other foreign nations in Southern Africa (Chagnon, 2022). This shows that the continents' diplomatic engagement is weak and vulnerable to predatory structures of the international political economy, as African countries are still entrapped in the snares and vestiges of coloniality of power, being, and knowledge.

Disregard of Domestic Resource Mobilization by Member States

African states adopted a tradition of depending on aid and loans to finance development projects in different sectors. This has resulted from the adoption of populist policies in the post-colonial era. Zeleza (2019) defined populist policies as policies aimed at promoting political legitimacy and, at the same time, draining the national purse. These policies include free education, free health care, and the provision of grants to citizens. Such policies are not investments but a guarantee to rule in perpetuity by African politicians. A welfarist state needs to have the financial capacity to bankroll social safety net programs, but in the case of Africa, the purpose is to sustain patrimonial politics and kleptocracy. As a consequence, post-colonial Africa is characterized by heavy borrowing from international financial institutions, private companies, and emerging economies (Moyo, 2009). The technocrats in the administration of public finances and economic planning failed to realize the effects of having policies that largely depend on the central bank in implementation. In 1980, the Republic of Zimbabwe adopted populist policies such as health for all and education for all as a trump card to gain support from the masses. The policies, however, intensify borrowing from international financial institutions and other countries. Therefore, this has resulted in a debt dilemma and debt trap.

The significance of debt is also strongly highlighted in developmental state theories. From the work of scholars like Keynes (1936), Lerner (1943), and Domar (1957), it is hardly imaginable that a government can achieve growth and sustained development without debt. The literature makes it clear that nothing is characteristically bad about government borrowing and that, in an ideal situation, macroeconomic policies must reflect pragmatism rather than a religious adherence to some ideology (Armstrong, 2019). The issue of the debt dilemma can be best described by Dambisa Moyo (2009) as the "dead aid theory," which provides critical epistemology of the negative contribution of aid to the development of post-colonial Africa. Moyo (2009) argued that, since 1960, African countries borrowed at least

USD 500 billion from the IMF and World Bank to fund their populist projects, programs, and policies. Therefore, the majority of African states are now heavily indebted countries as member states' development agendas rely on debts rather than developing self-sustainable programs for revenue creation. Chabal (2014) argued that post-colonial Africa is dominated by a crop of egoistic leaders who amass wealth for themselves at the expense of state development. Such a scenario has left the continent vulnerable to external exploitation. Thomas Sankara believed that aid was a subtle form of conquest, whereby the imperialist instrumentalized it to entrap the Global South countries into the snares of a matrix of coloniality of power, being, and knowledge (Harsch, 2013). The continent needs to upscale domestic resource mobilization (DRM) from mineral royalties, tourism, and trade, thus increasing government revenues through taxation and other non-debt income sources, which is essential in allowing countries to own and flexibly chart policies that address their specific development challenges while mitigating the risks of debt distress (Elsayid, 2016). Furthermore, member states need to build fiscal capacity with efficient monitoring, administration, and compliance institutions as well as to expand their tax bases.

The other aspect of concern is that African countries are typically characterized by "hard-to-tax" informal sectors (small/informal businesses or subsistence farmers), which provide ample opportunity for tax noncompliance due to the lack of information on revenues. The share of informal employment in Africa (85.8% of total employment) remains the largest in the world (ILO, 2018). The prominence of the informal sector in most African economies stems from the income-generation or employment opportunities it offers to the unemployed, in particular (Boly et al., 2020). The continent needs to be focused on streamlining tax administration and bringing the informal sector into the tax system. In the same vein, central governments should provide the same tax incentives to foreign and domestic companies. However, in the case of Zimbabwe, foreign companies are being given tax holidays that extend to ten years for bringing investment and employment, which disadvantages local companies' growth and competitiveness. Therefore, the continent needs to boost domestic resource mobilization (DRM) by increasing revenue, improving public spending efficiency, leveraging large pension fund markets and sovereign wealth funds, curbing illicit financial flows out of the continent, and harnessing partnerships. As is pointed out in the UNCTAD (2006) report, "even under a favorable external trading and financial environment, considerable domestic policy efforts would be needed to ensure that economies gradually become self-reliant in sustaining rapid growth."

Weak Regional Cooperation

South-South cooperation has been adopted as the panacea to circumvent the challenge of exploitation of the third world countries by the first world. For Wallerstein (1997), such cooperation provides an environment that insulates

Global South states from exploitation by the Global North. To achieve such an end, the Global South countries created regional bodies, exchange programs, and financial institutions to fund their development policies. According to Qobo (2007), it is widely acknowledged that Africa's integration efforts have thus far failed to bear satisfactory fruit. While other regions have successfully used their integration mechanisms to improve their economic welfare, Africa lags concerning gross domestic product (GDP) growth, per capita income, capital inflows, and general living standards (Dymski, 2018). This is a problem across most of the continent, despite the existence of a plethora of policy plans and grand visions. The first major blueprint for Africa's development—the Lagos Plan of Action and the Final Act of Lagos—was adopted almost three decades ago and set out a vision of an integrated African market by the year 2000. It was given further impetus by the Abuja Treaty, which was approved in 1991 and came into force in 1994. According to this treaty, the African Economic Community (AEC) would be in place by 2028. Some of its milestones would include the strengthening of existing regional economic communities and the formation of new ones (between 1994 and 1999); stabilization of existing tariffs; and integration and harmonization of economic sectors (1999–2007); establishment of a free trade area and customs union (2007–2017); harmonization of tariff systems across various regional economic communities (RECs) (2017–2019); the creation of a common African market and harmonization of monetary, financial, and fiscal policies; and the establishment of a pan-African economic and monetary union (2023–2028), (Qobo, 2007).

Despite the progressive plans propounded by African leaders, the bone of contention in this chapter is that little has changed since the 1990s to advance regional integration and ensure developmental progress on the continent. For Qobo (2007), Africa's elites seem to be focusing on the wrong set of priorities with too little genuine commitment towards the goal of Africa's development. For regional integration in Africa to be a success, there is a need for a paradigm shift where the continent's leadership has to move beyond grand gestures and abstract visions and be pragmatic and have a sense of urgency in action. Evidence shows that member states at the domestic level need to undertake bold and sustainable political and economic reforms, and the continent then pursues developmental coordination and gradual harmonization of policies and regulations, which could form the foundation for greater integration. As Percy Mistry contends: "African governments need to be less ambitious and more realistic and pragmatic about the objectives and intermediate targets for integration, taking into account the constraints and capacities of integrating national governments". The problem with African politicians is that they value the consolidation of political power at the expense of development. African leaders have had little success in their integration and development efforts. What persists is that individual leaders hope to achieve at the continental level what they had failed to do on the domestic level. Thus, integration as applied in Africa can only be viewed as a form of escapism from real challenges at the domestic level, as well as a strategy to consolidate alliances that would reinforce the political sovereignty of member countries.

Evidence shows that domestic successes precede continental successes through sound and functional policies at the domestic level. African countries remained largely internally unintegrated in the post-colonial period. Today, as then, national consciousness remains a state elite project rather than a process that is driven from the bottom up. As a result, there is no nationalism in the true sense of the word, but only elite nationalistic projects (Nye, 2004:112). This underscores the futility of attempting continental integration based on weak national foundations. Evidence notes that African integration remains slow, tortuous, and incomplete as member states are unwilling to cede sovereignty at the regional level by agreeing to a supranational body affecting the continent's bargaining power in the global financial system. African leaders require sustained efforts, political will, and a commitment to shared goals by strengthening regional institutions, promoting dialogue, and pursuing economic integration to enhance bargaining power and achieve more favorable outcomes through collective action.

Conclusion

Decolonizing the global financial architecture and working towards financial sovereignty in Africa is a crucial step towards dismantling the inequities that have perpetuated underdevelopment and dependency on the continent. It requires a comprehensive and multifaceted approach that challenges the Western-centric nature of the current system and empowers African nations to have greater control over their financial affairs. To achieve financial sovereignty, African countries must prioritize reforming international financial institutions, strengthening regional financial institutions, promoting local currency usage and regional trade, fostering domestic resource mobilization, enhancing financial inclusion and innovation, and increasing financial literacy and capacity building. It is true that decolonizing the global financial architecture and achieving financial sovereignty in Africa is a complex and long-term process. It requires collaborative yet radical efforts from African governments, regional organizations, civil society, and the international community. By challenging the Western-centric nature of the current system, Africa can assert its economic independence, promote sustainable development, and shape a financial architecture that serves the interests and aspirations of its people.

References

Afolabi, O. S. (2020). Globalisation, decoloniality and the question of knowledge production in Africa. *Journal of Higher Education in Africa/Revue de l'enseignement supérieur en Afrique, 18*(1), 93–110.

Alami, I. (2022). International financial subordination: A critical research agenda. *Review of International Political Economy, 30*(4), 1360–1386. https://doi.org/10.1080/09692290.2022.2098359

Amin, S. (1974). *Accumulation on a world scale: A critique of the theory of underdevelopment.* Monthly Review Press.

Amin, A. (Ed.). (2009). The social economy: International perspectives on economic solidarity. Bloomsbury Publishing.

Anzaldua, G. (1983). *Borderlands/La Frontera: New Mestiza.* Aunt Flute Publishers.

Apita, T., & Maududa, K. (2023). Importance of BRICS as region politics and policies. *Geo Journal, 88*(5), 5205–5220.

Armstrong, B. B. D. (2019). *Brass cities: Innovation policy and local economic transformation* (Doctoral dissertation, Massachusetts Institute of Technology).

Ban, C., & Blyth, M. (2013). The BRICS and the Washington Consensus: An introduction. *Review of International Political Economy, 20*(2), 241–255.

Barrow, R. J., & Lee, J. W. (2003). IMF programs: Who is chosen and what are the effects? *Journal of Monetary Economics, 52*(7), 1245–1269.

Boly, A et al. (2020). *Mobilizing domestic resource in Africa for inclusive growth.* Policy Brief.

Bonizzi, B., Kaltenbrunner, A., & Powell, J. (2022). Financialised capitalism and the subordination of emerging capitalist economies. *Cambridge Journal of Economics.* https://doi.org/10.1093/cje/beac023

Calomiris, C. W., & Neal, L. (2020). History of financial globalisation, Overview. *Handbook of Key Global Financial Markets, Institutions and Infrastructure.*

Chabal, E. (2014). Managing the postcolonial: minority politics in Montpellier, c. 1960–c. 2010. *Contemporary European History, 23*(2), 237–258.

Chagnon, C. W. (2022). From extractivist to global extractivist: the evolution of an organising concept. *The Journal of Peasant Studies.*

Chatterjee, M., & Naka, I. (2022). Twenty years of BRICS: political and economic transformations through the lens of land. *Oxford Development Studies, 50*(1), 2–13.

Duvisac, S. (2022). Decolonising practice: Pathways, insights, and experiences from the field of christian relief, development, and advocacy. *Christian Relief, Development, and Advocacy: The Journal of the Accord Network, 5*(1).

Dymski, G. (2018). *Developing economies, international financial integration and sustainable development.* Paper Presented at Intergovernmental Group of Experts on Financing for Development, 7–9 Movember 2018, Paris des Nations, Geneva.

Elsayid, E. (2016). *The Hidden Role of World Bank and International Monetary Fund in Developing Countries: Egypt, Malaysia and Turkey.* Saarbrucken: AV Akademikerverlag.

Fanon, F. (1967). *The wretched of the earth.* Paris: Penguin.

Fukuyama, F. (1992). Capitalism & democracy: The missing link. *Journal of Democracy, 3*(3), 100–110.

Grosfoguel, R. (2016). Epistemic extractivist: A dialogue with Alberto Acosta, Leane Betasamosoke Simpson and Silva Rivera Cusicangui. In B. Sausa-Santos & M. N. Meneses (Eds.), *Knowledge born in the struggle: Constructing the epistemologies of the Global South.* Routledge.

Gudynas, E. (2021). Extractivisnm: Johnson, D. 2009. Literary research and interdisciplinarity. In D. D. S. Correa & W. R. Owens (Eds.), *The handbook to literary research* (2nd ed., pp. 131–147). Routledge.

Guyer, J. I., & Pallaver, K. (2018). Money and currency in African history. In the oxford research encyclopedia of African history (pp. 1–28). Oxford University Press.

Hall, B. L., & Tandon, R. (2017). Decolonization of knowledge, epistemicide, participatory research and higher education.

Harsch, E. (2013). The legacies of Thomas Sankara: A revolutionary experience in retrospect. *Review of African Political Economy, 40*(137), 358–374.

ILO. (2018). *Women and men in the informal economy: A statistical picture.* ILO.

Kapuya, Z. (2019). *Phenomenology of decolonizing the university: Essays of contemporary thoughts in afrikology.* Mwanaka Media Publishing.

Koddenbrock, K., Kvangraven, I. H., & Sylla, N. (2022). Beyond financialization: The longue duree of finance and imperialism. *Cambridge Journal of Economics.* https://doi.org/10.31219/osf.io/pjt7x

Lienau, O. (2016). The challenge of legitimacy in sovereign debt restructuring. *Harvard International Law Review, 57*(1), 151–265.

Makumbe, J. (2011). *Zimbabwe: Political context study. RIPOCA Research Notes 10.*

Maldonado-Torres, N. (2018). Thinking through the decolonial turn: Post-continental interventions in theory, philosophy, and critique-an introduction. *Transmodenity: Journal of Peripheral Cultural Production of Luso-Hispanic World, 1*(2).

Marini, R. M. (1973). *La dialectica de la dependencia.* Ediciones Era.

Mbembe, A. (2015). Decolonizing knowledge and the question of the archive.

Mignolo, W. D. (2013). *The darker side of western modernity.* Duke University Press.

Moyo, D. (2009). *Dead aid: Why aid is not working in a better way for Africa.* Macmillan.

Moyo, G. (2024). *Africa in the global economy: Capital flight, enablers and decolonial responses.* Springer Nature.

Muhumed, M. M. (2016). The impact of microfinance on consumption in Bangladesh. *Journal of Economics and Sustainable Development, 7*(12), 105–114.

Muhumed, M. M., & Gaas, S. A. (2016). The World Bank and IMF in developing countries: Helping or hindering. *International Journal of African and Asian Studies, 26*, 39–49.

Musila, G. A. (2017). Part-time Africans, Europolitans and 'Africa Lite'. In *Afropolitanism: Reboot* (pp. 70–74). Routledge.

Musthaq, F. (2021). Dependency in a financialised global economy. *Review of African Political Economy, 48*(167), 15–31. https://doi.org/10.1080/03056244.2020.1857234

Nabudere, D. W. (2013). *Afrikology, philosophy, Wholeness. An Epistemology.* Institute of South Africa.

Naqvi, N. (2019). Manias, panics and crashes in emerging markets: An Empirical investigation of the post-2008 crisis period. *New Political Economy, 24*(6), 759–779. https://doi.org/10.1080/13563467.2018.1526263

Ndhlovu-Gatsheni, S. J. (2013). *Coloniality of power in post-colonial Africa: Myth or reality of decolonization.* Codeseria.

Nkrumah, K. (1965). *Neocolonialism. The last stage of imperialism.* Thomas Nelson & Sons.

Nye, J., Jr. (2004). *Power in the global information age: From realism to globalization.* Routledge.

Pigeaud & Sylla, N. S. (2018). Towards a political economy of monetary dependency: The case of the CFA franc in West Africa (No. 19/2). MaxPo discussion paper.

Powell, J. (2019). Towards a Marxist theory of financialized capitalism. In M. Vidal, T. Smith, P. Prew, & T. Rotta (Eds.), *Oxford handbook of Karl Marx* (pp. 629–650). Oxford University Press.

Prebisch, R. (1939). El Ciclo Economicoy la Politica Monetaria. In E. Garcia Vasquey (Ed.), *Obras de Raul Prebisch* (pp. 647–657). Fundacion Raul Prebisch.

Qobo, M. (2007). *The challenges of regional integration in Africa In the context of globalisation and the prospects for the United States of Africa.* ISS Paper 145, June.

Rey, H. (2015). *Dilemma not trilemma: The global financial cycle and monetary policy independence.* NBER Working Paper, 21162 (May 2015).

Saul, J. S. (2004). Globalization, imperialism, development: false binaries and radical resolutions. Socialist Register, 40.

Seth, S. (2023). *What is the SWIFT Banking System*, Investopedia?

Shiferaw, L. T. (2023). *Carving out Africa's role in the emerging global order Commentary* 23 October 2023.

Signé, L. (2022). Climate change, development, and conflict-fragility nexus in the Sahel. Brookings.

Signé, L., & Chris Heitzig, C. (2022). *Effective engagement with Africa: Capitalizing on shifts in business, technology, and global partnerships April 2022 Africa Growth Initiative.* The Brookings Institution.

Stuenkel, O. (2020). *The BRICS and the future of global order.* Lexingtin Books.

Sylla, N. S. (2021). Fighting monetary colonialism in francophone Africa: Samir Amin's contribution. *Review of African Political Economy, 48*(167), 32–49. https://doi.org/10.1080/03056244.2021.1878123
Tavares, M. (1985). A retomada da hegemonia Americana. *Revista De Economia Polıtica, 5*(2), 5–16.
Todaro, M. P. (2014). *Guide for Economic Development.*
UNCTAD. (2006). *FDI from developing and transitional economies: implications for development. World Investment Report 2006.* UNCTAD.
UNCTAD. (2019). *Handbook of statistics.* Switzerland.
Vernengo, M. (2006). 13. From capital controls to dollarization: American hegemony and the US dollar. Monetary Integration and Dollarization: No Panacea, 245.
Vom Hau, N., Scott, J., & Hulme, D. (2012). Beyond the BRICS: Alternative strategies of influence in the global politics of development. *The European Journal of Development.*
Wallerstein, I. (1997). Social science and the quest for a just society. *American Journal of Sociology, 102*(5), 1241–1257.
Williamson, J. (2008). A short history of the Washington Consensus. In N. Serra & J. E. Stiglitz (Eds.), *The Washington Consensus reconsidered: Towards a new global governance*. Oxford University Press.
Zeleza, P. T. (2019). Africa's persistent struggles for development and democracy in a multipolar world. *Canadian Journal of African Studies/Revue canadienne des études africaines, 53*(1), 155–170.

Arthur Fidelis Chikerema is a holder of a PhD in Public Administration from the University of Fort Hare, South Africa. He is currently a Senior Lecturer in the Department of Governance and Public Management at Midlands State University with extensive research interests, consultancy experience, and publications in areas of democracy and human rights, peacebuilding, public policy, local government, gender, international relations, and public debt.

Vincent Chakunda is a holder of a PhD in Public Administration from the University of Fort Hare, South Africa. He is currently a Senior Lecturer in the Department of Governance and Public Management and Coordinator at the Center for Public Policy and Devolution at Midlands State University, Zimbabwe, with extensive research interests, consultancy experience and publications in areas of public policy and governance, public debt, strategic management, devolution, local governance delivery (focusing on systems of accountability, transparency, equity, and inclusivity), elections, and democracy and intergovernmental fiscal equalisation.

Chapter 3
Specters of Global Financial Apartheid in Africa

Gorden Moyo

Abstract Global Africa is currently subjected to a perfect storm of global events including climate devastation, the ripple effects of the Russo-Ukraine war, the aftermaths of the scourge of the COVID-19 pandemic, and the resurgence of coups across the continent, as well as the lingering effects of the 2007 global financial crisis. The general response to this polycrisis by the archetypical global financial institutions such as the duo of the World Bank and the International Monetary Fund as well as by the powerful multilateral bodies including the G-7 and the G-20 countries has been to place global finance at the heart of the "imagined solutions." This has however resulted in far-reaching implications for African countries that were coercively inserted into the global financial system with all its colonial birth defects.

Introduction

Africa is currently subjected to a perfect storm of global events including climate devastation, the ripple effects of the Russo-Ukraine war, the aftermaths of the scourge of the COVID-19 pandemic, and the resurgence of coups across the continent, as well as the lingering effects of the 2007 global financial crisis. The general response to this polycrisis by the archetypical global financial institutions such as the duo of the World Bank and the International Monetary Fund (IMF) as well as by the powerful multilateral bodies including the G-7 and the G-20 countries has been to place global finance at the heart of the "imagined solutions." This has however resulted in far-reaching implications for African countries that were coercively inserted into the global financial system with all its colonial birth defects.

While the mainstream neoliberal economic thinkers (see Easterly, 2002; Sachs, 2005; Collier, 2007; Acemoglu & Robinson, 2012; Mills, 2023) put their faith on

G. Moyo (✉)
Faculty of Humanities, University of the Free State, Qwaqwa, South Africa

G. Moyo, S. J. Ndlovu-Gatsheni (eds.), *Global Storms and Africa in World Politics*, Global Power Shift, https://doi.org/10.1007/978-3-031-83868-2_3

global finance and financialization as solutions to many of the "global bads," this discussion is however, critical of the role played by global finance in the brutal histories of resource and knowledge extraction, exploitation and dispossession *gratis* from the time of slavery, through colonialism, imperialism, neocolonialism, neo-imperialism, globalism and globalization. There is hardly any doubt, at least from the perspective of the ordinary Africans, that today the continent remains marginalized globally as it was over five centuries ago. This fact, uncomfortable as it is, is practically represented by the concentrations of wealth in the global North and the concentrations of poverty in the global South as well as the flows of capital from global Africa to both, the global North, and the economically emerging global East. It is against this backdrop that this chapter focuses on the contemporary financial apartheid in Africa as a function of what Arewa (2023) referred to as "colonial hangover" or what some heterodox decolonial thinkers have variously called "coloniality of finance," "financial subordination," "financial subjugation," or simply "financial dependence." All these serve a binary role of being causes of, while at the same time, being results of financial apartheid.

The central proposition of this chapter is that the subordinate position of Africa in the global algebra of power, economy, trade, investment, and finance as well as epistemies, has hardly shifted since its conception over 500 years ago. The continent has remained locked at the bottom of the hierarchy of global financial and economic architecture despite the talk of post-colonialism, independence, freedom, and sovereignty as well as in spite of the much-lauded South-South cooperation meme. Africa and the other global South sub-regions continue to reel under a "global financial apartheid regime" that is inextricably linked to financial imperialism among the other cognate ills of the global North-controlled global financial system. Not surprisingly, the global financial architecture that is rooted in the ideology of financial apartheid/racial capitalism has not been able to resolve the financial problems of Africa and those of the other global South economies in general. Instead, global financial apartheid architecture is hard-wired to reproduce unequal global financial relations. This has served to exacerbate unequal and racialized financial relations with global Africa at the bottom while the fetishized global North countries and companies occupy the apex of financial modernity. This matrix of power explains the "Superior-Inferior relations" between the global North and the global South.

This Era of Global Storms/Crises, that has so far been marked by the eruption of the global financial crisis in 2007, COVID-19 in 2019, Russo-Ukraine war in 2022, and the recent spate of coups in West and Central Africa as well as the ongoing climate devastation, has ironically strengthened the power of the multilateral and bilateral lenders and creditors and against the economically vulnerable economies of the global South. For the record, these institutions including the World Bank and the IMF have been consistently designing and redesigning their geofinancial tools to protect their structural power over the borrowing African countries and the other global South economies that have essentially remained as debt colonies despite attaining their political freedom in the 1960s. A quick time series analysis will confirm the skewed nature of the Creditor-Debtor relations in Africa where the excolonizers are always the creditors/lenders while the excolonies are always the debtors. Viewed from this perspective, financial dependence, subjugation and subordination in Africa are not a happenstance but a part of a well-designed strategy whose *leit motif* is to keep Africa and the rest of the global South economies stuck in the lower rungs of the global pecking (dis)order and as the "altar boys" of the global North's "priestly" economies with the sole objective of ensuring structural dependence *ad infinitum.*

A few questions inform the subtext of the debates contained in this chapter: How are today's financial practices shaped by the brutal histories and biographies of colonialism and imperialism? What makes African countries continue to be financially subordinated to their excolonizers as well as to the emergent and emerging powers of the global East? What is it about the operations of global finance that continues to reproduce deeply unequal power relations between global Africa on one hand, and the global North and global East on the other? What are the factors that shape the global financial apartheid practices, and who benefits from them? Is the current global financial architecture fit for addressing coloniality of finance? And is a decolonial political economy of finance possible, and how would it look like?

It is hoped that by tackling these questions, this chapter will contribute toward enabling policy makers and shapers to better understand the more subtle contemporary forms of financial subjugation that have served to reproduce deeply entrenched global financial asymmetries over several years leading to the continued marginalization and pauperization of the African peoples. To develop this argument, this chapter invokes Afro-decolonial perspective as an analytical framework along with the other heterodox approaches such as dependency theories, world systems theory, and Marxist scholarship ranged against the neoliberal orthodox economic perspectives.

Global Financial Apartheid

Three interlinked and interdigitized themes namely; "global financial apartheid," "uneven global financial system," and "rigged global financial architecture" are treated in this chapter. Although the three themes are not synonyms, they are all deployed here to denote the ongoing systemic and structural financial deprivation suffered by African countries and the rest of the global South economies as a result of their historical relations with wealthier countries of the global North and more recently as a consequence of their interactions with the emergent and emerging capitalist economies of the global East including China, India, Russia, Turkiye, Saudi Arabia and United Arab Emirates (UAE), and the other Persian Gulf States.

For the avoidance of any doubt, global financial apartheid is a sequel of global apartheid, which describes an international system of minority rule as was the case in apartheid South Africa, and today, there are allegations that Israel is an apartheid regime in Palestine. In recent years, scholars and researchers have been advancing the notion that contemporary global financial system just like the colonial financial system, promotes geographical inequalities, racial inequalities, and differential access to finance capital as well as financial dependence of the peripheries including Africa and the other global South countries (Mutasa, 2007; Boberg, 2015; Sachs, 2023a, b; Moyo, 2024). The system does this by taking advantage of the financial and structural weaknesses in Africa and the global South in general. It penalizes African countries disproportionately and expresses itself as a tool for the historical powerful actors especially the United States, the United Kingdom, the EU, Japan, Canada, and Australia among the other core countries. In other words, the global financial system is the oil that lubricates the asymmetrical integration of Africa in the global economy.

Closely related to the notion of global financial apartheid and global financial system is global financial architecture. This describes a framework of institutions, policies, rules, and practices that govern the global financial system (Schultz, 2021; Kotzias et al., 2023). The architecture consists of a complex network of organizations including the IMF, the World Bank, and the World Trade Organization (WTO), regional and national banks, international commodity markets, as well as international credit rating agencies such as the Big Three namely; Fitch Investment, Standard, and Poor's and Moody's. On paper, the objective of this extensive network of financial, trade, and economic institutions is to promote economic growth, financial stability, and international cooperation in the management of the financial system. Paradoxically, history indicates that these fetishized institutions of the global North have presided over the opposite of what they purport to promote. Needless to say, financial instability, balance of payments deficits, inequalities, financial capital outflows, and many other financial and economic ills have taken root in Africa and the other global South countries under the watch of the international financial institutions (IFIs) especially the duo of the World Bank and the IMF.

The global financial and economic institutions have in their disposal the technologies of subjectivation including lending, neoliberal macroeconomic frameworks, structural adjustment programs (SAPs), austerity measures, and uneven exchange system that have been persistently and consistently imposed on the peripheries in order to keep them subdued and at the service of Western core powers and institutions. From an orthodox economic perspective, all these tools are meant to address the economic and financial challenges of the poor countries of the South. However, heterodox thinkers contest this position as simplistic and delusional. They argue that, in fact, these tools are purposed to ensure that African countries and the rest of the global South economies remain locked in the historical division of labor where they supply commodities in return of surplus capital, obsolescent technologies, and manufactured goods from the wealthier countries of the global North. As already mentioned, this practice was designed during the colonial era and has remained unchanged to this day. To this end, Africans have remained poor in a resource-rich continent.

For all intents and purposes, global financial apartheid and global financial architecture are two sides of the same coin. Their operations include the provisioning of grants, aid, concessional loans, development assistance, and more recently, climate financing and many other development finance mobilizing strategies. As previously mentioned, many critics (see Alami, 2019; Kvangraven et al., 2020; Paula, 2022; Alami et al., 2022), contest that the global financial architecture was designed to lift the peripheries out of their financial dependence, poverty, and debt colonialism in mind. Instead, they contend that the architecture was designed to enable indebted countries to be able to perpetually service their debts without ever being able to pay them off. Put differently, the solutions that are prescribed by the IFIs especially the IMF and the World Bank, are only meant to recover loans offered to the borrowing countries. This tends to keep these IFIs in "business" and their staffers as the most highly paid international public servants.

For some strange and twisted logic, the IFIs have been unwilling to drop the conditionalities they impose on cash-hungry countries of the South despite the overwhelming evidence against their relevancy and efficacy in resolving the financial heart attacks that are perennially affecting African countries. Even some global North scholars such as Joseph Stiglitz, Jefrrey Sachs, and Greg Mills have expressed some level of disdain about the efficacy of some of the conditionalities that are imposed on weak economies of the South. As Mutasa (2007) argues, despite the many arguments against conditionalities attached to multilateral lending and development assistance from bilateral donors, the conditionalities such as those relating to austerity measures, privatization, deregulation, destatization, desubsidization, and decontrol have instead intensified. This gives credence to the assertion that the global financial architecture is part of the hidden agenda to keep African countries poor, weak, and marginalized in the global economy (Nanga, 2015). In this regard, the current global financial architecture can be best described as unfit, unjust, and harmful to Africa's development aspirations.

Broadly speaking, many policies that have been developed, marketed, and exported by the Euro-Western countries and institutions to alleviate Africa's financial woes have in fact proved to be accentuators rather than ameliorators of financial apartheid and periodic financial heart attacks. Examples of these include the IMF and the World Bank's Heavily Indebted Poor Countries (HIPC) Initiative of 1996; the G-7's launch of the Multilateral Debt Relief Initiative (MDRI) in 2005; and the G-20 Debt Service Suspension Initiative (DSSI) of 2020; as well as the G-20 Common Framework for Debt Treatments of 2020 plus many others in-between. However, not unexpectedly, neoliberal theorists (Acemoglu & Robinson, 2012; Moyo, 2018; Mills, 2023) have conveniently blamed the failure of all these mechanisms to address Africa's financial problems on the continent's weak institutions, mismanagement, misappropriation, embezzlement, high level corruption, and lack of accountability and transparency. Although all these do account for the troubles facing the continent today, they are superficial factors. The really problem in Africa, as ferociously and epistemically presented by African and Africanists scholars including Achille Mbembe, Adebayo Adedeji, Adebayo Olukoshi, Adebayo Adebajo, Amina Mama, Archie Mafeje, Bade Omnimode, Bernard Ngubane, Charles Abugre, Cheikh Anta Diop, Chinua Achebe, Claude Ake, Dani Nabudare, Demba Dembele, Dennis Brutus, Brian Raftopoulos, Eshetu Chole, Fantu Cheru, Frantz Fanon, George Nzongala-Ntalaja, Ibbo Mandaza, Issa

G. Shiviji, Jacques Delpechin, Jimi Adesina, Leonce Ndikumana, Kankwenda M'Baya, Kwesi Prah Mahmood Mamdani, Ngugi waThiong'o, Pauline Hountondji, Paul Tiyambe Zeleza, Peter Anyang' Nyong'o, Sabelo Gatsheni J. Ndlovu, Sam Moyo, Samir Amin, Steve Biko, Thandika Mkandawire, Toyin Falola, Tukumbi Lumumba-Kasongo, Valentine Mudimbe, Walter Rodney, Tao Graham, Yash Tandon, and Yasmine Fall (the list is endless), is structural and systemic and is currently driven by a network of financial and economic institutions that are apparently remote controlled by wealthy countries and a few powerful global elites.

Enablers and Beneficiaries of Financial Apartheid

Today a growing number of scholars and researchers (Nanga, 2015; Alami, 2019; Bernards, 2020; Alami et al., 2022; Moyo, 2024) have written tomes about the enduring relevance of slavery, colonialism, and imperialism in shaping the contemporary global financial system. These authors and researchers have highlighted how financial and economic institutions in the Transatlantic region have profited from colonial engagements with colonial ventures and slave trading. Building on the foundations of left leaning scholars including Vladimir Lenin, Rudolf Hilferding, Nikolai Bukharin, Rosa Luxemburg, Kwame Nkrumah, Andre Gunder Frank, Walter Rodney, and Samir Amin among others, the contemporary critical finance scholars' focus on how financial and monetary relations between Africa and the fetishized global actors continue to reinforce the longstanding patterns of uneven development on the African continent and the rest of the global South.

As explained, global financial subordination is currently sustained by a multitude of policies and practices churned out largely by the troika of the World Bank, the IMF and the WTO all of which have been acting as bulldozers paving the way for the multinational corporations (MNCs) and the transnational capitalist class (TCC) to easily and speedily transfer financial capital from the continent to the imperial capitals, tax havens and other secrecy jurisdictions where it remains inaccessible to Africa's tax authorities. In doing so, these institutions have been contributing toward deepening of inequalities between the global North and global South economies. At the same time, they have helped sustain a global financial system that promotes the financial strangulation of Africa and the rest of the global South by a handful of global elites, financial marauders, and financial oligarchs. In net, the IFIs have been expanding what some observers have mockingly described as the "global financial republic" that has kept the countries of the global South entrapped in the vicious cycle of debt (Gildea, 2019; Ndlovu-Gatsheni, 2023).

Although the World Bank and the IMF gained their notoriety in the 1980s and 1990s through their much advertised but dreaded epistemic framework of SAPs, the two were already major interlocutors of global geoeconomic and geofinancial governance since their establishment at the end of the Second World War. To this day, the triad of the IMF, the World Bank and the WTO remains the premier global institutions with overarching influence on global finance, foreign investment decisions, and international trade rules as well as intellectual property rights among the other geoeconomic tools that have been deployed to maintain and sustain the geoeconomic, geofinancial and diplomatic superiority of the Euro-Western powers and their juridical institutions that maintain their own levels of consumption, production and development by suffocating global Africa and other countries of the global South.

For the record, while the archetypical Euro-Western organizations namely the World Bank and the IMF were jointly formed to assist in the stabilization of the economy and reconstruction of Europe in the end of the Second World War, the duo is now more active in global South including Latin America, the Caribbeans, Middle East, Asia and Africa with less direct activities in the global North except for gifting their Euro-Western shareholders with opportunities for trade, investment and finance (Moyo, 2024). To be clear, the IFIs activities in the rich countries of the global North have been relatively of low key—the exception being their financial advice and bailout programs in Portugal, Ireland, Iceland, Greece and Spain (PIIGS) following the global financial "tsunami" which swept the Transatlantic states and the rest of the world in 2007. Otherwise, the IFIs have curiously been more active in Africa and the rest of the global South where they have been tutoring, urging, and cajoling the economically vulnerable countries to open up their economies to the Euro-Western businesses, investment, trade, and finance, thereby facilitating financial apartheid, financial subjugation, and financial imperialism.

To this extent, accessibility, availability, and affordability of critical finance in Africa is largely determined by the geofinancial network of institutions whose policy prescriptions including financial liberalization, privatization, and trade liberalization have resulted in financial subordination, debt colonialism and financial poverty as the defining features of the continent's financial and economic landscape. Only those countries and companies that embrace the austerity regime of the IFIs have access to funding from bilateral and multilateral creditors as well as from the global capital markets. Literature is replete with evidence demonstrating that African countries especially those that are considered to be deviant in the eyes of the West such as Sudan, Uganda, and Zimbabwe, are generally excluded from the Euro-Western "financial grace."

African leaders such as Kwame Nkrumah, Muammar Gaddafi, Patrice Lumumba, Amilcar Cabral, Chris Hani, Thomas Sankara and many other decolonial luminaries who refused to bow to the gods of racial capitalism, imperialism, apartheid, and neocolonialism were eliminated by the alliance of global imperialists working in cahoots with some of the African collaborators. A classical case was the fall of Col. Muammar Gaddafi in the hands of the US and its North Atlantic Treaty Organization (NATO) allies "coincidentally" following his plans to adopt a Pan-African Currency based on gold backed by the Libyan Dinars. It is instructive to also note that Col. Gaddafi was a fervent champion of the African Investment Bank and Africa's Central Bank as well as the United States of Africa. None of these have ever been supported by the global North powers and institutions. Sadly, the departure of Gaddafi from the scene has somehow derailed these decolonial programs much to the relief of many in the Transatlantic region as well as those from the emergent and emerging global East as will be explained anon.

As previously mentioned, the IFIs work hand in gloves with transnational capitalist class and the rich global elites as well as with domestic elites together who are the real beneficiaries of the financial subordinated Africa. Although the IFIs have repeatedly raised concerns against illicit financial flows as well as concerns over tax havens, the bottom line is that their financialization and liberalization policies have directly and indirectly facilitated the decapitalization of the African countries. Accordingly, African countries have become increasingly poor as they interact more and more with the IMF, the World Bank, and the WTO as well as with the MNCs. To be clear of all the countries across the globe that have been bailed out by the IMF, 11 have been dependent to it for over three decades; 32 have been trapped in a debt cycle for almost 30 years, and 31 countries have been using the IMF lines of credit for almost two decades (Tendulka, 2021). The majority of these countries are in the global South including Africa.

To this extent, the IMF and the other Western controlled institutions should be considered to be part of a financial ecosystem that nourishes the global powerful countries, institutions, and individuals at the expense of Africa and African peoples. All this is happening at a time when net inflows to Africa in the form of international aid, loans, grants, remittances, and foreign direct investments among others have declined as a result of a number of factors including diversion of funds by the Euro-Western powers toward the war in Ukraine as well as to support their own post-COVID-19 recovery programs among many other financial, economic and political factors that are not relevant in this discussion.

Moreover, the façade of aid to Africa should be stripped naked as it has been serving the purpose of fooling Africans into thinking that the external financiers including the IFIs are in a mission to save the continent from poverty and underdevelopment when in actual fact the reverse is true. The IFIs are the Deputy Sheriffs working for and on behalf of the powerful global actors including states, big corporations, banks, and global elites, among others. Overall, it worth reiterating that the global North, which has now been joined by the emergent and emerging global East economies enjoys the privileged position of being able to dictate the terms of international transactions through its proxies-the global agencies—the IMF, the World Bank, and the WTO, among others.

Rigged Global Financial System

The global financial system has an inbuilt discrimination mechanism against countries outside the oligarchical setup of the global North. This is one of the reasons why Africa is losing billions of US dollars through various capital transfers including profit shifting, illicit financial flows and debt repayments among many other global circuits that are directly and indirectly facilitated by financial globalization. As mentioned, most of the capital that has been spirited away from

Africa has found its way into tax havens and offshore financial centers (OFCs) most of which are historically located in the global North. Many of these secrecy jurisdictions were established at the end of colonialism when the departing excolonialists looted their former colonies and stashed the funds away from tax authorities of African countries and those of their own home countries (Okwechime et al., 2016; Moyo, 2024). Thus, the net resource transfers from the continent to the rest of the world have been an enduring practice since Africa's colonial encounters. This stands in direct contrast to the conventional narrative about Africa being a beneficiary of grace from the North through its official development assistance, grants, concessional loans, foreign direct investment, and remittances. However, the reality is that all these transfers are outweighed by the equalizing backwash effects resulting from a rigged financial system (Dutt, 2004).

It is broadly agreed in literature that the rigged global financial system is perpetuated by the systemic loss of wealth from the continent due to Africa's role in international division of labor as a provider of commodities and a consumer of processed imports. As explained, the genealogy of this role is traceable to the dynamics of transitioning from a colonial state to a "post-colonial state" in the 1960s. As elaborated by decolonial thinkers such as Archie Mafeje, Claude Ake, Frantz Fanon, and Sabelo Ndlovu-Gatsheni, the transitioning process was flawed, fake and fabled. Their central argument is that at independence the colonial structures of power, economy, production, and finance remained in *situ* thus; Africa has not changed its subordinate position in the hierarchized global geoeconomic system. This geographical imbalance is sustained today by tools of subjectivation including predatory lending and SAPs as well as the dominance of the US dollar which is used to discipline the weaker countries to submit to the US controlled international financial system.

Also, policies such as the Africa Growth and Opportunity Act (AGOA)—which is, a trade relationship between the US and African countries as well as the Economic Partnership Agreements (EPAs)—which is, the trade relationship between EU and Africa have been strategically deployed by the powerful North to maintain its dominant economic and trade relations with African countries. These relations are predicated on the histories of colonialism, imperialism, racialism, and globalism, among others. As previously mentioned, the current North-South financial relations are characterized by birth defects in which African countries were not represented at the table of the Bretton Woods Agreement in 1944 when the "modern" financial system was designed. Instead, the majority of the African countries were at the time under colonial administration. No fundamental changes were made to the Bretton Woods Institutions (BWIs) when they held their Annual Meetings in Africa for the first time in 1973 in Kenya. Again, there were no major changes made when the IFIs held their second meeting in Africa 50 years later, in Morocco in October 2023 (also see Kaboub, 2023). It is therefore not entirely unsurprising that African countries and other global South economies can hardly influence the global financial cycle, the amount of capital flows into the continent, and the prices of lead currencies and interest rates (Koddenbrock & Sylla, 2019). And by extension, it is also not surprising that practically no African country has ever transformed its economy as a result of implementing the policy prescriptions of the BWIs/IFIs.

One of the key characteristics of the rigged global financial architecture is the hierarchy of currencies that has helped determine how countries interact within the global economy (Stein & Rowden, 2021). The US is at the top of this currency hierarchy with the US dollar acting as a veritable *numeraire* currency. At the bottom of the global hierarchy of currencies are countries of the global South. In recent years, the US has weaponized its dollar to advance its national and geopolitical interests (Fofack, 2023). As such, several countries that are targeted by US sanctions are working out strategies for de-dollarization. This includes the BRICS (Brazil, Russia, India, China, and South Africa) countries that feel short-changed by the US dollar dominated financial system. African countries whose economies are weak and yet their debts are denominated in US dollar are even worse when it comes to the politics of hierarchy of international currencies. Unfortunately, it is hypothesized that the strength of the US dollar vis-à-vis other currencies could be retained in the foreseeable future despite the efforts of the BRICS + toward de-dollarization.

Perhaps the most pernicious driver of financial imperialism is debt colonialism. Heterodox theorists such as Rudolf Hilferding, Rosa Luxemburg and Andre Gunder Frank have long noted that lending practices have served the interests of the creditors and big powers behind them who push the debtor countries into a vicious circle of debt and financial dependence (Hilferding, 1910; Luxemburg, 1913). Many African countries including Chad, Ethiopia, Ghana, Mozambique, Sierra Leone, Zambia, and Zimbabwe have been trapped in debt slavery as they can barely manage to service their debts. To be sure, Africa's debt stock as of December 2022 stood at US$789 billion up from US$702 billion in 2021, compared to US$380.9 billion in 2012 (Moyo, 2024).

Despite the stratospherical accumulation of debt, the IMF and the World Bank along with the G-7 and G-20 countries have been reluctant or unwilling to cancel the debts of the debt distressed countries. Even the so-called Africa's "all-weather friend" China has been reluctant to cancel debts of the debt distressed "friends" such as Sudan and Zimbabwe. Instead, the lenders and creditors continue to pile more loans to the economically poor countries that are desperately in need of resources to rehabilitate their economies following their economic stagnation caused by the COVID-19 global pandemic, ecological devastation, and hyperinflation caused by the Russo-Ukraine war. Quite clearly, debt has been historically used as an instrument of domination, subjugation and marginalization as well as plunder and exploitation by lenders and creditors.

In line with their imperial impulses, lenders have little regard for the dire economic situation in Africa and elsewhere in the global South. For example, the World Bank has been charging higher interest rates for its so-called "concessional loans" and similarly the IMF has been charging high surcharges to its borrowers, while the international credit rating agencies (ICRAs) have downgraded countries such as Angola, Ghana, Nigeria, South Africa, and Zambia despite the economic challenges caused by external shocks including pandemics, climate catastrophes, coups, and wars. By so doing, the ICRAs have been undermining the efforts of the African governments to mend their ailing economies and stunted development. For this reason, the ICRAs and the other global North-controlled institutions should be viewed as "accessories," "architects," and "reproducers" of financial apartheid in Africa and the rest of the global South. Put slightly differently, they are the *missi dorminici* (envoys of the ruler) of the powerful global North countries. They are used to reproduce financial dependence, financial subordination and financial subjugation in Africa and the rest of the global South.

The Vain of Global North-centric Responses

It is ironic that the architects of financial apartheid in Africa and other parts of the global South have been parading themselves as the wielders of the solutions of the same problems that they have helped to cause. Unsurprisingly, most of the contrived global North-centric solutions to Africa's financial woes are in essence meant to reproduce financial domination -the very disease they purport to cure. As mentioned earlier, examples of the purported solutions include the HIPC Initiative, MDRI, the DSSI and the Common Framework for Debt Restructuring as well as Global Climate Finance among many others. While these initiatives have cumulatively written off hundreds of billions in sovereign debt, they have not resolved the world's debt problem which continues to break records. To be sure, as Mutasa (2007) pointed out, these debt initiatives have suffered problems of chronic underfunding, excessive conditionalities, inadequate debt relief, and cumbersome procedures and eligibilities restrictions. There has been no real political will by the global actors to address the deficiencies of the global financial architecture.

The ongoing discussions of the Conference of Parties (COPs) are illustrative of the deformities of the global climate financing architecture. While green solutions such as carbon offsets, carbon credits, green bonds, carbon sinks and many others are marketed as smart solutions to climate change, anecdotal evidence indicates that they are enabling the Euro-Western countries and corporations to extract super profits at the expense of the African countries that are disproportionately affected by climate crisis. Some of the effects of these interventions include displacement, domination, degradation and impoverishment of the ordinary people. While the global North call their interventions with lovely superlatives such as green capitalism and smart transition, some observers refer to them as green colonialism, carbon colonialism, and fossil capitalism, climate apartheid (Saltana, 2023).

The other vain attempt by the global North to address the financial challenges of the vulnerable economies is exemplified by the way the IMF has been allocating and issuing the Special Drawing Rights (SDRs). These are international reserve assets that were created in 1969 in anticipation of future financial crises. The SDRs are supposed to alleviate liquidity constraints of the countries across the globe but in practice they have served to reinforce inequalities between the wealthier countries and the economically vulnerable economies especially those from Africa (Fofack, 2023). The most recent example is that of the US$650 worth of SDRs that were issued by the IMF in 2020 to combat COVID-19 pandemic. Of the US$650 billion, Africa only received a paltry US$33 billion (4.3 percent), and the richer countries received a lion's share despite the fact that they did not need the SDRs to combat COVID-19—they had various other financing options at their disposal (Konokhova, 2023). For instance, the UK with a population of 67 million people got more SDRs than 27 low-income countries with a combined population of 611 million people (Fofack, 2023). The profound unequal distribution of finance resources such as SDRs is precisely what entrenches global hegemony through the global North-centric organizations (Gururagavendran, 2023).

It must be mentioned here that the global North prescribed policy responses to financing challenges have had adverse impact on the lives and livelihoods of the ordinary people. These include poverty, high unemployment rates, persistent gender gap, and lack of primary health delivery, high inflationary rates, and widening inequalities in the majority of the African countries. Ironically, in an attempt to lessen the economic difficulties and financial heart attacks that are experienced in Africa and the other vulnerable countries, both multilateral and bilateral lenders and creditors have been providing more loans that have also resulted in debt distress and colonialism. Hence the charge that the current global financial architecture is not suited for the job.

This has necessitated the African Ministers of Finance, the African Development Bank, and the United Nations Economic Commission for Africa (UNECA) and the United Nations Conference on Trade and Development (UNCTAD) and many other institutions as well as civil society organizations and academics to call for the reform of the current global financial architecture. The proposed reforms include: (a) increasing policy space for Africa and other global South countries which could be achieved through relaxation of policy conditionalities in the delivery of aid; (b) restructuring of the debt sustainability framework (DSF) of the World Bank which is viewed as subjective on what constitutes good policy; and (c) increasing the representation of Africa IFIs (Okwechime et al., 2016).

The problem with the above suggested reforms is that they give undue emphasis on external intervention for solutions to the financial and economic distress that have engulfed Africa. African and Africanists thinkers have long cautioned against reliance on external sources of finance as solution to Africa's problems. Reliance on external financing will almost always end up taking the continent round the vicious cycle (Okwechime et al., 2016). Worse still, the proposed reforms are framed within the neo-liberal policy paradigms with no discernable departure from the very structures that are responsible for debt colonialism, financial dependence, and financial subjugation. As will be explained in the following pages, Africa will need some form of delinking as suggested Samir Amin in the 1970s.

Mirage of the Global East Promise

Arguably, the traditional powers have been joined by the new creditors and lenders in keeping Africa marginalized in the global economy. The new global actors including China, Russia, and India have designed a variety of financial and monetary mechanisms, including currency swaps, reserve pooling arrangements, and credit lines as part of their dollar diplomacy to court African countries. In particular, China and India (Chindia) have expanded the capacities of their national development banks, many of which now dwarf the volume of lending of the World Bank, and regional multilateral development banks around the globe.

Admittedly, unlike the Euro-Western powers, China and other emerging economies dole out huge amounts of financial largesse, aid, grants, and loans to Africa and the other countries across the globe without conditionalities that can be equated to those of the West. In particular, unlike the West, China is not concerned with issues of human rights and democracy which are normally demanded by multilateral and bilateral lenders and creditors. However, despite China's rhetoric on non-interference doctrine, it should be noted that in fact Beijing has been bullying African countries to shut down the Taiwan embassies in pursuit of its One China Policy. For example, in the last two decades Taiwanese embassies in countries such as Burkina Faso, Chad, Central Africa Republic, Gambia, Guinea-Bissau, Liberia, Malawi, Nigeria and South Africa have been closed under-pressure from Beijing.

Thus, although African countries are extracting some benefits from their engagement with their new partners, the patterns of relationship are not fundamentally different from those of the West-Africa relations. It is therefore reasoned out here that, in practical terms, Africa's move from one external patron to another is akin to changing the character of dependency without changing the logic of global capitalist relations (Ndlovu-Gatsheni, 2017; Moyo, 2021, 2024). To this end, the activities of China and other emerging economies of the global East on the continent are viewed here as part of neo-imperialism. This stands in direct contrast to the narrative that pitches the global East as a benign force that is helping Africa to be evenly integrated into the global economy.

So far, the indications are that Beijing and the other emerging powers are seeking to be accommodated in the Western-governed global financial system so that they can also enjoy the benefits of global capitalism that has kept Africa confined in the margins of history, global governance, economy, and finance (Nanga, 2015; Moyo, 2021, 2024). This is not to say that the new powers are comfortable with the current global system. Far from it. The fact is that the global financial and economic structures and institutions were designed to support the economies and politics and security of the Transatlantic states at the expense of the rest of the world. As such, the global governance system is as pernicious to the global East emergent and emerging economies as it is pernicious to African countries and other poor economies of the South.

However, it seems where the emergent economies led by China extract gains from the skewed relations with Africa and other vulnerable global South countries;

they have no incentive to change that system least they also lose out from the benefits of an asymmetrical integrated region into the global economy. As Moyo (2021) correctly observed, 'while the emerging and re-emerging powers seek to undermine the absolute Euro-Western superiority, they do not question its teleology of the markets, neoliberal designs and global coloniality'. So far, the rise of China has not addressed the deep historical and structural factors that keep Africans poor in a resource-rich continent. Instead, like the excolonizers, the Asian giant is generally concerned with markets, commodities, and sources of energy for its own industrialization program. The demand for raw materials by China and other BRICS countries has apparently increased the dependence of some of the African states on extractive industries a phenomenon that is hardly different from the practices of the West and its MNCs. Stein and Rowden (2021) confirm that the structure of trade between China and Africa is not fundamentally different from that of the West and Africa—it is all about the traditional division of labor where Africa is exporting commodities while importing finished products.

Viewed from this perspective, the new global powers have actually become new underwriters of Africa's marginalization. Take for example the IMF reforms of 2010 where two big African economies Nigeria and South Africa had their voting power reduced by 41 percent and 21 percent respectively while that of China increased by 35 percent, Brazil, India, and Russia by 23, 11 and 8 percentage points respectively (see Bond, 2015). This was despite the fact that African countries were in the forefront in the fight for the reforms of the IMF and the World Bank and yet the reforms benefited the new powers while disenfranchising Africa. What is troubling is that the reduction of Africa's voting powers in the IMF did not arouse any protest from the global East powers who instead celebrated their own new voting powers which they got at the expense of Africa. Considering the IMF reforms example, it is doubtful that Africa is gaining out of the emerging multipolar world system. So far, the hard fact is that Africa's position in the emerging multipolar world system has not changed.

It is also instructive to note that while a number of African countries are looking up to China and other global South middle powers for development partnerships, Beijing is leading the creation of a parallel international financial system focusing on its own interests. For instance, Beijing has established the China led Asian Infrastructure Investment Bank (AIIB) which is molded to rival the IMF. Again, along with Brazil, Russia, India and South Africa, China has established the New Development Bank (NDB) and the Contingence Reserve Arrangement (CRA) as well as its own international credit rating agency—the Dagong (also see Murithi, 2017; Moyo, 2024). Quite clearly, these institutions are not alternatives to the global capitalist institutions that have been undermining Africa in the global economy. In a way China is emulating the USA of the post-World War 2 which established financial, political, and economic institutions to reinforce its hegemony.

Needless to say, more than 10 years after the establishment of the NDB very little can be said about its impact to the African economies. If anything, its design has ironically served to empower the IMF by compelling countries that want to access more than 30 percent of their borrowing quota to first sign up to an IMF SAP (Bond,

2023). This gives credence to the claims that the emergence of China and others does not mark the demise of financial apartheid but instead it denotes that financial imperialism is entering a new phase where it is also implemented by those that profess to be acting against it. It would be therefore a fatal error for African leaders to place the hope for the continent's development journey on external institutions including those designed by the global East actors.

Dismantling Global Financial Apartheid Strictures

Hopefully, it is clear from the foregoing discussion, that this analysis rejects minimalists reforms to the global financial architecture that are favored by the Euro-Western powers and their juridical institutions such as the IMF and the World Bank as well as some of those represented by the emergent powers led by China. Some of the said reforms so far have been piecemeal, tokenistic, and ambivalent to say the least. This is particularly because the reforms have been led by the potential beneficiaries of the status quo. Some of the purported reforms are nothing but mere evolution within the capitalist paradigm rather than attempts to radically change the exploitative global capitalist system as well as the dysfunctional global financial architecture. Take for example, the arrangement by the G-7 and the G-20 and their allies to relieve poor countries of the debt burden in the light of the COVID-19 global pandemic. To this day, no African country is known to have resolved its debt crisis through following any of the prescriptions of the DSSI and the G20 Common Framework.

Clearly, the global North countries want minimalist reforms to the global financial system that are just enough to contain the pressure for radical reform while they reap massive profits. Unfortunately for Africa and the other global South countries such minimalist reforms, as noted by Gathii (2023), only serve to kick the can down the road as they do not challenge the unequal global financial relations. It is for this reason that this discussion argues in favor of comprehensive structural and systemic reforms in order for the continent to reinvent itself from the ashes of colonialism, imperialism, neocolonialism, globalism and globalization.

One of the most crucial steps for Africa is to delink itself from the capitalist constructed financial black hole as well as from the new imperialist 'false paradise'. This means desisting from blindly embracing neo-liberal policies that have served to enrich foreign investors and MNCs at the expense of the African peoples. In other words, there is an urgent need to decolonize the global financial system. This includes integrating more decolonial, anticolonial, feminist, antiracist and anticapitalist critiques struggles into the global financial system and practices in order to address the ongoing subjugation, exploitation, oppression, and marginalization of the continent (also see Saltana, 2023).

At the same time, African governments should urgently deal with the label of being viewed as passive recipients of external traditions, axiologies, institutions, ideas, policies, practices, systems, and epistemies. This includes rebelling against externally inspired financial, economic and development templates that serve to continuously entrench the continent as a supplier of raw materials and cheap labor and consumer of finished products from the industrialized and industrializing economies. Rather than depending on Euro-Western type solutions, African leaders and policy makers should harness the natural, material, and intellectual resources of the continent to ensure that African economies are not perpetually and structurally entrenched at the bottom rung of the global pecking order. By so doing, they will be able to improve the continent's well being while standing as a bulwark against the bullying tactics of the agents of financial apartheid.

The other key tool against global financial apartheid is the mobilization of the masses. Bond (2008) was right in claiming that the solution to the looting, marginalization, and imperialization of Africa is to be found in the self-activity of progressive Africans themselves including their campaigns, declarations and struggles ranged against an exploitative, extractive, and uneven global economy. Again, Hickel et al. (2022) were correct in asserting that 'structural transformation will only be achieved through political struggles from below, including anticolonial and environmental justice movements that continue to fight against imperialism'. To be sure, well mobilized masses have the potential to contribute toward dismantling the technologies of subjectivation including commodity dependence, financial subordination, and debt colonialism among others-with the object of creating a fair and inclusive financial, economic, and political system. This approach resonates very well with that of Roos (2018) who maintains that the only way to begin dismantling imperialist relations of domination and truly liberate the new debt colonies from their economic and financial subjugation is for the working class and social movements to stand united against impositions of global finance.

While noting the importance of the national efforts, it is also argued here that the fight against global financial apartheid cannot be won without global solidarity from the rest of the like-minded people and institutions across the globe. It is an established fact that the poor and the peasants across the globe are victims of capital accumulation by the TCC. Thomas Sankara of Burkina Faso had his finger on the pulse when he noted that those who want to exploit Africa are the same as those who want to exploit Europe (cited in Roos, 2018). This includes a few rich global elites constitutive of owners and managers of MNCs and other big business corporations that are benefiting from the current global financial system. Accordingly, global South leaders from across the spectrum should forge networks and collaborations across the globe in pursuit of the fight against imperial globality. Just like the war to end slavery, apartheid and administrative colonialism involved a large swath of actors including states, democracy campaigners, peasants, civil society, academics, and financiers across the globe, the fight against the ongoing financial apartheid in Africa and elsewhere in the global South, will need to be supported by all the like-minded global progressivists.

Conclusion

This chapter traces the colonial genealogies and biographies of the current financial apartheid regime in Africa back to the structural defects caused by colonialism and extractive dependence. It argues that the global financial system has consigned African countries and those of the economically vulnerable countries of the global South to dependencies such that they now lurch in the morass of vicious cycle of financial dependence, financial subordination, and subjugation. As such, nothing short of radical transformation will resolve the problem of financial apartheid in Africa. Without radical transformation, patterns of financial apartheid are unlikely to change, and existing patterns of financial dependence, domination and subjugation will likely continue defining the future of the continent.

References

Acemoglu, D., & Robinson, J. A. (2012). *Why nations fail: The origins of power, prosperity, and poverty*. Crown Business.

Alami, I. (2019). Global finance capital and third world debt. In I. Ness & Z. Cope (Eds.), *The Palgrave encyclopedia of imperialism and anti-imperialism*, https://doi.org/10.1007/978-3-319-91206-6_123-1.

Alami, I., Alves, C., Bonizzi, B., Kaltenbrunner, A., Koddenbrock, K., Kvangraven, I., & Powell, J. (2022). International financial subordination: A critical research agenda. *Review of International Political Economy, 30*(4), 1360–1386.

Arewa, O. (2023). Colonial hangover in global financial markets: Eurobonds, China and African debt. *Imperialism and the Political Economy of Global South's Debt*, 38.

Bernards, N. (2020). *How do colonial legacies shape the contemporary global political economy?*

Boberg, J. (2015). *Finance imperialism in British India: Profits from India equity on the London Stock Exchange 1900–1930*. https://gupea.ub.gu.se/handle/2077/53155.

Bond, P. (2008). Looting of Africa. In G. Lechini (Ed.). *Globalization and the Washington consensus: Its influence on democracy and development in the South*. Consejo Latinoamericanao de Ciencias Sociales (CLACSO). http://bibliotecavirtual.clasco.org.ar/ar/libros/sursur/ech/07bond.pdf

Bond, P. (2015). Uneven Citizen Advocacy within the bricks within global governance. *OHCHR*. https://www.ohchr.org/sites/default/files/Documents/Issues/IntOrder/GlobalGovernanceSpaces/PatrickBond.pdf.

Bond, P. (2023). *The BRICS Johannesburg Summit's Hype, Hope and Hopelessness*, (18 August), CADTM.

Collier, P. (2007). *The Bottom Billion: Why the poorest countries are failing and what can be done about it*. Oxford University Press.

Dutt, A. K. (2004). Uneven development, convergence and north-south interaction. In P. O'Hara (Ed.), *Global political economy and the problems of nations: Performance, institutions, problems and policies*. Routledge, Taylor and Francis Group.

Easterly, W. (2002). How did heavily indebted poor countries become heavily indebted? Reviewing two decades of debt relief. *World Development, 30*(10), 1677–1696. https://www.academia.edu/download/31561638/decades_of_debt..Easterly.pdf

Fofack, H. (2023). *Decolonising global finance*.

Gathii, J. T. (2023). Introduction. In J. T. Gathii (Eds.), *Reform the global and financial architecture*, Sheria Publishing House. ISBN: 979-8-9885111-0-6.

Gildea, R. (2019). *Empires of the mind: The colonial past and the politics of the present*. Cambridge University Press.
Gururagavendran, B. (2023). The coloniality of sovereign debt in the global south. In J. T. Gathii (Ed.), *The global debt and financial architecture*. Sheria Publishing House.
Hickel, J., Dorninger, C., Wieland, H., & Suwandi, I. (2022). Imperialists appropriation in the world economy: Drain from the global south through unequal exchange, 1990–2015. *Global Environmental Change, 73*(March).
Hilferding, R. (1981, 1910). *Finance capital: A study of the latest phase of capitalist development*. London: Routledge and Kegan Paul.
Kaboub, F. (2023). *Decolonising the global economic architecture: The prerequisite for a just transition*.
Koddenbrock, K., & Sylla, N. S. (2019). *Towards a political economy of monetary dependency: The case of the CFA in West Africa*, Maxpo Discussion Paper, No. 19/2, Max Planck Sciences Po Center on Coping with Instability in Market Societies, Paris.
Konokhova, M. (2023). *African countries push for changes as global financial architecture 'failing the world'*.
Kotzias, M., Micozzi, M., Ryfisch, D., & Niedermayer, R. (2023). *Reform the international financial architecture: A primer*.
Kvangraven, I. H., Koddenbrock, K., & Sylla, N. S. (2020). Financial subordination and uneven financialisation in 21st century Africa. *Oxford University Press and Community Development Journal* (pp. 1–22).
Luxemburg, R. (1913). *The accumulation of capital*. Routledge and Kegan Paul. https://marxists.org/archive/luxemburg/1913/accumulation-capital/
Mills, G. (2023). *Rich state, poor state: Why some countries succeed and others fail*. Penguin Random House: South Africa.
Moyo, D. (2018). *Edge of Chaos: Why democracy is failing to deliver-and how to fix it*. ABACUS.
Moyo, G. (2021). *African agency, finance and developmental states*. Macmillan Palgrave.
Moyo, G. (2024). *Africa in the global economy: Capital flight, financial subordination and decolonial responses*. Springer Nature.
Murithi, T. (2017). *Africa and the remaking of global order*. Institute for Justice and Reconciliation.
Mutasa, C. (2007). *Global apartheid continues to haunt global democracy*. CADTM. www.cadtm.org/Global-Apartheid-Continues-to-Haunt-Democracy/
Nanga, J. (2015). *New capitalist domination and imperialism in Africa* (9 November), CADTM.
Ndlovu-Gatsheni, S. J. (2017). Whither dependency theory? In U. Kufakurinani, I. S. Kvangraven, F. Santana & M. S. Styve (Eds.), *Dialogues on development*, 1, 34–41. https://developingeconomics.files.wordpress.com/2017/06/chapter-4-whither-dependency-theory.pdf
Ndlovu-Gatsheni, S. J. (2023). Beyond the coloniser's model of the world: towards reworlding from the Global South. *Third World Quarterly, 44*(10), 2246–2262. https://doi.org/10.1080/01436597.2023.2171389
Okwechime, I., Yange, J. T., & Aduloju, A. A. (2016). *World review of political, 7*(2, Summer).
Paula, L. F. (2022). *Financial subordination of peripheral emerging economies: A Keynesian-Structuralist Approach*. Discussion Paper 32/2022. The Institute of the Economy.
Roos, J. (2018). *The new debt colonies* (February 1), Viewpoint Magazine.
Sachs, J. (2005). *The end of poverty: How we can make it happen in our lifetime*. Penguin Books.
Sachs, J. (2023a). *How to end global financial apartheid: The poor countries are demanding an end to a world dominated by the rich – as well they should*.
Sachs, J. (2023b). *Financial apartheid, poverty trap: Replacing the system with a win-win proposition*. www.laprogressive.com
Saltana, F. (2023). Decolonising climate coloniality. In R. Solnit & T. Y. Lutunatabua (Eds.), *Not too late: Changing the climate story from despair to possibility*. Haymarket Books.
Schultz, C. (2021). *Postcolonial financing: The political history of 'risks-versus-rewards' investment in emerging markets*. https://doi.org/10.3167/th.2021.681603
Stein, H., & Rowden, R. (2021). *Global finance and the COVID-19 Pandemic in Africa*.
Tendulka, A. (2021). The international monetary fund: A vehicle for modern day imperialism. *International Policy Digest*.

Gorden Moyo (PhD) is currently the Senior Research Fellow in the Department of Sociology, Faculty of Humanities at the University of the Free State (UFS) in South Africa; Senior Lecturer in the Faculty of Social Sciences and Humanities at Lupane State University (LSU) in Zimbabwe; Member of the Editorial Board of the Sabella Abidde Publishing House, University of Alabama (USA); Director of the Public Policy and Research Institute of Zimbabwe (PPRIZ); Associate Member of the International Society for Development and Sustainability (ISDS) in Japan; the President of the Development Studies Association of Zimbabwe (DeSAZ); Member of the Southern African Development Parliamentary Forum Technical Group on Public Financial Management; ex-Minister of State in the Prime Minister's Office, ex-Minister of State Enterprises and Parastatals, and ex-Member of Parliament of Zimbabwe (2009–2013); ex-British Council Facilitator of the Pan-African Leadership Interaction Programme in 19 countries across Africa including Botswana, Cameroon, Eritrea, Ethiopia, Eswatini, Ghana, Kenya, Lesotho, Liberia, Malawi, Mauritius, Namibia, Nigeria, South Africa, Tanzania, Uganda, Zambia, and Zimbabwe. He is a Chevening Scholar whose primary research interests are in global finance, international economic relations, developmental states, public leadership, military commercialism, Africa-China relations, and African Agency among others. He has published several articles in peer-reviewed journals and several book chapters. His most recent books include *African Agency, Finance, and Developmental States* (Palgrave McMillan, 2021); *Making Politics in Zimbabwe's Second Republic: The Formative Project by Emmerson Mnangagwa* (Springer, 2023) co-edited with Prof Kirk Helliker; and *Africa in the Global Economy: Capital Outflows, Enablers and Decolonial Responses* (Springer, 2024).

Chapter 4
Development Under Threat: The Return of the Debt Crisis in Africa

Sizo Nkala

Abstract Africa finds itself in a debt crisis similar to that witnessed in the 1980s through the 1990s. Since 2010, Africa's debt has increased by 183 percent to over US$1.8 trillion. The median public debt-to-GDP ratio in Africa grew from 28.8 percent in 2012 to 59.1 percent in 2022. While the figure of US$1.8 trillion seems low since Africa's debt makes up only 2 percent of the total, the majority of African countries do not have the capacity to handle their debts thus rendering them unsustainable and inimical to Africa's development. About six countries have defaulted on their debts since 2020, while eight countries have been classified as debt-distressed and 13 more are facing a high risk of debt distress. This chapter argues that the current measures namely the Debt Service Suspension Initiative (DSSI) and the Common Framework for Debt Treatment Beyond the DSSI introduced to mitigate the debt crisis have proved ineffective. Urgent solutions including an improved international debt treatment mechanism, continental initiatives like the African Credit Rating Agency and the African Debt Monitoring Mechanism, and the capacitation of national debt management offices are needed to address the debt crisis in Africa.

Introduction

The world is in the midst of a polycrisis and multiple global storms. Climate change, global poverty on the rise, wars and instability, geopolitical tensions, erosion of multilateralism, and a devastating debt crisis affecting especially the low-income countries the majority of whom are in Africa are some of the storms wreaking havoc across the world. This chapter addresses the latter storm in relation to Africa. Since 2010, Africa's debt has increased by 183 percent to over US$1.8 trillion. The median public debt-to-GDP ratio in Africa grew from 28.8 percent in 2012 to 59.1 percent

S. Nkala (✉)
Department of International Relations and Politics, Centre for Africa-China Studies, University of Johannesburg, Johannesburg, South Africa

G. Moyo, S. J. Ndlovu-Gatsheni (eds.), *Global Storms and Africa in World Politics*, Global Power Shift, https://doi.org/10.1007/978-3-031-83868-2_4

in 2022 (UNCTAD, 2023). This means that half of the African states have a debt-to-GDP ratio above 59 percent. According to the International Monetary Fund's (IMF) Debt Sustainability Analysis (DSA), 21 African countries were either in debt distress (8) or facing a high risk of debt distress (13) which translates into 455 million African citizens living in debt trapped countries (IMF, 2023). In 2023, countries in the region paid over US$69 billion in debt service payments which is more than all the aid received in 2021. The size of Africa's external debt is equal to 29 percent of its GDP and 140 percent of its export revenue. Just six years before the lapsing of the Sustainable Development Goals (SDGs) deadline in 2030, 25 countries in Africa spent more money on interest payments than on health, while in seven countries, interest expenditure exceeded spending on education. More than half of Africa's population (751 million people) lives in countries where the government spends more on interest payments than on health and education (UNCTAD, 2023). That said, this paper delves into the dynamics of the debt crisis in Africa and its implications. The first section places the crisis in a historical perspective by demonstrating how colonialism structured African economies to be dependent on external finance and the export of primary commodities with volatile prices. This economic structure makes African countries particularly vulnerable to the debt trap. In the second section, I highlight the dynamics of the debt crisis and its contributing factors such as the 2014 oil price shocks, the COVID-19 pandemic, the Russia-Ukraine war, and the rise in global interest rates which fueled debt accumulation at a time when the capacity to service those debts was rapidly diminishing. The structure of the African debt stock, noting the composition of the creditors (especially the emergence of China and the private lenders), the degree of concessionality, and the phenomenon of resource-based loans (RBLs) and their implications, is discussed in section "Africa's Debt Crisis". The succeeding section is an assessment of the debt relief initiatives namely the Debt Service Suspension Initiative (DSSI) and the Common Framework for Debt Treatment Beyond the DSSI. These initiatives have proved ineffective and inadequate in addressing the continent's debt crisis. The final section proposes a plethora of possible solutions to the debt crisis including the improvement of the Common Framework, rebuilding debt management systems in African countries, the reform of the global financial system, and the setting up of the African Debt Monitoring Mechanism and the African Credit Rating Agency. However, a more long-term solution lies in the structural transformation of African economies which could be achieved through the implementation of the African Continental Free Trade Area (AfCFTA).

The History of Africa's Debt Problem

Just less than 20 years after African countries were rescued from a devastating debt crisis through the intervention of the Highly Indebted Poor Countries (HIPC) initiative and the Multilateral Debt Relief Initiative (MDRI), the continent finds itself once again with a debt burden too heavy to bear. At the G8 Summit in 2005 in

Gleneagles, Scotland, US$130 billion of debt was canceled for poor countries after a high-profile public campaign spear-headed by celebrities (Christianson, 2023). Under the 1996 HIPC initiative, developed countries wrote off debt for poor countries while the multilateral lenders restructured 44 percent of African debt. Coulibaly et al. (2019) point out that as a result of debt forgiveness, the median debt-to-GDP ratio for Africa was 31 percent in 2012 but it rose to 53 percent by 2017. Some countries such as Sierra Leone, Malawi, Ghana, and Liberia had their debt stock substantially reduced by up to 90 percent. Zambia had over US$2.5 billion of debt written off between 1998 and 2010 which saw its debt-to-GDP ratio declining from 161 percent to 17 percent. Nonetheless, the ratio had shot up to 140 percent in 2022. Ghana's debt-to-GDP ratio had reached 88 percent in 2022 from 25 percent in 2006 when the HIPC ended. Its debt service-to-revenue ratio stood at a worrying 117.6 percent (Kumah-Abiwu & Haynes, 2023; IMF African Department, 2023). In a short space of time, Africa seems to have come full circle from the debt crisis of the 1980s and 1990s. More than anything, that Africa is dealing with another debt crisis in a few short years is an indictment on the effectiveness of the HIPC as a debt-relief mechanism which did not go far enough to address the fundamental factors driving Africa's perpetual debt trap (Sanubi, 2006).

Before delving into the dynamics of the current debt crisis, it is necessary to explore the history of the continent's debt problem to put the current situation into a historical perspective. Africa's endemic problem with debt has its roots in the colonial era (Alemayehu, 2003; Omotola & Saliu, 2009; Okeke, 2001; Danso, 1990). When colonialism reached the African shores in the latter part of the nineteenth century, African territories were forcibly integrated into the world economy as suppliers of various raw materials such as cotton, copper, gold, sisal, rubber, tobacco, phosphate, manganese, cocoa, and coal among other things to European factories which were at the forefront of the industrial revolution (Danso, 1990; Alemayehu, 2003). Thus, African economies were incorporated into a world economic system characterized by an asymmetric relationship between the core (global North) and the periphery (global South) (Wallerstein, 1974; Gunder-Frank, 1972). Nkala (2019: 74) argues that "Zimbabwe was incorporated into the global economy at the inception of colonialism as a peripheral and dependent player… the modern mining industry in Zimbabwe was born of capital raised in the London and New York financial markets. Its umbilical cord is tied to the capitalist centers in the Western capitals." Mamdani (1977) showed how British colonizers coerced Uganda into producing cotton for the textile industry in Manchester. Consequently, the colonial economies were structured to produce one or two primary products to be sold to the metropoles in Europe. The international division of labor positioned Africa to supply raw materials without any capacity for processing them resulting in a disarticulated economy that produced what Africans did not consume (Danso, 1990; Omotola & Saliu, 2009). The nature of the colonial economy meant that African countries depended on the European countries not only for markets but for finance as well to maintain the export economy.

As such, when they emerged from colonialism in the 1960s, the newly independent African states inherited commodity-based and export-oriented economies that depended on trade with the developed countries and also determined the terms of trade. Ramose (2006: 3) was dismayed that the decolonization process left the economic power of the colonizers intact and contended that this constituted "a very grave concern over the structural economic dependency of contemporary Africa." Hence, after independence, African countries had no option but to borrow to finance development projects (Okeke, 2001). Financial dependence of the colonies on the metropoles continued as the new governments inherited the debt taken by colonial governments and continued to take out loans for major infrastructure projects (Zajontz, 2022). In the late 1960s and early 1970s, African governments could finance most of their development needs through their export earnings on the back of a commodity price boom. However, after the first oil price shocks of 1973–1974 when oil prices quadrupled African states' oil import bills are estimated to have increased by between US$800 million and US$1.3 billion which was enough to capsize their development plans (Johnson & Wilson, 1982). The situation turned from bad to worse when the huge oil import bills were compounded by declining forex earnings as a result of the subsequent fall in commodity prices. For example, copper prices declined from US$1.40 per pound in the 1960s and early 1970s to just US$0.53 cents per pound in 1974 dealing a body blow to countries like Zaire and Zambia (Callaghy, 1984). According to Cooper and Robert (1975), prices of commodities like sugar, beef, coffee, and grains fell by 21 percent between May 1974 and June 1975. Industrial materials like iron ore, rubber, coal, and lumber fell by 40 percent between April 1974 and June 1975. African countries had huge national accounts deficits which forced them to accumulate debt to keep their development projects alive. Believing that African countries were going through a liquidity crisis and that the commodity price slump was cyclical, European banks and governments were happy to avail credit to African sovereign borrowers (Lipumba, 2002). African external debt ballooned from just US$6 billion in 1970 to US$14 billion in 1973. It reached US$83 billion in 1983 and almost doubled in a year to US$150 billion in 1984 and stood at US$230 billion four years later in 1988 (Callaghy, 1984; Adedeji, 1990). Another oil price increase in 1979–1980 and the subsequent interest rate hike in the US and other industrialized countries aimed at combatting inflation pushed African countries deep into the economic doldrums. The resultant increase in real interest rates and the deteriorating terms of trade combined with a severe drought in 1982 plunged the continent into a debt crisis.

As early as 1977, Tanzania's debt obligations exceeded its exports. In 1982, six countries—the Central African Republic (CAR), Chad, Mali, Mauritania, Sudan, and Tanzania had arrears above 20 percent of their exports (Lipumba, 2002). While in 1978, only two countries had stabilization agreements with the IMF, between 1979 and 1982, 36 countries had an agreement of one kind or another with the IMF including standby agreements or the extended fund facility as they struggled with the balance of payments. Buckling under the pressure of debt servicing, about 27 African countries underwent numerous repeat nonconcessional debt rescheduling processes with the Paris Club in conjunction with IMF lending based on the implementation of the Structural Adjustment Programs (SAP) (Callaghy, 1984). However, debt rescheduling did not work as debt arrears continued to pile up. Upon realizing that Africa was facing a solvency crisis rather than a short-term liquidity crisis, new measures were introduced in the mid-1980s to address the debt problem. These included the 1985 Baker Plan, and the so-called Toronto, London, Naples, and Lyon terms in 1988, 1991, 1994, and 1995 respectively which sought to reduce the countries' debt stock by various amounts ranging from one-third to 80 percent on condition that debtor countries adopt neoliberal macroeconomic policies (Omotola & Saliu, 2009). However, these measures were not effective as Sub-Saharan Africa's debt stock was only reduced by 20 percent between 1985 and 1995. Smith (2021) observed that between 1983 and 1990, African countries paid a total of US$180 billion in debt service compared with a total debt stock of US$140 billion in 1982. While per capita incomes had grown at 1.4 percent per year in the 1970s, they regressed to −0.4 percent and −0.2 percent in the 1980s and 1990s as a result of the debt crisis (Smith, 2021).

With the traditional approaches of IMF stabilization programs and debt rescheduling having failed, the Highly Indebted Poor County (HIPC) initiative was introduced in 1995. The HIPC initiative was underpinned by six conditions: improving debt sustainability on a case-by-case basis; putting debt relief to good use; measures to build on the Paris Club mechanisms; coordination of all creditors to provide debt relief on an equitable basis; preservation of preferred creditor status of the MFIs who also provide debt relief; and new external financing on concessional terms. Countries would be eligible for debt forgiveness upon the successful implementation of economic reforms for three years. Of the 41 HIPC-qualifying countries, 33 were in Africa. After the implementation of the HIPC and the 2005 Multilateral Debt Relief Initiative (MDRI)—a G7 scheme which canceled the debt of the HIPC countries owed to the IMF, the World Bank, and the African Development Bank—the public debt-to-GDP ratio for 26 qualifying countries in Africa fell from an average of 104 percent before the interventions to an average of 27 percent after the interventions (Mark & Merotto, 2012). Nonetheless, the 2020s look set to be a dejavu of the 1980s as African economies are on the brink of collapse once again under debt distress. The next section is an assessment of the current debt situation in Africa.

Africa's Debt Crisis

Since the beginning of the COVID-19 pandemic in 2020, several countries namely Chad, Ethiopia, Mali, Ghana, Zambia, and Malawi defaulted on their debt payments due to acute fiscal imbalances (Pellegrini, 2023). About 30 African countries joined the G20's Debt Service Suspension Initiative (DSSI) in a bid to free up resources to tackle the pandemic. These were the signs that the debt crisis had begun in earnest. In 2022, Africa's total public debt was well over US$1.8 trillion which represented an increase of 183 percent from 2010 (UNCTAD, 2023). The public debt growth rate far outpaced economic growth as it grew four times faster than the GDP between 2010 and 2022. The size of Africa's public debt, albeit making up just 2 percent of the global public debt, far exceeds what the majority of the region's economies can handle (Mo Ibrahim Foundation, 2023). The global economic recession following the advent of the COVID-19 pandemic had many countries in a precarious position. The IMF noted that although the public debt-to-GDP ratios and external public debt service-to-revenue ratios are not at the level they were in the 1990s (the public debt-to-GDP ratio reached 89 percent in 1995) that prompted the introduction of the HIPC and the MDRI, they have reached levels that undermine debt sustainability (Ngugi et al., 2023; IMF, 2023). The IMF and the World Bank's Debt Sustainability Analysis (DSA) for 2023 classifies eight countries as debt distressed, 13 display a high risk of debt distress, and 16 show moderate risk. The number of African countries at high risk of or in debt distress in the DSA list decreased from 23 in 2022 to 21 in 2023. Nonetheless, this still leaves nearly 455 million people in the continent living in countries that are either facing a high risk of debt distress or are already debt distressed. About 18 countries had debt levels above 60 percent of their GDP before the COVID-19 pandemic. This number rose to 27 in 2020 after the pandemic before declining to 24 in 2022 (The United Nations Conference on Trade and Development, 2023).

The making of the current debt crisis could be traced back to the 2008 financial crisis and the 2014–2015 oil price collapse. Before the 2008 global financial crisis, African countries ran a primary fiscal surplus reaching an average of 3.5 percent of the GDP. However, after the financial crisis, most countries experienced deficits averaging 1.6 percent of the GDP (Coulibaly et al., 2019). African countries had enjoyed a commodity price super-cycle which saw many governments adopt lax fiscal policies banking on the continuation of high commodity prices. When the super-cycle came to an end in 2014, most governments found it politically impossible to switch to prudent fiscal policies thus placing public finances under pressure. The collapse in commodity prices drove the primary deficit to 3.5 percent of GDP between 2014 and 2017 (Coulibaly et al., 2019). This was particularly pronounced in oil-exporting countries which underwent rapid debt accumulation. The poor state of macroeconomic conditions in most African countries also drove them to the debt trap. To arrest debt accumulation and escape the debt trap, African governments needed to improve their current accounts, fiscal balances, and inflow of foreign direct investment. However, in all these indicators in the 8 years from 2015 to 2022, Africa was underperforming (Mukhopadhyay, 2022). Both the fiscal balance and current accounts stood at negative 4.7 percent and 3.7 percent of the GDP respectively while the net foreign direct investment was only 1.8 percent of GDP in 2022 (Mukhopadhyay, 2022).

Sustained budget deficits combined with the trade imbalance and low FDI inflows locked most low-income countries into a vicious cycle of low development in which they could not stop debt accumulation. Although the situation was already looking bleak, the COVID-19 pandemic and the Russia-Ukraine war pushed many countries into the red (Pellegrini, 2023). As COVID-19 lockdowns ground the global economy to a halt and the global commodity demand shrunk rapidly, many countries in Africa were left with little choice but to borrow at high interest rates to raise funds to address the public health emergency and to protect the millions of vulnerable people who lost their incomes. The continent faced its worst recession in decades when the real GDP shrunk by 2.1 percent in 2020. Increased debt vulnerabilities saw 11 countries' sovereign credit status being downgraded during the pandemic due to reduced revenues, growing fiscal deficits, shrinking foreign exchange receipts, and fluctuating exchange rates (Mukhopadhyay, 2022; Moreira, 2023). This was also exacerbated by the disruption of the global energy and food supply chains following the outbreak of the Russia-Ukraine conflict in February 2022 which increased many countries' food and energy import bills. The large import bills could only be met through issuing more debt. The high borrowing induced by the pandemic and the sluggish global economic recovery threw the region's public finances off-balance.

In 2023, countries in the region paid over US$69 billion in debt service payments which is more than all the aid received in 2021 (Smith, 2023). In Nigeria alone, 59 percent of government revenue was dedicated to debt repayment. Africa's external public debt is equivalent to 29 percent of its GDP and represents 140 percent of the continent's export revenue (UNCTAD, 2023). The mismatch between export revenues and external debt has seen many countries struggling to service their debts due to the shortage of foreign currency. Moreover, African countries also have to face significantly high borrowing costs because of the risk perception. The average cost of financing for Africa is 11.6 percent, which is way above the 3.1 percent risk-free rate (UNCTAD, 2023). The high-risk levels bar many countries from participating in the financial markets or participating at a significantly high cost. Interest rates on Africa's sovereign bonds were six percentage points higher than loans from bilateral and multilateral lenders in 2021. Consequently, 21 countries in the region make interest payments which make up more than 10 percent of their revenues (UNCTAD, 2023).

The IMF (2023) noted that the proportion of government revenues directed toward interest payments increased in 34 African countries and by over 10 percentage points in 13 countries. This diverts a significant amount of the already limited budgets from critical services like education, health, and water and sanitation. In the depths of the 1980s debt crisis, the former Tanzanian President Julius Nyerere (1985: 2) remarked that poor countries pay interests from their "poverty, not from abundance. The high, and often floating interest rates are a form of Taxation without Representation-taxation of the poor for the benefit of the rich." In the last 10 years, interest payments have increased by 132 percent which is almost double the rate of other developing countries where interest payments increased by 64 percent. About 25 countries in Africa spent more money on interest payments than on health, while in seven countries, interest expenditure exceeded spending on education. More than half of Africa's population (751 million people) lives in countries where the government spends more on interest payments than on health and education (UNCTAD, 2023). As Okeke (2001) rightly argued, spending significant shares of government revenue on debt servicing while starving essential services such as health, education, and sanitation of funding is a violation of international human rights law. The high interest rates are largely due to a rigged system of international finance. African countries are automatically slapped with a 2.9 percent premium when they borrow because of the continent's risk perception (Otieno, 2023). Moreover, during the COVID-19 pandemic, 41 percent of countries in Africa received a negative credit rating which made borrowing even more expensive (Smith, 2023). The credit rating agencies such as S&P, Moody's, and Fitch which rate 90 percent of the market, influence how lenders price African risk yet they don't have sufficient expertise in low-income countries. Only two of the agencies have offices in Africa and both of them are located in Johannesburg, South Africa.

Africa's struggling exports and the US Federal Reserve's decision to increase interest rates saw private creditors shunning African sovereign bonds while investing more in bonds from developed countries due to the prospects of increased returns (Christianson, 2023). The unholy confluence of the COVID-19 pandemic, the Russia-Ukraine war, the rise in global interest rates, and the decline in concessional finance from official lenders plunged Africa into a full-blown debt crisis. It is a crisis that has left many governments with the grim choice of repaying debts or providing essential services for their citizens. Structural issues that constrain sustainable development financing remain a factor. Domestic savings in African countries have been depressed at 15 percent of GDP on average since 2000 because of low revenue collection, rampant profit shifting by multinationals, illicit financial flows, and weak natural resource governance (Coulibaly et al., 2019).

The Structure of the African Debt

The structure of African debt has evolved over the years with far-reaching implications on debt treatment processes and debt sustainability. The creditor profile of African countries is one dimension of the African public debt that changed dramatically in the past two decades. While the creditor composition used to be dominated by multilateral and Western bilateral actors, private creditors and non-Paris Club members are becoming increasingly important. Private creditors' share of Africa's debt stock increased from just 17 percent in 2000 to 30 percent in 2010 and reached a record 44 percent in 2021 (Mo Ibrahim Foundation, 2023). This development corresponded to Africa's increased access to the Eurobond market beginning in the late 2000s. Since 2007, African governments gained access to the capital markets and started issuing Eurobonds which by 2021 made up US$144 billion of the continent's debt stock (Christianson, 2023). Moreira (2023) observes that 21 African countries had issued Eurobonds in 2020 up from just 3 in 2001. The issuance of African sovereign bonds increased significantly from an average of US$10 billion annually in the 2000s to US$80 billion between the years 2016 and 2020. Although commercial debt is characterized by shorter maturities and high interest rates, African countries took credit from the private sector as they were trying to avoid the policy conditions that come with loans from the MDBs and Western countries (Mo Ibrahim Foundation, 2023). The short-term maturity and high interest rates associated with commercial debt make it unsuitable for funding infrastructure projects whose returns are distributed over a long time. On the other hand, bilateral debt moved in the opposite direction, declining from 52 percent in 2000 to just 25 percent in 2021. This is most likely because of the financial crisis which plunged most of the traditional bilateral lenders into a recession in 2008.

Multilateral debt did not change much having moved from 36 percent in 2009 to 34 percent in 2022 (See Adesina, 2023). Domestic creditors comprising commercial banks and pension funds have also become more prominent as their share of the debt stock has now reached 55 percent—which represents an increase of more than 100 percent since 2007. This demonstrates the successful development of the local capital markets on the one hand but also the challenges that African countries have faced in accessing the international market leaving them with no choice but to resort to local banks on the other (Pellegrini, 2023). Another significant development in the structure of African debt has been the emergence of Chinese credit from both official and private sources. The debt from private Chinese creditors increased from 2.3 percent (US$5,3 billion) in 2009 to 3.7 percent (US$24,39 billion) in 2022. Chinese official credit grew from 4.2 percent (US$9,27 billion) in 2009 to 9.6 percent (US$62,89 billion) in 2022 (Adesina, 2023). The bulk of Chinese finance is directed to infrastructure projects in the energy, transport, and information and communication technology sectors. The rise of China represents the emergence of non-Paris Club member's official creditors whose rules and norms may be different thus potentially adding more complications to debt treatment and debt resolution processes (Mukhopadhyay, 2022).

Further, African public debt has been described as uniquely burdensome because most of the lenders are foreign and they issue credit in international currencies. In contrast, over 70 percent of the public debt in Canada, China, the US, and the UK is domestic and is issued in their own currencies, yet Africa has over 70 percent of its public debt denominated in US dollars (Mo Ibrahim Foundation, 2023). Accepting loans in foreign currency means that debtor countries have to shoulder the risk of interest rate changes which leaves them having to cough out more money toward debt payments at the expense of development expenditure (Thompson, 2023). There has also been an emergence of natural resource-backed loans (RBLs) over the years. RBLs are defined as "loans that are secured by using a country's natural resources to serve either as a direct source of repayment or as an underlying guarantee for repayment of the loans." Between 2004 and 2018, there were 30 natural resource-backed loans signed by African states namely Angola, Chad, Ghana, Niger, Sudan, and Zimbabwe among others and their lenders worth a total of US$66 billion.

The natural resources could include mineral deposits, oil, and commodities. Angola leads African countries in terms of the number of RBLs with six followed by Ghana and the Republic of Congo with five each while Zimbabwe and South Sudan are a joint third with three RBLs each. Most of the RBLs are sourced from the Chinese policy banks such as the China Development Bank (CDB), China Export and Import Bank (Exim Bank), while some are sourced from commercial lenders. For example, Chad secured a loan from Glencore in 2014 to be serviced by future oil revenues. However, due to commodity price volatility, the borrowers can find themselves having to sell higher volumes of their commodity in order to service the loans (Coulibaly et al., 2019). Debt restructuring negotiations become even more complex due to the lack of data on collateralized or syndicated debt which gives creditors control of specific assets or revenue streams in the event of debtor countries defaulting on their debt. Creditors holding collateralized debt will be reluctant to restructure (Christianson, 2023). Further, the degree of concessionality in Africa's debt stock is another important feature. The proportion of concessional loans varies with each source. Among Africa's creditors, multilateral lenders lead with respect to concessional finance. Around 63 percent and 45.5 percent of loans from the World Bank and the AfDB are issued under concessional terms with an average interest rate of 1 percent. This compares to 40 percent for Paris Club lenders and just over 5 percent for China with average interest rates of 1.2 percent and 3.2 percent respectively (Mo Ibrahim Foundation, 2023). Chinese loans are attractive to African governments because they are underpinned by the principle of noninterference and usually go to the transport, energy, and mining sectors. However, Chinese finance has been criticized for being tied to the use of Chinese companies, materials, and labor in the funded projects (Nkala & Eyita-Okon, 2023).

Debt Service Suspension Initiative and the Common Framework

Moreira (2023) laments the absence of an international debt resolution framework which has seen the international community relying on late, ad hoc, and temporary debt-relief interventions such as the 2020 Debt Service Suspension Initiative (DSSI) and the G20 Common Framework. It seems nothing has been learned from the HIPC/MDRI experience. Although African countries had been languishing in debt crises since the 1980s, the HIPC was only approved in 1996 while the MDRI was finalized in 2005 and both initiatives would take a decade to implement. The HIPC required compliance with a three-year IMF Program before a country was accepted into the initiative. If, after the program, a country still had debt stocks regarded as unsustainable, a two-thirds debt-stock reduction was effected (Alemayehu, 2003). Although the debt stock of African countries was significantly reduced after these interventions, their implementation was late and slow. The 1980s and 1990s have been branded lost decades in terms of development because of the failure to address the debt problem with urgency.

The DSSI was introduced by the Group of 20 (G20) in 2020 to provide relief for African countries and other low-income countries struggling with debt repayments owing to the challenges brought by the COVID-19 pandemic. The scheme offered debt service moratoriums on bilateral loans for 73 eligible developing countries including 37 from Africa. However, the initiative achieved limited success. Although 30 of the 37 eligible African countries participated and benefited from the suspension of debt service, the actual savings of US$1.8 billion realized for the period May–December 2020 were way below the expected figure of US$5.5 billion (Mukhopadhyay, 2022). The initiative was limited in scope as it only covered debt from official creditors while excluding private lenders. Independent Chinese State-owned enterprises (SOEs) did not participate in the initiative which rendered it a damp squib (Otieno, 2023; Mo Ibrahim Foundation, 2023). Moreover, a lack of clear communication on the financing costs and sovereign credit rating saw some debtor countries opting not to participate.

The G20 also introduced the Common Framework for Debt Treatment Beyond the DSSI in November 2020. The Common Framework was designed to expedite and negotiate debt treatment for countries eligible for the DSSI and aimed to secure the participation of all creditors including the private sector. While the onus is on the debtor country to request debt treatment, the necessity of treatment is to be determined by the IMF and the World Bank's Debt Sustainability Analysis and the collective evaluation of the creditors. The Common Framework requires the debtor country to provide all the necessary information to all creditors in the spirit of transparency but with due respect to commercially sensitive information. All official creditors including those outside the G20 and the Paris Club who are owed by the debtor country are free to participate in the debt treatment negotiations first separately and then jointly with other creditors to decide on the key parameters of the treatment program. The key parameters of the Common Framework include: the changes in nominal debt service over the IMF program period; debt reduction in net present value terms if applicable; and the extension of the duration of the treated claims.

The framework stressed that these parameters will enhance burden-sharing among creditors by ensuring that all creditors including those in the private sector extend comparable treatment to the debtor country in terms of changes in nominal debt service, size of debt stock, and the duration of treated claims. The debtor country is required to seek comparable treatment from all creditors. However, because the framework is based on general principles, its application to specific cases has been difficult and time-consuming. It is also not clear whether China, a major bilateral creditor, will abide by the parameters set according to the IMF and World Bank's DSA or defer to its Belt and Road Initiative (BRI) Debt Sustainability Framework which is underpinned by higher risk parameters than those of the DSA (Cooray & Walker, 2023). China and other private creditors complained about the lack of flexibility and the exclusion of the debt owed to the IMF and the World Bank in the perimeter of the debt to be restructured (Pellegrini, 2023). It will be very difficult to move forward with debt restructuring if the creditors do not agree on common rules. These delays will leave debtor countries facing crippling economic uncertainty and undermine the probability that they will ever be able to pay back their debts. Another issue with the Common Framework is that debtor countries have not been willing to apply for the treatment due to the risk of being downgraded.

Only four countries namely Zambia, Ethiopia, Chad, and Ghana applied for debt treatment under the Framework. Chad reached an agreement in December 2022 after two years of negotiations while Zambia's negotiations are still ongoing almost 3 years on (Ngugi et al., 2023). Chad's debt treatment deal was criticized for failing to reduce its external debt of US$3 billion but instead just postponing the country's debt service to the future. This means that Chad still has a debt overhang that will constrain economic growth as revenues will still be channeled to the creditors at the expense of investment (The African Sovereign Debt Justice Network, 2022). In addition, Chad's debt treatment is underpinned by the erroneous assumption that the oil-exporting country is just going through a liquidity crisis yet all indications, not least Chad's previous multiple debt restructuring agreements, point to the fact that it is insolvent. Instead of debt rescheduling, the Common Framework should prioritize debt reduction or outright cancelation. Zambia's debt treatment negotiations also suffered a major setback that underscored the weaknesses inherent in the Common Framework. Having defaulted on its debt payments since 2020, Zambia applied for debt treatment and started negotiations with its creditors in 2021. A deal was reached with the bilateral creditor committee cochaired by China and France to restructure the US$6.3 billion debt owed to official creditors in June 2023. Zambia also concluded and agreed on a debt treatment deal with private creditors who hold US$3 billion of debt in October 2023. However, the Zambian government was forced to pull out of the deal because the official creditors cried foul claiming that the private bondholders had secured a better deal (Fabricius, 2023). Both deals collapsed and Zambia had to go back to the drawing board thus keeping the country in a debt trap. Zambia's access to a US$1.3 billion bailout depends on the success of the restructuring process (Gbadamosi, 2023). It also highlights the Common Framework's failure to provide a firm guideline for the debt treatment process which leads to disagreements among creditors and delayed relief for debt-distressed countries. Perhaps the most crucial weakness of the Framework is that its terms and recommendations are nonbinding and leave the restructuring discussions to take place on a case-by-case basis.

In 2021, the IMF approved a Special Drawing Rights (SDR) allocation of US$650 billion as a response to the liquidity crisis induced by the COVID-19 pandemic. The G20 committed to channel US$100 billion of SDRs to low-income countries. However, by the end of 2023, only US$82 billion had been committed. At the New Global Financial Pact in June 2023, the industrialized countries pledged to allocate their SDRs to the newly created US$100 billion climate finance fund (Mo Ibrahim Foundation, 2023). According to Adesina (2023), the African Development Bank can use SDR rechanneling to increase the financing for African countries. The AfDB claimed that US$5 billion worth of SDR can be leveraged to deliver US$20 billion in financing. Moreover, the AfDB can also ramp up the use of partial credit guarantees to help African countries issue sovereign bonds with longer maturities and lower interest rates. The G20 and the IMF introduced the Global Sovereign Debt Roundtable in February 2023 which seeks to bring together official and bilateral creditors with debtor countries to try and resolve issues undermining the effectiveness of the Common Framework. Smith (2023) is of the view that the solution to the debt crisis is held back by the differences between major players viz. China, private creditors, and the US and its G7 partners. The US has blamed China for delaying the conclusion of negotiations on debt restructuring because of its use of a different system of development finance which has been characterized as fragmented, opaque, and transactional.

The Way Forward

Bringing the debt debacle to an end is an urgent matter that cannot be delayed any longer. The world will not be able to respond effectively to the global challenges of climate change, global poverty, illegal immigration, and political instability if the majority of low-income countries do not find a way out of their debt trap. Perhaps the first and most important step would be for the international community to improve the Common Framework and make it fit for purpose. This would entail providing clear procedures and timelines for bilateral creditors, providing incentives for private lenders to cooperate, and detailing how the principle of comparable treatment would be applied in debt restructuring processes. Especially important is to bring the official and private creditors together in the debt restructuring negotiations in order to improve trust and transparency the lack of which led to the breakdown of Zambia's negotiations. Moreover, the multilateral development banks (MDBs) and other international institutions like the IMF must come to the fore in the debt resolution efforts by providing an analysis of a country's debt situation, recommending the extent of relief needed, and providing low interest funds to help countries struggling with debt. The involvement of MDBs in the HIPC and MDRI initiatives was key to the successful reduction of debt for African countries in the 2000s. It is also necessary that debt servicing is frozen during restructuring negotiations as it will not only provide much-needed cashflow relief to the debtor countries but also encourage creditors to facilitate debt negotiations expeditiously.

There is a need to build capacity at the national, regional, and international levels to enhance debt management and prevent over-indebtedness. It is crucial that there is transparency in debt practices including debt contracts, terms, and conditions so as to promote responsible borrowing, lending, and effective debt management in line with the African Borrowing Charter. Omotola and Saliu (2009) point out that a sustainable debt strategy includes a functional Debt Management Office (DMO) with qualified staff, state-of-the-art IT equipment, and other performance enhancers to collect and store information regarding internal and external borrowings. In most African countries, the DMOs are dysfunctional due to the lack of human resources. At the African Climate Summit in 2023, participating countries committed to establishing an African Debt Monitoring Mechanism in 2024 which will act as a repository of data on debt and will go a long way in helping African countries with debt negotiations and increasing transparency. Contractual terms that include using natural resources as collateral for the loan should also be disclosed (Otieno, 2023; Bradlow & Masamba, 2022). Institutions such as the African Development Bank and the IMF have an important role to play in providing training and technical assistance to national debt management officials. On their part, African governments should do more to consult the public in making decisions on borrowing and debt management. As argued by Chikerema and Chakunda in Chap. 2 of this volume, African countries also need robust domestic resource mobilization systems that will boost government revenues and help reduce debt accumulation. Debtor countries should ensure that they treat all creditors comparably to make restructuring a success. Creditors will be keen to strike a restructuring deal if they believe that their participation would help the debtor country rather than other creditors (Bradlow & Masamba, 2022). There has been talk of establishing an African Credit Rating Agency to provide alternative assessments about the nature and extent of risk in Africa (Mo Ibrahim Foundation, 2023). An African Credit Rating Agency would disrupt the monopoly of the Big 3 rating agencies (Moody's, S&P, Fitch) whose assessments are widely believed to be inaccurate and contribute to inflating the cost of borrowing for African countries. In the final analysis, a more permanent and sustainable solution to the endemic debt problem lies in addressing the colonial legacy of commodity export economies by transforming and diversifying the African economy. The African Continental Free Trade Area (AfCFTA) which was launched in 2021 could serve as a critical catalyst for the structural transformation of African economies through forging new regional value chains and attracting foreign investment. However, it is disappointing that three years since it was launched to much fanfare, not much progress seems to have been registered toward making it a reality.

Conclusion

African countries are suffocating under a heavy debt burden. Debt accumulation intensified in the 2010s as a result of a growing infrastructure finance gap, access to the Eurobond market, the oil-price shock in 2014, the COVID-19 pandemic, and the Russia-Ukraine war and its disruption of critical global supply chains. As such, the continent has seen its debt explode yet its capacity to service the debt has been shrinking just as fast. The debt crisis, coming as it does in the aftermath of a deadly pandemic and only six years before the lapsing of the Sustainable Development Goals deadline in 2030, presents an enormous challenge for the continent and the world at large. Already, African countries are forced to spend more on interest payments than on essential services such as health, education, water and sanitation, and infrastructure. If this situation persists, then, just like the 1980s and the 1990s, the 2020s look set to be another "lost decade" for Africa. In the meantime, the G20 international forum and the Paris Club have proposed debt relief measures namely the DSSI and the Common Framework. However, these interventions have met with limited success due to, among other things, the lack of private sector participation, nonbinding nature of the initiatives, mistrust between the Paris Club (western government lenders) and non-Paris Club members like China, and the lack of clarity on the application and operation of the principle of comparable treatment. Therefore, going forward, the Framework must be made more inclusive by inviting the private sector and China, more transparent, and the debt treatment parameters be determined equitably. Moreover, African countries need to enhance their debt management systems, improve their revenue collection mechanisms, and act to reduce corruption and illicit financial flows. At the continental level, the establishment of the African Debt Monitoring Mechanism and the African Credit Rating Agency will be worthy additions to the suite of instruments for combatting the debt crisis. More importantly, the AfCFTA, if fully implemented, can be an effective remedy to the debt crisis. The free trade regime, which seeks to establish the largest free trade area in the world, has the potential to foster new regional value chains, expand Africa's manufacturing base, and redress the colonial legacy of commodity export economies which are the root cause of Africa's endemic debt trap.

References

Adedeji, A. (1990). Africa's debt problem. *African Journal of Political Economy, 2*(5), 1–7.

Adesina, A. (2023). *Evolution of debt landscape over the past 10 years in Africa*. 20 June, Paris Club, Paris. Available from https://www.afdb.org/en/news-and-events/speeches/evolution-debt-landscape-over-past-10-years-africa-keynote-speech-dr-akinwumi-adesina-president-african-development-bank-group-delivered-paris-club-june-20-2023-62308

Alemayehu, G. F. (2003). The historical origin of African debt crisis. *Eastern Africa Social Science Research Review, 19*(1), 59–89.

Bradlow, D., & Masamba, M. (2022). Debt distress in Africa: Biggest problems, and ways forward. *The Conversation*, 11 May. Available from https://theconversation.com/debt-distress-in-africa-biggest-problems-and-ways-forward-182716

Callaghy, T. (1984). Africa's debt crisis. *The Journal of International Affairs, 38*(1), 61–79.

Christianson, D. (2023). Africa's debt crisis: No Gleneagles moment ahead. *Tralac*, 29 June. Available from https://www.tralac.org/blog/article/16040-africa-s-debt-crisis-no-gleneagles-moment-ahead.html

Cooper, R., & Robert, L. (1975). *The 1972–75 commodity boom*. Brookings Papers on Economic Activity 671–723. Brookings. Available from https://www.brookings.edu/wp-content/uploads/1975/12/1975c_bpea_cooper_lawrence_bosworth_houthakker.pdf

Cooray, M., & Walker, R. (2023). The G20's approach on debt has failed. *The Interpreter,* 16 November. Available from https://www.lowyinstitute.org/the-interpreter/g20-s-approach-debt-has-failed

Coulibaly, B., Gandhi, D., & Senbet, L. (2019). *Is sub-Saharan Africa facing another systemic sovereign debt crisis?* Policy Brief. Africa Growth Initiative at Brookings. Available from https://www.brookings.edu/wp-content/uploads/2019/04/africa_sovereign_debt_sustainability.pdf.

Danso, A. (1990). The causes and impact of the African debt crisis. *The Review of Black Political Economy, 19*, 5–21.

Fabricius, P. (2023). *Pilot Zambian debt relief collapses*. The Institute for Security Studies. Available from https://issafrica.org/iss-today/pilot-zambian-debt-relief-collapses (Accessed 12 January 2024).

Gbadamosi, N. (2023). What's causing Africa's debt crisis?. *Foreign Policy*, 1 February. Available from https://foreignpolicy.com/2023/02/01/africa-debt-crisis-yellen-georgieva-imf/

Gunder-Frank, A. (1972). *Lumpen-bourgeoisie: Lumpen-development*. Monthly Review Press.

Johnson, W., & Wilson, E. (1982). The "oil crises" and African economies: Oil wave on a tidal flood of industrial price inflation. *Daedalus, 111*(2), 211–241.

Kumah-Abiwu, F., & Haynes, J. (2023). Ghana: Soaring Public Debt and Democratic Challenges. *Democracy in Africa*, 18 October. Available from https://democracyinafrica.org/ghana-soaring-public-debt-and-democratic-challenges/

Lipumba, N. (2002). *Debt relief and sustainable development in sub-Saharan Africa*. Paper presented at the Fifth Expert Group Meeting on Finance for Sustainable Development, Nairobi, Kenya, December 1–4 1999.

Mamdani, M. (1977). *Politics and class formation in Uganda*. Heinemann.

Mark, T., & Merotto, D. (2012). African debt since debt relief: How clean is the slate? *World Bank Blog*, October 4. Available from https://blogs.worldbank.org/africacan/african-debt-since-debt-relief-how-clean-is-the-slate

Mo Ibrahim Foundation. (2023). *Global Africa: Africa in the world and the world in Africa*. Forum Report. Available from https://mo.ibrahim.foundation/sites/default/files/2023-07/2023-forum-report.pdf#page=71

Moreira, E. (2023). *Debt dynamics and financial stability in Africa*. Policy Brief. Policy Center for the New South. Available from https://www.policycenter.ma/sites/default/files/2023-06/PB_25-23_Emmanuel%20Pinto%20Moreira%20VF.pdf

Mukhopadhyay, A. (2022). *The search for sustainable solutions to debt accumulation in sub-Saharan Africa*. ORF Occasional Paper No. 349. Observer Research Foundation. Available from https://www.orfonline.org/research/the-search-for-sustainable-solutions-to-debt-accumulation-in-sub-saharan-africa

Ngugi, R., Kiriga, B., Karima, L., Mwangi, A., & Rono, Z. (2023). *Africa's debt priorities: A sustainability perspective and required support from the G20*. Policy Insights. South African Institute for International Affairs. Available from https://saiia.org.za/research/africas-debt-priorities-a-sustainability-perspective-required-support-from-the-g20/

Nkala, S. (2019). *Decolonization, class struggles and economic empowerment in post-colonial states: An appraisal of Zimbabwe's post-independence indigenization project in the mining sector*. PhD Thesis, University of KwaZulu Natal. Available from https://researchspace.ukzn.ac.za/handle/10413/17710

Nkala, S., & Eyita-Okon, E. (2023). The belt and road initiative and the build back better world: Implications on Africa's infrastructure development. In B. Ndzendze & D. Monyae (Eds.), *Perspectives on Africa-China infrastructural and industrial cooperation*. Springer. https://link.springer.com/chapter/10.1007/978-3-031-38395-3_13

Nyerere, J. (1985). Africa and the debt crisis. *African Affairs, 84*(337), 489–497.

Okeke, C. (2001). The debt burden: An African perspective. *The International Lawyer, 35*(4), 1489–1505.

Omotola, S., & Saliu, H. (2009). Foreign aid, debt relief and Africa's development: Problems and prospects. *South African Journal of International Affairs, 16*(1), 87–102. https://doi.org/10.1080/10220460902986180

Otieno, E. (2023). *Breaking the cycle of debt: Addressing the reasons behind high indebtedness in Africa and recommendations for sustainable solutions*. African Forum and Network on Debt and Development. Available from https://afrodad.org/breaking-the-cycle-of-debt-addressing-the-reasons-behind-high-indebtedness-in-africa-and-recommendations-for-sustainable-solutions/

Pellegrini, G. (2023). *Rising debt: Is the biggest obstacle to African development back?* Italian Institute for International Political Studies. Available from https://www.ispionline.it/en/publication/rising-debt-is-the-biggest-obstacle-to-african-development-back-137441

Ramose, M. (2006). Philosophy and Africa's struggle for economic independence. *Politeia, 25*(1), 3–17.

Sanubi, F. (2006). International politics of debt relief to sub-Saharan Africa: A theoretical restatement. *The Indian Journal of Political Science, 68*(3), 629–638.

Smith, G. (2021). *When credit is due: How Africa's debt can be a benefit not a burden*. Oxford University Press.

Smith, G. (2023). Millions will fall into extreme poverty if the U.S. and China can't come together on the African debt crisis. *Forbes*, April 12. Available from https://www.forbes.com/sites/gaylesmith/2023/04/12/millions-will-fall-into-extreme-poverty-if-the-us-and-china-cant-come-together-on-the-african-debt-crisis/?sh=6c42f8367684

The African Debt Justice Network. (2022). Sixty second sovereign debt news update: Chad becomes the first country to reach a Debt Treatment Agreement with official and private creditors under the G20 Common Framework. *Afronomics Law*, 31 December. Available from https://www.afronomicslaw.org/category/african-sovereign-debt-justice-network-afsdjn/sixty-second-sovereign-debt-news-update-chad.

The International Monetary Fund. (2023). *Debt dilemmas in sub-Saharan Africa: Some principles and trade-offs in debt restructuring*. In Regional economic outlook: Sub-Saharan Africa—A light on the Horizon? Washington DC. Available from file:///C:/Users/sizos/OneDrive/Documents/debt-note2.pdf

The International Monetary Fund African Department. (2023). *Ghana: Request for an arrangement under the extended credit facility—debt sustainability analysis*. IMF Staff Country Reports, Issue 168. https://doi.org/10.5089/9798400244322.002.

The United Nations Conference on Trade and Development. (2023). *A world of debt*. Available from https://unctad.org/publication/world-of-debt/regional-stories

Thompson, W. (2023). Explainer: The making of Africa's sovereign debt crisis – Part Two. *Finance Uncovered*, 26 June 26. Available from https://www.financeuncovered.org/stories/explainer-africa-sovereign-debt-crisis-ghana-education

Wallerstein, I. (1974). The rise and future demise of the world capitalist system: Concepts for comparative analysis. *Comparative Studies in Society and History, 16*(4), 387–415.

Zajontz, T. (2022). Debt, distress, dispossession: Towards a critical political economy of Africa's financial dependency. *The Review of African Political Economy, 9*(171), 173–183.

Sizo Nkala is a Postdoctoral Research Fellow at the University of Johannesburg Centre for Africa-China Studies. He holds a PhD in Political Science from the University of KwaZulu-Natal where he also served as a lecturer for three years teaching undergraduate and postgraduate classes across different disciplines including international relations, public policy, and contemporary African politics. He has worked as an external consultant for In On Africa (formerly Consultancy Africa Intelligence). He is a Laureate of the Council for Social Science Research in Africa (CODESRIA) and the Centre for African Studies Basel (CASB) Summer School. His research interests include China-Africa relations in the technology, media and economic spheres, African political-economy, immigration, and global politics. He has published several articles in local and international peer-reviewed journals.

Chapter 5
Creditor Contributions, Benefits, and Solutions to Debt Crisis in Africa

Janet Mudzviti-Zhou

Abstract The debt crisis in Africa has become a major concern, with significant implications for the continent's economic development and social progress. This chapter critically examines how creditors are contributing to and benefiting from Africa's debt, while also exploring how their proposed solutions have exacerbated, rather than resolved, the underlying problem. The chapter begins by addressing the role of creditors in Africa's debt crisis. By using the political economy conceptual framing, it highlights the historical context, tracing the origins of the crisis back to unsustainable lending practices by international financial institutions and external creditors, bilateral and multilateral as well as new and traditional creditors. Through a comprehensive analysis of debt accumulation patterns, it becomes evident that creditors have played a significant part in causing the current storm in Africa of the debt burden, often through irresponsible lending practices and inadequate debt management frameworks.

Introduction

The debt crisis in Africa has become a major concern, with significant implications for the continent's economic development and social progress. This chapter critically examines how creditors are contributing to and benefiting from Africa's debt, while also exploring how their proposed solutions have exacerbated, rather than resolved, the underlying problem. The chapter begins by addressing the role of creditors in Africa's debt crisis. By using the political economy conceptual framing, it highlights the historical context, tracing the origins of the crisis back to unsustainable lending practices by international financial institutions and external creditors, both bilateral and multilateral as well as new and traditional creditors. Through a comprehensive analysis of debt accumulation patterns, it becomes evident that creditors have played a significant part in causing the current storm in Africa of the debt burden, often

J. Mudzviti-Zhou (✉)
Harare, Zimbabwe

G. Moyo, S. J. Ndlovu-Gatsheni (eds.), *Global Storms and Africa in World Politics*, Global Power Shift, https://doi.org/10.1007/978-3-031-83868-2_5

through irresponsible lending practices and inadequate debt management frameworks. The chapter analyses ways in which creditors benefit from Africa's debt—spotlighting on the exploitative nature of certain lending arrangements, such as the issuance of loans with high interest rates, conditionalities, and collateralization of strategic assets, as already alluded to in previous Chap. 3 by GordenMoyo and Chap. 4 by Sizo Nkala.

The escalation of geopolitical tensions, mainly emanating from the Russia-Ukraine war, is leading to tighter global financial conditions, higher global inflation, lower growth, and higher stress on public finances, exerting massive adverse implications for low and middle-income countries' debt dynamics. These factors compromise developing nations' ability to react to unforeseen contingencies, tackle climatic shocks, and invest in citizens. This was quite evident during the COVID-19 as Africa suffered the so-called vaccine apartheid and the global village collapsed as countries focused to their internal needs first. Second, an unequal global financial architecture makes access to financing by developing nations inadequate and expensive. As alluded to earlier, debt overhang constrains development through limited access to concessionary funding, currency devaluations, rising cost of money (interest rates), and sluggish economic growth. As such, nations have the impossible choice of serving the people or servicing their debts. Gorden Moyo aptly describes it as "rigged global financial architecture."

Historical Overview

Africa's excessive debt of the 1970s and early 1980s, which skyrocketed from US$140 billion in 1982 when the issue first surfaced to over US$270 billion in 1990, has been driven by many factors (Mutero, 2020). It is sufficient to say that, contrary to the dominant narratives of the creditors, Africa's debt conundrum, is not solely the result of imprudent economic policies, corruption, protracted civil wars, a lack of democratic checks and balances on government borrowing and spending, excessive population growth, and poor governance. All of these factors have undoubtedly played a significant role and mismanagement and misgovernance cannot be underplayed (see Hanlon, 2021; Mutero, 2020). However, the debt crisis has been worsened by other exogenous factors, including irresponsible over-lending by private and official creditors during the commodity boom of the 1970s. Also, persistent negative real interest rates during most of the 1970s in global financial markets fueled by accommodative monetary and fiscal policies in industrialized nations made it economically irrational for developing countries not to borrow externally for consumption and development programs (see Kasekende & Ali, 2019). In addition, the crisis was also fueled by the deliberate targeting of developing nations in general and oil exporters in particular as main export markets to receive cheap credit to facilitate industrialized nations' adjustment to the oil shocks of 1973 and 1979 (Geda, 2003). The crisis has roots in the global monetary shock of 1979–81 aimed at curbing the world of inflation but had the collateral impact of inducing a deep and prolonged recession, particularly in debt-ridden developing countries, causing commodity markets and prices to collapse.

Between 1979 and 1983, African governments relied excessively on foreign savings due to their unwillingness to reduce domestic consumption and increase domestic savings. This was due to their mistaken belief—which the international financial institutions (IFls) had encouraged in some instances, such as in Zambia-that the collapse in commodity prices would be temporary (Fondad, 1992). Up to now countries that produce raw materials always bank on the volatility of commodity prices and the belief that prices always shoot up after drastic falls (this is the current scenario with Lithium which has plummeted to by 80% between 2022 and December 2023). A protracted and catastrophic drought between 1981 and 1984 seriously hindered the development of cash crops and agriculture on the continent, causing significant harm to output and the weak financial systems of African countries. The 1980s experienced high, positive real interest rates, worsening Africa's debt service and accumulation loads.

Furthermore, Berg and Hussain (2019) submit that the US currency depreciated between 1985 and 1990, causing volatile exchange rate fluctuations that increased the dollar value of Africa's outstanding obligations. Almost half of these debts were denominated in currencies or composites that rose in value relative to the US dollar. For countries like Zimbabwe, who currently use the USD as their base currency since 2009 due to the currency crisis, the impact would be more devastating. In the early years of the debt crisis, several public and private rescheduling frequently had severe terms attached. This led to a significant increase in the outstanding debt while offering brief but completely insufficient cash flow relief. Poor management of the same governments' external debt records, policies, and priorities resulted in multiple missed opportunities to improve their circumstances. Additionally, inadequate and unrealistic advice regarding the amount of debt-relief African governments needed to negotiate and how they might adjust was provided by creditors.

The accumulation of severe arrears that debtors have been allowed to the point where it is more detrimental to the restoration of orderly debtor-creditor relations than it would have been had they first taken more reasonable steps to lower debt and debt service obligations. Protectionism in global markets for low-tech and agricultural items makes it particularly difficult for African nations to diversify and boost exports to markets that accept hard currency, making it even more difficult for them to escape the debt trap (Ezenwe, 1993). Fast forward to the twenty-first century, debt continued to be fueled by many factors, including frequent climatic shocks, the 2007/8 global financial recession, the COVID-19 pandemic, and the Russia-Ukraine war. The debt crisis will continue to worsen without real action to reform the global financial architecture to lower borrowing costs and bail out developing nations, as discussed in the previous sections by Nkala and Moyo and in the next sections.

Africa's debt is at its highest in over a decade. Primarily due to the pandemic, war in Europe, and rising inflation, African nations have had to take more debt. As a result, the rise in debt stock of low and middle-income countries (LMICs) has outpaced economic growth, thus raising concerns about these nations' ability to service their debts (World Bank International Debt Report, 2023). The situation is troubling, particularly for the poorest nations eligible for International Development Association (IDA) resources, as their external debt stocks have spiked faster than other LMICs. This decade-long asymmetry between economic growth and debt accumulation has created or exacerbated debt vulnerabilities in many LMICs, and actions to address these vulnerabilities have become increasingly urgent. The 2023 International Debt Report shows that about 60% of IDA-eligible countries are assessed at high risk of debt distress or are already in debt distress.

For the first time since 2015, the external debt stock of LMICs plunged by 3.4% from US$9.3 trillion in 20,211 to US$9 trillion in 2022 (World Bank Debt Report, 2023). The decline is linked to negative debt outflows (disbursements minus principal repayments) and the appreciation of the USD against other major currencies. Long-term and short-term debt stocks decreased at the same pace; the decline in the former was primarily due to a 5% reduction in obligations to private creditors. Altogether, the external debt stock of IDA-eligible countries spiked by 2.7% in 2022 to an all-time high of US$1.1 trillion, doubling the 2012 levels (World Bank Debt Report, 2023).

In 2022, the external debt stock of IDA-eligible countries increased by 2.7% to a record US$1.1 trillion, more than double the 2012 level. Public and publicly guaranteed (PPG) debt stock, including the IMF, increased 1.7% in 2022 to US$728 billion, whereas long-term private non-guaranteed (PNG) debt rose much faster, increasing 4.1% to US$225 billion. The World Bank statistics further show that when viewed from a creditor perspective, the long-term PPG debt stock composition of IDA-eligible countries was 50% multilateral creditors, 29% bilateral creditors, and 21% private creditors. This mix has shifted somewhat since 2012, as creditor groups have accounted for 56%, 33%, and 10%, respectively (World Bank, 2021). Public and private sector borrowers' total debt stock owed to private creditors remained steady for the IDA-eligible countries, with a 1.2% increase to US$377.4 billion in 2022. The increase was driven by lending from commercial banks and other private creditors, which increased by 2.2% to US$279.1 billion in 2022, whereas the debt stock owed to bondholders fell 1.5% to US$98.3 billion (World Bank Debt Report, 2023).

Overall, Africa's external debt has grown significantly over the last decade. The total external debt was US$655.59 billion, consisting of bilateral debt (excluding China) of US$86.22 billion and bilateral (China) of US$62.89 billion), multilateral creditors of US$223.74 billion, private (excluding China) of US$258.34 billion, and private (China) of 24.39 billion. Africa's external debt rose rapidly between 2014 and 2020 as a percentage of GDP. However, in the last two (2) years, external debt-to-GDP has decreased from 24.3% in 2021 to 22.8% in 2022 (World Bank Debt Report, 2023). Today, 23% of external debt is owed to bilateral creditors, with major creditors being China US$60.9 billion, France US$15 billion, Saudi Arabia US$11.9 billion, Kuwait US$9.6 billion, Germany US$9.5 billion, and Japan US$8.5 billion. China has become Africa's biggest bilateral lender. Its public lenders held almost US$63 billion of Africa's external debt in 2022, and its private lenders held over

US$24 billion of Africa's external debt (World Bank Debt Report, 2023). In 2022, Africa's annual debt service—interest plus principal payments on public and publicly guaranteed (PPG) debt—was US$67.5 billion. This constituted 12% of government spending, far exceeding health expenditures as a percentage of government spending estimated at 7% in 2020 (World Bank Debt Report, 2023).

Creditor Contributions to the Debt Crisis

Africa is trapped in debt, sustaining high poverty and inequality levels, as governments fail to cope with the citizens needs and fulfillment of social and economic rights. High indebtedness heavily constrains the countercyclical effects of fiscal policies and impedes domestic capital accumulation by heightening interest, tax, and inflation rates. As shall be highlighted, creditors have played a significant role in burdening developing countries with unsustainable debt burden. This can only be linked to the historical design of the present-day global financial system (GFS). The GFS encompasses a complex network of financial institutions, markets, and instruments that enables the flow of capital and resources within a country and across international borders (Buckley, 2024). It outlines rules of engagement between nations through the balance of payments and their monetary authorities, such as central banks, treasuries, and stabilization funds managing them. From this, it is clear that the GFS plays a crucial role in facilitating global investment, promoting international trade, and distributing wealth among nations. While GFS is critical for sustaining economic growth and stability in developing countries, it can be a potential source of financial instability and contagion risks if poorly managed.

Historically, the rise in finance was caused by two significant factors: long-lived productive assets and long-distance trade. To bridge the time lag between concluding a trade agreement and the final delivery of actual goods or services between nations, the market (goods, assets, and services) required some form of finance. Literature shows that a surge in global capital flows in the late nineteenth century fueled financial globalization to the extent that between the 1870s and the outbreak of World War 1, the globe experienced an era of increased interconnectedness and speedy expansion of the global financial system (Berg & Hussain, 2019; Fofack, 2014).

Between the 1870s and 1914, nations adopted and followed the Gold Standard Monetary System. Under this system, a nation's currency was directly convertible to gold. According to Bloomfield (1981), a unit of the national currency was defined in terms of a given quantity of gold; the central bank or treasury stood ready to buy and sell gold at the resulting fixed price in terms of the national currency; gold was freely coined, and gold coins formed a significant part of the circulating medium; and gold could be freely exported and imported. The preceding conditions implied nearly fixed exchange rate regimes between local currencies of nations following the gold standard. Gold was used broadly because of its long history of use as a store of value bolstered by its malleability, portability, aesthetic appeal, virtual indestructibility, universal acceptance, liquidity, and rarity.

However, the aftermath of the First World War resulted in significant disruption of economic activity, and the gold standard was temporarily suspended. Attempts were made in the 1920s to revitalize the gold standard but were frustrated by the Great Depression of the 1930s (Pettinger, 2009). This Great Depression posed widespread economic growth challenges (overspending and debt accumulation in earlier years), currency devaluations, and protectionist policies. In a bid to establish a stable, multilateral post-World War 2 economic order based on consensual decision-making and cooperation in trade and economic relations, about 43 allied nations convened for a conference in Bretton Woods, New Hampshire, in 1944—leading to the creation of the International Bank for Reconstruction and Development (now part of the World Bank) and the International Monetary Fund (IMF). The IMF would create a stable climate for global trade by harmonizing its members' monetary policies and maintaining exchange stability. It could provide temporary financial assistance to countries encountering difficulties with their balance of payments. The World Bank, on the other hand, would serve to improve the capacity of countries to trade by lending money to war-ravaged and impoverished countries for reconstruction and development projects. Under the Bretton Woods System, nations pegged their local currencies to the United States dollar (USD), which was convertible to gold.

The global community relies on an international financial architecture dating back to 1945, primarily developed for and by advanced nations for post-war recovery. During the establishment of the Bretton Woods institutions, developing countries were not represented as many, mainly African nations, were still under colonial rule. Bordo and Eichengreen (1991) summed up Bretton Woods institutions' shortcomings by positing that there were divergent views on post-war economic order: The US wanted an open and non-discriminatory global trading system while Britain for reasons of political expediency and economic vulnerability, resisted the abandonment of the imperial preference system and the sterling bloc. Also, European countries had reservations about a liberal economic order advocated by the US over such matters as empire, spheres of influence, and regionalism. As such, Bretton Woods institutions were made from a compromise that only served the socioeconomic goals of the US and Europe. In this context, the interests of the Global South were not considered when these multilateral institutions were formed.

The contemporary global financial architecture perpetuates systemic inequalities through its quota-based governance structure, which fails to reflect evolving global power dynamics. This resonates with Moyo's analysis (Chap. 3) comparing it to "global financial apartheid." A critical examination of the IMF quota system reveals multiple dimensions of power imbalance: it determines member contributions, voting rights, resource access limits, and Special Drawing Rights (SDR) allocations (United Nations, 2023a, b). While the quota formula ostensibly attempts to balance countries' payment capacity with potential resource needs, its static nature fails to adapt to global economic shifts, thereby entrenching existing power disparities in the international financial system.

Contemporary developing economies face an intersecting web of challenges that reflect deep structural inequalities in the global economic system. Beyond traditional development challenges, these nations now confront intensifying climate vulnerability, systemic financial risks, and persistent gender inequalities, all exacerbated by geopolitical tensions. Recent global shocks have transformed previously manageable debt into unsustainable burdens. UN data reveals an alarming picture: approximately 40% of developing nations (52 countries) currently face severe debt challenges (United Nations, 2023a, b). While these nations represent only 2.5% of global GDP, they encompass 15% of the world's population and include over half of the most climate-vulnerable countries. This statistical disparity underscores the profound inequities in global economic structures.

The political economy of global financial markets severely constrains African nations' access to affordable capital, undermining their capacity for sustainable development and economic recovery. This financial constraint has far-reaching implications for addressing societal inequalities, climate action, and essential social services. Data from 2023 illustrates this structural inequality: 14 nations faced sovereign bond yields exceeding US Treasury bonds by over 10 percentage points, while 21 countries confronted premiums of at least 6 percentage points (United Nations, 2023a, b). Panizza's (2022a, b) analysis suggests that developing nations experiencing debt crises might have maintained solvency had they accessed financing at rates comparable to wealthy nations, highlighting the systemic nature of global financial inequalities.

The existing financial architecture fails to support the mobilization of stable and long-term financing needed to fight rising global debt challenges and achieve the United Nations (UN) Sustainable Development Goals (SDGs) for all people. Instead, creditors charge higher interest rates on loans provided to developing nations, with many governments forced to allocate a high share of revenue to debt service payments instead of investing in critical social services like education, health care, and social protection. Also, because of high indebtedness leading to defaults, many African countries are experiencing high borrowing costs, including excessive interest on arrears and penalties. Yet, without fair, rules-based global financial architecture, debt resolution has typically been too little, too late. The debt restructurings offered by creditors are inadequate to provide a clean slate and avoid repeat crises, which often materialize too late with protracted high social costs.

The current global financial architecture has massive variations in countries' liquidity access during crises. In 1968, the IMF created the SDR system to supplement official reserves and facilitate global liquidity. According to the IMF's Articles of Agreement, SDR allocations should be considered every five (5) years, referred to as the "basic period," and the Fund is allowed to allocate SDRs in response to "unexpected major events."[1] However, of the 12 basic periods that lapsed since the introduction of SDR, there have been only four (4) general allocations and one (1) special allocation. This is the case despite deteriorating

[1] https://www.imf.org/external/pubs/ft/aa/

global macroeconomic conditions warranting more frequent SDR allocations. In addition, the allocation of SDRs tends to disproportionately benefit countries that are less in need of them as they are distributed in proportion to existing IMF quotas.

As alluded to earlier, the IMF quota system is primarily a function of an economy's size and relative position in the world economy. For instance, in 2021, the IMF issued a record US$650 billion in SDRs to help member countries combat the devastating impacts of the COVID-19 pandemic. However, rich nations least likely to require or utilize SDRs got approximately US$450 billion. The allocation constituted 70% of the total general SDR allocation. At the same time, Africa, with a population exceeding 1.4 billion, got fewer SDRs than Germany, with a population of 83 million (UNECA, 2023).[2] Many advanced countries' SDRs are never fully utilized and are kept as reserves. Yet developing nations struggling with debt distress were forced to borrow more to meet the demands created by the pandemic. For instance, World Bank statistics show that the debt burden of more than 70 low-income nations increased by a record 12% to US$860 billion in 2020 (UNECA, 2023). This exacerbated the debt crises and further subdued the capacity to service and repay the debts.

The debt provided by almost all creditors has some conditions attached. Dreher (2004) posits that the design of IMF-supported programs has conditions: macroeconomic, structural, fiscal, and monetary policies. The performance of these areas serves as a tool to monitor progress in a recipient country of IMF loans. Also, these measures serve as insurance for the Fund by ensuring that the imposed conditions on the borrowing nation remain favorable to avoid debt default. The IMF reviews, evaluates, and keeps track of borrower compliance using three primary instruments. One instrument related to macroeconomic indicators, including foreign reserves, fiscal balances, external borrowing, and credit and money aggregates, is the Quantitative Performance Criteria, or QPCs. Through this evaluation, the IMF determines whether the borrower complies with the government's primary balance requirement and the borrowing cap.

Although the Indicative Targets method is also designed to monitor quantitative indicators, it is more effective at capturing outcomes when there is uncertainty surrounding economic patterns. The ITs monitor how well borrowers are fulfilling their obligations to pay the required minimum amount of domestic revenue and for social assistance. Finally, the Structural Benchmarks are an alternative non-quantifiable IMF tool that measures borrowers' economic reforms. The Structural Benchmarks focus on measuring whether the country is improving financial sector operations, building social safety nets, or strengthening public financial management.

Despite justification for setting loan conditions, policies championed by multilateral institutions like the World Bank and IMF are viewed skeptically in many developing nations. The ensuing austerity measures from these policies entail increases in taxes, including high user fees in the education and health sectors, deregulation, and downsizing of government through withdrawal of subsidies,

[2] UNECA stands for United Nations Economic Commission for Africa.

reduction of civil service, and commercialization and privatization of critical state-owned enterprises. Without establishing strong social safety nets, these reforms disproportionately impact low-income people who rely heavily on public services. This was significantly attested by the IMF-led Economic Structural Adjustment Program (ESAP) implemented by Zimbabwe in the 1990s.

In Zimbabwe, these reforms contributed to deindustrialization, increased informalization, high unemployment, increased exchange rate depreciation, rampant inflation, and increased poverty and marginalization (Marabuka, 2013). The countries implementing these IMF-sponsored "blanket policies" would end up borrowing more for social protection to cushion vulnerable citizens and marginalized and underserved communities. Even, prominent American economist Stiglitz argued that the IMF fails to take the best policy to improve developing countries' welfare as its policies reflect the interests and ideology of the Western financial community (Guilherme, 2008). The IMF has also been criticized for imposing policies with little or no consultation with affected countries. Moreover, the technical complexity of macroeconomic policies that the IMF addresses has often dissuaded civil society groups from voicing criticism of the Fund's measures (Pereira, 2008).

Most of the debt provided by creditors did not fund global public goods like climate action and pandemic preparedness. Also, for a long time, the debt sustainability analyses by GFS failed to incorporate climate risks and their impact on long-term investments to gauge the positive effects of these investments on productivity and resilience on debt sustainability. More so, the debt sustainability assessments did not reflect countries' SDG financing needs as they failed to incorporate fiscal space for investments in the SDGs. The current seniority system prioritizes payments to external creditors instead of giving seniority to social protection obligations and payments related to other pressing domestic needs. Although giving seniority to social protection obligations would increase the risk of default, it would more accurately reflect how much of a write-down is necessary when defaults occur (UN, 2023). As such, multilateral institutions should change business models to ensure all their lending has a sustainable development impact. This can include reorientation of allocation of concessional finance to indicate vulnerabilities such as climate disasters and support for conflict-prone countries.

Due to high indebtedness, several African countries, including Angola, Ghana, Chad, the Democratic Republic of Congo, and Zimbabwe, among others, have experimented with the Resource-backed Loan (RBL) model (ZIMCODD, 2021). In this model, natural resources can serve as payment in kind, the resource of an income revenue stream used to make repayments or an asset that serves as collateral. In other words, RBLs are loans given to a government where repayment is either made directly from natural resources or a resource-related future income stream. The debt overhang has directly impacted capital inflows and led to a vicious debt cycle in Africa—the cycle of continuous borrowing, accumulation of payment burden, and eventual default (ZIMCODD, 2021). This has caused borrowing countries to lose access to global capital markets and suffer higher borrowing costs, in addition to harming growth and investment. So, to reduce the impact of the debt cycle, the resource-backed loans have become more appealing to cash-strapped

African governments that are already trapped in debt distress. At the same time, predatory creditors are taking advantage of a debt crisis in Africa, thus aggravating the situation.

While proponents of the resource-backed loans model posit that it has often provided much-needed infrastructure, including roads and hydro-dams, critics point out that this model has led to crippling levels of debt, and the risk of losing collateral is worth more than the value of the loan. In 2006, for instance, Zimbabwe borrowed US$200 million from China, a loan secured by 26 million ounces of platinum reserves in Selous (ZIMCODD, 2023). However, these RBLs are dangerous as they also exert dire developmental impacts by fueling corruption and unsustainable resource extraction, leading to environmental degradation, pollution (air and water), forced displacements of communities, farmer-miner conflicts, and human-wildlife conflicts, among other challenges (also, ZIMCODD, 2023). The mining activities are not bringing tangible development to mining-host communities through corporate social responsibility (CSR), such as maintaining roads and constructing new schools and clinics. In addition, the unsustainable extraction of natural resources is an injustice to future generations by depriving them of the value of nature, causing the benefits of nature to humanity to be distributed unequally across time (Soga & Gaston, 2021). Hence, future generations will be less likely to experience wildlife and unable to reap nature's economic, ecological, and psychological benefits.

Creditors as Beneficiaries of Debt Crisis

The section explores the predatory nature of some of the creditors, highlighting how Africa loses out in various creditor-led debt-relief initiatives. This section also highlights the linkages of debt, trade, markets, and natural resources, among other sectors—the emergency of the debt conundrum and the global storm in Africa.

In 1988, there was a growing consensus that the international debt strategy needed a significant reorientation that would bring about a more balanced approach to support the still-struggling debtor nations, whose development had been severely harmed by the debt crisis. Japan and France made some intriguing suggestions in 1988 to revitalize the approach by direct and widespread public support of debt and debt service reduction. But Nicholas Brady, the Secretary of the Treasury, was the one who made the bold move (Griffith-Jones et al., 2021). Announced in March 1989, Brady's proposal—later dubbed the Brady Plan—became the new paradigm for handling the commercial bank debt of emerging nations, namely those in Latin America.

About seven (7) years later, the HIPC Initiative was introduced by the International Monetary Fund (IMF) and World Bank in 1996, the main idea being to ensure that the poorest countries in the world are not overwhelmed by unmanageable or unsustainable debt burdens. This initiative has evolved with time as it was broadened in 1999 and later supplemented by the Multilateral Debt Relief Initiative (MDRI) in 2005, where a HIPC country can get 100% debt relief on eligible debts to help accelerate progress toward the attainment of the United Nations (UN)'s Sustainable Development Goals (SDGs).

The G20 Common Framework is the Common Framework for Debt Treatments beyond the Debt Service Suspension Initiative (DSSI). Advanced countries announced it in November 2020 to deal with the issue of unsustainable debts faced by various countries due to the COVID-19 pandemic. The framework recognizes that efficient debt resolution requires a case-by-case approach and strong coordination among creditors. The goal is to facilitate timely and orderly debt treatment for countries eligible for the DSSI, including participation from official creditors and the private sector. The process begins when a debtor country requests debt treatment. The need for debt treatment is determined based on an IMF-WBG Debt Sustainability Analysis (DSA) and the participating official creditors' assessment. The eligible debt includes public and publicly guaranteed debts with an original maturity of more than one year. The treatment considers the cut-off date in the 2020 DSSI term sheet, protecting new financing provided after March 24, 2020.

Current debt-relief mechanisms, while seemingly progressive, reveal significant limitations in addressing systemic debt challenges. The G20's Debt Service Suspension Initiative (DSSI), though important, provides insufficient relief and faces implementation challenges. Its temporary nature and limited scope—covering only 73 of the poorest nations—excludes numerous struggling middle-income countries. Private creditors' reluctance to participate further undermines its effectiveness. This situation demands a comprehensive approach combining debt restructuring, new financing mechanisms, and fundamental reforms to the global financial architecture.

The Common Framework's structural limitations manifest in several critical areas: timeliness of response, eligibility criteria, and equitable treatment across creditor classes. A particular challenge lies in the absence of effective mechanisms to ensure comparable treatment between private and official creditors, highlighting the need for more robust and inclusive debt resolution frameworks. Without improvements to establish inclusive and representative sovereign debt authority independent of debtor and creditor interests, there will be no orderly, timely, and fair debt resolution. The shortage of rules-based systems breeds inefficiency—too little, too late restructurings—with exorbitant social costs and market uncertainty increasing risk premium. A lack of bankruptcy procedures strengthens holdout creditors while disadvantaging other claimants on sovereign resources like workers and pensioners.

Undoubtedly, whether whole or partial, debt relief can stop capital flight from Africa; some empirical studies have indicated a negative relationship between economic growth and development and a positive association between capital flight and external debt. For decades, African nations have been forced to allocate a sizable amount of their yearly budgets to debt service. African countries still pay back over US$20 billion in debt annually, "a stark reminder that aid is not free," notwithstanding the robust debt-relief programs. The expectation is that when debt is reduced, more money will be available to fund development initiatives.

Similarly, debt reduction is thought to encourage more saving and domestic investment. This could spur economic expansion and lessen poverty, resulting in better living conditions. This is particularly true if the money obtained from debt relief is used to improve the national economies of African governments. Although there is some truth to this optimistic approach, it has also been noted that the much-discussed debt relief has been biased and selective. For example, different countries are subject to varied qualifying and classification requirements under the various loan treaties. Even worse, these requirements were created exclusively by the Paris Club and affiliated organizations working in the West's, especially the US', best interests.

Fundamentally, the incredibly rosy expectations for Africa's development under the new debt reduction are overly sanguine. For example, almost all of the strategies developed by the World Bank and IMF to manage Africa's external debt have been based on terms like devaluation, privatization, deregulation, and political and economic liberalization. The HIPC programs similarly strongly emphasized these requirements, limiting program participation to nations undergoing political, economic, social, and other reforms. However, these circumstances, like the Structural Adjustment Programmes (SAPs) regime, will likely have many unforeseen repercussions that could offset the intended gains, just as similar programs have in the past.

The management of the debt-relief solutions is also critical. Many African nations give the impression of being democratic, but this is only because multi-party elections are held there, frequently with little to no voter choice. Implicitly, fundamental components of a democratic society like accountability, oversight, widespread engagement, empowerment, and constitutionalism continue to be widely mocked. The question of whether African leaders whose nations have benefited from the debt-relief package will provide a satisfactory explanation for such generosity is raised by this trend. More politicians would be ready to invest in their constituents' welfare through effective governance and management of debt reduction, which would improve general infrastructure development, health care, education, energy distribution, and job creation. However, considering African nations' widespread opportunistic and corrupt culture, it is questionable whether much can be accomplished in these critical sectors.

When all of the above is considered, it begs the issue of whether debt reduction is really what Africa needs. The debt reduction program is being implemented to give the impression that the West is providing special treatment to Africa. This should not be the case. Decades of exploitation of Africa through colonialism and the slave trade are primarily to blame for the continent's growing dilemma and tensions. Years of marginalization and ongoing exploitation of African resources by the neo-colonial enterprise were to follow. This resonates with the decoloniality theory and concept as explained in earlier chapters in this nook by Gatsheni & also Chakunda and Chikerema. Instead of being viewed as help, perhaps the HIPC could be seen as a meager portion of meeting a Western debt to Africa. In light of this, the idea of debt relief—or, worse yet, debt forgiveness—offends.

Trade and entrepreneurial development are far more critical to Africa than debt reduction. Debt relief is a good place to start. Still, the real problem is how to loosen the restrictive international trade laws that force Africa and many other developing nations into precarious situations. The high expectations accompanying the debt relief granted to some African countries will remain expectations for years to come unless the proper conditions are created for a genuinely liberal international trade, where there is no longer discrimination and double standards on trade barriers. However, Africa's problems have worsened due to the mounting global economic crises. Due to these crises, most African nations are experiencing a decline in the demand from around the world for natural resources that account for most of their income. Other anticipated effects include reduced remittances, drying up of vital foreign direct investment, and flight of foreign capital out of vulnerable local stock exchanges as international investors seek safer havens. In addition, Africa should anticipate a decrease in direct funding from wealthier countries that are currently busy with their own economic issues and the Russia-Ukraine war.

Strategies and Solutions for Alleviating the Debt Crises

Studies have shown that the burden of debt constrains economic growth, undermines development efforts, and perpetuates cycles of poverty in Africa (see Ndikumana & Boyce, 2008). Addressing these challenges requires comprehensive strategies and innovative solutions that go beyond short-term or "strait jacket" fixes. This section explores scholarly perspectives on the strategies and solutions for alleviating the debt crises in Africa. Evidence shows that addressing the debt crises in Africa requires a multifaceted approach that encompasses debt restructuring, domestic resource mobilization, enhanced debt management, economic diversification, and inclusive growth policies (Fofack, 2014; Kasekende & Ali, 2019). Fundamentally, sustainable debt management practices and innovative financing mechanisms are vital to ensure long-term fiscal stability and promote sustainable development across the continent. By implementing these strategies and solutions in concert with international cooperation and support, African nations can chart a path toward decoloniality, independence, debt sustainability, and economic prosperity.

Debt restructuring and relief initiatives are key for African countries to alleviate their debt burdens that have made them vulnerable and incapable of fulfilling their basic duties to provide public services for their citizens. This encompasses renegotiating terms with creditors, extending repayment periods, and reducing interest rates to make debt servicing more manageable. International financial institutions such as the IMF and the World Bank can be pivotal in coordinating debt-relief efforts and providing technical assistance to indebted countries. Berg and Hussain (2019) argue that debt-relief initiatives, on the other hand, aim to address the unsustainable debt burdens faced by HIPCs and low-income developing nations. These initiatives often involve canceling or reducing debts owed by eligible countries, allowing them to allocate more resources toward poverty reduction, healthcare, education, and infrastructure development.

IMF claims that debt restructuring and relief initiatives are crucial in promoting economic stability and development. By alleviating debt burdens, countries can redirect financial resources toward productive investments, thereby stimulating economic growth and poverty alleviation. Moreover, reduced debt obligations enhance a country's capacity to access international capital markets, fostering investor confidence and attracting foreign direct investment. The success of debt restructuring and relief initiatives can be observed in various case studies. For instance, the HIPC and the Multilateral Debt Relief Initiative (MDRI) have significantly reduced the debt burdens of eligible countries, enabling them to reallocate resources toward critical development priorities. Countries like Uganda, Mozambique, and Tanzania have experienced tangible improvements in social indicators and economic performance following debt-relief interventions. However, despite their notable benefits, debt restructuring and relief initiatives have been criticized based on the associated moral hazard, where countries may engage in reckless borrowing practices with the expectation of future debt forgiveness (Fofack, 2014). In the same context, the conditionality imposed by creditors and international financial institutions as part of debt-relief programs has been criticized for impacting national sovereignty and policy autonomy.

Mutero (2020) submits an argument for prioritizing domestic resource mobilization as a panacea to reducing reliance on external borrowing and bolstering fiscal sustainability. This involves widening tax bases, improving tax administration, combating illicit financial flows, and enhancing revenue collection mechanisms. By harnessing domestic resources effectively, African governments can mitigate the need for excessive borrowing and foster economic self-reliance. In arguing for domestic resource mobilization relative to debt, the African Development Bank Group (2019) stated that African countries, including Zimbabwe, have often resorted to external borrowing to finance budget deficits and development projects. However, heavy reliance on external loans exposes these nations to various risks, including currency fluctuations, high interest rates, and conditionalities imposed by lenders such as international financial institutions and bilateral creditors. Enhanced domestic resource mobilization offers a more sustainable alternative by tapping into the domestic economy's potential.

Mutero (2020) identified four (4) primary strategies for enhancing domestic resource mobilization: the first one involves strengthening tax systems. African countries can improve tax compliance, broaden the tax base, and enhance revenue administration to increase tax revenues. Progressive taxation policies can ensure that the burden falls equitably across different income groups while minimizing tax evasion and avoidance. The second strategy widely supported by the African Development Bank Group (2019) is harnessing natural resources. Mutero (2020) submits that African nations, including Zimbabwe, possess abundant natural resources that can generate significant revenue if managed effectively. Transparency and accountability governance frameworks and sustainable exploitation practices can maximize the contribution of natural resource revenues to national development.

The third strategy involves promoting financial inclusion. This is attained through facilitating increased access to financial services for underserved populations and hence fostering savings, investment, and entrepreneurship. Eventually, this leads to the expansion of the tax base and stimulating economic growth. The fourth one involves combating illicit financial flows. Addressing illicit financial flows through measures such as enhancing transparency, strengthening anti-money laundering mechanisms, and promoting international cooperation is essential to preserve domestic resources and combat corruption. For instance, the Reserve Bank of Zimbabwe Financial Intelligence Unit (2022) reported that between 2000 and 2021, Zimbabwe lost an estimated US$179 billion through illicit financial flows.

IMF (2020) argues that sustainable development and economic diversification are critical for reducing vulnerability to debt crises and fostering inclusive growth. African countries should prioritize investments in critical sectors such as agriculture, manufacturing, renewable energy, and technology to diversify their economies, create employment opportunities, and reduce dependence on volatile commodity markets. Moreover, sustainable development strategies should prioritize environmental sustainability, social equity, and resilience to external shocks. Fofack (2014) advocates for debt-relief programs that link debt reduction to health, education, and infrastructure investments, aligning with sustainable development objectives. Such investments can enhance human capital, foster economic productivity, and create conditions conducive to sustainable growth while simultaneously addressing debt sustainability concerns. According to Mutero (2020), the economic benefits of transitioning to low-carbon economies are reducing greenhouse gas emissions and investing in climate adaptation measures. Integrating environmental considerations into debt management frameworks can mitigate climate-related risks, enhance resource efficiency, and promote long-term economic sustainability.

Economic diversification involves broadening economic activities and reducing dependency on a single sector, mitigating risks associated with commodity price volatility and external shocks. The IMF (2020) argues that economic diversification increases resilience to external shocks, fosters innovation, and promotes inclusive growth. Mutero (2020) added that diversified economies possess the capacity to withstand downturns in specific sectors and capitalize on emerging opportunities, reducing reliance on debt financing for stabilization purposes. It is fundamental to note that promoting economic diversification entails targeted investments in sectors with high growth potential, conducive regulatory frameworks, and supportive infrastructure. Recommendations are that African governments should leverage debt financing to generate private sector investment in key sectors, develop human capital, and upgrade technological capabilities.

Through diversification of economies, nations can reduce vulnerabilities, enhance competitiveness, and create sustainable pathways for economic development, thereby strengthening their debt management capacity. The IMF (2020) views promoting sustainable development and economic diversification as not mutually exclusive but complementary within debt management strategies. According to Mutero (2020), governments can pursue debt-for-nature swaps, debt-for-climate swaps, and debt-for-equity swaps to finance investments in sustainable infrastructure, environmental conservation, and renewable energy projects. The conclusions by Fofack (2014) are that fostering economic diversification contributes to achieving sustainable development objectives by creating employment opportunities, reducing income inequalities, and promoting social cohesion. Policies aimed at encouraging small and medium enterprises (SMEs), enhancing access to finance for marginalized groups, and fostering innovation ecosystems can unlock new sources of economic growth while advancing sustainable development goals.

Effective governance mechanisms and transparency are essential for addressing systemic issues of corruption, mismanagement, and fiscal opacity that contribute to debt crises in Africa. Governments must strengthen institutions, enforce anti-corruption measures, enhance public financial management systems, and promote accountability and transparency in debt-related transactions. Civil society organizations, the media, and international watchdogs promote transparency and hold governments accountable for their fiscal policies and debt management practices. The IMF (2020) submits that governance covers the institutional frameworks, policies, and processes that guide decision-making and resource allocation within a country. In the context of debt management, governance plays a pivotal role in shaping fiscal discipline, promoting accountability, and mitigating the risks associated with debt accumulation.

Gelbard and Leite (1999) emphasized the importance of good governance in managing public finances and debt. They argued that transparency and accountability frameworks governance structures enhance the credibility of debt management policies, fostering investor confidence and reducing the likelihood of fiscal mismanagement and corruption. According to Fofack (2014), effective governance frameworks facilitate the formulation and implementation of prudent debt management strategies, including establishing debt ceilings, debt sustainability analyses, and mechanisms for monitoring and evaluation. Mutero (2020) underscored the role of transparency in promoting economic efficiency, accountability, and democratic governance. The argument is that transparency fosters public trust, enables citizens to hold policymakers accountable, and reduces information asymmetry between borrowers and lenders in financial markets.

Numerous empirical studies support the proposition that strengthened governance and transparency contribute to improved debt management outcomes. A study conducted by the IMF and the World Bank underlined the positive correlation between governance indicators, such as control of corruption and rule of law, and debt sustainability. Countries that implemented reforms to enhance governance and transparency in debt management have experienced tangible benefits. For instance, Ghana introduced the Fiscal Responsibility Act and the establishment of a Public Debt Management Office. This led to greater fiscal discipline, reduced borrowing costs, and improved debt sustainability (IMF, 2020). In the same context, Chile illustrates the value of proactive measures in enhancing transparency in debt management. Examples include the publication of comprehensive debt reports and the establishment of independent oversight mechanisms. Mutero (2020) submits that these measures bolster investor confidence and facilitate access to international capital markets.

Zimbabwe is a case example of how governance has to underpin efforts to reduce the debt burden, clear arrears and move toward debt sustainability. Following decades of failed and false starts to debt resolution, in 2022 efforts were renewed through a High-Level Debt dialogue platform. The platform is facilitated by former Mozambican President Joachim Chissano and the Africa Development Bank President Dr. Akinwumi Adesina. It composes of all stakeholders from within Zimbabwe and the creditors. Three reform areas were developed namely; governance reforms, economic reforms, and land tenure reforms. This shows that governance is at the center of any debt resolution package and reforms therein are the seed for the success of the other areas. In understanding this notion, it is imperative to accept that governance and the reform agenda is a two-way traffic which calls on both the creditors and debtors to be responsible in their lending, borrowing, and finding sustainable solutions to the poly crisis ensuing.

Global cooperation plays a pivotal role in facilitating debt reduction initiatives. As argued by Mutero (2020), addressing the root causes of debt requires concerted efforts by the international community to promote transparency, accountability, and good governance practices in debtor countries. Multilateral institutions such as the IMF, World Bank, and regional development banks are crucial in coordinating debt-relief programs and providing financial assistance to heavily indebted nations. Fofack (2014) added that by fostering dialogue and collaboration among stakeholders, global cooperation enhances the effectiveness of debt reduction strategies and promotes equitable burden sharing among creditors and debtors.

Berg and Hussain (2019) submit that multilateral approaches provide a framework for designing comprehensive debt reduction strategies that address the unique challenges faced by debtor countries. The HIPC Initiative is an example of a multilateral approach toward debt relief to the poorest countries (IMF, 2020). Through debt restructuring, grants, and concessional loans, the HIPC Initiative has assisted in alleviating the debt burden of eligible countries, enabling them to redirect resources toward poverty reduction and human development. Despite notable progress from global cooperation and multilateral initiatives, several challenges continue in debt reduction. Mutero (2020) noted implementation bottlenecks, bureaucratic hurdles, and political obstacles can impede the effectiveness of debt relief programs, undermining their impact on poverty reduction and economic development. In addition, the COVID-19 pandemic worsened the debt vulnerabilities of several developing countries, compelling greater international cooperation, and innovative financing mechanisms to address the evolving debt crisis.

Case for the IFIs Reforms

Debt sustainability is a major concern among African nations. A plethora of factors, among other things, weak governance structures, volatile commodity prices, and the impact of global economic shocks worsen this. Whereas IFIs have a crucial role in providing Africa with financial assistance and debt relief, the current framework necessitates a comprehensive re-evaluation to resolve the persistent challenges and drive long-term sustainability. The section explores pertinent reforms necessary for promoting debt sustainability in Africa within the context of IFIs. Reforming IFIs is a critical subject in global governance and development. These institutions, such as the IMF and the World Bank, provide financial assistance, shape economic policies, and promote global financial stability. The following are key considerations in reforming IFIs.

A critical aspect of reforming IFIs is addressing governance and representation issues. Hanlon (2021) submits that governance and representation play key roles in determining the effectiveness and transparency of IFIs. Mutero (2020) argues for the voting power and decision-making authority within IFIs that are skewed toward countries in the global North. Efforts of the reform process should focus on increasing developing countries' voices and participation, ensuring a more equitable and inclusive decision-making process. Fofack (2014) views that weak governance structures within IFIs can lead to opaque decision-making processes, lack of accountability, and inefficiency in resource allocation. Despite competing arguments, Hanlon (2021) argues that governance matters within IFIs contribute to perpetuating unsustainable lending practices and inadequate debt management strategies in the context of debt sustainability in the global South. This is exacerbated by the absence of effective oversight mechanisms that enable IFIs to enforce conditionalities and loan terms that align with the long-term interests of African countries. This perpetuates a cycle of debt dependency and undermines efforts to achieve sustainable development goals.

Whitfield and Behuria's (2019) views on the representation of African countries within IFIs are that these factors influence the formulation of policies and strategies related to debt sustainability. Mutero (2020) stresses the importance of inclusive decision-making in international economic governance. Nevertheless, the global South remains underrepresented in key decision-making bodies of IFIs. Fundamentally, the lack of adequate representation constrains the voice of the global South in shaping policies that directly impact their economies and debt dynamics. As a result, the policy prescriptions offered by IFIs may not fully consider African countries' unique challenges and priorities, leading to one-size-fits-all approaches that fail to address the root causes of debt distress. To Hanlon (2021), strengthening the voice and participation of Africa in the design and implementation of debt management strategies is important in fostering ownership and sustainability. Arguments have thus been proffered on the necessity of empowering regional institutions such as the AU and the ADB to play a more prominent role in debt negotiations, and policy formulation can also contribute to more equitable outcomes.

Mutero (2020) argues that transparency and accountability within the governance structures of the IFIs are essential pillars in promoting responsible lending and borrowing practices. Such transparency and accountability frameworks should include greater disclosure of information, improved evaluation and monitoring of programs and projects, and mechanisms for holding IFIs accountable for their actions and outcomes. Fofack (2014) asserts that increased transparency and accountability encourage trust and allow stakeholders to assess the effectiveness and impact of IFI policies and interventions in the African context; opacity in debt contracts and the lack of accountability mechanisms have contributed to unsustainable debt burdens. According to Mutero (2020), enhancing transparency in debt processes and transactions is a central pillar for preventing IFFs and ensuring that borrowed funds are utilized for productive purposes rather than being siphoned off through corruption. Robust debt management frameworks are, therefore, crucial in monitoring debt levels, tracking borrowing trends, and assessing repayment capacity. Scholars have affirmed the importance of strengthening institutional capacities within African governments to negotiate transparent debt contracts and conduct comprehensive debt sustainability analyses as a panacea for mitigating risks associated with excessive borrowing.

Debt restructuring measures are important in addressing unsustainable debt burdens through renegotiating debt terms, reducing debt levels, and restoring fiscal stability. In the context of high debt-to-GDP ratios and limited fiscal space in Africa, effective debt restructuring mechanisms are essential in restoring macroeconomic stability and creating conditions for sustainable development. Mutero (2020) argues that current debt restructuring mechanisms within IFIs fundamentally lack flexibility and lack measures for addressing challenges peculiar to African countries. As submitted by Hanlon (2021), rigid debt repayment schedules and punitive measures can exacerbate economic hardships and impede long-term development prospects. Fofack (2014) argues that to address the array of debt challenges confronting African nations, IFIs should embrace flexible and inclusive debt restructuring frameworks that are aware of the unique socioeconomic realities of African nations.

These arguments justify advocacy for the establishment of sovereign debt restructuring mechanisms to facilitate orderly and timely debt workouts while safeguarding the interests of both creditors and debtors. Fundamental to note is that the participation of private creditors in debt restructuring initiatives is vital to achieving comprehensive debt relief. As framed by Kasekende and Ali (2019), the involvement of the private creditor in multilateral debt restructuring frameworks promotes burden sharing and enhances the effectiveness of debt-relief efforts. Fofack (2014) further discusses fostering inclusive and participatory dialogue among member countries, civil society organizations, academia, and other stakeholders. This can be done through regional consultations, thematic forums, and conferences to gather diverse perspectives and input on the reform agenda.

Conclusion

In conclusion, the issue of creditor contributions, benefits, and solutions to the debt crisis in Africa underscores a complex interplay of economic, political, and social factors. The continent's debt burden has been a longstanding challenge, exacerbated by factors such as poor governance, corruption, unsustainable borrowing practices, and external shocks. The chapter shows that creditor contributions to Africa's debt crisis have been multifaceted. While international financial institutions and bilateral creditors have provided much-needed financial assistance, the terms of loans and debt restructuring lack transparency, conditionality, and have the potential to exacerbate debt dependency. This is further exacerbated by the involvement of private creditors and the proliferation of non-concessional loans that have introduced additional challenges, including higher interest rates and less favorable terms for debtor countries. On the other hand, some debt-relief initiatives such as the HIPC and the MDRI have provided some debt relief and fiscal space for investment in poverty reduction and development programs. Additionally, debt-for-development swaps and innovative financing mechanisms have emerged as promising avenues for addressing development priorities while managing debt sustainability. However, the chapter reveals that addressing the debt crisis in Africa requires comprehensive and sustainable solutions. These include the need for enhanced transparency, accountability, and responsible lending practices among creditors and debtor countries alike, strengthening debt management capacities, improving governance frameworks, and fostering greater dialogue and cooperation between creditors and debtors. Added to the above, promoting economic diversification, inclusive growth, and sustainable development is essential for reducing Africa's vulnerability to debt distress. The chapter further reveals the value of investing in human capital, infrastructure development, and productive sectors as a way of unlocking the continent's growth potential and creating opportunities for debt sustainability. In capping this chapter, it is fundamental to note that while the debt crisis in Africa poses significant challenges, it also presents an opportunity for collective action and transformative change. By addressing the root causes of the crisis, fostering responsible lending and borrowing practices, and promoting inclusive and sustainable development, Africa can chart a path toward debt sustainability, economic resilience, and shared prosperity for its people and future generations.

References

African Development Bank Group. (2019). *Domestic revenue mobilization in Africa: Progress, prospects, and challenges*. African Development Bank Group, downloaded from https://www.afdb.org/, dated 06/02/2024.

Berg, A., & Hussain, M. F. (2019). *The African continental free trade area: Economic and distributional effects*. IMF Working Paper, 19(117).

Bloomfield, A. (1981). Gold standard. In D. Greenwald (Ed.), *Encyclopedia of economics* (p. 452). McGraw-Hill.

Buckley, D. (2024). *What is the global financial system?* Accessed from https://www.daytrading.com/global-financial-system

Dreher, A. (2004). *IMF and economic growth: The effects of programs, loans, and compliance with conditionality*. Research Paper Series, ThurgauerWirtschaftsinstitut.

Ezenwe, U. (1993). The African debt crisis and the challenge ofdevelopment. *Intereconomics*, ISSN 0020-5346, Nomos Verlagsgesellschaft, Baden-Baden, 28(1), 35–43, https://doi.org/10.1007/BF02928100.

Fofack, H. (2014). *Financing Africa's infrastructure and agricultural development*. The World Bank.

FONDAD. (1992). *African debt revisited: Procrastination or progress?* FONDAD, The Hague. Accessed from: www.fondad.org

Geda, A. (2003). The historical origin of African debt crisis. *Eastern Africa Social Science Research Review, 19*, 59–89. https://doi.org/10.1353/eas.2002.0012

Gelbard, E., & Leite, C. A. (1999). *Measuring default risk premia on African sovereign debt*. World Bank Policy Research Working Paper, (2179).

Griffith-Jones, S., Gallagher, K., & Volz, U. (2021). *Debt relief by private creditors: Lessons from the Brady plan*. Published by Heinrich Böll Foundation, Center for Sustainable Finance (SOAS, University of London), and Global Development Policy Center (Boston University) as Background Paper to the Debt Relief for Green and Inclusive Recovery Project.

Guilherme, R. S. (2008). *IMF conditionalities for the least developed countries*. Policy Brief No. 19.

Hanlon, J. (2021). Mozambique: Who owes what? *Review of African Political Economy, 48*(159), 279–292.

IMF. (2020). *Enhancing domestic revenue mobilization*. International Monetary Fund. Downloaded from https://www.imf.org/en/ Date 05/02/2024.

Kasekende, L., & Ali, Z. (2019). *Domestic revenue mobilization in sub-Saharan Africa: The role of tax policy and administration*. International Monetary Fund.

Marabuka, E. (2013). *What are the effects of ESAP on Zimbabwe?* Lupane State University https://www.academia.edu/8614456/Effects_of_ESAP_in_Zimbabwe.

Mutero, J. (2020). *Revenue performance in Zimbabwe: What needs to be done*. Zimbabwe Economic Policy Analysis and Research Unit, downloaded from https://www.zeparu.co.zw/

Ndikumana, L., & Boyce, J. (2008). *New estimates of capital flight from sub-Saharan African countries: Linkages with external borrowing and policy options*. Working Paper Series, No. 166, Political Economy Research Institute.

Panizza, U. (2022a). *Long-term debt sustainability in emerging market economies: A counterfactual analysis*. Graduate Institute of International and Development Studies International Economics Department Working Paper Series, No. HEIDWP07-2022.

Panizza. (2022b). *The logic and risks of climate linked debt instruments*. Graduate Institute of International Development Studies.

Pereira, N. M. (2008). *The IMF maintains its grip on low-income governments*. European Network on Debt and Development.

Pettinger, T. (2009). *Economics help: Gold standard explained*. https://econ.economicshelp.org/2009/02/gold-standard-explained.html.

Soga, M., & Gaston, K. J. (2021). Towards a unified understanding of human–nature interactions. *Nature Sustainability, 5*, 374–383.

UN. (2023). *UN chief reinforces call for multilateral reform, outlines next steps*. https://news.un.org/en/story/2023/10/1141892

UNECA. (2023). *African Ministers call for reforms of the IMF's Special Drawing Rights system*. https://www.uneca.org/stories/african-ministers-call-for-reforms-of-the-imf-sdr-system

United Nations. (2023a). *Financing for sustainable development report 2023*. New York: Interagency Taskforce on Financing for Development.

United Nations. (2023b). *World economic situation and prospects 2023*. New York, United Nations Department of Economic and Social Affairs.

Whitfield, L., & Behuria, P. (2019). Mozambique: Debt, illicit financial flows, and the systemic implications of corruption. *Third World Quarterly, 40*(6), 1064–1086.

World Bank. (2021). *Mozambique economic update: Debt sustainability and economic recovery*. World Bank.

World Bank. (2023). *International debt report*. Accessed on https://www.worldbank.org/en/programs/debt-statistics/idr/products

ZIMCODD. (2021). The bane of resource-backed loans: Implications for debt sustainability. Accessed on https://zimcodd.org/wp-content/uploads/2021/02/The-Bane-of-Resource-Backed-Loans-Implications-for-Debt-Sustainability.pdf

ZIMCODD. (2023). *Monthly economic review, October 2023*. Accessed on https://zimcodd.org/?sdm_process_download=1&download_id=6610

Janet Mudzviti-Zhou is a pan-Africanist feminist, a practitioner and activist with over 15 years of experience in the civil society sector in Southern Africa. She is an expert in applying human rights and political lens in policy analysis, debt justice and gender studies. She is the former executive director of Zimbabwe Coalition on Debt and Development (ZIMCODD) and currently the country manager (Zimbabwe) of Southern Africa Trust.

Part II
Global Climate Crisis

Chapter 6
Climate Colonialism in Africa

Vincent Chenzi, Nyasha Trishia Murau, and Washington Mazorodze

Abstract This chapter seeks to reposition the emerging anthropogenic (human-caused) climate change discourse alongside the global storms debate. It asserts that climate change like the three global storms (The 2008 financial crisis, the 2019 Covid-19 pandemic, and the February 2022 Russia–Ukraine conflict) has shaped and reconfigured relations between the global south and its more affluent northern counterpart. Despite the fact that global warming-driven climate change is a contemporary phenomenon, its manifestation and management however mirrors the political divide that has existed between the global north and south whereby the north continues to exploit the south in what can best be described as climate colonialism. The study argues that climate colonialism reproduces the horrors of colonialism and imperialism in the form of global north-backed initiatives that only further ravage the post-colony. In particular, climate financing, climate adaptation, carbon offsetting, green policing, natural resource exploitation, and smart solutions to climate change.

Introduction

Climate change, stemming from natural events like volcanic eruptions or shifts in the sun's activity, as well as anthropogenic activities such as deforestation and fossil fuel burning significantly impacts weather patterns and contributes to extreme climate events (Stern & Kaufmann, 2000). Contemporary projections on climate change posit that Global Warming Levels (GWLs) are anticipated to increase by at least 1.5 °C by the year 2100 above pre-industrial temperatures. There are basically four Global Warming Level scenarios, 1.5 °C, 2 °C, 3 °C, and 4 °C, and these represent distinct assumptions, with the first two aligning with the Paris Agreement

V. Chenzi (✉)
Department of Peace Security and Society, University of Zimbabwe, Harare, Zimbabwe

N. T. Murau · W. Mazorodze
Peace and Security Studies, Zimbabwe Defence University, Harare, Zimbabwe

G. Moyo, S. J. Ndlovu-Gatsheni (eds.), *Global Storms and Africa in World Politics*, Global Power Shift, https://doi.org/10.1007/978-3-031-83868-2_6

thresholds and the latter pair depicting potential worst-case situations (Mateyisi et al., 2024; Raftery et al., 2017).

Notwithstanding, climate change has already ravaged the globe by intensifying and even triggering disasters in the form of heat waves, floods, droughts, cyclones, desertification, and the rise in sea levels (IPCC, 2023). Africa has already witnessed extreme climate events including severe droughts, floods, wildfires, and cyclones which have affected all economic sectors (Marumbwa et al., 2020). However, the African continent has been disproportionately affected by these climate change processes which have been punctuated by altered weather patterns, rising temperatures, and extreme weather events (Chenzi et al., 2024). The continent is particularly vulnerable not only because a large portion of its population lives in impoverished conditions but there are also historical and administrative conditions that makes the continent's inhabitants more vulnerable especially to what can best be referred to as climate colonialism. Hence, the incommensurate encumbrance of climate destruction is largely descending on erstwhile colonized, brutalized, and racialized milieus in the global south, signalling the strong presence of colonization through the climate crisis sustained by the development industry and globalization (Sultana, 2022).

There exists a strong relationship between colonialism and climate change. Colonialism is broadly defined as the control by one power over a dependent region or people involving the use of violence, murder, displacement, and/or marginalization of the existing population (Chenzi, in press; Christopher, 2023). Although colonialism is as old as human history dating back to ancient empires like ancient Egypt, Greece, Rome, and Phoenicia, nevertheless two principal waves of colonialism have persisted and also manifest presently as climate coloniality. That is, the fifteenth and nineteenth century European colonization of North and South America, and the Scramble for Africa, respectively (Chamberlain, 2014). These two colonial periods have been responsible for centuries of harmful extractive practices across global south regions particularly in Africa, Asia, and Latin America that have driven wealth to the global north, and poverty to the global south (which is largely a reference to post-colonial and occupied states). In this regard, climate colonialism manifests as a structural practice where countries in the global north exploit and trounce states in the global south to increase their power and control of less powerful nations, under the pretence of reducing global carbon emissions and building green technology. This has manifested itself through uneven distribution of extracted resources, public and private acquisition of land, and the unceasing violence, pillaging, trauma, and exertion of power over communities with less resource power (Ober & Sakdapolrak, 2020).

Hence, climate coloniality brings forth the horrors of colonialism and imperialism via climate effects in the post-colony (situated mainly in the tropics and subtropics where climate-evoked disasters and changes have been dominant for some time). Consequently, climate change exposes both the colonialism of the past and an ongoing coloniality that controls and structures lives of global southerners which are intrinsically linked to the processes of capitalism, imperialism, and international development (Sultana, 2022). The jagged and mismatched vulnerabilities and marginalizations of deaths and devastation between global north and south denizens draws attention to colonial continuities from the past into the present and future.

Coloniality depends on racial supremacy and hierarchical dealings entrenched during active colonialism and currently manifesting in post-colonial space times, where the colonial enclosure of power endures. Thus, climate coloniality takes place where Eurocentric racial capitalism, hegemony, neocolonialism, uneven consumption, and military dominance are co-constitutive of climate effects experienced by diversely racialized populations who are disproportionately made vulnerable and expendable (Sultana, 2022; Solnit et al., 2023; Ober & Sakdapolrak, 2020). Contemporary climate coloniality manifests itself in the form of commodification, rapacious displacement, creation of sacrifice zones, dispossessions through colonial–capitalist extractivism, subtle racism and continued 'othering', and inordinate exposures to traumas from anthropogenic climate-induced disasters.

On a similar note, climate colonialism is also evidenced by the Western hegemonization of climate narratives, financing, and solutions. By exploring the uneven and unjust impacts of climate change, climate coloniality reveals how differently located populations encounter, react to, and contend with the climate change crisis and its concomitant vulnerabilities in radically different approaches. That is, post-colonial states continue to be marginalized in international forums where power matrices of control are exerted through narratives on climate change by former colonial powers. This means that former colonized regions in the global south, especially in Latin America and the African continent, continue to experience the worst effects of the climate crisis regardless of their limited contribution to global warming. Hence, the coloniality of climate is an indispensable feature of everyday life curtailing opportunities and possibilities sustained by global racial capitalism, colonial dispossession, and climate debts (Sultana, 2022; van Ryneveld, 2021). Accordingly, it has been argued that it is the failure of Africa to overcome the Euro-North American coloniality hegemony that persist in barring the possibilities of African agency (Ndlovu-Gatsheni, 2012, 2013). Hence, the best way forward in addressing climate coloniality is by decolonizing climate and its associated discourses currently dominated by the neo-colonial global north military industrial complex.

In order to appreciate the emerging forms of colonialism taking shape in the global south in general and Africa in particular, the chapter was guided by three research questions. In particular, what is the relationship between the historical process of colonialism and climate change? How do contemporary western climate solutions perpetuate colonialism in Africa? and What are the most appropriate approaches to address the challenge of climate colonialism? For the purpose of addressing these pertinent questions, the study is divided into five broad sections apart from the introduction. The first segment examines emerging studies on climate colonialism across the globe. The second portion of the chapter consists of the conceptual analysis and it adopted the World Systems Theory and decolonial epistemic position. The third and fourth sections analysed the relationship between climate change and colonialism and the role of global north-based solutions to climate change towards entrenching climate colonialism in Africa, respectively. The fifth and final section concludes the chapter by focusing on possible remedies to address climate coloniality in Africa.

Climate Colonialism

There is a steadily growing body of literature on climate coloniality which focuses on a plethora of issues. Chief among the discourse is critique of existing neo-liberal climate mitigation approaches (Sultana, 2022; Cabello & Gilbertson, 2012; Dhanarto, 2016; Parola, 2020); benefits of indigenous knowledge systems as a way of overcoming the climate crisis (Emeagwali & Shizha, 2016; Acabado & Kuan, 2021; Whyte, 2017); and studies on decoloniality as an emancipator against climate colonialism (Quijano, 2000; Mignolo & Walsh, 2018). Other studies have also focused on the negative effects of climate coloniality, especially land grabs on marginalized communities (Busscher et al., 2018). These studies argue that existing vulnerabilities were considered to be more pressing than climate induced land grabs (Busscher et al., 2020).

On the critique of global north-based capitalist climate mitigation approaches, the Reducing Emissions from Deforestation and forest Degradation, conservation, sustainable management of forests and enhancing of carbon stocks (REDD+), a global programme introduced in 2010 through the United Nations Framework Convention on Climate Change (UNFCCC) has strongly been debunked (Streck, 2020). Proponents of climate coloniality contend that REDD+ is formulated within an epistemological perception which views forests and lands in the global south as tools that bankroll the subjugation of nature by global northerners for profit, regardless of financial input, governance, and/or participation from communities (Cabello & Gilbertson, 2012; Dhanarto, 2016). This has been used as the major reason why REDD+ has largely failed to effectively address the climate crisis. Critics have associated global north-based climate crisis mitigation policies especially REDD+, biofuel production, carbon offsetting, and green policing as being synonymous with land grabbing also referred to as ‘climate grabbing’ (Borras et al., 2020; Haller et al., 2020; Parola, 2020). Contrary to the above position, several global north-based studies have argued that these measures can be improved by ameliorating challenges in governance, finance, and/or community engagement initiatives (Morris, 2010; Corbera & Schroeder, 2011; Larson & Petkova, 2011).

Likewise, the United Nations’ (UN) carbon-offsetting scheme under the Clean Development Mechanism (CDM) as expounded by the Kyoto Protocol which seeks to reduce Green House Gas (GHG) emissions through hydropower whilst fostering sustainable development has also been heavily criticized. The carbon-offsetting dams have been accused of camouflaging carbon colonialism by exacerbating asymmetries of causation and burden-sharing (Erlewein, 2014; Baird & Green, 2020; Birch, 2020). That is, overdeveloped countries invest in dam construction in the global south which result in the destruction of livelihoods, ecosystems, and also engender forced displacements whilst the investing entities continue to produce huge amounts of Green House Gas emissions.

Studies on indigenous communities and climate concur that anthropogenic climate change greatly affects indigenous groups compared to other communities the same way laws, policies, colonial institutions impacted these communities during the colonial episode (Maldonado et al., 2014; Cameron, 2012; Stuhl, 2016; Whyte, 2017). Therefore, contemporary investigations of indigenous climate vulnerability needs to inculcate the history and present practices of colonialism and capitalism on indigenous communities. Nevertheless, local knowledge possessed by disaster prone communities has been proven to be critical in the fight against anthropogenic climate change hazards (Ford et al., 2020; Chenzi & Chihobo, in press). This indigenous knowledge has been used in predicting the location, intensity, occurrence, manifestation, frequency, and duration of disasters prevalent in those communities (Iloka, 2016; Lunga & Musarurwa, 2016; Muga et al., 2021). However, climate coloniality has resulted in policy-makers in the global south to continuously depend on western scientific mitigation measures whilst overlooking locally accessible and inexpensive Indigenous Knowledge Systems (IKS) in their fight against the anthropogenic climate crisis. This oversight has resulted in failed disaster mitigation efforts.

Notwithstanding, although this literature on climate coloniality is very insightful in terms of understanding how the contemporary global system has perpetuated colonialism even in addressing the climate crisis; nonetheless much of this literature has mainly investigated climate coloniality in Latin America, Asia, and BIPOC regions in the global north whilst nuances of climate coloniality in the African continent have largely been ignored. Therefore, this chapter emphasized the dynamics of climate coloniality in Africa since it is the worst affected and the least prepared region despite scholarly oversight.

World Systems Theory and Decolonial Praxis

This chapter draws upon the World Systems Theory and decolonial epistemic perspectives. The World Systems Theory posits that rich core capitalist societies succeed by exploiting poorer peripheral ones (Chirot & Hall, 1982). The periphery therefore can only advance through a global revolution that will end the world capitalist system. The World Systems Theory thus provides a model of human interaction that cuts across political, economic, and social dimensions. In addition, World Systems Theory is multiscalar, that is, it assesses the connection between different levels in a regional and interregional system. It adopts a holistic methodology to scrutinize the globe as an interdependent system; and it tries to overcome narrow disciplinary specialization in the social sciences. Its main goals are to explain unequal development and wealth between societies in the modern capitalist world since 1500, and to understand the cyclical patterns of expansion and contraction that characterize the world system. World Systems Theory stresses that poorer, or 'peripheral' societies have been systematically underdeveloped by the rich and powerful 'core', and they stand little chance of prospering without world revolution (Chirot, 2001).

In this current study, the World Systems Theory is used in articulating the existing global setup between the global north and south and how this not only causes but sustains the current climate crisis. By using the World Systems Theory, it becomes clear that historical differences position colonial and imperial countries at greater advantage over post-colonial and presently occupied countries. In other words, colonial perceptions of extractivism persist through neocolonial and development interventions. Hence, the study argues that the environmentally uneven dealings between the global south and north, current extractive capitalism, the imperial structures of global trade, and supremacy in establishing policies and ideologies, all contribute towards maintaining climate coloniality (Sultana, 2022). This results in the creation of historically exploitative overdeveloped economies, whereby geopolitical and economic processes sustain assorted colonial practices of extraction and dispossession. Accordingly, Farhana Sultana (2022) posited that:

> Legacies of imperial violence live on not only exacerbating environmental degradations but increased climate-induced disasters. As frequencies and strengths of climate-fuelled natural hazards such as tropical cyclones grow, the structural violences of colonialism are further felt corporeally, communally, politically, economically, and ecologically. Slow but compounding violence intensify vulnerabilities that maintain climate coloniality and extends it into the future. Some lives and ecosystems are rendered disposable and sacrificial, whereby structural forces, both historical and contemporary, fuel it....

Therefore, coloniality is practiced through continued environmental degradations that are both open and secret, episodic and creeping such as toxic waste, mining, pollution, desertification, deforestation, disasters, and land erosion, among others. These depredations are produced by global capitalism's development and economic growth ideologies that recreate various forms of colonial racial harms to entire countries in the global south and communities of colour in the global north (Baer, 2012). In this regard, climate coloniality persists because contemporary governance arrangements are undergirded by centuries of colonial and imperial power systems and ideologies, whereby currently a global network of corporations, nation-states, and elites dominate discursive framings around climate and the material outcomes therein (Sultana, 2022).

Decoloniality is therefore used in the study as a viable solution in addressing the current colonialities that sustain the global outlook which brought benefits to the colonizer but drawbacks for the local populations. By applying decoloniality perspectives, the chapter contends that colonialism is not just in terms of formal political domination, but is much deeper especially the relationship between power and knowledge which cascades into the present, in relation to all aspects of knowledge, power, and culture in both economic and political realms (Ndlovu-Gatsheni, 2015). Nevertheless, decolonization involves restructuring existing relationships to ecologies (water, land, and communities), by uncovering, dismantling, and reassessing colonial structures and discourses by making them non-universal. In addition, demonstrating the hegemony imposed historically via racialized colonial praxis, and exposing the everyday tactics of subjugation and empire-building is also critical.

Climate Change and Colonialism

Colonialism and climate change are intrinsically linked. However, the connection between climate change with colonization can best be established by acknowledging that the historic injustices that were perpetrated during the colonial period are not consigned to history but that their legacies have persisted. In other words, the historic causes of climate change are deeply rooted in colonialism.

The beginning of the industrial revolution in Great Britain in 1750 which quickly proliferated into Western Europe established a fossil fuel-based capitalist system. This nascent capitalist system had a high demand for raw materials, cheap labour, and markets. In order to meet the high demand, the establishment of colonies in the global south became a critical policy for the system to work properly. Subsequently, colonies were established and designed to provide the necessary raw materials, cheap labour, and markets especially in the Caribbean, Latin America, Asia, and Africa.

However, the industrial revolution in Europe led to the widespread emission of GHGs which began the process of artificially increasing global temperatures leading to anthropogenic climate change. Therefore, the global north is intrinsically responsible for the contemporary climate crisis which is rooted in the exploitative colonial activities and practices yet, the global south is disproportionately impacted by the crisis. These observations were also made by the United Kingdom (UK)-based Greenpeace organization which stated that the current environmental emergency is a direct legacy of colonialism (Lewis, 2023). It is this perceived injustice that has sparked a wave of calls for climate reparations, basically, calling on wealthy nations in the global north (that have caused climate change) to financially bankroll nations in the global south (that have done the least to cause the climate crisis) in responding to its effects.

Western Solutions to Climate Change

On the enquiry pertaining to how contemporary western climate solutions perpetuate colonialism in Africa, the chapter states that the bulk of contemporary global north-based climate crisis solutions are not only unrealistic to say the least but they also perpetuate conditions of colonialism and dependency. In order to trenchantly understand how climate solutions to climate change perpetuate climate colonialism; contemporary reports, resolutions, and recommendations from western-backed international organizations responsible for investigating, addressing, and reporting the causes, manifestation, and effects of climate change were utilized. These international establishments include the Intergovernmental Panel on Climate Change (IPCC), Multihazard Mitigation Council (MMC), Sendai Framework for Disaster Risk Reduction (SFDRR), United Nations Climate Change Secretariat (UNCCS), United Nations Office for Disaster Risk Reduction (UNDRR), World Food Programme (WFP), UNFCCC, among others.

The reports from these organizations demonstrate that the framing of climate change causes, effects, and solutions perpetuates climate colonialism in the global south in general and Africa in particular. These international bodies deliberately exempt the global north as the main culprit behind the pollution-based climate alteration. Furthermore, the global north proposed solutions to climate change further entrench widespread exploitation and marginalization of the south whilst intensifying climate change effects. These sentiments were also echoed by several climate justice scholars who argued that the multinational climate associations waver in addressing the climate crisis by not holistically minimizing hyper-consumption, fossil fuel dependency, and growth models, along with the systems that sustain them (Cottle, 2009; Oglesby, 2010). Instead, these forums are nothing more than plays where the elites perform by erasing historical, spatial geopolitics, and power relations that perpetuate climate coloniality.

Farhana Sultana (2022) also posited that the alleged solutions to climate change are counterfeit, and are merely a form of upholding colonialism via land grabs, extraction, displacement, and dispossession. These alleged solutions include climate financing, carbon offsetting, and green policing, among others. However, the neocolonial nature of these trumped-up climate solutions is a critical aspect that is seldom mentioned, it is nonetheless critical towards understanding how climate colonialism manifests itself between the global north and south (Ramachandran, 2021). These solutions are provided under the guise of development projects and they usually involve wholesale displacement of indigenous people from their ancestral lands leading to widespread human and land rights abuses reminiscent of the colonial era.

Carbon offsetting for example is a typical western panacea to the ravages of climate change. It is a practice whereby wealthy states acquire the right to release larger amounts of Green House Gases beyond the stipulated amount by paying huge sums of money towards investment in carbon integration facilities in the global south as compensation (Watt, 2021). Hence, carbon offsetting provides unconditional rights to rich nations and organizations to pollute the atmosphere as normal simply because they can afford to do so. This approach disproportionately affects Black, Indigenous, and People of Colour (BIPOC), especially in the global south who are either forced to relocate or experience livelihood loses from green offset initiatives (Watt, 2021). Consequently, what green offsetting simply does is to deny economic agency to global south inhabitants whilst providing it to global north regions a similar custom which was practiced under colonialism.

In the same vein, funds drawn from carbon offsetting usually result in global north-backed climate change rehabilitation programs, especially afforestation and reforestation which have been discovered to involve violent land grabs and human rights abuses against Black, Indigenous, and People of Colour, especially in Africa,

Latin America, and parts of Asia. This inhumane process has widely been referred to as 'green policing'. Members of Non-Governmental Organizations (NGO) constitute the bulk of green police personnel (Nurse, 2013). Activities done under green policing include forced displacement of communities from their homes for conservation purposes and the shooting or incarceration of people who enter the forests they had lived in for generations.

In Mozambique, for example, a Norwegian-based company Green Resources' afforestation project for carbon offsetting obstructed local communities from gaining access to water sources, rivers and roads. It further broke its promises of job creation and infrastructure development soon after hoodwinking indigenous leaders to sign contracts leasing their land rights to the organization knowing fully well that they did not fully understand the terms and conditions of the contracts (Ramachandran, 2021). Such underhand dealings whereby duplicitous western agents waylay unsuspecting indigenous African leaders by misleading them into ceding their territories in return for empty promises are not new. Such double-dealing machinations were a popular weapon of choice among western colonialists during the heydays of the scramble for Africa (Boddy-Evans, 2012). The difference between contemporary colonial tendencies and the nineteenth century scramble for African colonies is the tendency to hide behind the climate rhetoric despite striking similarities in the mode of operation between the two.

Climate financing is also another global north-backed solution to climate change which also upholds climate colonialism. The precept for climate financing is principally based on the argument by global south nations that they shoulder the brunt of carbon emissions emitted by their wealthier counterparts in the global north despite contributing very little in terms of carbon emissions. Furthermore, territories in the impoverished global south furnished the resources that overdeveloped the global north for centuries via colonialism, imperialism, and neocolonialism. Consequently, most states in the former were rendered incapable of extenuating the climate crisis impacts.

The global north is currently responsible for over 92 percent of cumulative carbon emissions compared to 2 percent from the rest of the African continent. Nevertheless, the global south suffers the most from extreme weather events especially countries like Mozambique, Zimbabwe, Myanmar, and Haiti (Ramachandran, 2021). In Zimbabwe, prior to 2020 an average of two cyclones used to affect the country annually. Especially in Manicaland and Mashonaland East provinces (World Data, 2023). However, because of the human-induced climate change effects, the frequency of cyclones affecting Zimbabwe has increased to an annual average of five. This basically means that Zimbabwe and its Southern African neighbours have to brace up for more devastating disasters brought about by cyclones and therefore urgently require a robust disaster governance and resilience mechanism (Chenzi et al., 2024). Similarly, droughts have frequented Southern Africa, and have been increasing in their scope and intensity with increasing uncertainty in rainfall patterns (Chitongo et al., 2024). This socio-spatial discrimination regarding who is sacrificed by being forced to endure the incommensurate price of climate perturbation, and who is spared has broadly been referred to as climate apartheid. This form of ecological apartheid is evident between and across the global south and north at multiple levels, especially at the intersectionality of race, class, and gender, whereby Black, Indigenous, and People of Colour groups are exposed to ecological trauma and toxic environments.

Therefore, nations throughout the global south have demanded for climate reparations for years and in 2009, their strong demand at the Copenhagen's Conference of Parties (COP 15) prompted a pledge of US$100 billion annually by global north countries to assist them in adapting to the changing climate. Notwithstanding, a 2020 report by the Organisation for Economic Co-operation and Development (OCED) established that the affluent nations have never reached the US$100 billion pledge despite a yearly increase in climate finance by richer to poorer nations (WFP, 2021). Moreover, developing nations alone will require US$140–300 billion annually by 2030, and US$280–500 billion per year by 2050 towards adapting to climate change. However, between 2015 and 2016, an annual average of just US$22 billion was invested globally towards adaptation (Chenzi et al., 2024).

In addition, much of the climate adaptation funding is spent on mitigating climate change shocks rather than investing towards adaptation. The Organisation for Economic Co-operation and Development (OECD) also found that out of the US$78.9 billion which was mobilized for developing nations towards climate finance in 2018, through the UNFCCC, 70 percent was reserved for mitigation whilst only US$16.8bn was channelled towards adaptation. More so, the 46 poorest nations were also found to only account for 17 percent of the climate finance scheme between 2016 and 2020 (UNCCS, 2017; UNDRR, 2019). Worse still, instead of providing the promised funds, the bulk of the climate finance from high-income nations to low-income countries takes the form of loans (Lee, 2022). This debt burden is a typical neo-colonial scheme that guarantees the perpetual enslavement of global south nations to their rich counterparts in the north.

Another proposed solution by the global north which only facilitates climate colonialism is the green agenda or the introduction of smart solutions to the climate crisis. Rich nations have been campaigning to switch to clean energy sources including electric vehicles, hydroelectric dams, and solar power generation to mitigate the increase in greenhouse gas emissions (UNGC, 2011). However, this smart technological trajectory also demands natural resources including cobalt, lithium, sunlight, and water sources which are mainly found in the global south. This has resulted in wholesale exploitation of resources in the global south, creating an asymmetry of causation and burden-sharing whereby the global south shoulders the burden of supplying resources at the expense of the natural environment and livelihoods whilst the global north entities enjoy the dividends (Erlewein, 2014). In this regard, the onus on reducing the GHG emissions rests with the poor across the global south, yet there is no equilibrium between luxury and survival emissions despite repeated calls. This colonization of the atmosphere by the global north means that there is no accountability between luxury emissions and survival emissions and increasingly less atmospheric space is left for greenhouse gas emissions and ecosystems further weighing down historically oppressed and impoverished communities (Clark & York, 2005).

In 2019, a group of Congolese families sued Apple, Google, Dell, Microsoft, and Tesla for aiding in the death and injury of their children working in cobalt mines. These inhuman activities are reminiscent of colonial exploitation which led to the death and injury of tens of thousands of Africans in the Congo who worked in rubber plantations. The complainants argued that these corporations were aware of child labour in the supply chain but they did not do anything to address the situation. Again, the Russia–Ukraine war further increased the demand for energy sources including fossil fuels such that coal exports from South Africa to Western Europe alone increased by 720 percent (Banya, 2022).

Another western climate mitigation initiative that has been strongly critiqued as a purveyor of climate colonialism is REDD+. It is packaged within an epistemological understanding which views forests and lands as instruments which assist the domination of nature by humans for economic profit (Sapinski, 2015). Consequently, it enables powerful capitalist states and corporations to maintain their present levels of production, consumption, and, therefore, pollution by making it possible for them to purchase the 'right to pollute'. Thus, rich entities will carry on consumption of energy generated by sources that produce more and more greenhouse gas emissions. This is despite the fact that these same entities are historically responsible for the emergence of the climate crisis in the first place. Furthermore, REDD+ strips the authority of traditional communities of their autonomy in the management of their territories which further increase their vulnerability to the climate crisis.

The global resolution to embrace the use of alternative energy sources, particularly biofuels and agrofuels, to minimize the production of Carbon Dioxide (CO^2) and greenhouse gases has also been proven to exacerbate climate change. Greenhouse gas emissions have been reported in all production phases of the bio and agrofuels especially if they are grown intensively, using nitrogen-based fertilizers and machinery, or if the processing demands large inputs of (fossil) energy (Parola, 2020). For example, the processing of corn or sugarcane (ethanol), or palms or soybeans (biodiesel) produces between 17–420 times more CO^2 than the annual savings from replacing fossil fuels (Giampietro et al., 2009). Furthermore, apart from the fact that monocultural practices of converting rainforests, peatlands, savannas, and grasslands as part of 'carbon saving' further jeopardizes entire ecosystems, production of biofuels has other challenges including land rights, working conditions, shortages of food stocks, the rise of food prices, and the mass evictions of rural peoples globally.

Looking Ahead

Climate change is currently shaping how humans relate to the environment and will increasingly do so in the near future if urgent action is not taken. What is further hindering action towards addressing climate change is the dominance by the global north on how it should be addressed and who should address it. Historical colonialism has remained intrinsically connected with the causes, manifestation, and the proposed neo-liberal solutions to the anthropogenic climate crisis. Unfortunately, these western concocted remedies are nothing more than a sinister pro-colonial greenwashing agenda with a facade of environmental friendliness, whilst in reality these remedies are responsible for wholesale displacement, impoverishment, and increase in greenhouse gas emissions. Furthermore, prevailing discourses around the climate crisis have been counter-productive since they are conducted in an apolitical environment which misrepresents the current discriminatory reality.

More so, the pro-western forums approach the climate crisis as if it is a mere physical phenomenon which can be fixed with proper financial and technological investments in the global south. Consequently, these platforms act as depoliticized techno-economist utopias that never deliver where deflection, delay, co-optation, and performativity without concrete outcomes is a recurrent feature annually (Sultana, 2022). Instead, unrealistic solutions to the climate crisis are constantly proposed. These entail green capitalism and market-based technocratic involvement, philosophies of net-zero carbon rather than real/negative zero carbon, and pro-capitalist methods which do not resolve structural and systemic challenges. Subsequently, sustainable solutions to the climate crisis remain elusive because of the misconstrued assumption that all states operate on a level playing field on the global scene. In reality, unbalanced negotiating power dominates not just at the Conference of Parties (COPs) but in bilateral and multilateral agreements, trade treaties, climate finance schemes, and development interventions (Squeff, 2023).

There are however a number of measures that can be adopted by the global south to effectively address climate coloniality. Therefore, as part of the third enquiry on how to address the anthropogenic climate coloniality crisis, decolonization of climate needs to take centre stage (See also Chap. 7). However, the goal towards decoloniality is not a one way street since there is no single blueprint for decolonizing climate. Moreover decolonization is a procedure and not a singular event as it involves ongoing unlearning to relearn over time and place that bear results. This gradual process will then be used in addressing the complexities of capitalism, colonialism, imperialism, and geopolitical development which sustains the replication of contemporary colonialities through current global governance systems, discursive framings, imagined solutions, and interventions (Sheller, 2023). Thus, the domination of climate narratives by the capitalist fossil fuel industry, powerful states, and elite allies needs to be challenged and dealt with by global south entities.

Engaging indigenous communities to address climate colonialism is also a critical pathway towards climate decoloniality. Colonialism and lack of proper documentation of indigenous knowledge systems on climate hazards are the main reasons behind the failure of in-cooperating Disaster Risk Reduction (DRR) indigenous knowledge to institutional policies in the global south. One of the most crucial steps towards this goal is the need to combine local knowledge with external/scientific methods in order to strike a balance so as to maximize on opportunities presented by both. Indigenous peoples were found to adapt to the impacts of climate change in creative ways. In Zimbabwe, inhabitants of lower Muzarabani utilized indigenous knowledge systems to adapt to the flood prone region. These indigenous knowledge systems predated colonialism but enabled them to predict, mitigate, and adapt to disasters in the region enabling them to live in harmony with the environment (Chenzi & Chihobo, in press). Therefore, climate crisis solutions must embrace indigenous people's teachings of the land which they possess so as to empower them in decision-making (Lee, 2022).

On a similar note, the adoption of other diverse knowledge systems will broaden the global debate on the climate crisis and redress the effects of climate change (Chenzi et al., 2024). Currently, coloniality has discursively limited the scope of the anthropogenic climate change discourse by destroying other epistemologies whilst simultaneously entrenching the hegemony of global north knowledge of and about climate change including what actions are possible. This has created cognitive coloniality among global south entities by subtly deciding for them what is knowable and what has value. Cognitive coloniality also co-exists with epistemic violence in knowledge production and valuation of expertise whereby Black, Indigenous, and People of Colour knowledge is suppressed, ignored, and denied expression. Therefore, overcoming cognitive coloniality requires challenging epistemic violence through epistemological and ontological shifts from capitalist universality towards pluriversality. This is attained by acknowledging and embracing the existence of collective approaches to enlightenment and existence across the globe such that the Eurocentric colonial model becomes one of many approaches of existing and relating to socio-ecologies.

Deracializing climate is another critical measure to address climate colonialism. It is through racialized othering that climate change proceeded and proceeds. This is worsened by viewing humanity as undifferentiated in persistent narratives of the Anthropocene. Universalism of the Anthropocene obscures both historical and contemporary power arrangements and obligations. These imbalances are evident through extraction and hierarchical imperialist practices which engender asymmetrical political economies fuelled by global market systems. Legacies of colonialism continue the racist ecological uneven exchange whereby global south regions are controlled through development regulations and financial domination from imperial entities. Consequently, self-serving climate solutions contrived by the global north that promote extractivism and creation of sacrifice zones in historically impoverished countries of the post-colonial world are universally imposed (Giampietro et al., 2009). This universal racialization of climate also manifests through carbon colonialism evidenced by deep ocean floor mining, rare earth mineral grabs, enclosures of commons, and the wholesale destruction of BIPOC communities and ecosystems. Hence, climate colonialism is a cancerous and present reality in the global south in general and the African continent in particular.

Conclusion

In the final analysis, the colonial legacy that has long defined the relationship between the global north and south remains deeply rooted in the climate crisis debate. Currently, the global South nations continue to embrace and adhere to the hegemonic influence of the global north in terms of how climate change should be understood, interpreted, and addressed. This has however ensured a perpetual subjugation of the global south particularly the African continent. The African colonial experiences of the nineteenth century though subtle, are gradually repeating themselves through the auspices of the contemporary climate change discourse whose dominance by the global north has evidently proven to be not in the best interests of the global south. Therefore, decolonizing climate change is the best way forward for African states to overcome systemic colonialities that continue to pity the global south against the north.

References

Acabado, S., & Kuan, D. (2021). *Indigenous peoples, heritage and landscape in the Asia Pacific: Knowledge co-production and empowerment*. Routledge.

Baer, H. A. (2012). Global capitalism and climate change. In *Handbook on international political economy* (pp. 395–414).

Baird, I. G., & Green, W. N. (2020). The Clean Development Mechanism and large dam development: Contradictions associated with climate financing in Cambodia. *Climatic Change, 161*(2), 365–383.

Banya, N. (2022). South African coal exports to Europe surge, shipments to Asia decline. *Reuters*. https://www.reuters.com/world/africa/safrican-coal-exports-europe-surge-shipments-asia-decline-2022-08-15/

Birch, S. (2020). *Carbon offsetting guilt-free flying?*

Boddy-Evans, A. (2012). *What caused the scramble for Africa?* African History.

Borras, S. M., Jr., Franco, J. C., & Nam, Z. (2020). Climate change and land: Insights from Myanmar. *World Development, 129*, 104864.

Busscher, N., Parra, C., & Vanclay, F. (2018). Land grabbing within a protected area: The experience of local communities with conservation and forestry activities in Los Esteros del Iberá, Argentina. *Land Use Policy, 78*, 572–582.

Busscher, N., Parra, C., & Vanclay, F. (2020). Environmental justice implications of land grabbing for industrial agriculture and forestry in Argentina. *Journal of Environmental Planning and Management, 63*(3), 500–522.

Cabello, J., & Gilbertson, T. (2012). A colonial mechanism to enclose lands: A critical review of two REDD+-focused special issues. *Ephemera: Theory & Politics in Organization, 12*(1/2), 162–180.

Cameron, E. S. (2012). Securing Indigenous politics: A critique of the vulnerability and adaptation approach to the human dimensions of climate change in the Canadian Arctic. *Global Environmental Change, 22*(1), 103–114.

Chamberlain, M. E. (2014). *The scramble for Africa*. Routledge.

Chenzi, V. (in press). The New Scramble for Africa': Unpacking the dynamics of Chinese Foreign Investment in Zimbabwe's Mining sector Under the Second Republic, 2017–2023. In E. Kioko,

M. Chuhila, & T. F. Theodory (Eds.), *Infrastructuring Africa: Mega projects as Game Changers or Doom for African Futures?* Elservier.

Chenzi, V., & Chihobo, M. D. (in press). Harnessing local knowledge for resilience building: The case study of lower Muzarabani. In I. Chirisa & R. Kasimba (Eds.), *Disaster risks and hazards: Perspectives in the context of consilience and practice for resilience*. Springer Nature.

Chenzi, V., Mateyisi, M., Nangombe, S., & Maoela, M. A. (2024). Emerging adaptation patterns in rural Southern Africa. In M. Matsa, L. Chapungu, & G. Nhamo (Eds.), *Climate change resilience in rural southern Africa: The dynamics, prospects & challenges*. Springer Nature.

Chenzi, V., Murau, N. T., & Ndamba, A. (in press). Decolonizing climate change discourses through indigenous adaptation approaches: Perspectives from the African continent. In E. Chitando & O. B. Mlambo (Eds.), *The Palgrave handbook of decolonising knowledge in Africa*. Palgrave.

Chirot, D. (2001). World systems theory. In N. J. Smelser & P. B. Baltes (Eds.), *International encyclopedia of the social & behavioral sciences* (pp. 16609–16613). Pergamon.

Chirot, D., & Hall, T. D. (1982). World-system theory. *Annual Review of Sociology, 8*(1), 81–106.

Chitongo, L., Chenzi, V., & Blazer-Mapitsa, C. (2024). Climate governance and resilience action. In M. Matsa, L. Chapungu, & G. Nhamo (Eds.), *Climate change resilience in rural Southern Africa: The dynamics, prospects & challenges*. Springer Nature.

Christopher, A. J. (2023). *Colonial Africa* (Vol. 15). Taylor & Francis.

Clark, B., & York, R. (2005). Carbon metabolism: Global capitalism, climate change, and the biospheric rift. *Theory and Society, 34*, 391–428.

Corbera, E., & Schroeder, H. (2011). Governing and implementing REDD+. *Environmental Science & Policy, 14*(2), 89–99.

Cottle, S. (2009). Global crises in the news: Staging new wars, disasters and climate change. *International Journal of Communication, 3*, 494–516.

Dhanarto, P. (2016). *REDD+ and Indigenous Dayak in Central Kalimantan, Indonesia: A new form of colonialism?* Master of International Development thesis, 2016.

Emeagwali, G., & Shizha, E. (2016). African Indigenous knowledge and the sciences: Journeys into the past and present. In *African indigenous knowledge and the sciences*. Brill.

Erlewein, A. (2014). The promotion of dams through the Clean Development Mechanism: Between sustainable climate protection and carbon colonialism. In *Large dams in Asia: Contested environments between technological hydroscapes and social resistance* (pp. 149–168).

Ford, J. D., King, N., Galappaththi, E. K., Pearce, T., McDowell, G., & Harper, S. L. (2020). The resilience of indigenous peoples to environmental change. *One Earth, 2*(6), 532–543.

Giampietro, M., Smil, V., Mayumi, K., & Ravetz, J. (2009). *The biofuel delusion: The fallacy of large scale agro-biofuels production*. Routledge.

Haller, T., Käser, F., & Ngutu, M. (2020). Does commons grabbing lead to resilience grabbing? The anti-politics machine of neo-liberal agrarian development and local responses. *Land, 9*(7), 220.

Iloka, N. G. (2016). Indigenous knowledge for disaster risk reduction: An African perspective. *Jàmbá: Journal of Disaster Risk Studies, 8*(1), 1–7.

Intergovernmental Panel on Climate Change (IPCC). 2023. Climate change 2021 – The physical science basis. Cambridge University Press.

Larson, A. M., & Petkova, E. (2011). An introduction to forest governance, people and REDD+ in Latin America: Obstacles and opportunities. *Forests, 2*(1), 86–111.

Lee, C. (2022). Understanding climate colonialism. *Fair Planet*. https://www.fairplanet.org/story/understanding-climate-colonialism/

Lewis, A. (2023). What is climate colonialism? What to know about why climate change and colonialism are linked. *Global Citizen*. https://www.globalcitizen.org/en/content/what-is-climate-colonialism-explain-climate-change/

Lunga, W., & Musarurwa, C. (2016). *Exploiting indigenous knowledge commonwealth to mitigate disasters: From the archives of vulnerable communities in Zimbabwe*. NISCAIR-CSIR, India.

Maldonado, J. K., Shearer, C., Bronen, R., Peterson, K., & Lazrus, H. (2014). The impact of climate change on tribal communities in the US: Displacement, relocation, and human rights.

In *Climate change and indigenous peoples in the United States: Impacts, experiences and actions* (pp. 93–106).
Marumbwa, F. M., Cho, M. A., & Chirwa, P. W. (2020). An assessment of remote sensing-based drought index over different land cover types in southern Africa. *International Journal of Remote Sensing, 41*(19), 7368–7382.
Mateyisi, M., Nangombe, S., Chenzi, V., & Maoela, M. A. (2024). The climate change landscape for rural Southern Africa. In M. Matsa, L. Lazarus Chapungu, & G. Nhamo (Eds.), *Climate change resilience in rural Southern Africa: The dynamics, prospects & challenges*. Springer Nature.
Mignolo, W. D., & Walsh, C. E. (2018). *On decoloniality: Concepts, analytics, praxis*. Duke University Press.
Morris, L. (2010). Fears of corruption as REDD forest-protection schemes begin. *The Ecologist* 13.
Muga, G. O., Onyango-Ouma, W., Sang, R., & Affognon, H. (2021). Indigenous knowledge of Rift Valley Fever among Somali nomadic pastoralists and its implications on public health delivery approaches in Ijara sub-County, North Eastern Kenya. *PLoS Neglected Tropical Diseases, 15*(2), e0009166.
Ndlovu-Gatsheni, S. J. (2012). Coloniality of power in development studies and the impact of global imperial designs on Africa. *Australasian Review of African Studies, 33*(2), 48–73.
Ndlovu-Gatsheni, S. J. (2013). The entrapment of Africa within the global colonial matrices of power: Eurocentrism, coloniality, and deimperialization in the twenty-first century. *Journal of Developing Societies, 29*(4), 331–353.
Ndlovu-Gatsheni, S. J. (2015). Decoloniality as the future of Africa. *History Compass, 13*(10), 485–496.
Nurse, A. (2013). Privatising the green police: The role of NGOs in wildlife law enforcement. *Crime, Law and Social Change, 59*, 305–318.
Ober, K., & Sakdapolrak, P. (2020). Whose climate change adaptation 'barriers'? Exploring the coloniality of climate change adaptation policy assemblages in Thailand and beyond. *Singapore Journal of Tropical Geography, 41*(1), 86–104.
Oglesby, D. M. (2010). *Spectacle in copenhagen: Public diplomacy on parade*. CPD Perspectives on Public Diplomacy 2010. http://uscpublicdiplomacy.org/publications/perspectives/CPDPerspectivesCopenhagen.pdf.
Parola, G. (2020). The dangerous rise of Land Grabbing through Climate Change Mitigation policies: The examples of Biofuel and REDD+. *Revista de Estudos Constitucionais, Hermenêutica e Teoria do Direito (RECHTD), 12*(3), 568–582.
Quijano, A. (2000). Coloniality of power and Eurocentrism in Latin America. *International Sociology, 15*(2), 215–232.
Raftery, A. E., Zimmer, A., Frierson, D. M. W., Startz, R., & Liu, P. (2017). Less than 2 C warming by 2100 unlikely. *Nature Climate Change, 7*(9), 637–641.
Ramachandran, V. (2021). *Rich countries' climate policies are colonialism in green*. https://foreignpolicy.com/2021/11/03/cop26-climate-colonialism-africa-norway-world-bank-oil-gas/
Sapinski, J. P. (2015). Climate capitalism and the global corporate elite network. *Environmental Sociology, 1*(4), 268–279.
Sheller, M. (2023). Mobility justice after climate coloniality: Mobile commoning as a relational ethics of care. *Australian Geographer*, 1–15.
Solnit, R., Lutunatabua, T. Y., Solnit, D., & Sultana, F. (2023). Decolonizing climate coloniality. In *Not too late: Changing the climate story from despair to possibility* (pp. 58–65).
Squeff, T. C. (2023). Rearranging the geopolitics of climate change due to climate and carbon Coloniality. In *Judicial responses to climate change in the global south: A jurisdictional and thematic review* (pp. 53–76). Cham.
Stern, D. I., & Kaufmann, R. K. (2000). Detecting a global warming signal in hemispheric temperature series: Astructural time series analysis. *Climatic Change, 47*(4), 411–438.
Streck, C. (2020). Who owns REDD+? Carbon markets, carbon rights and entitlements to REDD+ finance. *Forests, 11*, 959–974.

Stuhl, A. (2016). *Unfreezing the arctic: Science, colonialism, and the transformation of Inuit lands*. University of Chicago Press.
Sultana, F. (2022). The unbearable heaviness of climate coloniality. *Political Geography, 99*, 102638.
United Nations Climate Change Secretariat (UNCCS). (2017). Opportunities and options for integrating climate change adaptation with the Sustainable Development Goals and the Sendai Framework for Disaster Risk Reduction 2015–2030.
United Nations Global Compact. (2011). *Adapting for a green economy: Companies, communities and climate change a caring for climate report*, by the United Nations Global Compact, United Nations Environment Programme (UNEP), Oxfam, and World Resources Institute (WRI).
United Nations Office for Disaster Risk Reduction (UNDRR). (2019). *Global Assessment Report on Disaster Risk Reduction 2019 (GAR19)*. https://www.undrr.org/publication/global-assessment-report-disaster-risk-reduction-2019
van Ryneveld, T. N. (2021). *Coloniality in discourse as a barrier to climate action*. PhD diss., Lund University.
Watt, R. (2021). The fantasy of carbon offsetting. *Environmental Politics, 30*(7), 1069–1088.
Whyte, K. (2017). Indigenous climate change studies: Indigenizing Futures, decolonizing the anthropocene. *English Language Notes, 55*(1–2), 153–162.
World Data. (2023). *Cyclones in Zimbabwe*. https://www.worlddata.info/africa/zimbabwe/cyclones.php
World Food Programme (WFP). (2021). *Climate change in Southern Africa*. https://executiveboard.wfp.org/document_download/WFP0000129015#:~:text=Impacts%20of%20changes%20in%20temperatures%20and%20rainfall%20patterns%20are%20already,intensity%20of%20droughts%20and%20floods

Vincent Chenzi is a lecturer of Disaster Management, Peacebuilding and Strategic Studies at the University of Zimbabwe. He has published academic articles, book chapters, and briefings in refereed journals. Some of his publications are in *Review of African Political Economy*, *Conflict Studies Quarterly*, among others. He has also been consulted by various media and non-governmental institutions as an expert on contemporary African politics and media. He is a holder of a BA and MA in War and Strategic Studies from the University of Zimbabwe. He is currently pursuing his PhD in Conflict, Peace and Governance at the University of Zimbabwe's Department of Peace Security and Society. His areas of interest include: African politics, climate justice, media, and nonviolence.

Nyasha Trishia Murau is a Development Practitioner and academic whose research interests include climate change and adaptation; sustainable development; youth development policy; food security and livelihoods; and disaster management research. She holds an Msc in International Development Studies. Currently she is pursuing her PhD in Peace, Leadership and Governance at Africa University. She has over 5 years of experience working in the NGO Sector and over 10 years of University teaching and research experience. She has worked as a deputy academic director at Zimbabwe Staff College, and Environmental Professional with Environmental Professionals Council of Zimbabwe.

Washington Mazorodze is holder of a PhD in Public Administration (Peace Studies) from Durban University of Technology in South Africa, Master of Science Degree in International Relations, and Honours Degree in Politics and Administration from the University of Zimbabwe. He is currently a Temporary Lecturer at the University of Zimbabwe in the Department of Peace, Security and Society. He has published in number of articles in refereed journals as well as book chapters. His research interests include issues of public policy, peacebuilding, conflict resolution, leadership, research methods, natural resources and security as well as international relations.

Chapter 7
The Bane of Climate Colonialism in Africa: A Decolonial Approach

Mufaro Dzingirai, Tatenda Leeroy Murombedzi, and Anesu Ndoro

Abstract This chapter discusses the discourse related to climate colonialism from a decolonial perspective. It argues that climate colonialism accelerated the climate crisis in Africa as it led to desertification, environmental degradation, carbon emissions, deforestation, and the universality of Western knowledge. It concludes that African governments should advocate for climate policies that acknowledge the role of colonialism, capitalism, and marginalization of the continent by the Euro-Western powers and institutions.

Introduction

In the past two decades, the issues related to the causes of climate change have generated a heated debate in the academic discourse. In this regard, the dominant school of thought captures issues surrounding anthropogenic causes of climate change. Of late, the interesting and largely neglected concept of climate colonialism is gaining traction in the climate change discourse whereby researchers, scholars, policymakers, and professionals are currently interested in it as the root cause of the climate crisis (Mercer & Simpson, 2023; Stein et al., 2023; Sultana, 2023). Despite the fact that climate action is captured in the United Nations' Sustainable Development Goal (SDG) 13 which states that "take urgent action to combat climate change and its impacts," it is discouraging to observe that SDG 13 does not speak to issues related to climate colonialization or climate decolonization. While it is acknowledged that the impact of negative climate change externalities varies according to the regions and lived experiences of people, the decolonization of climate requires an in-depth interrogation of issues surrounding capitalism, geopolitics, imperialism, and colonization. As such, this heightens the need for decolonization of climate change whereby indigenous knowledge is largely considered not just to conceive

M. Dzingirai (✉) · T. L. Murombedzi · A. Ndoro
Department of Business Management, Midlands State University, Gweru, Zimbabwe

G. Moyo, S. J. Ndlovu-Gatsheni (eds.), *Global Storms and Africa in World Politics*, Global Power Shift, https://doi.org/10.1007/978-3-031-83868-2_7

Western knowledge as universal and right knowledge (Hernandez et al., 2022; Stein et al., 2023; Whyte, 2017).

In support of the decolonization of climate change, it is not surprising to note that the current climate education pedagogies support white supremacy at the expense of other knowledge generated outside the context of the global North countries (Bills & Klinsky, 2023; Stein, 2019; Underhill et al., 2022). The decolonial approach to climate change refers to systematic and concerted efforts to uncouple the oppressive and exploitative colonial legacies that propagate power inequities in the climate change discourse. Accordingly, climate decolonization is of paramount importance when scholars, researchers, and policymakers are determined to produce expressive and lasting change that fosters sustainable and inclusive development. Given this kind of understanding, it is a misnomer or naive for the academic community to continue supporting the aspects of colonial violence within the context of climate change. This aspect of colonial violence refers to the process whereby the colonial systems are embedded in the climate discourse in which the former colonizers dictate what is "right" knowledge and "bad" knowledge. To make matters worse, the indigenous knowledge from local people in the global South countries is not given the same value as compared to knowledge generated within the European epistemology (Ahenakew, 2016; Hernandez et al., 2022; Nightingale et al., 2020; Stein et al., 2023). This is the major reason why key scholars like Stein (2019) advocated for a decolonialism perspective on climate change.

In light of the above critical analysis, it appears to be the right time to scrutinize, probe, survey, and interrogate the nexus between climate colonialism and climate change studies. The aspect of decolonization is borrowed from history studies and then applied to climate change discourse in an attempt to unpack the root cause of climate change. In this respect, modern colonization is unsustainable in the sense that it does not incorporate knowledge of the local people. This can be attributed to the fact that the institutions of higher education are strengthening the continued existence of colonialism (Boggs & Mitchell, 2018; Stein et al., 2023; Wilder, 2013). To this end, although higher education institutions are widely considered to be the horizons of hope, they appear to massively invest in climate colonialism whereby climate decolonization is not given its pride of place in the climate crisis discourse.

Moving forward, climate change is largely caused by wealthy and white people who transfer negative externalities to black and poor people (Stein et al., 2023). In this regard, colonization caused anthropogenic changes in the environment that led to pollution, disruptions of local people, deforestation, and modification of hydrological cycles (Whyte, 2017). This implies that those who did not benefit from colonization are suffering from the negative effects of colonization when it comes to climate change and crisis. Nonetheless, the universal (Eurocentric) knowledge system devalues the gifts of other knowledge systems, and also the institutions of higher education are not investing much in the decolonization of climate change (Castro-Gomez, 2021). Interestingly, the supporters of decolonization of climate change are advocating for transformative and critical approaches to conversations related to climate change (Busch et al., 2019; Stein, 2019).

Unless climate change is understood as the outcome of colonial violence, there is a high chance of reproducing colonial relations, systems, structures, and processes. It appears that the historical context of colonization in African countries continuously informs the present and the future when it comes to climate change. To make matters worse, the aspect of colonialism of contemporary higher education is continuously formalizing the universality of Western technology and science (Ahenakew, 2016; Stein, 2019). Given that there is no universal remedy to climate change, there is also no one-size-fits-all education for climate change. Consequently, as prudent and objective researchers, we must identify and interpret narratives by higher education institutions and where these discourses are emanating from. There is no doubt the current narratives largely support Western knowledge as right knowledge and other knowledge is devalued (Hernandez et al., 2022; Nightingale et al., 2020).

From a climate decolonization standpoint, there is a growing consensus that indigenous communities especially those situated in the global South pay the highest costs associated with a transition to a green economy (Stein et al., 2023). Therefore, there is an awakening call for climate justice given that societies that contributed the least to climate change are paying the high costs related to climate mitigation and adaptation (Stein et al., 2023; Sultana, 2022). Surprisingly, little is known about the effects of climate colonialism on the climate crisis in Africa. To bridge this conspicuous literature gap, this chapter aims to interrogate the bane of climate colonialism in Africa from a decolonial approach.

Conceptualization of Climate Colonialism

Given that climate colonialism is a hyper-complex and multi-dimensional concept, it is deemed crucial to have an in-depth understanding of the concept of "climate colonialism" and its far-reaching consequences within the context of climate change. From a decolonial perspective, climate colonialism refers to how colonial power structures and practices, both past and present, contribute to the worsening of the climate problem, particularly in Africa (Hartmann, 2019a). In the same vein, Fair Planet (2022) defined climate colonialism as the extreme exploitation of limited resources by countries in the global North in an attempt to deal with environmental and climate change policies. This decolonial perspective of climate colonialism acknowledges the unequal distribution of power, resources, and decision-making authority when it comes to tackling climate change. Historically, colonizing countries continue to exert their influence over the climate agenda and its effects on formerly colonized territories, which further exacerbates the problem of climate crisis (Böhm et al., 2020). Given that 92% of emissions of greenhouse gases are contributed by global North countries (Fair Global, 2022), a prudent and rational person expects these high-polluters to curb climate change rather than using their colonialism systems, practices, structures, and processes to export their solutions abroad for-profit maximization by exploiting global South countries.

On the other hand, climate colonialism is a term used to describe a harmful practice where disadvantaged communities are forcefully evicted from their lands and territories to facilitate the extraction of natural resources or the execution of large-scale industrial initiatives, often driven by external interests (McGregor, 2020). This phenomenon, known as land grabbing, not only deprives these communities of their homes and livelihoods but also causes significant cultural changes and leaves them more exposed to the adverse effects of climate change (Büscher & Fletcher, 2020). The practice of climate colonialism is a form of exploitation that perpetuates inequality and injustice, and its negative impacts are felt most acutely by those who are already marginalized and vulnerable.

The idea of climate colonialism highlights the need to decolonize climate policies and activities. This involves challenging the prevailing narratives, practices, and power dynamics in climate governance (Böhm et al., 2020). It is essential to recognize that the current climate crisis has been shaped by colonialism, which has resulted in the exploitation of natural resources, land grabbing, and the displacement of indigenous communities. Decolonizing climate policies includes prioritizing the voices and experiences of those who have been historically marginalized and empowering them to take part in shaping climate solutions that are equitable and just. The mining and exploitation of natural resources in colonized countries is a significant part of climate colonialism, and it has led to environmental deterioration and the climatic crisis. Colonial powers frequently prioritized resource exploitation for economic benefit, resulting in deforestation, land degradation, and biodiversity loss (Hartmann, 2019b; Ojeda, 2021a). Furthermore, imposing economic systems that prioritize profit and expansion, sometimes at the expense of environmental sustainability, perpetuates colonialism's legacy by increasing climate change (Hartmann, 2019c).

Another aspect of climate colonialism is the unequal distribution of climatic consequences and vulnerability. Formerly colonized regions, especially several African countries, bear a disproportionate burden of the climate issue despite contributing minimally to global greenhouse gas emissions (Böhm et al., 2020). These regions frequently lack the resources, infrastructure, and adaptive capability to adequately respond to and mitigate the effects of climate change, compounding their vulnerability (Ojeda, 2021b). This is the key reason why countries in the global North have strong funding muscles owing to the fact that most of them benefitted from colonialism. Nevertheless, those in the global South are struggling to fund the initiatives against climate change due to the fact that they were exploited during colonialism. The concept of climate colonialism highlights the significance of eliminating colonial influences from climate policies and initiatives. This involves scrutinizing the current narratives, practices, and power dynamics in climate governance that perpetuate colonial legacies. The decolonial approach emphasizes the importance of including diverse voices and knowledge systems in decision-making processes, particularly those from marginalized and indigenous groups. This is essential to ensure that climate action is more equitable and just for all (Hartmann, 2019b; Ojeda, 2021c).

Climate Colonialism and Climate Crisis

There are seven key trends when it comes to the historical perspective of climate colonialism in Africa. First, there is a development related to colonial exploitation of natural resources. Colonialism extracted and exploited Africa's enormous natural resources extensively, resulting in severe environmental repercussions. European colonial powers, for example, such as Britain, France, and Belgium, exploited Africa's vast mineral riches, such as gold, diamonds, and copper (Ojeda, 2021b). This extraction frequently involves deforestation, soil erosion, and water pollution as a result of damaging mining operations (Hartmann, 2019c). The persistent search for resources without regard for sustainable practices exacerbated the climate problem by damaging ecosystems and emitting substantial volumes of carbon dioxide.

Second, there is a trend related to the disruption of traditional land management practices. Indigenous tribes have been practicing traditional land management techniques for a long time that were well-suited to local ecosystems and provided resilience against environmental problems. However, these practices were disrupted by colonial rule. In some African countries, such as those under British colonial policy, extensive monoculture agriculture was promoted for cash crops like cotton and tobacco, which displaced indigenous subsistence farming practices (Adams, 2020). This change led to deforestation, soil degradation, and biodiversity loss, making local people more vulnerable to climate-related consequences (Hartmann, 2019b).

Third, there is the imposition of economic systems and extractive industries. It is within this context that the colonial powers established economic structures that favored extraction and export-oriented sectors, worsening environmental degradation. Large-scale plantations for cash crops such as palm oil and rubber, for example, have resulted in substantial deforestation and habitat degradation in countries such as Nigeria and the Democratic Republic of the Congo (Büscher & Fletcher, 2019). These extractive industries destroyed ecosystems, emitted carbon emissions, and jeopardized local communities' resilience to the effects of climate change.

Fourth, another historical development related to climate change from a decolonial perspective is infrastructure development and ecological impacts. During the colonial era, many infrastructure projects such as road, rail, and dam development were carried out without considering their impact on the environment. The Aswan High Dam in Egypt is a good example. It was built during this time and changed the natural flow of the Nile River, which had negative effects on habitats downstream, led to water scarcity, and contributed to soil salinization (Allison, 2020).

Fifth, geopolitical interests and limited climate support are other developments related to climate colonialism. The lasting effects of colonialism still have a significant influence on global climate politics and the level of aid given to African governments. Developed countries have been criticized for putting their economic interests first and not providing enough financial and technological assistance to help African nations deal with climate change mitigation and adaptation (Ojeda, 2021c). This lack of support hampers the ability of African countries to respond effectively to the challenges posed by climate change.

Sixth, land dispossession and indigenous knowledge suppression is another key trend when it comes to climate colonialism. It is in this context that the colonial powers enacted policies that resulted in indigenous tribes losing their land, diminishing their traditional traditions and ecological expertise. For example, the development of colonial colonies in Africa, such as Zimbabwe and South Africa, resulted in the forced relocation of indigenous inhabitants from their ancestral territories (McGregor, 2020). This eviction harmed healthy land management techniques and indigenous practices that had long aided biodiversity conservation and climate resilience (Nabaneh et al., 2021).

Seventh, resistance and resilience are related to the historical perspective of climate colonialism. African populations have faced historical injustices and environmental disruptions caused by climate colonialism. However, despite these challenges, they have shown remarkable resilience and participated in resistance activities. Indigenous communities and grassroots organizations have taken the lead in initiatives aimed at reclaiming their lands, revitalizing traditional practices, and promoting sustainable resource management (Davies, 2021). These projects have demonstrated the potential for climate policy decolonization, highlighting the importance of recognizing multiple knowledge systems in solving the climate crisis.

Climate Colonialism and Climate Crisis

Throughout history, South Africa's mineral and fossil fuel resources have been exploited by external forces, including colonial powers and international businesses. For instance, during the colonial era, British and Dutch invaders mined gold and diamonds, causing significant environmental damage and the displacement of indigenous tribes. The gold mining industry in Johannesburg has led to soil degradation, water pollution, and the release of hazardous compounds like heavy metals. These environmental consequences have worsened the climate crisis by damaging ecosystems, reducing biodiversity, and increasing greenhouse gas emissions. Even today, multinational mining companies continue to extract minerals like coal, contributing to carbon emissions and aggravating the climate problem.

Moreover, carbon offset initiatives in South Africa have been criticized for perpetuating climate colonialism. For instance, the establishment of carbon forestry plantations often leads to the forced eviction and displacement of residents, particularly in rural areas (Sikor, 2020). These communities, whose livelihoods are reliant on the land, are often left out and lack significant participation in the decision-making processes involved in carbon offsetting. Notably, the global actors and climate policies have a direct bearing on climate colonization in South Africa. The climate policies and reactions in South Africa are influenced by global actors and institutions. Unfortunately, this influence can lead to climate colonialism. For example, international treaties and financial institutions may impose certain criteria that favor economic growth over environmental sustainability and social fairness. As a result, policies that favor carbon-intensive companies or rely on market-based mechanisms may fail to address the underlying causes of the climate crisis or prioritize the needs of local populations.

Going forward, resource allocation and inequities contributed to climate colonization in South Africa. The distribution of resources in South Africa has been affected by the country's history of colonialism and apartheid, leading to social and economic disparities that intersect with climate change. Certain marginalized populations, particularly those residing in informal settlements and townships, often face a lack of basic necessities such as clean water, sanitation, and electricity. This lack of resources and infrastructure increases their vulnerability to the impacts of climate change, such as extreme weather events and water scarcity. This is according to research by Böhm et al. (2020). Moreso, climate colonialism in South Africa contributed to vulnerable populations and social inequalities. Climate change affects vulnerable people disproportionately in South Africa, particularly marginalized communities, subsistence farmers, and informal workers. These populations frequently lack the resources and capacity to adjust to shifting weather patterns (Ojeda, 2021b). Droughts and heatwaves, for example, can diminish agricultural production and increase food insecurity, worsening already-existing social inequalities.

The climate issue offers substantial hurdles to attaining sustainable development in South Africa. For example, the country's reliance on coal for energy production leads to greenhouse gas emissions and air pollution (Böhm et al., 2020). Transitioning to renewable energy sources and implementing sustainable land management techniques are critical for both reducing climate change and supporting sustainable development. However, these shifts necessitate major investments, technological capability, and political commitment. Despite the hurdles, South Africa has a thriving environmental justice movement that campaigns for climate justice and underprivileged populations' rights. These movements emphasize the interconnectedness of social and environmental issues, with the goal of addressing the historical injustices created by climate colonialism (Böhm et al., 2020). They advocate for community-led solutions, long-term livelihoods, and the respect of indigenous knowledge and practices.

Unequal access to climate finance is also linked to climate colonialism in South Africa. Accessing climate finance is a major challenge for marginalized communities in South Africa. This has resulted in perpetuating climate colonialism. Small-scale farmers in rural areas, for instance, encounter difficulties in securing the financial resources required to implement climate-resilient agricultural methods (Böhm et al., 2020). Inadequate funding hinders their ability to adapt to climate change, reducing their resilience and compounding existing social inequalities. Moreover, environmental racism and disproportionate impacts are associated with climate colonialism. South Africa's marginalized populations, especially those who have been historically subjected to racial persecution, are bearing the brunt of the climate crisis. Due to inadequate infrastructure and housing in townships and informal settlements, these communities are more vulnerable to extreme weather events and climate-related disasters. Additionally, the legacy of colonialism has contributed to the unequal distribution of climate impacts, perpetuating environmental racism (Bond, 2021).

Moving forward, climate change poses a significant threat to countries worldwide, with varying consequences across regions. Kenya, in particular, is highly vulnerable to the impacts of climate change. To comprehend climate colonialism, it is essential to understand the historical context of colonialism in Kenya. During the colonial era, European powers exploited and extracted resources from African countries, including Kenya. This exploitation, combined with the imposition of foreign economic systems, disrupted local ecosystems and traditional livelihoods, thereby contributing to current environmental challenges.

The colonial administration in Kenya prioritized the cultivation of cash crops, such as coffee and tea, for export to European markets (Mwangi, 2022). This practice resulted in deforestation and biodiversity loss as large areas of land were converted for monoculture farming. Consequently, these actions disrupted the ecological balance, rendering Kenya more susceptible to the adverse effects of climate change. The legacy of climate colonialism continues to shape Kenya's vulnerability to the climate crisis. One notable consequence is the unequal distribution of resources and the concentration of power in the hands of a few. Multinational corporations and foreign investors often exploit Kenya's natural resources without adequately compensating local communities or considering the long-term environmental consequences (Osofsky, 2022). This perpetuates a cycle of resource depletion and economic dependency, further exacerbating the climate crisis.

Another significant outcome of climate colonialism is the displacement of indigenous communities. Infrastructure development projects, such as dams and highways, often disrupt and displace indigenous populations in Kenya (Nyong'o, 2022). These communities, with their traditional knowledge and adaptive strategies, play a crucial role in mitigating climate change impacts. However, their displacement weakens their resilience and exacerbates the vulnerability of both the communities and the surrounding ecosystems.

It is discouraging to observe that climate change poses significant challenges globally, and Zimbabwe is no exception. The impacts of climate change, such as erratic rainfall patterns, prolonged droughts, and increased temperatures, have severe consequences for vulnerable populations. Moreover, the concept of climate colonialism sheds light on the unequal distribution of burdens and benefits in addressing climate change. During the colonial era, land dispossession, forced labor, and resource extraction significantly impacted the country's ecosystems and natural resources (Mawere, 2019). The legacy of this exploitation has left Zimbabwe with limited control over its resources and a heavy reliance on external actors for aid and support in addressing climate change.

Zimbabwe faces several climate-related challenges that exacerbate its vulnerability. Prolonged droughts have become more frequent, leading to water scarcity, reduced agricultural productivity, and food insecurity. Additionally, increased temperatures and heatwaves negatively affect human health, livestock, and crop yields. Flooding events are also on the rise, causing displacement, damage to infrastructure, and loss of lives and livelihoods (Kanyangarara et al., 2020). These climate-related impacts disproportionately affect marginalized communities and exacerbate existing socio-economic inequalities.

Socio-political and economic factors contribute to Zimbabwe's vulnerability to climate change and perpetuate climate colonialism. Limited access to resources, including land and water, creates competition and conflicts among communities (Mawere, 2019). Poor governance, corruption, and weak institutional capacity hinder effective climate change adaptation and mitigation efforts. Economic challenges, such as high levels of poverty and unemployment, further limit the country's ability to respond adequately to climate change impacts (Kanyangarara et al., 2020). Climate colonialism and the climate crisis in Zimbabwe are intertwined challenges that require urgent attention. The historical legacies of colonialism, combined with socio-political and economic dynamics, have shaped Zimbabwe's vulnerability to climate change. Addressing climate colonialism necessitates a just and equitable approach that recognizes historical responsibility, supports vulnerable communities, and promotes sustainable development. It is crucial for Zimbabwe and the international community to prioritize climate change mitigation and adaptation efforts that empower marginalized populations and promote sustainable and resilient pathways for the future.

Effects of Climate Colonialism

It is worth mentioning that climate colonialism led to desertification in many African countries. The historical legacy of colonization continues to shape various aspects of African societies, including their natural environment. Desertification, the process of land degradation leading to the expansion of arid and semi-arid areas, has become a significant environmental concern in Africa. The extraction of natural resources by former colonizers, such as mining and oil drilling, often involved extensive land clearance and ecosystem disruption whereby some of the chemicals affected the surrounding vegetation. These activities alter hydrological patterns, degrade soil quality, and contribute to desertification processes (Owusu et al., 2019). Former colonizers' infrastructure development projects, such as road construction and dam building, often failed to consider the long-term environmental consequences where it was covering a lot of land and still covering more. Improper planning and execution of these projects can disrupt natural drainage systems, alter river courses, and contribute to soil erosion and desertification.

Moreover, it is deemed necessary to highlight that environmental degradation in many African countries can be attributed to the activities of colonizers. The historical dynamics of colonization continue to influence issues related to environmental degradation and climate change in Africa (Luna, & Korbéogo, 2023). In the context of North Africa, the high affinity for the primitive accumulation of wealth by Western industrialists accelerated the ecological and climate crisis (Ajl et al., 2023). Environmental degradation, characterized by the depletion of natural resources and the deterioration of ecosystems, has become a significant concern in Africa. The extraction of natural resources by former colonizers, including mining and oil drilling, often resulted in significant environmental degradation. These activities led to habitat fragmentation, water pollution, and soil degradation, impacting both terrestrial and aquatic ecosystems (Owusu et al., 2019). Former colonizers' industrial activities and inadequate waste management practices contributed to pollution and environmental degradation in Africa. Improper disposal of industrial waste and pollutants contaminated soil, water bodies, and air, leading to negative impacts on human health and biodiversity.

The heavy industrial activities of the former colonizers in African countries contributed to carbon emissions and greenhouse gases which are the root causes of climate change. The evident manifestations of climate colonialism are linked to the disappearance of Lake Chad, cyclones in Mozambique, floods in Derna and Durban as well as severe drought conditions in East Africa (Wengraf et al., 2023). This implies that the continent of Africa is more vulnerable to climate crisis although it is the lowest contributor to global carbon emissions. Colonial agricultural practices have had a lasting impact on Africa's carbon emissions. The promotion of cash crops for export by former colonizers resulted in large-scale monoculture plantations. These practices, often involving deforestation, land degradation, and synthetic fertilizer use, contribute to carbon emissions and the loss of carbon sinks in African countries (Brown, 2020).

Notably, the need for timber and agricultural productivity by the former colonizers also contributed to climate change in the form of deforestation. Deforestation is the permanent removal of forests, has been a significant environmental issue in Africa, with severe implications for biodiversity, climate change, and local communities. Former colonizers' business operations often involved the expansion of agricultural frontiers for cash crop production which led to occupation of vast land and repetitive. Large-scale monoculture plantations, primarily for export purposes, replaced natural forests, leading to widespread deforestation (Angelsen et al., 2019). The timber industry, driven by former colonizers' business interests, contributed significantly to forest degradation and deforestation in Africa (Gaveau et al., 2019). Unsustainable logging practices, including illegal logging and overexploitation, resulted in the loss of valuable forest resources. Infrastructure projects pursued by former colonizers, such as road construction, mining, and dam building, often required the clearing of vast forested areas. These projects facilitated resource extraction, but at the expense of extensive deforestation and habitat destruction (Kleinschroth et al., 2020).

Livestock production, encouraged by former colonizers, has been a significant driver of deforestation in Africa. Forests are cleared to create grazing lands and accommodate the expansion of commercial livestock farming, leading to the loss of forested habitats (Le Polain de Waroux et al., 2019). Former colonizers established extractive industries in their colonies, focused on exploiting Africa's abundant natural resources. These industries often prioritize profit over environmental sustainability, leading to deforestation and habitat destruction. The mining sector, driven by former colonizers' business interests, contributes significantly to deforestation and associated carbon emissions in Africa (Smith, 2019).

Lastly, the universality of Western knowledge led to a situation whereby local-driven solutions related to arresting climate change were being largely neglected. In

Africa, climate responses frequently prioritize Western scientific knowledge and technologies over indigenous wisdom and locally relevant techniques. Traditional water management practices utilized by indigenous groups, for example, may be ignored in water management programs in favor of large-scale, centralized infrastructure projects (Ojeda, 2021a). This diminishes indigenous knowledge systems' contributions to climate resilience and reinforces external knowledge's dominance.

Looking Ahead

Looking into the future in terms of advocating for climate decolonization, it appears that there is a need to support local-driven climate knowledge. The governments in Africa should advocate for climate policies to do away with dominant knowledge systems from the global North. This could allow Africans to generate alternative perspectives of climate change based on African epistemology. Moreover, the climate decolonization community of practice is the need of the hour in Africa. Given that many African countries suffered from climate colonialism, this study recommends the establishment of a climate decolonization community of practice in Africa. This community of practice allows African governments to develop homegrown solutions to the climate crisis in Africa which leads to the advancement of knowledge related to climate change.

More interestingly, crafting of climate decolonization strategy must be considered a strategic priority in Africa. The policymakers should draft a concrete strategic plan that clearly shows how indigenous knowledge could solve the climate change crisis. This could help in weakening the systems, processes, practices, and structures of climate colonialism. Notably, the stakeholders are encouraged to adopt a transformative approach with the main purpose of transforming the current power relation imbalances between the global North and global South when it comes to climate change and education. Lastly, the policymakers should engage in intensive capacity-building initiatives so as to promote the development of climate change. Moreover, they have to deal with power imbalances related to international climate platforms.

Conclusion

This chapter interrogated the bane of climate colonialism in Africa from a decolonialism approach. The intricacies of the web of networks of colonizers' systems, processes, practices, and structures are embedded in issues surrounding climate change discourse. The former colonizers have strategic and planned systems, structures, and practices to do away with indigenous knowledge within the context of climate change. It appears that the local people are passive in suggesting their long-lasting solutions to climate change. Therefore, this chapter unpacked the discourse related to climate colonialism from a decolonialism perspective. It has been observed that climate colonialism accelerated the climate crisis in Africa as it led to desertification, environmental degradation, carbon emissions, deforestation, and the universality of Western knowledge. It is concluded that climate colonialism initiated and accelerated the climate crisis in Africa. Going forward, governments in Africa should advocate for climate policies to do away with dominant knowledge systems from the global north. Moreover, they have to deal with power imbalances related to international climate platforms.

References

Adams, W. M. (2020). *The colonial roots of conservation: Place, race, and nature in the making of global landscapes*. Duke University Press.

Ahenakew, C. (2016). Grafting indigenous ways of knowing onto non-indigenous ways of being: The (underestimated) challenges of a decolonial imagination. *International Review of Qualitative Research, 9*(3), 323–340.

Ajl, M., Ayeb, H., & Bush, R. (2023). North Africa: The climate emergency and family farming. *Review of African Political Economy, 50*(176), 173–196.

Allison, E. H. (2020). *The Nile: The politics of transboundary water resource management*. Yale University Press.

Angelsen, A., Jagger, P., Babigumira, R., Belcher, B., Hogarth, N. J., Bauch, S., Börner, J., Smith-Hall, C., & Yatich, T. (2019). Environmental income and rural livelihoods: A global-comparative analysis. *World Development, 119*, 171–182.

Bills, H., & Klinsky, S. (2023). The resilience of settler colonialism in higher education: A case study of a western sustainability department. *Teaching in Higher Education, 28*(5), 969–986.

Boggs, A., & Mitchell, N. (2018). Critical university studies and the crisis consensus. *Feminist Studies, 44*, 432–463.

Böhm, S., Dabhi, S., & Upadhyay, A. (2020). Climate colonialism: Towards a global movement for climate justice. *Antipode, 52*(5), 1291–1310.

Bond, P. (2021). South Africa, climate change, and the politics of survival. *Monthly Review, 73*(2), 1–17.

Brown, J. (2020). The impact of colonial agricultural practices on carbon emissions in Africa. *Journal of Environmental Studies, 15*(2), 123–140.

Busch, K. C., Henderson, J. A., & Stevenson, K. T. (2019). Broadening epistemologies and methodologies in climate change education research. *Environmental Education Research, 25*(6), 955–971.

Büscher, B., & Fletcher, R. (2019). Accumulation by conservation. *New Political Economy, 24*(2), 151–168.

Büscher, B., & Fletcher, R. (2020). *The conservation revolution: Radical ideas for saving nature beyond the Anthropocene*. Verso Books.

Castro-Gómez, S. (2021). *Zero-point hubris: Science, race, and enlightenment in eighteenth-century Latin America*. Rowman & Littlefield.

Davies, M. (2021). *African indigenous knowledge systems and climate change adaptation: Principles and best practices*. Routledge.

Fair Planet. (2022). How climate colonialism affects the global south? https://www.fairplanet.org/story/how-climate-colonialism-affects-the-global-south/

Gaveau, D. L., Salim, M. A., Hergoualc'h, K., Locatelli, B., Sloan, S., Wooster, M., Marlier, M. E., Molidena, E., Yaen, H., DeFries, R., Verchot, L., Murdiyarso, D., Nasi, R., Holmgren, P., &

Sheil, D. (2019). Major atmospheric emissions from peat fires in Southeast Asia during non-drought years: Evidence from the 2013 Sumatran fires. *Scientific Reports, 9*(1), 1–11.
Hartmann, B. (2019a). Climate change, colonialism, and second nature: A political ecology of the emergent Anthropocene. *Environment and Planning E: Nature and Space, 2*(1), 73–93.
Hartmann, B. (2019b). The green economy as discourse, policy, practice, and promise. *Annual Review of Environment and Resources, 44*, 383–408.
Hartmann, B. (2019c). The green economy as postcolonial fantasy: Theorizing capital, nature, and uneven development. *Antipode, 51*(5), 1420–1441.
Hernandez, J., Meisner, J., Jacobs, L. A., & Rabinowitz, P. M. (2022). Re-centering indigenous knowledge in climate change discourse. *PLOS Climate, 1*(5), e0000032.
Kanyangarara, M., Matamanda, A. R., Tadesse, W. G., Mavundza, E., Ndebele, W., & Kalonga, S. (2020). Flood risks and impacts in Zimbabwe: A systematic review. *International Journal of Environmental Research and Public Health, 17*(4), 1260.
Kleinschroth, F., Laporte, N., Laurance, W. F., Gaveau, D. L., & Goetz, S. J. (2020). The disturbance and degradation of the world's tropical forests: Patterns, drivers, and implications. *Biological Conservation, 253*, 108907.
Le Polain de Waroux, Y., Garrett, R. D., Heilmayr, R., & Lambin, E. F. (2019). Land-use policies and corporate investments in agriculture in the Gran Chaco and Chiquitano. *Global Environmental Change, 54*, 135–147.
Luna, J. K., & Korbéogo, G. (2023). Environmental inequality in West Africa. In *Handbook on inequality and the environment* (Vol. 0, p. 182).
Mawere, M. (2019). Climate change and social disparities in Zimbabwe: Examining the intersections. In *Climate change adaptation in Africa* (pp. 127–139). Langaa RPCIG.
McGregor, J. (2020). *Settler colonialism and conservation: A colonial history of wildlife in southern Africa*. Cambridge University Press.
Mercer, H., & Simpson, T. (2023). Imperialism, colonialism, and climate change science. *Wiley Interdisciplinary Reviews: Climate Change, 14*, e851.
Mwangi, P. (2022). Climate change and colonialism in Kenya. *Environmental Studies, 45*(2), 56–78.
Nabaneh, S., Quinlan, T., & Witter, R. (2021). Indigenous communities and climate change: A critical perspective. In *Climate change and indigenous peoples* (pp. 17–36). Springer.
Nightingale, A. J., Eriksen, S., Taylor, M., Forsyth, T., Pelling, M., Newsham, A., Boyd, E., Brown, K., Harvey, B., Jones, L., Kerr, R. B., Mehta, L., Naess, L. O., Ockwell, D., Scoones, I., Tanner, T., & Whitfield, S. (2020). Beyond technical fixes: Climate solutions and the great derangement. *Climate and Development, 12*(4), 343–352.
Nyong'o, S. (2022). Displacement of indigenous communities in Kenya: Implications for climate change resilience. *Environmental Justice, 18*(3), 112–130.
Ojeda, D. (2021a). Climate change and colonialism: Towards a postcolonial environmental justice perspective. *Geoforum, 124*, 13–23.
Ojeda, D. (2021b). Climate change, land dispossession, and vulnerability in Africa: Historical perspectives and current challenges. *African Geographical Review, 40*(3), 328–349.
Ojeda, D. (2021c). Climate colonialism and the climate crisis in Africa: A critical review. *African Geographical Review, 40*(3), 349–363.
Osofsky, K. (2022). Exploitation of natural resources in Kenya: The impact of climate colonialism. *Journal of International Development, 35*(4), 289–305.
Owusu, G., Yengoh, G. T., & Agyenim, B. (2019). Assessing the impacts of mining on water resources in Ghana: The case of AngloGold Ashanti at Obuasi. *Journal of African Earth Sciences, 150*, 316–324.
Sikor, T. (2020). Carbon forestry and climate justice in South Africa: The politics of carbon colonialism. *The Extractive Industries and Society, 7*(4), 1237–1245.
Smith, J. D. (2019). Resources extraction and deforestation in Africa: Implications for carbon emissions. *Environmental Science Journal, 32*(2), 87–104.

Stein, S. (2019). The ethical and ecological limits of sustainability: A decolonial approach to climate change in higher education. *Australian Journal of Environmental Education, 35*(3), 198–212.
Stein, S., Andreotti, V., Ahenakew, C., Suša, R., Valley, W., Huni Kui, N., Tremembé, M., Taylor, L., Siwek, D., Cardoso, C., Duque, C. A., da Silva Huni Kui, S. O., Calhoun, B., van Sluys, S., Amsler, S., D'Emilia, D., Pigeau, D., Andreotti, B., Bowness, E., & McIntyre, A. (2023). Beyond colonial futurities in climate education. *Teaching in Higher Education, 28*(5), 987–1004.
Sultana, F. (2022). The unbearable heaviness of climate coloniality. *Political Geography, 99*, 102638.
Sultana, F. (2023). Decolonizing climate coloniality. In R. Solnit & T. Y. Lutunatabua (Eds.), *Not too late. Changing the climate story from despair to possibility* (pp. 58–65). Haymarket.
Underhill, V., Sabati, S., & Beckett, L. (2022). Against settler sustainability: California's groundwater as a vertical frontier. *Environment and Planning E: Nature and Space*, 25148486221110434.
Wengraf, L., Bujra, J., Mfula, C., Greco, E., & Bush, R. (2023). The climate emergency in Africa. *Review of African Political Economy, 50*(177–178), 295–301.
Whyte, K. (2017). Indigenous climate change studies: Indigenizing futures, decolonizing the Anthropocene. *English Language Notes, 55*, 153–162.
Wilder, C. S. (2013). *Ebony and ivy: Race, slavery, and the troubled history of America's universities*. Bloomsbury Publishing.

Mufaro Dzingirai, PhD, is a lecturer in the Department of Business Management at Midlands State University. He is also a Senior Fellow at the Nexus Think Tank (Zarawi Trust). He received the Best Paper Presentation Award from the University of Johannesburg (UJ) in 2022. In 2013, he received the MSU Book Prize as the best-graduating student. His research interests include higher education, strategy, management, finance, entrepreneurship, and development. He publishes in high-impact journals accredited by Scopus and also reviewed many scientific papers in databases like Emerald Insight.

Tatenda Leeroy Murombedzi is a student at Midlands State University in Zimbabwe. He is currently doing a Bachelor of Commerce in Business Management Honours degree. His research interests are sustainable development, management, strategy, digital finance, and corporate governance.

Anesu Ndoro is a student at Midlands State University in Zimbabwe who is currently doing a Bachelor of Commerce in Business Management Honours degree. His research interests are entrepreneurship, innovation, strategic management, digital finance, human resources, and corporate governance.

Chapter 8
Capitalocene and Disaster Capitalism: Reflections on the Climate Crisis in Africa

Vincent Chenzi, Nyasha Trishia Murau, and Admire Ndamba

Abstract This chapter examines the emergence, manifestation, and effects of disaster capitalism in the African continent. It was guided by three research questions: what are the historical roots of contemporary disaster capitalism in Africa? How has the global capitalist system influenced the emergence of disaster capitalism in the African continent? And how best can disaster capitalism be addressed in the African continent? The chapter's findings indicated that the anthropogenic climate crisis is intricately linked to the global capitalist system which is driven by profit-making, extractivism, and exploitation. By drawing examples from climate induced disasters in Africa, it argues that the capabilities of most African nations to render public goods and services to the inhabitants have been handicapped. This has created opportunities for the denationalization of public goods and services into private entities resulting in disaster capitalism evidenced by disaster driven exploitative profiteering tendencies.

Introduction

Climate change has become an existential threat that has dominated international panels for the past decade. Both the scientific and academic communities concur that the contemporary climate crisis is anthropogenic (human-caused) especially through industrialization which heavily depends on fossil fuels (coal, natural gas, and oil). The fossil fuel-based industrial complex has been responsible for producing Green House Gases (GHG) that have been slowly raising the earth's temperature. Consequently, global temperatures since the 1960s have been slightly warmer than the preceding decade and this trend is set to increase in the coming decades (Mateyisi et al., forthcoming). The summer of 2023 was earth's hottest since global

V. Chenzi (✉)
Department of Peace Security and Society, University of Zimbabwe, Harare, Zimbabwe

N. T. Murau · A. Ndamba
Peace and Security Studies, Zimbabwe Defence University, Harare, Zimbabwe

G. Moyo, S. J. Ndlovu-Gatsheni (eds.), *Global Storms and Africa in World Politics*, Global Power Shift, https://doi.org/10.1007/978-3-031-83868-2_8

records began in 1880, and summers in the coming years are expected to be much hotter than the 2023 record (Carrington, 2023). There are basically four climate change projections by the year 2100. These generally assume that global temperatures are going to rise by either 1.5 °C or 2 °C according to the Paris Agreement thresholds. In the worst-case scenario, temperatures are expected to even rise by 3–4 °C if the current Green House Gas emissions are not drastically reduced (Subramanian et al., 2023).

This rise in global temperature is already triggering serious challenges across the African continent. Rural communities in Africa are at the forefront of the climate crisis and they are confronted by a threefold threat which is punctuated by rise in sea levels, shifting weather patterns, and the increase in frequency and intensity of extreme weather events including droughts, heatwaves, heavy rainfall, and tropical storms (Epule et al., 2021). Consequently, these climate change driven disasters have acted as risk multipliers leading to far-flung crisis affecting millions especially in the form of population displacement and food insecurity across the region. In 2019, for example, Cyclone Idai, one of the deadliest storms to ever hit the continent affected Zimbabwe, Mozambique, and Malawi killing more than 1200 while displacing 2.2 million and ruining 800, 000 hectares of arable land, crops, and seed stock (WFP, 2021). Again, the 2016 El Nino evoked drought was the continent's worst in 35 years. Zambia was also struck by one of its worst droughts in decades following the erratic 2018–2019 rainfall season. Likewise, between 2021 and 2022, Southern Madagascar came across intense drought conditions that drove 1.35 million Malagasies to the brink of starvation (Ngoma et al., 2023; Rabezanahary Tanteliniaina & Andrianarimanana, 2023).

However, the measures currently being adopted to address the emerging anthropogenic climate change disasters in Africa and other parts of the global south have resulted in disaster capitalism. Evidence from the African continent demonstrates that disaster capitalism manifests itself as an extreme version of capitalism whereby both natural and anthropogenic disasters are transformed into profitable business schemes for corporate interests; and provide opportunities for political elites to enforce infamous policies that serve the peculiar interests of capital (Faas, 2018; Nasong'o, 2021). In Zimbabwe, South Africa, and Morocco, there is evidence suggesting that disaster capitalism is systematically being promoted by the state and individuals acting on behalf of the state. Currently, capitalism's profiteering tendencies aided by state agents and policies has further aggravated the effects of the anthropogenic climate crisis. This approach considers disasters as economic opportunities to amass wealth via insurance and compensation mechanisms suggested by the World Bank emphasizing on alleged "post-recovery activities." In this perspective, events that take place in the aftermath of disasters, whether natural, economic, or political are all considered as ripe for making profits (Amouzai, 2023). This disaster capitalism complex if left unchecked will replace core functions of government with its own profitable enterprises such that all climate crisis related functions will be performed by private corporations at a profit (Klein, 2007).

In order to curb the spiraling climate crisis and its related disasters, the industrialized states have been lobbying the World Bank to immediately ban all financial aid and investments toward fossil fuel energy projects across the African continent (Ramachandran, 2021). However, this chapter argues that the proposed solution is nothing short of climate colonialism since the anthropogenic climate crisis is a creation of the industrialized states through colonialism and the neoliberal capitalist economic system. Therefore, there is need to historicize the current climate crisis in the context of colonialism since these two are intricately linked. That is, western capitalists are largely responsible for climatic changes that have triggered natural and environmental disasters (Mafa, 2019). Hence, this lobbying to end fossil fuel energy sources in Africa is nothing short of racial capitalism whereby racial devolution is not parallel, or impertinent to, but is intrinsic to the process of capitalism in ways that cannot merely be relegated to class alone. In this regard, racial capitalism becomes the operation where capital encroaches on racial hierarchies via exploitation and extraction of surplus wealth from racialized labor, locally and globally, by the capitalist elite caste for profit. Hence, the construct of racial capitalism helps in acknowledging the relationship between the mistreatment of Black, Indigenous, and People of Color (BIPOC) globally and the social relations of climate breakdown.

However, disaster capitalism is deeply rooted in Africa's colonial past. Hence, the historical research design was deployed in the chapter to establish the relationship between Africa's colonial past and contemporary manifestations of disaster capitalism. Thus, the historical research design enables the research to corroborate, verify, and integrate evidence from the past to gain an understanding of current events and defend or refute a hypothesis given about a particular time period (Porra et al., 2014). This research design was very appropriate for the study as it was used to create historical connections between colonialism, disaster capitalism, and anthropogenic climate change and its ensuing disasters in Africa. By using this approach, the study was able to critique current efforts by the global north to address the climate crisis since they are historically responsible for the entire climate crisis. Furthermore, the historical approach was able to identify colonial continuities in the current climate discourse.

Colonialism frequently created intrusions for the expansion of capitalism, or an economic ideology founded on wage-labor that gave precedence to development in monetary earnings for the proprietors of the assets as the implicit focus, incentive, and purpose of major human social endeavors. Jointly, capitalism and colonialism established key elements of the groundwork for industrialization and militarization, or in this case "carbon-intensive economics." These created the drivers of contemporary anthropogenic climate change, from massive petrochemical technologies that burn fossil fuels for energy to deforestation for commodity agriculture (Whyte, 2017).

In Africa, nineteenth century colonial encroachment triggered anthropogenic environmental alterations that quickly disrupted most of the indigenous inhabitants. These were in the form of pollution, modification of hydrological cycles, deforestation, and the expansion of soil-use and terraforming for specific types of commercial activities including grazing, transportation, farming, and residential, commercial, and government infrastructure (Fuentes-George, 2023; Singh, 2023). These colonially-induced environmental modifications transformed the environmental conditions that sustained indigenous inhabitants' health, economies, cultures, and political autonomy. Although indigenous groups in most societies possess long histories of adjusting to change, colonialism initiated rapid changes such that most indigenous populations were made vulnerable to dangers. These ranged from health challenges caused by dietary changes, cultural erosion, and destruction of indigenous diplomacy. Therefore, indigenous peoples view their vulnerability to climate change as a consequence of increased colonially-induced environmental changes (Ford et al., 2020).

Furthermore, climate science itself as a discipline is deeply rooted in imperialism and colonialism. For example, it was Habsburg imperialist politicians that assisted scientists in developing an understanding of the relationship between development of local storms and atmospheric circulation. This also includes the bulk of historic meteorological data that contemporary climate scientists rely on, which was also produced by colonizing powers (Mercer, 2023). The data were extracted by scientists from the logbooks of mid-nineteenth century English ships. This information was recorded as part of an effort to better connect territories colonized by the British Empire and speed up the exploitation of other people's territories and waterways (Coen, 2020). What is worrying is that it is still the same colonial entities of the past that still dominate the contemporary climate discourse.

Hence, colonialism haunts the past, present, and future via climate while imperialism is perpetuated by racial capitalism, development interventions, education, neoliberalism, training, and media. Climate coloniality is thus declared in assorted forms, including neoliberal growth and development models, hyperconsumptive and wasteful lifestyles, fossil fuel capitalism, and also through structures, systems, and epistemologies built and sustained by powerful global alliances. Moreover, anthropogenic hegemony, institutional unaccountability, neocolonial approaches to "resources," and coloniality of global governance structures, all coalesce to make colonialities of climate (Sultana, 2022). The chapter therefore strongly argues that there is urgent need to deconstruct climate colonialities in order to critically understand how climate change acts as a phenomenon that not only situates the material realities and didactics around nature-society relationships, but also the epistemic violences that precede in its aftermath (Kelly, 2013). This will facilitate the creation of futures not haunted by the past and present colonialities.

This chapter is very critical toward situating historical colonial experiences within the contemporary disaster capitalism and the climate crisis. It also helps in understanding how neoliberal policies are not only responsible for causing anthropogenic climate change and its ensuing disasters but it also sheds light on how the same polices are thwarting ex-ante and ex-post disaster response efforts through disaster capitalism. The chapter was guided by three research questions. What are the historical roots of contemporary disaster capitalism? How has the global capitalist system influenced the emergence of disaster capitalism in the African continent? and How best can disaster capitalism be addressed in the African continent?

In order to address the demands of these questions, the chapter is divided into six segments including the introduction which establishes a connection between colonialism and contemporary disaster capitalism. Global appreciation of literature on disaster capitalism forms the second portion and it identifies gaps in literature on contemporary disaster capitalism across the globe. Conceptualization of disaster capitalism forms the third segment of the chapter. The exploration of disaster capitalism in the African continent and the implications form the fourth and fifth portions of the chapter, respectively. The sixth part identifies possible approaches to address disaster capitalism in Africa.

Global Reflections on Disaster Capitalism

Globally, studies about the historical implications of disaster capitalism are scant and are even fewer in the African continent. Nevertheless, this scant literature concurs that disaster capitalism is salient in both public and private sectors and it is evident through the interaction between capitalist neoliberal reforms, practices, and disasters. There has been minor research on the role of public and private sectors in the (re)production and assemblage of disaster risks from a disaster capitalism lens, both in the academic and policy realms (Sandoval et al., 2020). This chapter reacts to this disparity by providing a preliminary continental overview of the root causes, behavior, and consequences of disaster capitalism, its contribution to disaster risk creation, and its role in the systemic nature of risks that manifest in the African continent. The chapter analyses diverse ex-ante and ex-post experiences of disaster capitalism in the African continent in the post-2000 period by linking them with the nineteenth century colonial past to identify historical continuities and discontinuities.

Disaster capitalism has been explained as a scenario whereby a complete overhaul of economies and economic regulations in service of capitalist interests supplants state-run institutions under the cover of environmental crisis (Klein, 2007; Faas, 2018). In Iraq, disaster capitalism came as a consequence of the first and second gulf war, maladministration under Saddam Hussein, and years of United Nations sanctions (UN), which resulted in wholesale destruction of public amenities paving way for disasters such as floods, famine, disease epidemics, and extreme poverty. Consequently, private companies took over by rendering the services which the failed regime was no longer able to execute at exorbitant rates such that only the most affluent could afford them (Klein, 2007, pp. 47–48).

Likewise, studies conducted by the United Nations office for Disaster Risk Reduction (UNDRR) in Chile, Italy, and Brazil demonstrated that the coordinated neoliberal reforms and practices engendered profiteering tendencies against disaster struck populations; privatization of critical public amenities; and liberation of environmental protection schemes (UNDRR, 2022). Subsequently, such capitalist tendencies led to the intensification and emergence of new risks. In the United States of America (USA), survivors of the 2005 Hurricanes Katrina and Rita and the subsequent floods and levee failures were said to suffer from "chronic disaster syndrome" after spending more than 4 years without rehabilitation in the aftermath of the disasters (Adams et al., 2009). Chronic disaster syndrome is said to be a by-product of the crucial variables that create and sustain conditions of displacement. In particular, the permanent displacement of the most vulnerable populations from the social landscape as a sensible solution that unwittingly exacerbates the syndrome; long-term effects of personal trauma (these may include near death experience during a disaster, and death of close family members, loss of homes, jobs, community, financial security, and well-being); and finally the destruction of social arrangements that enable the smooth functioning of disaster capitalism which results in a disaster scenario being prolonged as a way of life (Adams et al., 2009; Fernández, 2019).

Other studies have sought to problematize the term "disaster capitalism," by arguing that since its launch in 2005 by activist journalist Naomi Klein, its proliferation in media and social movements has jeopardized its meaning by confusing and weakening its core concept and critiques. In order to stem this impending dilution, ethnographic case studies from the 2010 British Petroleum (BP) Deepwater Horizon Oil Disaster in the Gulf of Mexico and the 2010 Haiti earthquake were used to exemplify the phenomenon of disaster capitalism in practice (Schuller & Maldonado, 2016). Notwithstanding the above, disaster capitalism has also been argued to be a phenomenon that exists not only among Non-Governmental Organizations (NGO), governments, and powerful global corporations but can also be an evident trait among local victims of disasters (Gahman et al., 2021). By using the example of Ecuador in the aftermath of Mt. Tungurahua eruption, a new variety of disaster capitalism was discovered. That is, the creation of petite capitalist locals who were former victims of the disaster empowered by NGOs and the state via initiation into the capitalist enterprise. The role of disaster capitalism as a catalyst that creates petite capitalists demonstrates the limits of neoliberal economics' inability to envision disaster recovery except via self-serving, individualistic, entrepreneurial endeavors (Faas, 2018).

The sequence of disaster capitalism experiences across the globe demonstrates that there is need for meticulous effort when crafting solutions to disasters especially challenging the predominant socio-cultural and politico-economic circumstances that contributed toward creating the challenges in the first place (Radetzki, 2010). It appears that across the globe, addressing anthropogenic climate change has become a boom industry in its own right by acting as a source of substantial growth in a variety of sectors. Consequently, neoliberal capitalism is playing the dual role of precipitating disasters and utilizing the same disasters as opportunities to facilitate its expansion (Fletcher, 2012). Hence, there is need to identify how this situation is manifesting itself in the African continent through the use of case studies of contemporary anthropogenic climate change disasters.

Conceptualizing Disaster Capitalism Through the Postcolonial Theory

This chapter utilizes the postcolonial theory to establish the role that capitalism has played in Africa both in its colonial past and presently in the form of disaster capitalism fueled by the anthropogenic climate crisis. The postcolonial theory is a collection of opinions primarily focused on accounting for the historical, aesthetic, economic, political, and social impact of European colonial rule around the globe from the eighteenth century through to the twentieth century (Childs & Williams, 2014; Mikulewicz, 2020). Postcolonial theory assumes various forms and engagements which all share a cardinal theme; that the current global setup is impracticable to navigate let alone comprehend except by relating it to the history of imperialism and colonial rule (Hill et al., 2020). This implies that it is unfeasible to conceptualize European philosophical systems, literature, or past as entities existing in the absence of Europe's colonial overlap and subjugation across the globe (Williams & Chrisman, 2015). It also purports that the colonized regions are at the forgotten center of global modernity.

Furthermore, the prefix "post" for "postcolonial theory" has also met strong opposition, but it has never been interpreted to mean that colonialism has ended; alternatively, much of the postcolonial theory is focused on the lingering forms of colonial authority after the formal end of Empire (Ahmad, 1997). For over a generation, it has persisted in simultaneously investigating colonial domination in the first half of the twentieth century while also focusing on contemporary politics and justice across the globe. This means that it has assumed aggregate forms including political and aesthetic agency; explaining globalization and global modernity; reimagining politics and ethics from underneath imperial power, an effort that remains committed to those who continue to suffer its effects; and perpetually endeavors to discover and theorize new forms of human injustice, from environmentalism to human rights (Baldwin, 2017). Postcolonial theory has influenced the way we read texts, the way we understand national and transnational histories, and the way we understand the political implications of our own knowledge as scholars. Despite frequent critiques from outside the field (as well as from within it), postcolonial theory remains one of the key forms of critical humanistic interrogation in both academia and in the world.

Anthropogenic Climate Crisis and Disaster Capitalism in Africa

Regarding the first two questions that inquired on the historical roots of contemporary disaster capitalism and the role of the global capitalist system toward influencing the emergence of disaster capitalism in the African continent, evidence points out that there is a direct relationship between capitalism and the current climate crisis. Furthermore, the management of climate related disasters in Africa is hindered by disaster capitalism which has become a major challenge that not only threatens lives and livelihoods but has become a source of disasters at both ex-ante and ex-post disaster phases (Jacobs, 2021). Agents of disaster capitalism have included state-run institutions, NGOs, private business enterprises, and individuals. These entities prey upon disaster ridden denizens creating a vicious cycle of disaster situations compounded by climate change complications and neoliberal interventions that further jeopardize the lives and livelihoods of the citizens.

In Zimbabwe, for example, decades under the Mugabe and Mnangagwa regime's corrupt tendencies left the social support system devastated (Hove & Chenzi, 2020; Chenzi, 2021). Consequently, pertinent services including healthcare, education, housing, and water and electricity supply were staggered. The anthropogenic climate crisis further complicated the situation such that the water crisis has resulted in months without tap water in the country's urban settlements due to collapsed water reticulation infrastructure and low rainfall from climate change. This situation has led to the emergence of "water barons" consisting of both individual and private companies providing borehole drilling, well digging, or even supply of clean water charged per liter (Chidakwa, 2020). Those who cannot afford to drill boreholes, wells, or buy bulk water are forced to access water from surrounding water bodies. Consequently, Zimbabwe has recorded frequent waves of cholera epidemics in 2008, 2018, and 2023 (Chigudu, 2020; Al Jazeera, 2023).

Again, the post-2000 economic crisis in the country resulted in rural-urban migration and overcrowding in the urban regions. The 2005 state-backed "Operation *Murambatsvina*" (clean up the filth) meant to decongest the cities suspected of being political opposition strongholds only worsened the land crisis. Consequently, dubious land barons emerged both private and state-backed who sold settlement land to people in unsafe zones prone to flooding, landslides, and mud slides (Rwodzi & Muzorewa, 2023). The emergence of climate change induced disasters further complicated the situation by exposing people to climate hazards. Prior to 2020, Zimbabwe recorded an annual average of two tropical cyclones especially in Manicaland and Mashonaland East provinces (World Data, 2023). However, because of the anthropogenic climate change effects, the frequency of cyclones affecting the country has increased to an annual average of five. The emergence of Cyclone Idai between the fourth and 21st of March 2019 was compounded by the disaster capitalist tendencies of the land barons. The tropical cyclone caused catastrophic damage, and a humanitarian crisis in Mozambique, Madagascar, Zimbabwe, and Malawi, leaving more than 1500 people dead and many more missing while displacing more than 2 million inhabitants within the region (Chitongo et al., forthcoming; Chapungu, 2020). Several victims and survivors of the cyclone claimed that they were allocated stands by the Chimanimani council within the convergence zone. This was a direct breach to a state regulation which stipulates that buildings should be constructed at least 50 m away from rivers and water bodies (See Chap. 9). At Kopa, however, houses, shops, and local administrative offices were constructed in the very midst of the convergence zone where more than 280 victims were all swept away by the flooded rivers including houses, offices, vehicles, and property. Buildings including a police station, veterinary offices, shops, teachers, and agricultural inspectors' houses were situated in the high-risk zone and were all swept away with the occupants. The authorities simply suppressed the information that people were once settled there thus ultimately denying them a chance to access help from stake-holders (Chitongo et al., forthcoming). Again, in December 2023 alone, hundreds of homes constructed in wetlands were flooded leading to the death of 51 people (Pindula News, 2023). Hence, these disasters could have been avoided if residential land had been allocated away from the high-risk zones.

In Morocco, the earthquake that occurred on the eighth of September 2023, which killed more than 3, 000 and injured thousands more also demonstrated the evils of disaster capitalism (Amouzai, 2023). The earthquake's impact was most severe in the country's most marginalized regions particularly in the countryside. The state's relief response to the earthquake was negligible and sorely lacking with deadly consequences. This lackadaisical state response was attributed to a number of reasons including the neoliberal hollowing out of the state; commodification of relief efforts compounded by the liberalization of the insurance sector; the privatization of public services; and the dictation of policies encouraged for decades by International Financial Institutions (IFIs) such as the World Bank and the International Monetary Fund (IMF). Consequently, such policies exposed millions of vulnerable Moroccan workers to ravages of natural disasters, especially floods, wildfires, droughts, and earthquakes (Oduoye et al., 2023). Morocco ranks top among states most vulnerable to geological and climatic hazards in the Middle East and North Africa (MENA) region. Subsequently, it is experiencing the effects of climate change, which will gradually escalate the impact of accompanying disasters. Contemporary predictions imply that by 2030, approximately 42% of Morocco's coastal regions will encounter high risk of flooding and erosion especially in the coastal cities of Tangier and Rabat. More so, 77% of the population is anticipated to settle in these disaster-prone urban regions by 2050 (Agharroud et al., 2023; Raja et al., 2023).

In South Africa, the energy crisis which began in 2007 was also a by-product of disaster capitalism, where private interests swept in to profiteer in the wake of a disaster. Although in this case, the disaster was anthropogenic and took decades in the making, it was nonetheless intensified by the climate crisis. That is, the dependence of South Africa on thermal electricity resulted in artificial coal shortages, environmental protest against using coal-based electricity, coupled with underinvestment in power generation resulting in chronic load shedding. This artificial coal shortage led to the authorization of US $900 million in overpriced coal contracts by the Special Investigating Unit. These contracts were grabbed by opportunistic capitalists and state actors ultimately increasing the price of electricity by 500% (Lenferna, 2022). Worse still, the haphazard construction of Medupi and Kusile, the biggest coal plants ever constructed further intensified South Africa's energy crisis (Cole et al., 2022, 2023). The initiative was environmentally and economically imprudent in the face of both a global anthropogenic climate crisis primarily caused by over-dependence on fossil energy sources and progressively cheaper renewable energy sources. Consequently, South Africa has lost Hundreds of billions of Rands to address the energy crisis and is still confronted by crippling electricity shortages. This energy crisis has resulted in the proposed privatization of the energy sector by introducing private players to provide environmentally friendly renewable energy. This will further disenfranchise the majority poor since 10% of the population owns more than 80 percent of the wealth (Clarno & Vally, 2023). Hence, in the near future, the majority of South Africans who face poverty and unemployment will be largely excluded from the dividends and ownership of renewable energy.

Global North and Disaster Capitalism in Africa

Disaster capitalism in Africa is not only promoted by the state and its unscrupulous agents, global north governments and organizations are also responsible for promoting disaster capitalism in the continent. However, the capitalist driven solutions to climate change are frequently the main purveyors of western backed disaster capitalism in Africa. These alleged solutions demonstrate the insincerity of the western neoliberal philosophy toward addressing the anthropogenic climate crisis and its associated disasters. For example, one solution to the climate crisis which was proposed by the Norwegian government alongside seven other Nordic and Baltic states to the World Bank was the banning of all financing of natural gas projects in Africa and elsewhere by 2025. At the Conference of Parties (COP26) summit held in 2021, 20 more countries even pledged to halt all fossil fuel projects in the developing world by 2022 (Smith et al., 2022; vanAsselt & Green, 2023). These states suggested that in order to halt GHG emissions, the World Bank should only invest in clean energy interventions in the developing world especially green hydrogen and smart micro-grid networks (Ramachandran, 2021).

Such policy suggestions imply that developing regions are expected to use green hydrogen which is the most complex and expensive energy technology in existence or solar energy and wind powered electrical sources which are insufficient to meet the current energy needs without subsidizing with fossil fuels, of which gas is the cleanest by far. Furthermore, Africa has huge offshore gas fields and is populated by the world's poorest nations (Kriström, 2023; Margulis et al., 2023). Therefore, halting the funding of gas projects would literally cripple investment toward the construction of critical energy infrastructure essential in aiding economic development and improving the standard of living for the denizens. This includes halting electricity supply for homes, schools, and factories; industrial capacity for processing steel and cement; a drop in the supply of carbon dioxide, an indispensable ingredient for synthetic fertilizer; and liquefied gas for transportation and cooking. In other words, this proposed solution is a death sentence to Africa's citizens. This would further increase the annual death rate from 3.8 million due to indoor air pollution caused by exposure to toxic smoke due to indoor fire wood, coal, charcoal, or animal dung for cooking according to the World Health Organization (WHO) (Ritchie & Roser, 2023). The current promotion by India, China, and the United Nations (UN) is saving countless lives in the developing world but may be reversed if the current proposal by the capitalist developed world is adopted. Vijaya Ramachandran (2021) also concurred that:

> Many who support restrictions on poor countries do so, ironically, in the name of climate justice, rightly noting the global poor are most at risk from climate impacts. Yet how will the global poor become more resilient to extreme weather events and other effects of climate change if not through development? The global poor are most at risk because they cannot afford adaptation measures such as air conditioning and irrigation.

Therefore, the current lobbying for green energy by developed nations is merely advancing green colonialism since it is not in the best interest of the developing nations in anyway because developed nations account for 92% of greenhouse gas emissions (Smith, 2016; Scales, 2017). On the other hand, over 1 billion inhabitants from 48 African nations south of the Sahara Desert are sorely responsible for less than 1% of cumulative global greenhouse gas emissions. Moreover, even in the unlikely scenario that these countries trebled their electricity generation exclusively from natural gas, global emissions would only increase by roughly 1% (Ramachandran, 2021; Busk & Reynolds, 2023; Moore, 2023). Hence, denying access to affordable energy sources to the 1 billion multitude only generates more poverty thereby making them more vulnerable to global warming which was created by developed nations in the first place.

Therefore, lobbying for clean energy should be imposed on developed nations who also have the economic capacity to bankroll the initiative. In Africa, over 400 million inhabitants survive on less than US$2 per day and the current green energy technologies cannot meet their energy needs since they are too costly for African governments' financial capacity (Azzarri & Signorelli, 2020; Chenzi & Ndamba, 2023). However, these expensive energy subsidies can be borne in affluent nations, which also account for the bulk of the globe's historical and current GHG emissions. Furthermore, there are no affordable and environmentally friendly alternatives in the production of cement, fertilizer, and steel. Apart from the provision of electricity, fossil fuels are also very vital toward Africa's development. For example, modern agriculture, transport system, and construction are heavily dependent on fossil fuels. Therefore, banning the use of these energy sources in the global south by developed nations is barbarous, merciless, and disgraceful. Hence, the current trajectory is a ploy by rich nations to keep the global south in a perpetual state of poverty and dependency by repackaging development in the form of climate-related transfers.

This capitalist hypocrisy is further evidenced by developed nations that continue to rely on fossil fuels but frantically desire to deny the same to struggling developing nations. Norway, for example, is a fossil fuel-reliant developed nation-state with crude oil and natural gas accounting for 41%, 14%, 14%, and 7% of its exports, Gross Domestic Product (GDP), government revenues, and national employment, respectively. To the chagrin of African states, Norway intends to ban fossil fuels by 2050 providing itself ample time to adjust while denying the same option to African states (Bang & Lahn, 2020; Sun et al., 2022; Madsen et al., 2023). Furthermore, apart from being the world's third-largest exporter of natural gas it also houses the biggest hydrocarbon reserves in Europe. Unfortunately, Norway is not the only nation exhibiting the hypocrisy, USA also set up lofty GHG reduction targets while simultaneously calling on major oil and gas suppliers to increase production so as to meet its huge demand (Browning et al., 2023; Jenkins et al., 2021). Similarly, German also rolled out ambitious climate targets while providing Germans 20 years to ban coal in the country (Mengis et al., 2022).

Looking Ahead

The emerging challenges from disaster capitalism in the African continent require robust efforts to confront and address them. Unfortunately, African governments alongside western nation-states are also part of the problem. Currently the inhabitants of the African continent are being fleeced through disaster capitalism emanating from anthropogenic climate change effects, a problem which they nor their forefathers were not responsible for. Instead, they were victims then and now of capitalism and neoliberal racialized disaster capitalism. However, there are a number of measures that can be adopted to address the scourge of disaster capitalism. Chief among these solutions is decolonizing climate epistemologies in the African continent (See Chap. 7 of this volume).

Establishing a democratic and community-led process for Disaster Risk Reduction (DRR), climate adaptation, and recovery is a crucial step toward addressing disaster capitalism. Since disaster capitalism emanates from international or national institutions and their agents excluding the affected communities, decision-making and local governance must therefore be spearheaded by those directly impacted by the disaster. Moreover, key economic assets and natural resources critical for disaster mitigation must be placed within local community-control. Klein (2007) also argued that disaster capitalism is not an inevitable outcome of climate change or disasters but is a phenomenon that is deliberately allowed to manifest when the disaster response initiative is hijacked by external forces instead of the communities affected by the disaster (Klein, 2007). There are several steps that can be taken to safeguard communities against disaster capitalism and these include: reviewing zoning codes and local statutes to consider changing environmental conditions; aligning participatory climate change planning with participatory budgeting activities in order to assign funds equivalent to the climate vulnerabilities of different communities. Preventing development initiatives that can potentially displace communities into climate vulnerable regions; investing in drought, flooding, and forest fire prevention strategies and removing financial and political obstructions to climate change adaptation and disaster-response for vulnerable and impacted regions (Adams et al., 2009; Imperiale & Vanclay, 2021).

Likewise, guaranteeing community-led rebuilding processes with transparent governance and resource allocation is very vital in preventing disaster capitalist tendencies in disaster affected communities. Steps such as ensuring that residents of disaster-impacted communities have the right to return to their former homes;

establishing community-governance programs to manage and distribute aid resources and necessitating development projects to commit to a Community Benefits Agreement are of importance in safeguarding communities from predatory disaster capitalist tendencies (Güney, 2022).

Investing in critical public infrastructure especially sewer systems, water reticulation, electricity, communications network and health that will support evacuation, migration, and survival during disasters such as cyclones, wildfires, droughts, floods, epidemics, and pandemics is crucial (Bajracharya, 2024). This is usually because of the absence or scarcity of public infrastructure that encourages the emergence of private, state, and international entities to takeover service provision leading to disaster capitalism. Therefore, repairing roads, bridges, rails, and strengthening water and sewer systems should be prioritized. Constructing community emergency centers that can resist extreme weather conditions and equipped with the energy and resources essential for supporting communities without power and water must also be prioritized.

Last but not least, rich nations must first take the initiative by abruptly banning fossil fuels since they are the major polluters and are therefore sorely responsible for the rise in global temperature and its subsequent disasters. Therefore, instead of delaying the use of green energy in their countries and forcing it on Africa whose contribution to greenhouse gas emissions is minuscule, they should make big investments in clean technology and infrastructure to support poor countries. Rather than trying to ban the funding of natural gas projects in Africa, they should instead facilitate such for at least the next two decades in order to lift Africa out of poverty. Currently, global northerners are merely pursuing climate ambitions by burdening the least capable continent to shoulder their green agenda. Consequently, social justice has been hollowed out since the global south in general and Africa in particular still does not have access to funding to harness its energy resources to increase incomes, resilience, and quality of life.

Conclusion

In conclusion, the anthropogenic climate crisis that has become an endemic pathology across the continent is both a product and creation of western capitalist colonial system which continues to expand and trigger disasters while further impoverishing the continent's inhabitants. However, these disasters have become a new challenge for the continent by creating disaster capitalism which profits off the poorest members of society and is promoted by Western entities, African governments and state agents. Therefore, the historical injustices embedded within Africa's colonial past continue to morph and evolve into new forms of challenges that are now being driven by disasters which have come to characterize postcolonial Africa. What this means is that disaster capitalism may gradually increase to become a continental pathology in the near future since climate change driven disasters are anticipated to increase in frequency and strength if serious action is not taken.

References

Adams, V., Van Hattum, T., & English, D. (2009). Chronic disaster syndrome: Displacement, disaster capitalism, and the eviction of the poor from New Orleans. *American Ethnologist, 36*(4), 615–636.

Agharroud, K., Puddu, M., Ivčević, A., Satta, A., Kolker, A. S., & Snoussi, M. (2023). Climate risk assessment of the Tangier-Tetouan-Al Hoceima coastal region (Morocco). *Frontiers in Marine Science, 10*, 1176350.

Ahmad, A. (1997). Post-colonial theory and the 'post-'condition. *Socialist Register, 33*, 353–381.

Al Jazeera. (2023). Zimbabwe struggles to contain spread of cholera outbreak. https://www.aljazeera.com/news/2023/10/22/zimbabwe-struggles-to-contain-spread-of-cholera-outbreak

Amouzai, A. (2023). Disastrous capitalism in Morocco in wake of earthquake between the hammer of international financial institutions and the anvil of disaster capitalism. https://www.tni.org/en/article/disastrous-capitalism-in-morocco-in-wake-of-earthquake

Azzarri, C., & Signorelli, S. (2020). Climate and poverty in Africa South of the Sahara. *World Development, 125*, 104691.

Bajracharya, A. (2024). Countering local disaster capitalism: Lessons from Nepal's indigenous people. *Ecology, Economy and Society–the INSEE Journal, 7*(1), 105–135.

Baldwin, A. (2017). Postcolonial futures: Climate, race, and the yet-to-come. *ISLE: Interdisciplinary Studies in Literature and Environment, 24*(2), 292–305.

Bang, G., & Lahn, B. (2020). From oil as welfare to oil as risk? Norwegian petroleum resource governance and climate policy. *Climate Policy, 20*(8), 997–1009.

Browning, M., McFarland, J., Bistline, J., Boyd, G., Muratori, M., Binsted, M., Harris, C., Mai, T., Blanford, G., Edmonds, J., & Fawcett, A. A. (2023). Net-zero CO2 by 2050 scenarios for the United States in the energy modeling forum 37 study. *Energy and Climate Change, 4*, 100104.

Busk, L. A., & Reynolds, I. (2023). Climate change and the irrational society. *Theory & Event, 26*(3), 559–575.

Carrington, D. (2023). 'Smashed': Summer of 2023 the hottest ever recorded. https://www.theguardian.com/world/2023/sep/06/summer-of-2023-hottest-recorded-in-wake-up-call-to-cut-carbon-emissions

Chapungu, L. (2020). *Mitigating the impact of cyclone disasters: Lessons from cyclone Idai. Policy briefing: Climate change and migration*. South African Institute of International Affairs SAIIA.

Chenzi, V. (2021). Fake news, corruption, human rights, and the Mnangagwa regime, 2017–2021. *Journal of Diplomacy and International Relations, XXII*(1), 97–113.

Chenzi, V., & Ndamba, A. (2023). Surviving the Covid-19 lockdown: Zimbabwe's informal sector, 2020–2021. *Review of African Political Economy, 50*(176), 261–271.

Chidakwa, B. (2020). Water Barons Cash-in on desperation. https://www.herald.co.zw/water-barons-cash-in-on-desperation/

Chigudu, S. (2020). *The political life of an epidemic: Cholera, crisis and citizenship in Zimbabwe*. Cambridge University Press.

Childs, P., & Williams, P. (2014). *An introduction to post-colonial theory*. Routledge.

Chitongo, L., Chenzi, V., & Blazer-Mapitsa, C. (forthcoming). Climate governance and resilience action. In M. Matsa, L. Chapungu, & G. Nhamo (Eds.), *Climate change resilience in rural Southern Africa: The dynamics, prospects & challenges*. Springer Nature.

Clarno, A., & Vally, S. (2023). The context of struggle: Racial capitalism and political praxis in South Africa. *Ethnic and Racial Studies, 46*(16), 3425–3447.

Coen, D. R. (2020). The advent of climate science. In *Oxford research encyclopedia of climate science*.

Cole, M., Mthenjane, M., & van Zyl, A. (2022). The just transition and the coal mining sector in South Africa. *Journal of the Southern African Institute of Mining and Metallurgy, 122*(11), 637–638.

Cole, M. J., Mthenjane, M., & van Zyl, A. T. (2023). Assessing coal mine closures and mining community profiles for the just transition in South Africa. *Journal of the Southern African Institute of Mining and Metallurgy, 123*(6), 329–342.
Epule, T. E., Chehbouni, A., Dhiba, D., & Moto, M. W. (2021). The readiness index for climate change adaptation in Africa: The role of climate and adaptive capacity proxies. *Applied Sciences, 11*(20), 9413.
Faas, A. J. (2018). Petit capitalisms in disaster, or the limits of neoliberal imagination: Displacement, recovery, and opportunism in highland Ecuador. *Economic Anthropology, 5*(1), 32–44.
Fernández, A. M. (2019). Revolt, chronic disaster and hope. *City, 23*(4–5), 405–410.
Fletcher, R. (2012). Capitalizing on chaos: Climate change and disaster capitalism. *Ephemera: Theory & Politics in Organization, 12*(1–2), 97–112.
Ford, J. D., King, N., Galappaththi, E. K., Pearce, T., McDowell, G., & Harper, S. L. (2020). The resilience of indigenous peoples to environmental change. *One Earth, 2*(6), 532–543.
Fuentes-George, K. (2023). The legacy of colonialism on contemporary climate governance. *Georgetown Journal of International Affairs, 24*(1), 91–98.
Gahman, L., Thongs, G., & Adaeze Greenidge, A. (2021). Disaster, debt, and 'underdevelopment': The cunning of colonial-capitalism in the Caribbean. *Development, 64*, 112–118.
Güney, K. M. (2022). Earthquake, disaster capitalism and massive urban transformation in Istanbul. *The Geographical Journal, 190*(1), e12496. https://doi.org/10.1111/geoj.12496
Hill, R., Walsh, F. J., Davies, J., Sparrow, A., Mooney, M., Council, C.L., Wise, R. M., & Tengö, M. (2020). Knowledge co-production for indigenous adaptation pathways: Transform post-colonial articulation complexes to empower local decision-making. *Global Environmental Change, 65*, 102161.
Hove, M., & Chenzi, V. (2020). Social media, civil unrest and government responses: The Zimbabwean experience. *Journal of Contemporary African Studies, 38*(1), 121–137.
Imperiale, A. J., & Vanclay, F. (2021). Conceptualizing community resilience and the social dimensions of risk to overcome barriers to disaster risk reduction and sustainable development. *Sustainable Development, 29*(5), 891–905.
Jacobs, F. (2021). Beyond social vulnerability: COVID-19 as a disaster of racial capitalism. *Sociologica, 15*(1), 55–65.
Jenkins, J. D., Mayfield, E. N., Larson, E. D., Pacala, S. W., & Greig, C. (2021). Mission net-zero America: The nation-building path to a prosperous, net-zero emissions economy. *Joule, 5*(11), 2755–2761.
Kelly, E. (2013). Does deconstruction matter? Being 'at home' in the era of climate change. *Continuum, 27*(1), 41–53.
Klein, N. (2007, October). *Disaster capitalism: The new economy of catastrophe*. Harper's Magazine.
Kriström, J. R. (2023). *The global dangers of good intentions: Addressing the Swedish and Norwegian approaches to combat climate change*. Master's thesis, Nord universitet.
Lenferna, A. (2022). South Africa's energy transition is mired in disaster capitalism. https://jacobin.com/2022/08/south-africa-eskom-privatization-energy-renewables
Madsen, P. T., Hansen, D. S., Sperling, K., Houeland, C., & Jenkins, K. E. (2023). Abandoning fossil fuel production: What can be learned from the Danish phase-out of oil and gas? *Energy Research & Social Science, 103*, 103211.
Mafa, K. (2019). Zimbabwe: Cyclone Idai, sanctions and capitalism. https://socialistproject.ca/2019/04/zimbabwe-cyclone-idai-sanctions-and-capitalism/
Margulis, M. E., Hopewell, K., & Qereshniku, E. (2023). Food, famine and the free trade fallacy: The dangers of market fundamentalism in an era of climate emergency. *The Journal of Peasant Studies, 50*(1), 215 239.
Mateyisi, M., Nangombe, S., Chenzi, V., & Maoela, M. A. (forthcoming). The climate change landscape for rural Southern Africa. In M. Matsa, L. Chapungu, & G. Nhamo (Eds.), *Climate change resilience in rural Southern Africa: The dynamics, prospects & challenges*. Springer Nature.

Mengis, N., Kalhori, A., Simon, S., Harpprecht, C., Baetcke, L., Prats-Salvado, E., Schmidt-Hattenberger, C., Stevenson, A., Dold, C., El Zohbi, J., & Borchers, M. (2022). Net-zero CO2 Germany—A retrospect from the year 2050. *Earth's Futures, 10*(2), e2021EF002324.
Mercer, H. (2023). Colonialism: Why leading climate scientists have finally acknowledged its link with climate change. https://theconversation.com/colonialism-why-leading-climate-scientists-have-finally-acknowledged-its-link-with-climate-change-181642
Mikulewicz, M. (2020). The discursive politics of adaptation to climate change. *Annals of the American Association of Geographers, 110*(6), 1807–1830.
Moore, J. W. (2023). Our Capitalogenic world: Climate crises, class politics, and the civilizing project. *Annales Universitatis PaedagogicaeCracoviensis. Studia Poetica, 11*(1), 97–122.
Nasong'o, S. W. (2021). Disaster capitalism and political instability in Africa: The case of the perennial conflict in the DRC. https://www.maxwell.syr.edu/events/2021/10/26/default-calendar/disaster-capitalism-and-political-instability-in-africa-the-case-of-the-perennial-conflict-in-the-drc
Ngoma, H., Finn, A., & Kabisa, M. (2023). Climate shocks, vulnerability, resilience and livelihoods in rural Zambia. *Climate and Development, 16*, 1–12.
Oduoye, M. O., Rehman, L. U., Ubechu, S. C., Abdulkareem, L., Mourid, M. R., & Irfan, H. (2023). Urgent call to action: Supporting Morocco in the aftermath of the recent earthquake. *Journal of Global Health, 13*, 03065.
Pindula News. (2023). Flash floods damage 1600 houses countrywide. https://www.thezimbabwean.co/2023/12/flash-floods-damage-1-600-houses-countrywide/?tztc=1
Porra, J., Hirschheim, R., & Parks, M. S. (2014). The historical research method and information systems research. *Journal of the Association for Information Systems, 15*(9), 3.
Rabezanahary Tanteliniaina, M. F., & Andrianarimanana, M. H. (2023). Projection of future drought characteristics in the Great South of Madagascar using CMIP6 and bias-correction spatial disaggregation method. *Theoretical and Applied Climatology, 155*, 1–13.
Radetzki, M. (2010). The fallacies of concurrent climate policy efforts. *Ambio, 39*(3), 211–222.
Raja, H., Omar, W., Mounsif, I., & Duc, M. (2023). Coastal cliff failures hazard along the Safi coastline (Morocco): A methodology for shoreline change assessment and its forecast along with examination of the causes. *Environmental Earth Sciences, 82*(10), 255.
Ramachandran, V. (2021). Rich countries' climate policies are colonialism in Green. https://foreignpolicy.com/2021/11/03/cop26-climate-colonialism-africa-norway-world-bank-oil-gas/
Ritchie, H., & Max Roser, M. (2023). Indoor air pollution. In *Our world in data.*
Rwodzi, A., & Muzorewa, T. (2023). Land resettlement and elite monopoly in Peri-urban Harare: The colonial legacy of land ownership in post-colonial Zimbabwe, 2000–2019. *Southern Journal for Contemporary History, 48*(1), 82–104.
Sandoval, V., Gonzalez-Muzzio, C., Villalobos, C., Sarmiento, J. P., & Hoberman, G. (2020). Assessing disaster capitalism in post-disaster processes in Chile: Neoliberal reforms and the role of the corporate class. *Disaster Prevention and Management: An International Journal, 29*(6), 831–847.
Scales, I. R. (2017). Green capitalism. In N. Richardson Castree, M. F. Goodchild, W. Kobayashi Liu, & R. A. Marston (Eds.), *The international encyclopedia of geography.*
Schuller, M., & Maldonado, J. K. (2016). Disaster capitalism. *Annals of Anthropological Practice, 40*(1), 61–72.
Singh, N. (2023). Climate justice in the global south: Understanding the environmental legacy of colonialism. In *Global climate justice.*
Smith, R. (2016). *Green capitalism: The god that failed.* College Publications.
Smith, P., Beaumont, L., Bernacchi, C. J., Byrne, M., Cheung, W., Conant, R. T., Cotrufo, F., Feng, X., Janssens, I., Jones, H., & Kirschbaum, M. U. (2022). Essential outcomes for COP26.
Subramanian, A., Nagarajan, A. M., Vinod, S., Chakraborty, S., Sivagami, K., Theodore, T., Sathyanarayanan, S. S., Tamizhdurai, P., & Mangesh, V. L. (2023). Long-term impacts of climate change on coastal and transitional eco-systems in India: An overview of its current status, future projections, solutions, and policies. *RSC Advances, 13*(18), 12204–12228.

Sultana, F. (2022). The unbearable heaviness of climate coloniality. *Political Geography, 99*, 102638.
Sun, Y. Y., Gössling, S., Hem, L. E., Iversen, N. M., Walnum, H. J., Scott, D., & Oklevik, O. (2022). Can Norway become a net-zero economy under scenarios of tourism growth? *Journal of Cleaner Production, 363*, 132414.
United Nations office for Disaster Risk Reduction (UNDRR). (2022). *The role of public and private sectors in disaster capitalism*. UNDRR.
vanAsselt, H., & Green, F. (2023). COP26 and the dynamics of anti-fossil fuel norms. *Wiley Interdisciplinary Reviews: Climate Change, 14*(3), e816.
Whyte, K. (2017). Indigenous climate change studies: Indigenizing futures, decolonizing the Anthropocene. *English Language Notes, 55*(1–2), 153–162.
Williams, P., & Chrisman, L. (2015). Colonial discourse and post-colonial theory: An introduction. In *Colonial discourse and post-colonial theory* (pp. 1–20). Routledge.
World Data. (2023). Cyclones in Zimbabwe. https://www.worlddata.info/africa/zimbabwe/cyclones.php
World Food Programme. (2021). *Climate Change in Southern Africa*. https://executiveboard.wfp.org/document_download/WFP0000129015#:~:text=Impacts%20of%20changes%20in%20temperatures%20and%20rainfall%20patterns%20are%20already,intensity%20of%20droughts%20and%20floods

Vincent Chenzi is a lecturer of Disaster Management, Peacebuilding and Strategic Studies at the University of Zimbabwe. He has published academic articles, book chapters, and briefings in refereed journals. Some of his publications are in *Review of African Political Economy*, *Conflict Studies Quarterly*, among others. He has also been consulted by various media and non-governmental institutions as an expert on contemporary African politics and media. He is a holder of a BA and MA in War and Strategic Studies from the University of Zimbabwe. He is currently pursuing his PhD in Conflict, Peace and Governance at the University of Zimbabwe's Department of Peace Security and Society. His areas of interest include: African politics, climate justice, media, and nonviolence.

Nyasha Trishia Murau is a Development Practitioner and academic whose research interests include climate change and adaptation; sustainable development; youth development policy; food security and livelihoods; and disaster management research. She holds an Msc in International Development Studies. Currently she is pursuing her PhD in Peace, Leadership and Governance at Africa University. She has over 5 years of experience working in the NGO Sector and over 10 years of University teaching and research experience. She has worked as a deputy academic director at Zimbabwe Staff College, and Environmental Professional with Environmental Professionals Council of Zimbabwe.

Admire Ndamba is a lecturer of Disaster Management, Conflict and Security Studies at the University of Zimbabwe. He published articles with the Review of African Political Economy. He is currently pursuing his PhD studies in the field of Disaster Management at the University of Zimbabwe.

Chapter 9
Implications of Climate Crisis in Southern Africa

Gracsious Maviza, Divane Nzima, Siyaxola Enerst Gadu, and Ntobeko Ndlovu

Abstract This chapter discusses climate crisis within the framework of climate capitalism. Contrary to the conventional understanding of climate from an anthropocentric perspective, the discussion here emphasises fairness, equity, and inclusivity in crafting solutions that recognise the role of the history of colonialism and imperialism perpetuated by powerful countries and multinational corporations. Chapter concludes that only comprehensive strategies prioritising sustainability and inclusivity, beyond market-driven approaches will help build a more just and resilient future for Africa.

Introduction

The world is currently facing several global storms that are shifting the world as we know it. Climate change is one of the most notable and contentious of these. Southern Africa has been among the most affected regions with frequent and extreme weather events such as droughts, high temperatures, flash floods, cyclones,

G. Maviza (✉)
International Centre for Tropical Agriculture (CIAT), Pretoria, South Africa

Department of Sociology, University of Free State, Phuthaditjhaba, South Africa
e-mail: g.maviza@cgiar.org

D. Nzima
Department of Sociology, University of Free State, Phuthaditjhaba, South Africa
e-mail: nzimad@ufs.ac.za

S. E. Gadu
International Centre for Tropical Agriculture (CIAT), Pretoria, South Africa
e-mail: s.gadu@cgiar.org

N. Ndlovu
Institute of Development Sciences, National University of Science and Technology, Bulawayo, Zimbabwe
e-mail: ntobeko.ndlovu@nust.ac.zw

G. Moyo, S. J. Ndlovu-Gatsheni (eds.), *Global Storms and Africa in World Politics*, Global Power Shift, https://doi.org/10.1007/978-3-031-83868-2_9

and tropical storms. These have had an adverse impact on infrastructure, human settlements, food, and water systems (Tomaka et al., 2022). Given that most African countries are resource-constrained, it is anticipated that climate change and its associated shocks and hazards will remain a threat to the future viability of food, land, and water systems (Nhamo & Agyepong, 2019; Nzima & Maviza, 2023). In addition, climate change threatens to negatively impact the humanitarian-development-peace (H-D-P) nexus aimed at building sustainable economies and livelihoods through promoting development for peace and social cohesion. Contrary to the foregoing, the effects of climate change reinforce existing vulnerabilities, thus triggering disputes over resources with negative implications for peace and social cohesion. In most African countries, where economies are sustained through climate-sensitive natural resources, climate change exacerbates vulnerability and worsens economic woes with notable implications for peace (Lim et al., 2021).

The climate crisis has also resulted in climate coloniality (for further details on climate colonialism, see Chaps. 6, 7, and 8 of this volume), where an inequitable climate economy is emerging with African countries on the margins. Whereas African countries are the least contributors to the causes of climate change, they are the most affected by its effects, with limited access to climate financing to fund response strategies. According to Solnit et al. (2023), the traits of coloniality can be seen in the past, present, and future through the climate change discourse. Notwithstanding that climate change is a global problem, much of its adverse effects are disproportionately felt by former colonies in the Global South (Solnit et al., 2023). Given today's global geopolitical and economic power landscape, globalisation and transnationalism continue to perpetuate climate coloniality. The solutions to climate change such as moving away from fossil fuels to clean energy sources, such as solar and wind power, also perpetuate power imbalances. This new energy discourse creates a climate economy where those controlling capital profit from the climate crisis. In the recent past, there has been a significant discussion surrounding the unintended impacts of climate capitalism, often termed "'climate imperialism." This concept highlights how pursuing capital-intensive climate solutions without an equitable global financial infrastructure can unfairly favour powerful nations and corporations. Therefore, it exacerbates inequalities and vulnerabilities in disadvantaged regions and communities (Sapinski, 2015; Ponte, 2019). The global superpowers have managed to keep those most affected by climate change in perpetual dependency on the Global North with limited resources available either for mitigation or adaptation. The fronting of climate loans instead of grants in climate finance is a move that increases the debt burden of the already struggling countries.

Given the foregoing, this chapter seeks to highlight the adverse effects of extreme weather events in Southern Africa to demonstrate how climate change has been one of the global storms with implications on the humanitarian-development-peace nexus. In addition, the chapter discusses the response strategies and how some of these perpetuate climate coloniality through an uneven global funding infrastructure.

Extreme Weather Events in Malawi, Mozambique, and Zimbabwe

The Climate Risk Index of 2019 listed Malawi, Mozambique, and Zimbabwe amongst the ten countries most affected by extreme weather events. In addition, the 2021 German watch's Global Climate Risk ranked Mozambique first, Zimbabwe second, and Malawi fifth in the world's most affected countries, yet they are ranked 32nd, 108th, and 75th, respectively in relation to climate finance funds received (Mutizwa, 2023). These countries are some of the nations that were affected the most by the droughts that hit Southern Africa in 1992, Fall armyworm outbreaks in the mid-2010s, tropical cyclone Idai and Kenneth in 2019 (Mutsaka et al., 2019; Chesterman et al., 2020); and tropical cyclone Freddy in 2022 (Aderinto, 2023).

Tropical cyclones occur regularly in Mozambique and Malawi (Otto et al., 2022), and in the recent past, Zimbabwe has also been experiencing an increase in the frequency and severity of cyclones and tropical storms (Dembedza et al., 2022). The disastrous cyclones leave a trail of colossal destruction on property and infrastructure, massive displacements, devastating socio-economic impacts, and health risks (Tirivangasi et al., 2023). In Southern Africa, Mozambique is more vulnerable to cyclones between January and February (John & Vicente, 2020; Charrua et al., 2021). In 2019, certain regions in Malawi (Southern region), Mozambique (province of Sofala, Manica, Zambezia, and Tete), and Zimbabwe (Manicaland, Masvingo and Mashonaland East Province) suffered the devastating effects of tropical cyclones Idai and Kenneth (Chesterman et al., 2020; Odongo et al., 2022). Cyclone Idai and Kenneth happened within an unprecedented short period of about 1 month between them (Cook & Margesson, 2019; John & Vicente, 2020). The quick succession of cyclone Kenneth after cyclone Idai gave no room for recovery, trapping the affected areas to more wretchedness (Dembedza et al., 2022). The cyclones resulted in over 1300 deaths, displaced over 3 million people, affected millions of people and caused a humanitarian crisis across the three countries (Swain, 2021; Aderinto, 2023). In Mozambique, the cyclones resulted in over 600 deaths, displaced more than 17,000 people, and more than 2.2 million people were affected and required humanitarian assistance (Cubie, 2019; Canhanga et al., 2020; Muhala et al., 2021). Moreover, the cyclone destroyed more than 111,000 households (Hope, 2019). Out of the three countries, Mozambique suffered the most, in terms of human and economic losses (Kandawasvika et al., 2021).

Tropical Cyclone Idai is considered one of the most devastating natural disasters that has ever hit the region (Mavume et al., 2021). It caused unprecedented destruction of property and infrastructure (schools, towns and townships, roads, and bridges) to an estimated loss of around $274 million in Zimbabwe alone (Samutereko, 2021; Chikowore et al., 2019; Mutizwa, 2023). Cyclone Idai had adverse socio-economic impacts in all three countries, with damages and losses of more than $3 billion in Mozambique alone (Charrua et al., 2021; Mutizwa, 2023). The cyclone resulted in 344 recorded deaths, hundreds of reported injuries, hundreds of missing, and around 270,000 people were impacted in Zimbabwe (Chikowore et al., 2019;

Dembedza et al., 2022) (for further details on Cyclone Idai see Chap. 8 of this Book). In Malawi, it led to around 60 deaths, more than 670 injuries, displacement of more than 87,000 people, and almost a million affected people (Chikowore et al., 2019; Deprez & Labattut, 2020). Cyclone Idai is projected to have ruined crops covering hundreds of thousand hectares in Malawi, Zimbabwe, and Mozambique (Tevera et al., 2021), with a devastating impact on rain-fed agriculture (Macamo, 2021). In Mozambique, it had adverse effects on fisheries and aquaculture as almost 1500 fishermen of Sofala Province lost more than 160 fishponds, 67 boats, and 590 fishing vessels (Muhala et al., 2021). The governments of three countries, international and local NGOs collaborated in response to the crisis and the humanitarian situations created (Tevera et al., 2021).

Furthermore, from late 2021 to early 2022, the southern region of Malawi and the Sofala and Zambezia Provinces of Mozambique suffered the effects of cyclone Ana (Otto et al., 2022; Chaguza et al., 2023). In less than 2 months from the effects of cyclone Ana, Mozambique and Malawi were also hit by cyclone Gombe (Bagcchi, 2022; Adriano et al., 2023). For Malawi, Gombe is one of the largest cyclones ever recorded (Chaguza et al., 2023). Cyclone Ana alone resulted in 46 recorded deaths, displaced about 200,000 people, and affected almost a million people, with devastating damage and destruction to infrastructure and property in Malawi (Otto et al., 2022). As of March 2023, Malawi had reported 1578 deaths following cyclone Ana and Gombe in 2022 (Fischer, 2023). In Mozambique, it caused massive damage to almost 8000 homes, 23 water supply systems, 144 power poles, and roads (Otto et al., 2022). Moreover, cyclone Ana damaged 30 and 47 healthcare facilities in Mozambique and Malawi, respectively (Otto et al., 2022). Considering the foregone, significant scholarship indicates that cyclones have had major impacts on infrastructure across sectors. For example, in the health sector, in Mozambique and Malawi, cyclones have destroyed hospitals, resulting in challenges of accessing adequate healthcare services (Otto et al., 2022; Aderinto, 2023).

In 2023, the region was hit by another cyclone known as Tropical Cyclone Freddy (Aderinto, 2023). Cyclone Freddy was more severe in Malawi and Mozambique, with more devastating effects compared to cyclone Ana and Gombe combined. In Malawi alone, it resulted in the destruction of more than 83 health facilities, more than 600 deaths, and the displacement of almost 660,000 people (Adriano et al., 2023). Its effects had a compounded impact as it struck Mozambique and Malawi while they were combating a cholera outbreak (Aderinto, 2023). Moreover, following Cyclone Ana, Cyclone Gombe, and Cyclone Freddy, there was an increase in the number of cholera cases in Malawi. The reason was mainly that cyclones resulted in overcrowding and severe damage to water and sanitation systems, creating ideal environments for disease outbreaks (Bagcchi, 2022; Adriano et al., 2023; Chaguza et al., 2023). The displacement of people resulted in overcrowding, which put much pressure on Water, Sanitation, and Hygiene (WASH) facilities (Miggo et al., 2023), which also contributed to the cholera outbreaks. The dual burden of the effects of cyclones and the cholera outbreak placed Malawi in a Humanitarian crisis, forcing the country to seek assistance from various stakeholders and international organisations (Adriano et al., 2023). Thus, the three countries have experienced the devastating effects of cyclones and tropical storms in the past years, and floods are also common hazards.

The Southern African region is also prone to droughts due to diminishing rainfall patterns and extreme temperatures. The droughts have led to soaring levels of food insecurity for millions of people in the region. According to the International Federation of Red Cross and Red Crescent (IFRC) (2019), approximately 11 million people in Southern Africa were faced with food shortages and insecurity due to drought in 2019. Moreover, the availability of water is also a challenge due to droughts, causing livestock farmers to suffer losses due to lack of forage and drinking water for the animals. Malawi, Mozambique, and Zimbabwe are among the countries in the region prone to droughts. For example, the three countries were adversely affected by the 1992 drought that hit Southern Africa (Chesterman et al., 2020). In Mozambique, more than 1.3 million people were affected by food insecurity because of the drought (Chesterman et al., 2020), while in Zimbabwe, it was recorded as the worst and most devastating drought in living memory and recorded history (Samu & Akıntuğ, 2020; Maphosa, 1994) and in Malawi it affected 6.1 million people (Khamis, 2006). In Zimbabwe, the drought led to a 45% decrease in agricultural production and a 9% decline in manufacturing output, leading to a 11% drop in the GDP (Chesterman et al., 2020). As a result, Zimbabwe changed from having a food surplus to being a nation that imports food (Samu & Akıntuğ, 2020). In the subsequent years, severe droughts were further experienced in Malawi (Hamel, 2019) and Zimbabwe (Dembedza et al., 2022). For example, Zimbabwe experienced other severe droughts in 2002 (Dembedza et al., 2022), and in 2019 (Odongo et al., 2022), with the 2019 drought declared a national state of disaster by the government, as it resulted in severe crop yields decline, food insecurity, and an increase in food prices (Nyahunda & Tirivangasi, 2021; Odongo et al., 2022). Deprez and Labattut (2020) indicate that the drought left about 5.3 million people in need of humanitarian assistance and protection in Zimbabwe.

Temperatures have drastically increased in the Southern Africa region, particularly in the last two decades (Mafongoya et al., 2017; Kusangaya et al., 2014). Climate scholarship has shown that changes in climate have resulted in increasing temperatures and changing rainfall patterns in the past years in Southern Africa (Fitchett, 2021; Kusangaya, et al., 2014). Between 1961 and 2015, the mean annual air temperatures over the region increased by between 1.04 and 1.44 °C leading to a rise in very hot days over the last four decades, while cold extremes have declined in frequency (Trisos et al., 2022). For Fitchett (2021), extreme temperatures refer to extreme maximum/minimum temperatures that are a deviation from the norm over a longer-than-normal period. These come in the form of heat waves, and are dangerous to human beings, animals, and plants and may lead to deaths. In Southern Africa, the severity and frequency of these has been increasing. General projections indicate that the exposure to dangerous heat (over 40.6 °C) in most African cities will increase 20–52-fold compared to the historical periods. For Southern Africa, however, slower population growth and milder climate, will make the mean annual exposure of cities to dangerous heat conditions substantially lower than in other regions in the continent (Rohat et al., 2019). High temperatures often accompany drought, while particularly very hot days significantly increase the possibility of wildfires (Chesterman et al., 2020).

Furthermore, increases in temperatures and the resultant heatwaves sometimes result in an upsurge of pests, weeds, diseases, and decrease in water availability and quality. These impacts have dire consequences on crop yields, livestock, food availability, human health, and livelihoods (Mavume et al., 2021). In addition, Chesterman et al. (2020) indicate that heatwaves are a risk to human health in Southern Africa, as they can cause thermal stress. Although not so common, there has also been a notable increase in extreme cold temperatures in the region resulting in random incidences of snow in the most unlikely places.

During the 2015/2016 summer season, Central Zimbabwe and parts of Mozambique experienced over 70 °C more heat than expected. In Mozambique, one of the longest heatwaves was recorded in Tete Province during the summer of 2015/2016 (Meque et al., 2022). Marghidan et al. (2023), indicate that cities of Maputo, Beira, Nampula, and Tete have been exposed to more than 50 heatwaves between 1983 and 2016, and the number and duration of the heatwaves has increased significantly across the country.

Climate Change and Climate Security

Climate change often interacts with and exacerbates pre-existing challenges, which, compounded, may lead to heightened risks of violent conflicts or social instability (Smith & Vivekananda, 2009; Smith et al., 2021). The compounded pressure from increasing weather-induced disasters, continued marginalisation, and the socio-economic challenges related to poverty may increase social tensions and instability. This is even worse when governments fail to sufficiently respond to and meet the needs of their populations in humanitarian emergencies. In Southern Africa, climate change enhances the pre-existing economic, political, and security difficulties (Swain, 2021). Climate change is thus, a risk multiplier that may intensify conflicts and security risks in vulnerable contexts (Scheffran et al., 2019). This is mainly because Southern Africa is one of the regions that is adversely affected by the impacts of climate change (Hamel, 2019), and has a long history of violent political conflicts, high levels of poverty, and democracy deficits (Swain, 2021; van Nieuwkerk, 2012). For example, disasters and extreme weather events such as cyclones, droughts, and floods worsen food insecurity, poverty, and inequality, leading to heightened competition for resources. Relatedly, the adverse effects of extreme weather events on infrastructure often strain service delivery and reverse development strides that may have been registered, which in some instances may lead to conflicts over access to social services.

In addition, Smith et al. (2021) argued that climate change undermines political systems, weakens agricultural production, and worsens poverty levels. In this region, approximately 60% of the population live in rural areas and are dependent on rain-fed agriculture for food and livelihoods (Nhamo et al., 2018). Therefore, frequent climate change-induced disasters such as droughts and floods pose serious threats to the livelihoods and well-being of the population (Kamara et al., 2018). For example, Scheffran et al. (2019) indicate that regions highly dependent on rain-fed agriculture are more sensitive to civil conflict following droughts. In such contexts, human development and institutional processes are essential in strengthening conflict-sensitive adaptation and decreasing potential conflicts (Scheffran et al., 2019). Migration is one of the most common adaptation strategies to the compounded effects of climate change and other socio-economic factors in Southern Africa (Nzima & Maviza, 2023). However, although this may be a viable adaptation strategy, it also poses a challenge that may result in conflicts due to increased competition for basic needs, services, and livelihoods in host areas (Smith & Vivekananda, 2009; Kosec et al., 2022).

Therefore, climate-induced extreme weather events, together with other socio-economic factors worsen human security issues in Southern Africa (SADC, 2022). These lead to several structural drivers and triggers of instability and social unrest, especially in communities highly dependent on agro-based livelihoods (Raleigh et al., 2015; Morales-Muñoz et al., 2020). For example, in Malawi, Zimbabwe and Mozambique, climate impact-induced food insecurities have been shown to have far-reaching consequences (Maphosa, 1994). Some of these include an alarming rise in the likelihood of social tensions (Madurga Lopez et al., 2021). Within these countries, an increase in the intensity and frequency of droughts intensifies vulnerabilities, aggravates grievances, and increases the likelihood of social unrest (Ferré García et al., 2023). Compounded, these can potentially push local communities to engage in protests or natural resource disputes (Madurga Lopez et al., 2021).

Implications for the Humanitarian-Development-Peace Nexus

In the recent past, the world has been experiencing a surge in crises that have disproportionately affected communities and populations on the margins. According to Fanning and Fullwood-Thomas (2019), these crises have manifested through (1) a sharp rise in conflicts and conflict-related deaths, (2) intense climate-related shocks, and notable restrictions on personal freedoms and development opportunities driven by governance failures. To coordinate efforts to respond to these crises with urgency, the 2016 World Humanitarian Summit (WHS) adopted an approach that calls for a New Way of Working (NWoW) by leveraging on and linking the efforts of those working on humanitarian, development, and peace initiatives (Dūdaitė, 2018). Therefore, the NWoW embraces the humanitarian-development-peace nexus. The humanitarian-development-peace nexus creates opportunities to act expeditiously in a more holistic and simultaneous fashion in addressing inequalities and the needs of the marginalised (Barakat & Milton, 2020; Joireman & Haddad, 2023). Victims of crises who often require emergency relief are mostly the poorest in society. This is a reality that reminds us of the lived experiences of the marginalised and how structural inequalities and injustices manifest in our societies. Observing the most affected communities and the identity of their populations, also point to the reality that most of the crises are often a creation of inefficient and exclusionary development policies as well as inadequate investment in development (Fanning & Fullwood-Thomas, 2019). Therefore, the humanitarian-development-peace nexus can be deployed towards addressing systemic causes of humanitarian crises through emergency response and investing in long term development fostering positive peace. Given the political will and commitment from governments and other development actors, the humanitarian-development-peace nexus can minimise the recurrent shocks by creating stability which enables the achievement of sustainable development.

Most countries in Southern Africa inclusive of Malawi, Mozambique, and Zimbabwe that this chapter focuses on, still face challenges in meeting their developmental goals. Unfortunately, these countries are often faced with the need to respond to climate emergencies which usually cause a destabilising effect given their constrained resources (Scheffran et al., 2019; Chesterman et al., 2020; Samutereko, 2021). This highlights the need to have clear plans for responding to the climate crises all the while not diverting from their long-term development strategies (Fanning & Fullwood-Thomas, 2019; Joireman & Haddad, 2023). At present, there is little, if any, evidence that suggests that the humanitarian-development-peace nexus is being fully embraced, suggesting that humanitarian, development, and peace actors continue to operate in silos. However, there are practical implications that must first be emphasised for optimising the humanitarian-development-peace nexus, particularly in these three countries. The first consideration must be placed on the experiences of communities and their contextual realities which must be at the centre of all plans. For example, while all three countries have developmental and governance challenges, only Mozambique is currently facing military conflict that threatens peace in its Northern parts. On the one hand, Zimbabwe has been facing an economic crisis for over two decades which has also created an environment of political uncertainty resulting in disharmony that threatens national peace. While there is no armed conflict in Malawi and Zimbabwe, climate change creates conditions where competition for natural resources such as land and water between internally displaced persons (IDP) and locals can be sources of conflict (Barakat & Milton, 2020).

Therefore, this highlights the need to build in programming on peacebuilding such as, conflict resolution or prevention of conflict within development and humanitarian work during climate crises (Barakat & Milton, 2020; Joireman & Haddad, 2023). Given that these three countries regularly face climate crises such as those caused by tropical storms and cyclones as well as prolonged droughts, the humanitarian-development-peace nexus is even more relevant. However, looked at separately, the local experiences on humanitarian-development-peace are greatly varied between the three countries. Therefore, any humanitarian-development-peace nexus mix must be tailor made to meet the specific contextual needs of each country if it is to succeed particularly in responding to climate change and staying on course towards achieving long term development and peace objectives (Fanning & Fullwood-Thomas, 2019; Barakat & Milton, 2020).

For example, in Mozambique and Zimbabwe, extreme weather-related disasters destroyed infrastructure and led to intense food insecurity (Madurga Lopez et al., 2021). After cyclone Idai, affected populations were left without stable water, food, and energy supplies. The affected communities did not get sufficient humanitarian assistance to meet their immediate needs, and international aid stayed for too long with central government agencies or when distributed, it was not fairly distributed to the local areas. Moreover, the reconstruction efforts on the destroyed infrastructure were too slow and that sparked tensions within the communities. Similarly, in Malawi, corruption affected the flow of international aid as donors lost confidence in the government's ability to ethically respond to natural disasters and this generated social unrest (Banik & Chasukwa, 2016). Thus, when distribution of relief aid is compromised and development gains are slow after disasters, it can worsen existing inequalities and widen existing gaps and create a sense of injustice and marginalisation, aggravating grievances and undermining social cohesion and ultimately peace outcomes.

Another practical implication for a successful humanitarian-development-peace nexus is that institutions that command authority in any country must be engaged in driving processes and initiatives aimed at bringing relief during, and in anticipation of climate disasters (Fanning & Fullwood-Thomas, 2019). Therefore, it is crucial to identify and encourage participation from transformational actors within local governance structures. In many instances while governments are the main actors expected to drive the development agenda, most humanitarian and relief programming in response to climate disasters is driven by non-state actors and United Nations agencies. However, for effective programming, state actors must not be left behind because their coordination role is important in ensuring equitable distribution of resources and minimising duplication of roles and relief regimens. Equally, state actors, while driving the process, must leave room for all actors including local civil society and non-governmental organisations to come on board to maximise on the gains of the humanitarian-development-peace nexus through pulling resources together (Barakat & Milton, 2020).

Additionally, to maximise positive outcomes from the humanitarian-development-peace nexus working with multiple stakeholders, there is a need to centralise and be clear about who drives policy and technical direction on the general organisation and implementation of the nexus and its priorities (Fanning & Fullwood-Thomas, 2019). Governments can decide to take on this role if well capacitated; however, in the case of the three countries under review, it is not clear whether the government have adequate capacity, but they seem to be following the lead from UN agencies. Having clarity on who drives the policy direction is very important for ensuring clear and unambiguous coordination of programmes. Most importantly, to ensure the achievement of strategic outcomes there is a need for long term funding that is flexible to drive the implementation of the humanitarian-development-peace nexus (Barakat & Milton, 2020). The active role of government treasuries and development financing institutions in transforming the funding infrastructure cannot be emphasised enough. When Malawi was hit by the devastating floods because of cyclone Freddy in March 2023, a spotlight was cast on the global financing infrastructure as the country struggled to secure relief funding.

In addition, this highlighted the policy limitations for the country's long term development planning that considers climate disasters such as inadequate investment in early warning systems, emergency response systems, climate resilience, and adaptation programmes. While there is general agreement on the pressing need to realign the funding structures, the progress on this front has not moved at a desirable pace (Fanning & Fullwood-Thomas, 2019; Barakat & Milton, 2020; Joireman & Haddad, 2023). It is in this regard that conversations on climate coloniality through the uneven global funding infrastructure that perpetuates inequalities between the Global North and South have emerged.

Despite the many challenges in implementation, the humanitarian-development-peace nexus presents an opportunity to better coordinate humanitarian, development, and peace initiatives. There have been significant gains in moving communities affected by disasters and conflicts from perpetual dependence on relief (humanitarian aid) to building capacities for resilience (development), ensuring that households can self-sustain while also promoting peace. This is despite the concerns that the humanitarian-development-peace nexus can securitise humanitarian response and development initiatives. Most interventions implemented in affected communities using the humanitarian-development-peace nexus are anchored on food, land, and water systems, which are all climate sensitive. As such, climate-induced hazards and shocks may be detrimental to the gains made within the triple nexus, as the destruction of infrastructure, displacement of communities, water shortages, and low agricultural productivity, among others, keep communities in a vicious cycle of poverty and perpetual need for humanitarian assistance. It limits their capacities for resilience and compromises peace outcomes as they are pushed to compete for resources, thus eroding social cohesion and people's humanity. In view of the risks posed by climate change, it is important to embrace the humanitarian-development-peace nexus and fully cooperate towards optimising the strengths and opportunities that come with this new way of working.

As such, implementing climate capitalism within the humanitarian-development-peace nexus could widen societal disparities in Malawi, Mozambique, and Zimbabwe. While efforts are underway to address crises through this nexus, the emphasis on market-driven solutions might overshadow alternative approaches, such as regulatory measures or community-based strategies, which could offer fairer solutions (Ponte, 2019). The discourse on climate imperialism within the framework of climate capitalism underscores the need to reconsider how we approach climate change. There is a call to advocate for fairness, equity, and inclusivity in crafting solutions that genuinely benefit the environment and all segments of society—a concept described as "just sustainabilities" by Ponte (2019). Given these concerns, integrating the human development, disaster, and climate nexus becomes crucial to ensure that climate solutions do not inadvertently deepen inequalities and vulnerabilities within marginalised communities.

Looking Ahead

Given the current trends in climate change, it is clear that climate-related hazards and crises will continue in the foreseeable future. This is because climate change continues to be driven by anthropogenic activities, which release unprecedented amounts of greenhouse gases into the atmosphere. Although some solutions have been put in place to stop some of the activities responsible for extensive greenhouse emissions, a lot remains to be done to realise actual gains. For example, in the Global South, the efficacy of carbon sequestration as an example of measures to mitigate climate change by reducing greenhouse gas concentrations in the atmosphere remains a complex issue. In the Global South, where many countries face high vulnerability to climate change impacts and limited resources, the question of whether these regions can effectively implement and benefit from carbon sequestration strategies is a critical concern. Several challenges, such as financial constraints, technological limitations, and competing priorities for land use, may hinder the implementation of large-scale sequestration projects. Issues of land tenure, governance structures, and potential socio-economic impacts on local communities must be carefully considered to avoid exacerbating existing inequalities.

Moreover, in the context of climate imperialism, the future of climate change takes on a complex and often inequitable dimension. As the global community grapples with the consequences of a warming planet, the disparities in vulnerability and responsibility become glaring. Highly industrialised countries are the biggest contributors to greenhouse gas emissions and control the financial resources and technology to mitigate the impacts of climate change. However, they also inadvertently perpetuate climate imperialism by influencing and shaping international climate policies that prioritise their interests at the expense of the most vulnerable. This can lead to unequal distribution of adaptation and mitigation strategies, leaving vulnerable and less affluent regions disproportionately exposed to the harsh effects of the climate crisis. In the future, addressing climate change requires a commitment to global cooperation and justice, dismantling structures of climate imperialism to ensure that the burden of environmental challenges is shared equitably among nations, irrespective of their historical contributions to the crisis.

Conclusion

This chapter has demonstrated that climate change has devastating effects on economies by destroying infrastructure and adversely affecting food, land, and water systems. Over the years, significant gains have been made in Southern Africa on the humanitarian-development-peace nexus with notable advances from humanitarian to development-oriented assistance with peace-positive outcomes. However, the effects of climate change have significantly undone most of the gains as extreme weather events have led to extensive destruction of infrastructure and, in the process, weakening social protection and undermining social cohesion and stability. Climate change has kept communities in perpetual humanitarian relief mode characterised by precarity, hunger, and vulnerability. The repercussions of climate change extend beyond immediate environmental concerns. They disrupt people's livelihoods, trigger displacements, and fuel resource-based tensions, ultimately undermining the peace and stability fostered through various development initiatives. This underscores the challenge climate change poses not only to national governments but also international and local actors within the humanitarian-development-peace nexus, significantly impeding human security and overall development in Southern Africa. Moreover, the discourse on climate imperialism within the framework of climate capitalism emphasises the necessity to reassess our approach to climate change. Prioritising fairness, equity, and inclusivity in crafting solutions becomes imperative to safeguard both the environment and the diverse segments of society (Ponte, 2019). It becomes increasingly clear that comprehensive strategies prioritising sustainability and inclusivity, beyond market-driven approaches, are essential to build a more just and resilient future for the region.

Acknowledgements This work is carried out with support from the CGIAR Initiatives on Climate Resilience and Fragility, Conflict, and Migration. We would like to thank all funders who supported this research through their contributions to the CGIAR Trust Fund: https://www.cgiar.org/funders/.

References

Aderinto, N. (2023). Tropical Cyclone Freddy exposes major health risks in the hardest-hit Southern African countries: Lessons for climate change adaptation. *IJS Global Health, 6*(3), e0152.

Adriano, L. F., Nazir, A., & Uwishema, O. (2023). The devastating effect of cyclone Freddy amidst the deadliest cholera outbreak in Malawi: A double burden for an already weak healthcare system. *Annals of Medicine and Surgery, 85*(7), 3761–3763.

Bagcchi, S. (2022). Malawi takes on cholera outbreak amid cyclone devastation. *The Lancet Microbe, 3*(7), e480.

Banik, D., & Chasukwa, M. (2016). The impact of emerging donors on development and poverty reduction. In *Political transition and inclusive development in Malawi* (pp. 147–168). Routledge.

Barakat, S., & Milton, S. (2020). Localisation across the humanitarian-development-peace nexus. *Journal of Peacebuilding & Development, 15*(2), 147–163.

Canhanga, S., Munguambe, S., Chavango, H., & Macia, E. (2020). Impact of cyclone IDAI on the Hydrographic Services-The Case of Mozambique. *The International Hydrographic Review, 23*, 94–103.

Chaguza, C., Chibwe, I., Chaima, D., Musicha, P., Ndeketa, L., Kasambara, W., Mhango, C., Mseka, U. L., Bitilinyu-Bangoh, J., Mvula, B., & Kipandula, W. (2023). Genomic insights into the 2022–2023 Vibrio cholerae outbreak in Malawi. *Nature Communications, 15*(1), 6291. *medRxiv*, pp. 2023–06.

Charrua, A. B., Padmanaban, R., Cabral, P., Bandeira, S., & Romeiras, M. M. (2021). Impacts of the tropical cyclone Idai in Mozambique: A multi-temporal landsat satellite imagery analysis. *Remote Sensing, 13*(2), 201.

Chesterman, S., Neely, C., & Gosling, A. (2020). Historical analysis of climate change and agriculture events in the SADC region 1970–2020.

Chikowore, G., Nhavira, J. D., Munhande, C., Mashingaidze, T., & Sibanda, M. (2019). Natural disasters and development opportunities: Cyclone Idai, challenges, integration and development alternatives in Zimbabwe and sub-Saharan Africa in the New Millennium. *The Fountain: Journal of Interdisciplinary Studies, 3*(1), 1–14.

Cook, N., & Margesson, R. (2019). *Cyclones Idai and Kenneth in southeastern Africa: Humanitarian and recovery response in brief.* Congressional Research Service.

Cubie, D. (2019). Humanitarian Assistance and International Law (2018). *Yearbook of International Disaster Law Online, 1*(1), 409–418.

Dembedza, V. P., Chopera, P., Mapara, J., Mpofu-Hamadziripi, N., Kembo, G., & Macheka, L. (2022). Impact of climate change induced natural disasters on nutrition outcomes: A case of Cyclone Idai, Zimbabwe.

Deprez, S., & Labattut, E. (2020). Lessons learnt from CARE's shelter responses to Cyclone Idai in Malawi, Mozambique and Zimbabwe. https://www.dw.com/en/after-cyclone-idai-beira-has-found-itself-in-the-dark/a-48008877

Dūdaitė, G. (2018). *Humanitarian-development divide: Too wide to bridge?* (Doctoral dissertation, Masters Thesis, Aalborg Universitet).

Fanning, E., & Fullwood-Thomas, J. (2019). The humanitarian-development-peace nexus: What does it mean for multi-mandated organizations?

Ferre Garcia, T., Madurga Lopez, I., Sax, N., Liebig, T., Carneiro, B., Laderach, P. and Pacillo, G. (2023). How does climate exacerbate root causes of conflict in Zimbabwe? An impact pathway analysis. (Pending publication).

Fischer, N. (2023). Responding to the global cholera pandemic. *The Bulletin of the World Health Organization, 101*, 234–235.

Fitchett, J. (2021). Climate change has already hit Southern Africa. Here's how we know. *Global Citizen.*

Hamel, R. (2019). Drought-ravaged Malawi faces largest humanitarian emergency in its history. *Gates Open Research, 3*(504), 504.

Hope, M. (2019). Cyclones in Mozambique may reveal humanitarian challenges of responding to a new climate reality. *The Lancet Planetary Health, 3*(8), e338–e339.

International Federation of Red Cross and Red Crescent Newsroom. (2019, December 12) Southern Africa: Food crisis. Accessed December 16, 2019.

John, A., & Vicente, G. J. (2020). Institutional foundations of management of natural disasters: Lessons from the recent Cyclones in Mozambique.

Joireman, S. F., & Haddad, F. (2023). The humanitarian–development–peace Nexus in practice: Building climate and conflict sensitivity into humanitarian projects. *Current Opinion in Environmental Sustainability, 62*, 101272.

Kamara, J. K., Akombi, B. J., Agho, K., & Renzaho, A. M. (2018). Resilience to climate-induced disasters and its overall relationship to well-being in southern Africa: A mixed-methods systematic review. *International Journal of Environmental Research and Public Health, 15*(11), 2375.

Kandawasvika, G. Q., Thabethe, N., Dzangare, J., & Manangazira, P. (2021). Impacts of tropical cyclones Idai and Kenneth on public health in Southern Africa. In *Cyclones in Southern Africa: Volume 3: Implications for the sustainable development goals* (pp. 69–79).

Khamis, M. (2006). Climate change and smallholder farmers in Malawi. A report by ActionAid. ActionAid International, 1–8.

Kosec, K., Läderach, P., & Ruckstuhl, S. (2022). Fragility, conflict, and migration-proposal.

Kusangaya, S., Warburton, M. L., Van Garderen, E. A., & Jewitt, G. P. (2014). Impacts of climate change on water resources in southern Africa: A review. *Physics and Chemistry of the Earth, Parts a/b/c, 67*, 47–54.

Lim, K. S, K. T. C., Wang, J., Ayugi, B. O., Nooni, I. K., & Ongoma, V. (2021). Multi decadal variability and future changes in precipitation over southern africa. *Atmosphere, 12*,(6), 742.

Macamo, C. (2021). After Idai: Insights from Mozambique for climate resilient coastal infrastructure. *Policy Insights: African Perspectives-Global Insights, 110*, 1–22.

Madurga Lopez, I., Dutta Gupta, T., Läderach, P., & Pacillo, G. (2021). How does climate exacerbate root causes of conflict in Zimbabwe? An impact pathway analysis.

Mafongoya, P. L., Peerbhay, K., Jiri, O. & Nhamo, N. (2017). Climate scenarios in relation to agricultural patterns of major crops in Southern Africa. In *Smart technologies for sustainable smallholder agriculture* (pp. 21--37). Academic Press.

Maphosa, B. (1994). Lessons from the 1992 drought in Zimbabwe: The quest for alternative food policies. *Nordic Journal of African Studies, 3*(1), 6–6.

Marghidan, C. P., van Aalst, M., Blanford, J., Guigma, K., Pinto, I., Maure, G., & Marrufo, T. (2023). Heatwaves in Mozambique 1983–2016: Characteristics, trends and city-level summaries using high-resolution CHIRTS-daily. *Weather and Climate Extremes, 40*, 100565.

Mavume, A. F., Banze, B. E., Macie, O. A., & Queface, A. J. (2021). Analysis of climate change projections for Mozambique under the representative concentration pathways. *Atmosphere, 12*(5), 588.

Meque, A., Pinto, I., Maúre, G., & Beleza, A. (2022). Understanding the variability of heatwave characteristics in southern Africa. *Weather and Climate Extremes, 38*, 100498.

Miggo, M., Harawa, G., Kangwerema, A., Knovicks, S., Mfune, C., Safari, J., Kaunda, J. T., Kalua, J., Sefu, G., Phiri, E., & Patel, P. (2023). Fight against cholera outbreak, efforts and challenges in Malawi. *Health Science Reports, 6*(10), e1594.

Morales-Muñoz, H., Jha, S., Bonatti, M., Alff, H., Kurtenbach, S., & Sieber, S. (2020). Exploring connections—Environmental change, food security and violence as drivers of migration—A critical review of research. *Sustainability, 12*(14), 5702.

Muhala, V., Chicombo, T. F., Macate, I. E., Guimarães-Costa, A., Gundana, H., Malichocho, C., Hasimuna, O. J., Remédio, A., Maulu, S., Cuamba, L. & Bessa-Silva, A. R. (2021). Climate change in fisheries and aquaculture: Analysis of the impact caused by Idai and Kenneth cyclones in Mozambique. *Mozambique. Frontiers in Sustainable Food Systems, 5*, 714187.

Mutizwa, B. (2023). Climate change and human security in Zimbabwe. *Journal of Humanities and Social Sciences (JHASS), 5*(2), 53–64.

Mutsaka, B., Dlugosz, A., Kanike, B. G., Harris-Sapp, T., & Juillard, H. (2019). Real-time response review-DEC programme for cyclone Idai. *Synthesis Report*.

Nhamo, G., & Agyepong, A. O. (2019). Climate change adaptation and local government: Institutional complexities surrounding Cape Town's Day Zero. *Jàmbá: Journal of Disaster Risk Studies, 11*(3), 1–9.

Nhamo, L., Ndlela, B., Nhemachena, C., Mabhaudhi, T., Mpandeli, S., & Matchaya, G. (2018). The water-energy-food nexus: Climate risks and opportunities in southern Africa. *Water, 10*(5), 567.

Nyahunda, L., & Tirivangasi, H. M. (2021). Barriers to effective climate change management in Zimbabwe's rural communities. In *African handbook of climate change adaptation* (pp. 2405–2431). Springer International Publishing.

Nzima, D., & Maviza, G. (2023). Climate change and gendered migration patterns in Southern Africa: A review. In *Climate action in Southern Africa* (pp. 210–227).

Odongo, M. T., Misati, R. N., Kamau, A. W., & Kisingu, K. N. (2022). Climate change and inflation in Eastern and Southern Africa. *Sustainability, 14*(22), 14764.

Otto, F. E., Zachariah, M., Wolski, P., Pinto, I., Nhamtumbo, B., Bonnet, R., Vautard, R., Philip, S., Kew, S., Luu, L. N., & Heinrich, D. (2022). Climate change increased rainfall associated with tropical cyclones hitting highly vulnerable communities in Madagascar, Mozambique & Malawi. *Mozambique & Malawi, 41*.

Ponte, S. (2019). Green capitalism and unjust sustainabilities. *Samfundsøkonomen, 4*, 102–108.

Raleigh, C., Choi, H. J., & Kniveton, D. (2015). The devil is in the details: An investigation of the relationships between conflict, food price and climate across Africa. *Global Environmental Change: Human and Policy Dimensions, 32*, 187–199. https://doi.org/10.1016/j.gloenvcha.2015.03.005

Rohat, G., Flacke, J., Dosio, A., Dao, H., & Van Maarseveen, M. (2019). Projections of human exposure to dangerous heat in African cities under multiple socio-economic and climate scenarios. *Earth's Future, 7*(5), 528–546.

SADC. (2022). Synthesis report on the state of food security and vulnerability in Southern Africa 2022. Regional Vulnerability Assessment & Analysis Programme. Informing Resilient Livelihoods. Edited by SADC. SADC. Gaborone, Botswana.

Samu, R., & Akıntuğ, B. (2020). Pre-disaster planning and preparedness: Drought and flood forecasting and analysis in Zimbabwe. *Water Sa, 46*(3), 448–457.

Samutereko, E. Z. (2021). Disaster preparedness and response in Zimbabwe: The case of Cyclone Idai of March 2019 in Chipinge and Chimanimani. *Technium Social Sciences Journal, 21*, 877.

Sapinski, J. P. (2015). Climate capitalism and the global corporate elite network. *Environmental Sociology, 1*(4), 268–279.

Scheffran, J., Link, P. M., & Schilling, J. (2019). Climate and conflict in Africa. In *Oxford research encyclopedia of climate science*.

Smith, J. M., Olosky, L., & Fernández, J. G. (2021). *The climate-gender-conflict nexus*. Georgetown Institute for Women, Peace and Security.

Smith, D., & Vivekananda, J. (2009). *Climate change, conflict and fragility*. International Alert.

Solnit, R., Lutunatabua, T. Y., Solnit, D., & Sultana, F. (2023). Decolonizing climate coloniality. In *Not too late: Changing the climate story from despair to possibility* (pp. 58–65).

Swain, A. A. (2021). What issues arise from climate change in Southern Africa?

Tevera, D., Sibanda, M., Mamba, S. F., & Tivana, L. D. (2021). Assessment of cyclone Idai floods on local food systems and disaster management responses in Mozambique and Zimbabwe. In *Cyclones in Southern Africa: Volume 3: Implications for the Sustainable Development Goals* (pp. 59–68).

Tirivangasi, H. M., Nyahunda, L., Mabila, T., & Zingwena, T. (2023). Exploring Humanitarian response strategies in the aftermath of disasters induced by climate change in Zimbabwe. *Development Southern Africa, 40*(2), 313–328.

Tomaka, J., Lange, S., Gleixer, S., & Gornott, C. (2022) Climate risk profile: Zambia. Federal Ministry for Economic Cooperation and Development. Retrieved from https://agrica.de/wp-content/uploads/2022/08/GIZ_Climate-RiskProfile-Zambia_EN_final-1.pdf

Trisos, C. H., Adelekan, I. O., Totin, E., Ayanlade, A., & Efitre, J. (2022). Africa. In: H-O. Pörtner, D. C. Roberts, M. Tignor, E.S. Poloczanska, K. Mintenbeck, A. Alegría et al, (Eds.), *Craig Climate Change: Impacts, Adaptation and Vulnerability. Contribution of Working Group II to the Sixth Assessment Report of the Intergovernmental Panel on Climate Change*, (pp. 1285–1455). Cambridge: Cambridge University Press. https://doi.org/10.1017/9781009325844.011

Van Nieuwkerk, A. (2012). Towards peace and security in Southern Africa. *FES Peace and Security Series*, 6.

Gracsious Maviza, PhD, is a Research Scientist and the Southern African Regional Lead for the CGIAR FOCUS Climate Security Team at the International Centre for Tropical Agriculture (CIAT), one of the CGIAR research centres. She is also a Research Fellow in the Department of Sociology at the University of Free State, South Africa. Her research interest includes issues of migration, gender and inclusion, climate change, climate security, and livelihoods. She is also the co-founder of the Southern Women Academics Network (SWAN), a network inspired by her experiences and struggles as a female academic. Her chapter in this book was supported by CGIAR Initiative on Climate Resilience ClimBeR), and the CGIAR Initiative on Fragility, Conflict, and Migration (FCM). She would like to thank all funders who supported this research through their contributions to the CGIAR Trust Fund https://www.cgiar.org/funders/.

Divane Nzima, PhD, is a Senior Lecturer and Subject Head in the University of the Free State, Department of Sociology. He is an NRF-rated researcher who holds a Y2 rating. His research and teaching interests cut across various disciplines such as Sociology, Demography, and Development

Studies. He has published research on the intersection of migration and development, family dynamics and parenting, the wellbeing of the elderly in resource-constrained countries as well as artisanal mining and agricultural value chains. He has also taken an interest in political sociology with a keen interest on the nature and methods of political contestations to wield political power.

Siyaxola Enerst Gadu PhD, is a Climate, Peace and Security Specialist at the Alliance of Bioversity International and CIAT (ABC), which is part of CGIAR. He holds a PhD in Geography and Environmental Master's degree from the University of the Witwatersrand. His work experience includes 4 years of risk assessment in the insurance sector and a year of marketing in the agricultural industry. His research interests include environmental management, climate change adaptation, and climate change governance. The chapter where he is a co-author was carried out with support from the CGIAR Initiative on Climate Resilience (ClimBeR) and the CGIAR Initiative on Fragility, Conflict, and Migration (FCM). He would like to thank all funders who supported this research through their contributions to the CGIAR Trust Fund https://www.cgiar.org/funders/.

Ntobeko Ndlovu is a Research Fellow at the Institute of Development Studies of the National University of Science and Technology (IDS-NUST), Zimbabwe, and a PhD Candidate in Economics with the University of KwaZulu Natal. He holds a Master's Degree in Economics, specialising in Economic Development. His research interests include the economics of development, development finance, and climate finance, among others.

Part III
Global Health Crisis

Chapter 10
Vaccine Apartheid: An Indictment of Global Health System

Ephraim Chifamba

Abstract This chapter deploys Freire's Pedagogy of the Oppressed and the decolonial lenses to examine the linkage between capitalism and unequal access to COVID-19 vaccines. It argues that the public health sector has remained caught up in the global "vaccine apartheid" (gap in vaccine delivery between the global North and global South) which impedes inclusive delivery of health in the global South. Decolonial discussions have so far been limited to the area of political science and literature. Few studies have taken a systematic theoretical approach to the postcolonial discussions on the unequal delivery of COVID-19 medicines. To this end, the chapter proposes decolonization and deimperialization of the global health systems as viable options for addressing unequal access to drugs and vaccines between the global North and South.

Introduction

This chapter deploys Freire's Pedagogy of the Oppressed and the decolonial lenses to examine the linkage between capitalism and unequal access to COVID-19 vaccines. The public health sector has remained caught up in the global "vaccine apartheid" (gap in vaccine delivery between global North and global South) which impedes inclusive delivery of health in the global South. Decolonial discussions have so far been limited to the area of political science and literature. Few studies (Nissonke & Thorbecke, 2007; Matthewman & Huppatz, 2020) have taken a systematic theoretical approach to the postcolonial discussions on the unequal delivery of COVID-19 medicines. At the end of this chapter, decolonization and deimperialization of the global health systems are suggested as viable options for addressing unequal access to drugs and vaccines between the global North and South.

E. Chifamba (✉)
Rural and Urban Planning, Great Zimbabwe University, Masvingo, Zimbabwe
e-mail: echifamba@gzu.ac.zw

G. Moyo, S. J. Ndlovu-Gatsheni (eds.), *Global Storms and Africa in World Politics*, Global Power Shift, https://doi.org/10.1007/978-3-031-83868-2_10

Health apartheid has highlighted the global North's commitment to maintain the existing imperial status quo while relegating the global South's health system to collateral damage. To this, Sharpe (2016) argues that more often than not, the global health system is old wine in a new bottle. In this chapter, I provide evidence for holding this position. Navarro (2020) suggests that the objectification of the global South is driven by the materialist nature of the global health system and the "white savior complex" that humanity is a thing, and the global North owns it as an exclusive right. The current global health system is replete with numerous forms of colonial relics, ranging from ideologies and practices. Horton in his seminal work on *Its Time to End the Colonial Mindset in Global Health* pointed out that:

> Any Western medical institution more than a century old and which claims to stand for peace and justice has to confront the truth that its success was built on the savage legacy of colonialism. (Horton, 2023)

Thus, in order to fully decolonize the global public health system, systematic reforms must be taken that interrogate the fundamental assumptions of the global health system.

Global health is the latest de-historicized and depoliticized iteration of imperial linctus. Navarro (2020) posits that the "civilization agenda has been used as an excuse to advance neo-liberal programs". Furthermore, Roberts (2020) concludes that the biomedical "civilization project" endeavors to disassemble all medical and health systems of knowledge in the global South. In its place, the "civilization project" thrives to enforce colonial biomedical models. However, the global health system is often not understood within the context of avaricious global North's scientific initiatives, power dynamics, and modern imperial approaches that prioritize top-down global health programming and governance.

The COVID-19 pandemic showed existing inequities in the production and distribution of vaccines. McLaren (2020) states that pharmaceutical cartels and intellectual property rights regimes were promoted by the global North brought restrictions and shortages of COVID-19 vaccines in the global South. An abdication of such IP restrictions has been opposed by big pharmaceutical institutions from the global North. The vast majority of COVID-19 serums have been acquired by the global North (Ortega & Orsini, 2020) while countries in the global South have been compelled to wait for their turn; or, rely on the "generosity and benevolence" of the global North as they bequeath unused vaccines. Unfortunately, in Paulo Freire's (1994) words, "the oppressed internalize the image of the oppressor and adopt his guidelines, and become fearful of freedom."

The COVID-19 pandemic has exemplified how white hegemony, ableism, sexism, racism, and biocapitalism still persist as dominant and rationalizing lucidities for the global health sector. The administration of the COVID-19 pandemic indicates that colonial power is not simply a rarity event, but it has continued in a continuum that is modifying dimensions of supremacy to new forms of global health governance. Furthermore, while the delineations of capitalism were palpably clear in some cases of COVID-19 management, they also became concealed within the philanthro-capitalist arrangement.

Evolution of "Vaccine Apartheid"

Vaccination is perhaps the oldest and greatest deceiving instrument of the imperial agenda that even decolonialists regularly fail to identify. In this book, Ndlovu-Gatsheni and Moyo argue that Africa continues to exhibit fragility and vulnerability to global storms within a context in which it has consistently been made into an object rather than an agent of development. Within this context, Sharpe (2016) also posits that vaccination in the global South presents a benevolent appearance but has the soul of a fiend. The idealization of Western drugs veiled the real nature of the vaccination agenda (Ali et al., 2020). Freire's (1994) pedagogy of the oppressed exposes the accurate oddity of the hidden agenda behind the vaccination programs in the global South. Furthermore, Navarro (2020) and Roberts (2020) suggest that the evolution of immunization coincided with the growth of I-M-P-E-R-I-A-L-I-S-M, which is defined by McLaren (2020) as the Interposition of Monopolistic Power Exploiting the Resources of Impoverished Areas Leading to Increased Societal Misery.

The modern global health system and its overall designs is largely a creation of the global North. The global imperial architecture is explained by Ndlovu-Gatsheni (2013) who argues that:

> Global imperial designs, which have been in place since conquest by Western powers, did not suddenly evaporate after decolonization. Global coloniality as a leitmotif of the empire became the order of the day, with its invisible technologies of subjugation continuing to reproduce Africa's subaltern position, a position characterized by perceived deficits ranging from a lack of civilization, a lack of writing and a lack of history to a lack of development, a lack of human rights and a lack of democracy.

Global health has been delivered within the context of global coloniality of power and knowledge. Thus, global colonial design is a major challenge denying the global South space to create a conducive environment for inclusive vaccination programs. In Chap. 11 of this book, Chambiwa and Sakirai posit that the global South will find it difficult to wean itself from the yoke of vaccine dependence, which in turn affects its health systems.

With the advent of America as a superpower in the twentieth century, interlinkages between empire-building (Hudson &Mckittrick, 2014; Nissonke & Thorbecke, 2007) commerce (Levich, 2024) and the global public health system (Matthewman & Huppatz, 2020) were developed through numerous strategic mediating humanitarian organizations. These organizations used global public health to perpetuate the colonial socioeconomic and political architecture. While, significant progress was made to reduce tropical diseases and poverty (Sharpe, 2016), acts of munificence should not absolve global North and its agencies from liability for the obnoxious consequences of an unequal and questionable vaccination agenda.

Empire building and the need to find markets acted as an impetus toward the imperial vaccine agenda. During the beginning of the twentieth century, persistent economic challenges (Nunes, 2020) associated with mass vaccine production (Nissonke & Thorbecke, 2007) and consequent reduction in profits (Matthewman &

Huppatz, 2020) heightened the need to enlarge territories and markets. The proclivity toward annexation of countries to achieve global dominance by the global North became the major compelling factor for colonial expansion. Chilcote (2002) argues that colonization and primitive accumulation of resources were hidden behind the façade of "civilization" of colonized people or what Ortega and Orsini (2020) refer to as "colonial humanism."

The colonial agenda was affected by an increase in infectious diseases and deaths among the deployed civil servants, traders, and soldiers (Veracini, 2014). This challenge necessitated the development of medicines and vaccines that were financed by imperial powers. Nissonke and Thorbecke (2007) point out that vaccines were initially meant to protect individuals working for the imperialist power and ultimately for the entire inhabitants. Access to critical vaccines was structured in a form that exhibited a "caste system." However, Irogbe (2005) and Freire and Macedo (1987) suggest that higher mortality rate, lower life expectancy, and lower subjective health status were the major health outcomes of the caste system in the global South. In the same vein, Leroy (2016) discusses the expansion of the health system to include the colonized people within the context of huge profits derived from mass vaccination. However, the global South was made to believe that the expansion of the colonial health system was morally correct. In explaining the effect of accustomed oppression, Paulo Freire (1994) noted that:

> Conditioned by oppression to mistrust and undervalue themselves, the oppressed languish, submerged in the concrete reality of their oppression, thereby developing a false consciousness that is politically immobilizing.

Mass immunization was introduced as one of the major imperialist projects, despite the flawed reductionist idea behind them. Navarro (2020) raises a lot of questions about mass vaccination in the absence of appropriate useful and security confirmatory studies. The global North supported mass vaccination despite evidence of the adverse effects of various drugs on the health of the global South. Involuntary mass immunization programs have resulted in catastrophic consequences. For instance, Pradella (2014) notes that:

> … in the Philippines, before the United States took over in 1905, cases of death from smallpox increased remarkably. Furthermore, in Japan, after the introduction of compulsory vaccination between 1889 and 1908, 172,613 smallpox cases with 48,619 fatalities were recorded. The vaccination witnessed a 32 percent increase in death, thereby exceeding the death rate of the preimmunization era.

Vaccine apartheid and lower immunization rates in the global South have been well-documented in the previous pandemics. Regrettably, the global South has failed to mug up from historical errors resulting in history recurring in the context of the COVID-19 pandemic. If the lessons from history are to be learned, all stakeholders involved need to be reminded of their ethical duty and the fact that vaccine apartheid will further cause universal harm, which is not confined to the global South.

Post-World War Global Health Governance

The post-Westphalia sovereignty of 1648 was a turning point in the global health system. It fundamentally reshaped the global health framework by facilitating the emergence of a nascent transitional state, the proliferation of nonstate actors, and the decline of state power in the global South. World War II became another key transformative occasion of the twentieth century, with over 39.8 million deaths among Western Nations (Hudson & McKittrick, 2014). These two fundamental periods aligned public health philanthropy with the global North's colonial framework as liberal ideologies thrust "development" on the global South. Various foundations cooperated with allied agencies in funding numerous health projects meant to increase the extraction of raw materials while establishing lucrative markets for pharmaceutical products.

The Post-World War II Global Health Framework (GHF) was configured by both commercial security and the defense of domestic populations in the global North. For instance, the United States Institute of Medicine (USIM) designed programs to protect United States of America citizens (Irogbe, 2005). Furthermore, the institute asserted that the supply of new-fangled serums in the global South offered lucrative markets. The German Global Health Strategy also focused on the security of the German citizens and the commercial benefits of its export-oriented economy since 1945. The concept of global Health was configured from numerous imperial activities which began with the advent of "colonial medicine" and later transformed into Tropical Medicine.

The notion of Global Health Governance (GHG) was further popularized in the 1980s. The rapid expansion of the GHG as a system reflected the global North's interest in the collapse of the Soviet Union and the attainment of a unipolar world governance system. The global North wanted to diffuse the Soviet Union's influence while establishing ubiquitous supremacy to be exercised by various establishments of capitalism. Furthermore, in the early 1980s, the Structural Adjustment Programs (SAPs) decimated the global South's past investments in the public health sector. Global health governance strengthened with the neoliberal imposition of privatization, deregulation, and liberalization. The global South became incapacitated and weak in its attempt to deal with the health governance challenges.

The global North describes epidemics as unavoidable and disastrous to ensure interventions in the global South. This phenomenon started with the provision of medical facilities by the United States troops in Libya, Iraq, and Afghanistan and the Central Intelligence Agency's manipulation of vaccine campaigns in Pakistan to track down Osama Bin Laden. Leroy (2016) suggests that after the bombing of the Twin Towers between 9 and 11 September 2011, the global health framework was premeditated within the broader narrative of defense against terrorism. Global North's territorial insecurity provided a rare occasion to link international security to health. Western military forces began to be more organized as a rejoinder to emerging security threats. Western dominance and mediation in the health sector were glorified in the same manner as the Afghanistan "benign military intervention." Global private institutions such as Bill Gates and Merinda Foundation became instruments in the opaque global humanitarian health system.

The Bill & Melinda Gates Foundation (BMGF) is one of the biggest multinational institutions that is estimated to possess over 250 billion in assets (Thambisetty et al., 2022). The greater part of its global initiatives is devoted toward disadvantaged citizens of "imperialized communities." The bulk of their missions comprises malaria control, delivery of birth control medicines, and fighting communicable ailments. BMGF has become one of the influential philanthropic organizations which control global health governance. Bill Gates is the first private citizen outside government structures to give a keynote address at the World Health Organization's (WHO) general meeting of member nations. One representative at the WHO general assembly observed that: "Bill Gates is mollycoddled like a president, not only at the WHO general assembly, but also at other international meetings such as the G20." Another attendee at the same conference also retorted that "you can't cough, scratch your head or sneeze in the health sector without coming to the Bill Gates Foundation."

Furthermore, the BMGF exercises control not only through benevolent contributions to supra-territorial institutions but also through directing an ostentatious system of "partner institutions" including nongovernmental organizations, private institutions, and government agencies. The BMGF has become a leading benefactor to the United Nations' World Health Organization (WHO) and this has positioned it as a central player in the opaque worldwide health governance system.

The corporate hijacking of public health care among nations in the global South, with the complicity of the global North, deprives vulnerable persons of their right to equal access to health. The profit motive is the main enthralling issue in solving global health challenges. Deregulation, liberalization, and privatization of the health sector obliterated whatsoever residual reasonably priced basic needs accessible to the majority of the citizens in the global South. Under the guise of pecuniary expansion, big corporations have shattered community-empowering programs meant to alleviate poverty and promote health and climate robust interventions. This has subjected the global South to extreme social, physical, psychological, and biological stress. Under these conditions, infectious epidemics are destined to worsen.

Lessons from the COVID-19 Pandemic

The delivery of the COVID-19 vaccines to date is neither effectively planned nor inclusive. Pirtle (2020) posits that the global North is administering boosters whereas the rest of the global South has remained behind. Notwithstanding the urgent need to increase access to COVID-19 jabs, the global South has received inadequate vaccines from the international supply chain. Short (2023) provides a short and snappy analysis that:

> For instance, as of May 2023, out of more than 10 billion COVID-19 vaccine doses produced, Africa received around 610 million (approximately 6 percent of the COVID jabs, regardless of having 17.8 percent of the world's population). Approximately 310 million

> doses have been administered, leaving out 80 percent of Africans who have not been vaccinated. In other words, nearly 1.3 billion Africans have not been vaccinated and at the present inoculation rate, much of Africans may not receive the jab until 2024.

The disquieting geographical supply of COVID-19 vaccines further exposed the fallacy behind "COVID multilateralism" and "vaccine cooperation." Moyo and Moyo in Chap. 10 of this book suggest that there is a need to liberalize the vaccine supply chain and remove barriers to technological transfer. The global South should find alternative strategies for ensuring an inclusive future global health system. Without participation as equal partners in the global health ecosystem, the global South will remain behind.

The unequal supply of COVID-19 serums must be understood within the antique background of capitalism and the "othering" of the global South. Pirtle (2020) points out that recent BMGF and the Global Alliance for Vaccines and Immunization (GAVI) programs in the global South offer a case study in what is referred to as "pharmaceutical colonialism." For instance, COVID-19 financing mechanisms in Kenya raised borrowing costs and also increased debt interest bills (Zaman, 2024). This situation was common among most countries in the global South. The outcome of these structural bottlenecks resulted in an exclusive preoccupation with profit-making through vaccine manufacturing, distribution, and pricing at the expense of the humanitarian concern. The deliberate negligence of the global South provides a fertile ground for novel variants to emerge and spread, consequently contributing to new virus challenges in the future.

Distortions in the production distribution and pricing of COVID-19 serums created uncertainties in the supply chain among emerging economies. "Vaccine xenophobia" among high-income countries witnessed hoarding of available vaccines. It is within the context of unequal access to vaccines that Thambisetty et al. (2022) posit that:

> …apart from the ethical unfairness, the botches in the manufacturing and market supply were short-sighted. Without a significant and rapid increase in vaccine production and equitable global distribution, new COVID-19 variants will likely continue to emerge. Such variants may render existing vaccines less effective.

Furthermore, although Boris Johnson's ill-reputed statement that "let the bodies pile high in their thousands" (Smith & Judd, 2020) was unpleasant, it showed the tension that unfolded over the control and supply of COVID-19 vaccines across the globe. In effect, "vaccine xenophobia" is not just ethically inexcusable. Matthewman and Huppatz (2020) emphasize that the practice is clinically counterproductive, epidemiologically illogical, and self-defeating. In order to address the vaccine supply bottlenecks, Chabiwa and Sakirai in Chap. 11 of this book suggest that the global South should have its vaccine manufacturing industries and governments should prioritize the health sector.

COVID-19 vaccine manufacture, distribution, and access brought uncertainties across the globe. McLaren (2020) points out that those countries in the global South without COVID-19 vaccine manufacturing centers lack security of supply. Furthermore, Roberts (2020) highlights that among all countries in the global South, only India had adequate supply security during the year 2022. Numerous studies (Zaman, 2024; Houston, 2024; Torreele, 2024) reported a limited supply of COVID-19 vaccines between 2019 and 2023, with a devastating impact on the lives of people in the global South. Thambisetty et al. (2022) note that even in countries where the COVID-19 doses were manufactured, (for example, under the Johnson &Johnson-Aspen agreement in South Africa and Egypt), oodles of COVID-19 serums were exported to nations in the global North block.

From a purely economic point of view, the COVID-19 pandemic provided financial motivation for the monopoly of intellectual property rights. Manufacturers exhibited an immense penchant toward selling COVID-19 vaccines, as well as booster shots, to nations in the global South which could afford to pay the maximum charge, irrespective of the recipient nation's health requirements. Pecuniary securities clashed with what was expected to bring the COVID-19 pandemic to an end. Pirtle (2020) states that the average total fee of manufacturing the Astra-Zeneca COVID-19 vaccine was initially less than US$4, but a jab was sold at US$20. The "pandemic pricing" system yielded inequalities, upsetting the global South's access to the vaccines. Furthermore, pharmaceutical companies exercised unencumbered authority to decide which nation accessed COVID-19 vaccines and on what conditions.

The predacious competition in hoarding stockpiles of COVID-19 vaccines by the global North illustrated political and structural challenges that continue to perpetuate global health inequalities. Levich (2019) posits that in 2019, billions of medicines and associated provisions were required but delivery took a long period among most countries in the global South. The munificence of the global North came under strict scrutiny as doses of vaccines destined for the global South were destroyed because they became outdated during shipment (Wallace et al., 2020). The global north has resisted the lifting of pharmaceutical patents with negative ramifications on the health sector in the global South. The acts of charity from the global North are inadequate to set up the foundations for global health solidarity. In numerous ways, the conduct of the developed nations reflects a structure of imperial philanthropy, with no intention to modify the international regime of intellectual property rights.

Vaccine apartheid undermined national sovereignty in the sense that the global South breached drug control regulations and procedures in order to permit vaccinations into their countries. Smith and Judd (2020) note that big pharmaceutical companies such as Johnson & Johnson and AstraZeneca have a long history of piloting clinical trials in countries such as Kenya, South Africa, Nicaragua, and Zimbabwe among many other countries. However, some of the trials were conducted without the full consent and participation of local drug and medicine regulatory bodies such as the South Africa Health Product Regulatory Authority (SAHPRA) in South Africa, and the Pharmacy and the Poison Board (PPB) in Kenya (Horton, 2023). Thus, requisite procedures were grossly side-stepped under the excuse of dealing with a pandemic.

The Global North signed bilateral agreements with medical syndicates rather than acquiring the vaccines through the COVAX facility. This affected distribution and further entrenched vaccination disparities between the global North and South. The COVID-19 vaccine administration demonstrated that vaccine apartheid is a real construct that can be imposed in theory and practice upon nations against their will. Generally, citizens were immunized by governments, and deprived of their consensual approval. In order to control the spread of COVID-19, travelers were required to possess vaccination certificates prior to entry into the global North territories. Furthermore, the apartheid and nonmarket nature of vaccine production and distribution manifests in the abolition or disapproval of vaccines produced in the global South. For example, the Heberon Interferon-Alpha-2B produced in Cuba fell outside the COVAX Facility and hence was discriminated and debarred against in the global North. This is despite the fact that Cuba has been a member of the World Trade Organization since its launch.

The allotment of surplus COVID-19 vaccines, only once the global North had copiously met the internal requirements, altered the dream of international unity and collaboration into an altruistic project. Rather than use a supply model founded on justice, the global North utilized the COVAX arrangement as an instrument to dispose of their excess vaccines. The global North frequently reserved those handouts to certain nations for soft-power purposes, bypassing COVAX's transparent and ethical supply procedures. Thus, the global North destabilized COVAX and its initial values, thus reducing it into what Brown and Rosier (2023) in COVID-19 *Vaccines Apartheid and Failure of Global Cooperation* refers to as "a logistical body rather than an instrument of global equity."

Access to COVID-19 serum was turned into a political brokering tool. India, Japan, Russia, China, and Belarus used access to COVID-19 injections to build and strengthen ties with both foes and friends. However, Torreele (2024) suggests that the persuasion through the soft power of COVID-19 vaccines showed remarkable improvement compared to the use of military force. It is vital to note that the power inequities in these agreements cannot be overlooked. Zaman (2024) posits that:

> On one side is a low-income country snubbed by countries with higher incomes, facing a worsening pandemic and tired of waiting for COVID-19 vaccine doses, and on the other are large countries that have nationalist political agendas.

Stevano et al. (2021) further states that:

> The public health community's mantra for coping with COVID-19 encapsulates the systemic neglect of those living in poverty. The pithy advice to "stay home, socially distance, wash hands, and see a doctor in case of fever" highlights the plight of the vast numbers who can do none of these things. They have no home in which to shelter, no food stockpiles, live in crowded and unsanitary conditions, and have no access to clean water or affordable medical care. Far from being the great leveler, COVID-19 is a pandemic of poverty, exposing the perilous state of social safety nets for those on lower incomes or in poverty in the global South.

The COVID-19 vaccines are gradually considered global security chattels and resolutions concerning their usage have moved from health establishments to the central state institutions. The global North has militarized the manufacturing and distribution of COVID-19 vaccines to the detriment of people in the global South.

Furthermore, the COVID-19 pandemic has shown bewildering myths propagated in the prepandemic worldwide public health ecosystem. The misconception that pandemics and epidemics emerge from the global South and spread to the global North has been proved to be a futile attempt by the global North to allot the blame on emerging economies. The global South's "fragile economies" were linked with weaker public health systems and, consequently, more public health threats.

Toward Inclusive Future Global Health Systems

The global health system is an unjust scheme that lugs forward the relic of colonialism. Existing global North-South partnerships in the health sector benefit the global North. The resources provided by the global North bypass state health systems in most countries in the global South. Thus, the current health system has reproduced disparities in access to and utilization of COVID-19 vaccines. Unfortunately, the Paris Declaration on Aid Effectiveness and the Accra Plan of Action failed to address existing bottlenecks. Thus, there is a need to search for viable options to ensure an inclusive future global health system.

The global health collaboration should be founded purely on human rights-based approach and sound ethical beliefs. This should be premised on shared responsibility designed to guarantee equitable global supply of vaccinations without prioritizing some nations over others on the basis of geographical location. To achieve this, countries should reduce the power of private pharmaceutical institutions, control the enormous civic investments, and treat vaccines as public rather than private goods. Furthermore, the global South should be afforded a greater voice. There is also a need for states and regional bodies to enact enforcement mechanisms that promote the sharing of vaccines in the spirit of international solidarity.

A robust global health system is required to prevent the hoarding of vaccines by the global North, while the global South goes almost unvaccinated, as was the situation since 2019. The delivery of vaccines should be rule-based and transparent as compared to the COVAX facility, which was designated by the global North as a mechanism for "politicized benevolence." Needs-oriented facilities founded on the basis of sovereign impartiality should be designed. The COVID-19 era illustrated that aid protects lives, but according to Bajaj (2022) and Levich (2024), it embodies an inept, "painkilling" temporary amelioration rather than a viable durable strategy. Confronted with local cynicism, the global North should navigate through competing needs of selfishness by clarifying the choices to their populations and convince them of the durable option from both an ethical standpoint rather than yielding to elitist public beliefs. A global North-South win-win situation that balances global and national responsibilities for the common good is required urgently.

With COVID-19, lacking the capacity to produce its own serums has left the global South reliant on external brokers and, as a result, disproportionately affected by vaccine nationalism and instabilities in global vaccine supply chains. In turn, these challenges affected the global South's capacity to implement their vaccine rollout plans, safeguard their citizens, and in the end, rejoin the global economy. Thus, the development of medical research and innovation capacity and synchronization of vaccine registration and protocols in order to conform to the best international practices are critical factors which should be addressed. Institutions such as the African Vaccine Acquisition Task Team (AVATT) should not operate outside existing frameworks and governance systems. They should work within the confines of local legislative frameworks in the global South. Furthermore, the fight against corruption should be at the center of inclusive health provision in order to avoid resource leakages.

The global South has presented COVID-19 "vaccine equity" as a progressive step toward decolonization of the global health system. However, in the case of COVID-19, the decolonization agenda seems to be more worried about present disparities in terms of access to vaccines between the global North and South. In the process, the decolonial agenda has ignored the difference between *access to COVID-19* vaccines (as a broad challenge in the international health system) and *access to the correct vaccines* (a mediation that advances overall global health justice). The COVID-19 and COVAX vaccines have apparently become a battleground for the fight over vaccine access. However, the global South has failed to realize that access to vaccines should mirror the wants and anticipated health outcomes.

Conclusion

This chapter argues that justice and equity were not, and are not, the objective of the global health system regardless of the catholic utopic imprint of the health justice programs within the global health sector. The global health system has reproduced the colonial vintages of racism, white supremacy, sexism, and biocapitalism. This has created global North-South power dynamics that forecloses the capacity to realize global health equity. Equitable serum production and supply that does not debase people in the global South is long overdue. A de-colonial slant to the global health system requires a far-reaching paradigm shift. This includes undoing a euro-centric imperial approach that thrives to maintain and sustain racist, capitalist, and white supremacist structures of power. Thus, the time is now for the global South to reimagine, develop, and implement inclusive de-colonial global health systems that cater to the previously marginalized populations. Future studies can evaluate the lessons learned from the failure of global North-South collaboration to preclude COVID-19 vaccine apartheid.

References

Ali, S., Asaria, M., & Stranges, S. (2020). COVID-19 and inequality: Are we all in this together? *Canadian Journal of Public Health, 111*(3), 415–416.

Bajaj, S., Maki, L., & Stanford, C. F. (2022). Vaccine apartheid: Global cooperation and equity. *The Lancet., 399*(10334), 1452–1453. Retrieved July 1, 2023, from. https://doi.org/10.1016/S0140-6736(22)00328-2

Brown, S., & Rosier, M. (2023). COVID-19 vaccine apartheid and the failure of global cooperation. *The British Journal of Politics and International Relations, 25*(3), 535–554.

Chilcote, R. H. (2002). Globalization or imperialism? *Latin American, Perspectives, 29(6), 80–84.*

Freire, P. (1994). *Pedagogy of hope*. Continuum.

Freire, P., & Macedo, D. (1987). *Literacy: Reading the word and the world.* Bergin & Garvey.

Horton, R. (2023). *The COVID-19 Catastrophe. What's gone wrong and how to stop it happening again?* Polity Press.

Houston, A. R. (2024). *Pandemic, public health and the regulation of borders*. Routledge Press.

Hudson, P. J., & McKittrick, K. (2014). The geographies of blackness and anti-blackness: An interview with Katherine McKittrick. *The CLR James Journal, 20*(1), 233–240.

Irogbe, K. (2005). Globalization and the development of underdevelopment of the third world. *Journal of Third World Studies, 22*(1), 41–68.

Leroy, J. (2016). Black history in occupied territory: On the entanglements of slavery and settler colonialism. *Theory & Event, 19*(4).

Levich, J. (2019). Global health and US imperialism. In I. Ness & Z. Cope (Eds.), *Encyclopedia of imperialism and anti-imperialism*. Palgrave Macmillan.

Levich, J. (2024, November 2). The real agenda of the Gates Foundation, Liberation News.

Matthewman, S., & Huppatz, K. (2020). Sociology of COVID-19. *Journal of Sociology, 56, 19–39.*

McLaren, J. (2020). *Racial disparity in COVID-19 deaths: Seeking economic roots with census data (Report No. 27407).* National Bureau of Economic Research.

Navarro, V. (2020). The consequences of neoliberalism in the current pandemic. *International Journal of Health Services: Planning, Administration, Evaluation, 50*(3), 271–275.

Ndlovu-Gatsheni, S. J. (2013). *Empire, global coloniality and African subjectivity* (Vol. 288). Berghahn Books.

Nissonke, M., & Thorbecke, E. (2007). Channels and policy debate in the globalization-inequality-poverty nexus. *World Development, 34*(8), 1338–1360.

Nunes, J. (2020). The COVID-19 pandemic: Securitization, neoliberal crisis, and global vulnerabilization. *Cadernos de SaúdePública, 36*(5), 1–4.

Ortega, F., & Orsini, M. (2020). Governing COVID-19 without government in Brazil: Ignorance, neoliberal authoritarianism, and the collapse of public health leadership. *Global Public Health, 15*(9), 1257–1277.

Pirtle, W. N. L. (2020). Racial capitalism: A fundamental cause of novel coronavirus (COVID-19) pandemic inequities in the United States. *Health Education & Behavior, 47*(4), 504–508.

Pradella, L. (2014). New developmentalism and the origins of methodological nationalism. *Competition & Change, 18*(2), 180–193.

Roberts, S. E. (2020). I can't breathe: Race, violence, and COVID-19. *Annals of Surgery, 272*(3), e191.

Sharpe, C. (2016). *In the wake: On blackness and being*. Duke University Press.

Short, J. (2023). Bio-political economies of the COVID-19 pandemic. *TOPIA: Canadian. Journal of Cultural Studies, 41.*

Smith, J. A., & Judd, J. (2020). COVID19: Vulnerability and the power of privilege in a pandemic. *Health Promotion Journal of Australia, 31*(2), 158–160.

Stevano, S., Franz, T., Dafermos, L., & Waeyenberge, E. V. (2021). COVID-19 and the crises of capitalism: intensifying inequalities and global responses. *Canadian Journal of Development studies, 42*(1), 1–14.

Thambisetty, S., McMahon, A., McDonagh, L., Kang, H., & Dutfield, G. (2022). Addressing vaccine inequity during the covid-19 pandemic: The trips intellectual property waiver proposal and beyond. *The Cambridge Law Journal, 81*(2), 384–416.

Torreele, E. (2024). Tackling vaccine inequality in 2023: Have we made progress? *Expert Review of Vaccines Taylor and Francis, 23*(1), 1–4.

Veracini, L. (2014). Understanding colonialism and settler colonialism as distinct formations. *Interventions, 16*(5), 615–633.

Wallace, R., Liebman, A., Chaves, L. F., & Wallace, R. (2020). COVID-19 and circuits of capital. *Monthly Review, 72*(1), 1–15.

Zaman, K. (2024). Decolonising human rights law in the global health-the impacts of intellectual property law on access to essential medicines: A perspective from the COVID-19 pandemic. *Asian Journal of International Law, 19*(1), 1–18.

Ephraim Chifamba is an Associate Professor and lecturer in the department of Rural and Urban Planning at Great Zimbabwe University. He has several qualifications in Development studies, Rural development, and Project monitoring and evaluation. He has published numerous book chapters and papers in refereed journals. Prof Chifamba has vast research interests in sustainable development, decolonization, and rural livelihoods. He is currently editing a book titled: *Building Sustainable and Resilient Rural Communities in Southern Africa*

Chapter 11
Vaccine Imperialism

Chambiwa Elijah and Sakirai Gift

Abstract The exploitative transnational corporations are the ones producing vaccines, supposedly to save Africans from the COVID-19 pandemic. The West is not prepared to relinquish its hegemonic stranglehold on the global stage with vaccine production and distribution being a case in point. Resultantly, the Global South will always depend on the West for the sustenance of its health institutions. However, African efforts are being demonized and dismissed as frivolous undertakings, and an apt example is the Madagascan herbal cure for COVID-19 which was summarily dismissed, not necessarily because it was unsafe but because of vaccine imperialism which is being perpetrated by the Western world. The West wants to monopolize and certify everything because it does not want to be outflanked. Such behaviors point to the evidence of neo-imperial Western fundamentalism wherein everything African is demonized and dismissed.

Introduction

In recent years, the world has been reeling from the dire health crises which the COVID-19 pandemic wrought into existence. This scenario has brought to the fore the economic divide that exists between the West and the Global South. The geopolitical landscape between the two has always been fraught with incessant roguery which is primarily premised on racism and capitalistic practices whose roots can be traced back to colonialism. As such, an "us versus them" mentality has been

C. Elijah (✉) · S. Gift
Humanities and Social Sciences, Marymount Teachers College, Mutare, Zimbabwe

Languages, Marymount Teachers College, Mutare, Zimbabwe

Education, Marymount Teachers College, Mutare, Zimbabwe

G. Moyo, S. J. Ndlovu-Gatsheni (eds.), *Global Storms and Africa in World Politics*, Global Power Shift, https://doi.org/10.1007/978-3-031-83868-2_11

apparent in modern day global trends where the so-called advanced countries (the West) have persistently viewed the so-called developing countries (Africa and Asia) as "the Other" whose existential continuity is hinged upon the West's generosity and paternalism. This has led to the dehumanization of Africans in general and the Global South in particular. It is from this ideologically skewed background that the world fell into the clutches of the fore mentioned virulent COVID-19 pandemic which ran riot and killed people in their thousands. The existential uncertainty and angst which this scenario generated resulted in the hoarding of COVID-19 vaccines the moment that they became available. Incidentally, the wealthy Western countries created a capitalistic financial world order where profit takes precedence over human lives. COVID-19 nationalism came into being, and the Global South, being financially incapacitated due to the recession that followed, was left exposed without any form of protection.

Blackness and the Negation of Being

The centuries-old subjugation of the so-called people of color has primarily been predicated on a three-pronged system which entails language, race, and epistemological conceptions. These three factors have invariably been used to make the black race voluntarily defer to Western ontological precepts. For instance, language has been used as a tool for subjugation through making black people wish that they were white. Fanon (2008:8) underscores this fact when he posits that:

> To speak means to be in a position to use a certain syntax, to grasp the morphology of this or that language but it means above all to assume a culture, to support the weight of a civilization.

The above quote highlights how language can be used as a tool in the subjugation of a people. This brings to the fore the extent to which linguistic imperialism has embedded itself within the African land space and the need for a nomenclature and ideological perspective that is tailor-made for the African context. WA Thiongo (1994), in his seminal work entitled *Decolonizing the Mind*, calls for the renunciation of European languages for the decolonization process to be effective. Likewise, Fanon (1963:37) brings this out in his book entitled *The Wretched of the Earth* when he avers:

> Decolonization…influences individuals and modifies them fundamentally. It transforms spectators crushed with their inessentiality into privileged actors with the grandiose glare of history's floodlights upon them. It brings a natural rhythm into existence…and with it a new language and a new humanity.

Besides that, race has also been employed as a tool in the subjugation of black people the world over. DuBois (2008:1) underscores this fact when he asserts that the problem of the twentieth century is the problem of the color line. Though he limited his scope to the twentieth century, Dubois' assertion brings out the contentious nature of race and how it has been used to confer a degree of superiority by one race (whites) over another (blacks). Hence, for DuBois, the world is an essentially racialized entity. Incidentally, Ashcroft et al. (2007:33) have termed this phenomenon chromatism: which refers to the essentialist distinction between people on the basis of color. In line with the above, in his book *Black Skin White Masks*, Fanon (2008:9) argues that:

> The colonized is elevated above his jungle status in proportion to his adoption of the mother country's cultural standards. He becomes whiter as he renounces his blackness, his jungle.

This outlines the link that exists between race and subjugation. Since the white race is considered as the norm, the relegation and subsequent negation of all things black is a foregone conclusion. Lastly, as was highlighted earlier, the subjugation of black people is also premised on epistemological conceptions. Western knowledge systems take precedence over all other forms of knowledge. This fact is underscored by Sardar (2008: xv–i) who argues that:

> ...western history not only writes cannibalism in the very chromosomes of the non-West. History, both History of the West and History as perceived by the West, is transformed into a mighty river into which all the other histories flow and merge as mere minor and irrelevant tributaries.

This highlights how Western conceptions of knowledge have been used as a hegemonic tool in the subjugation of black people. It is at the backdrop of these three factors that we can understand the current form of self-loathing that is gripping black people in the contemporary world. So effective has been this centuries-old cultural distillation that most black people have utterly renounced their cultural heritage, language, and sense of national belonging. Incidentally, Fanon (2008:35) avers that we must see whether it is possible for the black man to overcome his feeling of insignificance. The monopoly of the Western nations over the epistemic space contributes to global storms.

Autochthony Titling as Conferment of Identity

In the Global South, land as a synecdoche of power has wrought a lot of polarization and animosity among different demographics. This has resulted in a lot of infighting, brickbats, and violence. In a bid to control land, this contestation has led to the acute racialization of the geopolitical African land space. As such, this power struggle has been extended to the health sector where the Western nations have unilaterally hoarded vaccines and have enacted innumerable machinations in a bid to legitimize, contest, or delegitimize opposing narratives. This contestation has created an environment that is inimical to any meaningful development. Various Western countries have tried to entitle themselves to the needful vaccines by whatever means. Colonial powers created extractive, resources based economies rather than building health, education, and other systems needed for Africa's sustainable development.

Within the Global South historical continuum, this was attempted through intoning autochthony, nomenclature, and titling as conferment of identity by the former colonial powers. With regard to autochthony, the erstwhile settler governments used it as a justification for acquiring land and subsequently dehumanizing the people who had subsisted in those land spaces for centuries.

This outlines how autochthony was used by the colonial regimes to justify their acquisition of the African land space. By asserting that both blacks and whites had no claim to indigeneity, the colonial regimes intended to rob the blacks of any claim to the countries. Hence, the settler regime entrenched itself into the African historical space and then bolstered it by coming up with racialized nations. Conversely, black Africans have always maintained and still maintain that the land is theirs by right; hence, they have always heavily contested the white people's assertions with regard to whom and what constitutes indigeneity. This has always culminated in the global storms across the globe.

Scholars from this camp have attacked the imperialistic tendencies of the settler regime and have also invariably termed them racist. Mugabe (2001:71) posits that:

> …We seek to complete the realisation of the objectives of our just struggle by dismantling everything that attenuates our sovereignty and sovereign right to our heritage and resources, principally land; by empowering our people through greater say and control over our resources: indeed by challenging a political economy which yields a two race nation, yields a colonial white leisure employer class while the black majority wallows in poverty, serfdom and indigence.

With this in mind, it may be duly noted that people in the Global South have been at the receiving end of the West, a state of affairs that they have been trying to do away with.

Curtailed African Agency

Coupled with the above discourse is also the apparent lack of agency that is invariably evident in the Global South, which is also a direct result of the skewed nature of the existential interface that has always subsisted between the West and the Global South. This lack of agency and resultant self-hate stem from overwhelming disempowering thought patterns whose incidence inevitably culminates in acute xenocentrism. This self-hate and intense desire to gravitate toward all things white may be termed the black curse.

The foregoing show of apparent self-hate among Africans is the ideological precipitate of a decades old existential distillation that has been taking place over time in most black people's lives who have also lived in arguably one of the most tumultuous epochs of their respective nations and the world at large with regard to race and identity in a world that is increasingly becoming one village. One may hazard to make the above declaration because despite assertions to the contrary, issues pertaining to race and identity have invariably pervaded the news and international fora the world over. These issues have ranged from never-ending xenophobic attacks in South Africa to race riots in the United States due to alleged police brutality to the land upheavals in Zimbabwe. It seems as if the question of identity has taken primacy over most other issues at the present moment. The question has manifested itself through a seemingly aggressive assertion of nationhood in the West, a phenomenon which has been played out through stringent anti-immigrant laws in countries like Australia, New Zealand, the United Kingdom, and the United States, among other countries.

These countries have brought forward so many reasons for their anti-immigrant stance which range from economic protectionism to fear of terror attacks. Recently, these countries, along with many others in that region, have added health reasons for their stringent anti-immigration laws due to the COVID-19 pandemic. Incidentally, it should be noted that the people who have been mainly targeted by the fore mentioned laws have been predominantly Africans, black Africans to be precise. Most whites find it considerably easy to move around the globe as long as they have the economic wherewithal to do so. Conversely, black people always have to overcome a plethora of odds despite the state of their finances. It seems as if there is an implicit consensus among Westerners that black people are a liability which must be eschewed at all costs.

Hence, one may argue that the beliefs of yester year about the superiority of the white race still persist even in the twenty-first century though it is no longer being broadcasted from rooftops. In the Global South, the situation is the same. Generally, its geophysical space is still racially configured. There are basically white areas and black areas and no gray area. There are no interracial interfaces, and the few that exist are purely in official settings where peremptory socialization is evident. Ideologically, black people are still second class citizens in their countries of birth. This is despite the fact that as a people, we have reclaimed our land, indigenized most companies, and come up with curricula that are hyped to be among the best in the world which also happens to have Afrocentric underpinnings.

All the above notwithstanding, black Africans still grovel in the presence of a white person. It should be noted that this phenomenon is not confined to the poor rustics who are still suffering from the colonial hangover which inculcated a thoroughgoing inferiority complex in them. Rather, sophisticated graduates who work in high paying jobs still regard white people with awe and are willing minions of the great white civilization. This group is always ready to point out how African countries have gone to the dogs and compares the progress that was achieved under colonial rule with the situation that is obtaining on the ground. They usually end their musings with the assertion that black people are naturally inferior to whites. As such, they argue that it is the white people's God-given right to rule over other races, particularly the black race.

One then wonders what would make someone hate themselves to this extent. Granted, most people are bitter due to the high rates of unemployment and corruption that are gripping most African nations along with the impunity that certain sections of our nations operate under. Admittedly, this might stir a lot of anger against our governments, but to forgo one's existential prerogative over a perceived sense of injustice! To really hate one's entire sense of being and wish to be someone else is really a tragedy, and the pity is this feeling has gripped most of the populace in the Global South, whether young or old. Resultantly, such sentiments have percolated into the cultural myth-pool from which we all drink as a people. We have come up with a lexicon that negates our sense of being and virtually relegates us to the periphery of culture and progress.

For instance, in Zimbabwe, any wrongdoing on the part of a black friend is usually surmised by the Shona phrase *Mabhoyianonetsa* (boys are a problem) which is a vestigial relic of the colonial period where all black men were referred to as boys irrespective of their age. Similarly, any problem that comes up in the social sphere is termed *chibhoyi* (African spiritualism), serving to underscore the evil that black culture and heritage is supposedly naturally adorned with. Likewise, anything good in life is termed *chirungu* (Western), and even a black person who is rich or doing relatively well is called *murungu* (White person).

All this serves to bring out the sense of superiority and high pedigree that white culture is conferred with and the disdain and distaste that black culture is viewed with.

Idioms of Exclusionary Memory

Language is arguably the most potent instrument that humans invariably use to make sense of their environment. We negotiate meaning through the use of language, and we interrogate, adapt to, navigate, and manage our diverse societies through language. It is the instrument which we use to construct meanings in our societies, and nationally, language encapsulates our aspirations, values, mores, and history. It is through language that we reach into the distant past and get a communal experience with our forebears. It goes without saying that without a language, a nation is doomed to fail and its people will lack an ideological foregrounding and historicity. Such a nation will be one in which people live in the moment without a philosophical cauldron within which they can place their heritage based nuggets of knowledge. Resultantly, such kind of a nation is bound to fail.

In our case, the Global South has got languages which are rich in idioms, proverbs, and heritage based knowledge which ensured the continuity of our nations up to the present. Be that as it may, that firm foundation of faith in our languages was shaken at the advent of colonization. We were taught to look down upon our indigenous knowledge systems and languages with utter disdain that borders on revulsion. Nowadays, most Africans gravitate toward the European languages of their erstwhile colonial masters even when they aren't obliged to do so. Some people even initiate their toddlers into foreign linguistic pools, and all this does is to alienate that toddler from his/her sociocultural milieu which creates a citizen with a tourist mentality in adulthood. Such people never really feel as if they belong to their country and are always eager to escape at the earliest opportunity. They feel as if they are marooned in a polity from which they must escape before they are overwhelmed with the burden of belonging to their country of birth indefinitely. If they do escape, they make it a point to sever all connections with their motherland and firmly disassociate themselves with anything African. In such cases, the nation would have lost a citizen for good, which is another tragedy.

If the people fail to escape, they subsist under an unshakeable cloud of despondency as they curse their stars for having been born black in Africa. This demographic group utterly fails to relate to their immediate environment and actively cultivates a xenocentric outlook which is heavily underlined by a reductionist ideological standpoint toward all things African. As such, they try the best they can under the circumstances to become white. They support European sport more than they support local sport and talent. Most of these people can name all the players in the English Premier League along with their footballing history. They are walking encyclopedias when it comes to English, Spanish, Italian, or German soccer. They talk about player transfers, coach hiring and firing, and all games that will be in play *kuchando* (the West) at any given time. On the other hand, they usually don't know about the local league or even teams that will be playing at their local pitch. At times, fights erupt among Africans due to games that are played in the English Premier League.

The working class black men fighting over teams whose connections to their lives is a weekly viewership of their games on a TV which will be mounted on the wall in some bar or nightclub in a forgotten part of the country: what a tragedy. Politically, such people follow English or US politics like citizens living in exile. They literally revere words that come out of the mouths of Western presidents. For such people, whites are angels, and their presidents are demigods who are entitled to do whatever they want with impunity: their physical appearance and "superior" languages clearly attest to their divine heritage.

Now, the damage that such kind of a mindset has on the young that these people interact with is irreparably deadly. The children in whose minds these sentiments are planted are forever gripped by a thoroughgoing inferiority complex which is coupled with self-hate. That same toddler whose mother immersed him/her in a colonial language is further dehumanized through the community's self-negating dictum that blackness is cursed and the people go further to substantiate their claim by talking about Noah's sons and the cursed Ham, the supposed forebear of the black race.

The argument about the inherent inferiority of the black race is further bolstered by snapshots from the contemporary world. *Have you ever seen a successful black state*? They ask visibly annoyed in the belief that their interlocutor will be missing something overly obvious. *Black people can't manage their affairs at all. Africa and the Caribbean are the bases for war, famine, coups, and countercoups and gross economic mismanagement. If anything, the West did us a favor by colonizing us; otherwise, we would have been running around barefooted in animal skins with no education and civilization to talk about.* Blackness and the negation of being. Here we have people who are willing participants of their own dehumanization. People who argue on behalf of their oppressors. These people reduce all history and the geopolitical matrix to a simple black and white sequence oblivious of the fact that so many things have precipitated Africa's seeming backwardness.

The unilateral imposition of foreign languages in Africa resulted in the decimation of local languages which they are yet to recover from. These languages were used in the relegation of black people from the epistemological and ontological spheres in their respective countries. As such, the colonized aspired to be white through the adoption of Western languages. This exclusionary linguistic approach was coupled with a history curriculum that extolled the exploits of Western figures at the expense of local ones. African historical personages were labeled as demonic, and their exploits were dismissed as infantile theatrics which were not worth recording. Hence, it was argued that Africa had no history to speak of. The contrivance of this exclusionary linguistic dispensation along with a selective cultural memory is what Africans are still grappling with to this day. As Africans, we are a living paradox: free but still laboring under the yoke of ideological oppression.

Health in the Global South

Though African nations have continuously made spirited attempts to effect total control within their respective nations through the absolute control of their national resources, such attempts have been invariably met with an unrepentant West which is not prepared to relinquish its hegemonic stranglehold on the global stage with vaccine distribution being a case in point. So thoroughgoing has been this financial and ideological subjugation that the Global South still depends on the West for the sustenance of its health institutions.

As such, the West has always orchestrated devious machinations which ensure that the Global South will never wean itself from the yoke of financial dependence, which in turn affects its health system. This has been achieved through corporate deals between pharmaceutical companies and Western governments. This fact is echoed by Laumas (2020) who argues that such partnerships reinforce vaccine sovereignty, a situation whereby wealth and power become the premise upon which access to vaccines is predicated as opposed to a needs-based approach. This shows how entrenched Western hegemony is within the modern day geopolitical spectrum. The Global South, being predominantly made up of developing nations, has interminably been the testing ground for the West's vaccines and other scientific endeavors in which human test subjects are required. This is done without the prerequisite research conditions which goes on to undermine the dignity of the research subjects. The effect this has on the polities in the Global South is literally unquantifiable. Helplessness and a sense of despondency result in the realization that one is a mere cog within another race's grand scheme of existence. Inevitably, a thoroughgoing loss of self-worth and a general disregard of one's health systems are the result of that onslaught.

This dovetails with Quijano's (2019) assertion that the development of vaccines in Africa cannot be divorced from imperialism since public health and medicine have been overly vital cogs within the colonial enterprise. This state of affairs has led to a developmental chasm where we have the wealthy nations on one side and the developing nations on the other. This state of affairs buttresses the health inequalities which exist between the West and the Global South leading to global storms. The actualization of COVID-19 vaccine nationalism is widening inequality between the rich and the poor at an individual, household, and national level.

In line with this view, Bajaj (2022) posits that ever widening gaps in global vaccine equity have led to a two track pandemic where the wealthy have all the mitigatory resources in place and the Global South in which the countries have to wait for hand-me-downs from high income nations. Subsequently, this will also result in parallel developmental trajectories which reflect the above scenario: wealthy nations, which also happen to have high incomes, doing relatively well as opposed to the developing ones.

From the above expose, it may be duly noted that the inequalities which exist between the Global South and the West are rooted in the colonial period where Africans were relegated to the periphery of the global sphere in all areas. This situation has also been largely realized in vaccine distribution in the fight against the corona virus.

"Epistemological Policemen" and COVID-19

The way human beings treat each other under the sun makes us all pawns in the grand scheme of things. The Western world used a process of marginalisation and denigration of Africans. This is called epistemicide of knowledge whereby the systems of colonialism and neocolonialism eclipsed their validity. Significantly, the epistemicide did not only occur among blacks; even the Western-based knowledge that challenged capitalism was suppressed (Bagdikian, 2004). The most fundamental problem with the West's attempt to establish ontology and epistemic homogeneity is that it limits our ability to investigate and understand the world. It also limits creativity in terms of providing solutions for global patterns (Mutambara, 2021). All this will lead to a situation where the so-called poor or underdeveloped nations will always be marginalized.

Santos (2016) states that beyond the knowledge structure within the academic discipline, we should consider how Western knowledge has endeavored to subvert all knowledge located beyond its geographical space. Western knowledge structures are regarded as modern, scientific, intellectually rigorous, and universally applicable and, therefore, superior in contrast to their perception of knowledge from Africa which is deemed primitive, unscientific, and culturally biased. This has allowed the West to define the characteristics of African countries as underdeveloped, unproductive, and primitive. Conversely, Western knowledge has been lauded as the best solution for all ailments in the world; hence, vaccines which were produced in the aftermath of COVID-19 were quickly produced and exported to African countries.

A number of reports have shown that Western states and institutions are fast-tracking COVID-19 vaccines. COVID-19 vaccines and therapeutics were being produced and approved in weeks and months (Mckibbin & Fernando, 2020). Thus, the US Food and Drug Administration agency has approved emergency COVID-19 vaccines which were produced by Pfizer/Biotech and by Moderna under the coronavirus treatment acceleration program (CTAD) (Singer 6 November 2020.) Westerners and their transnational corporations that produce COVID-19 vaccines were ironically given indemnity from lawsuits should their vaccines prove to be harmful to human beings. The Australian government promised to foot the bill for compensation if its citizens get harmed by the vaccine.

Likewise, the United States provides compensation to its citizens if they are harmed by the vaccine (Independent 2 December 2020). African states will not have the resources to compensate their citizens in the event that the vaccine is harmful. The African nations are at the receiving end since Western nations can impose vaccines upon them against their will. Gill (2013) points out that millions of people were going to be inoculated by governments without their consent due to the global external actors at play. Vaccine imperialism, like other forms of exclusionary philosophies and ideologies, is divisible and more lethal than COVID-19, thereby leading to global storms.

Britain's medical regulator granted temporary authorization for the usage of some coronavirus vaccines before full licenses were granted to them (Holton 31 August 2020). The United Nations, the World Health Organization, and the World Bank also supported the fast-tracking of COVID-19 vaccines. No African or black-owned company was producing COVID-19 vaccines. The African is an observer, a subject, and not participant in vaccine development. This highlights the state of global storms that are happening around the world.

Nhemachena et al. (2021) note that COVID-19 made the Africans' bottoms flat, disoriented, hierarchic, and heteronomous. While the core of empire is busy producing COVID-19 nanovaccines, the bottom of empire is patiently and flatly waiting to be penetrated and corporeally invaded with non-vaccines. We live under a system of global capitalism that is prepared to deny basic health protection to poor countries. Allison (2020) points out that the Astra-Zeneca vaccine was tested on the bodies of South Africans who volunteered to be part of the clinical test in Johannesburg. After contributing human beings for the vaccine trials, the WTO refused the Global South permission to produce the vaccine. This clearly shows the extent of the global storms.

The dominance of Western forms of knowledge coincides with colonial and post-colonial influences (Bernnett, 2009). The World Health Organization (WHO), as an international body that regulates and controls health information, is able to manipulate the media, thereby making certain kinds of dishonest information harder to detect. Singer (2020) note that the world mother body (WHO) creates rights and obligations for countries, including the requirement to report public health events. The regulations also outline the criteria to determine whether or not a particular event constitutes a public health emergency of international concern. This is as a result of trust in the WHO, which, as the mother body of health institutions, has the mandate of deciding what kind of advice to give and publish regardless of being biased and promoting or denigrating some agendas.

The emergence of COVID-19 opened a Pandora's box as far as health issues are concerned around the globe. Its existence was marred with different theories, and the leading world body did not give people the exact information concerning the virus—there were secrets that could have been hidden. Unfortunately for the masses, they only consume what is given to them by the mother body. According to Nhemachena (2021), the entire world was being persuaded to embrace controversial fast-tracked COVID-19 nanovaccines. The Western states and their international institutions were psyching up the world to accept their vaccines. These effects of structural favors resulted in an exclusive preoccupation with profit making through vaccine manufacturing at the expense of human concern (Galatas, 2017). Blank (2020) also argues that besides being used to sustain the colonial nature of power, the pandemic also provided an opportunity for the global pseudo philanthropic elite to amass soft power over nations, especially those in the Global South in the process, hence threatening their national sovereignties.

WHO media engagement makes it possible for the organization to quickly connect with people across the globe. The coverage includes digital and traditional TV and radio, wire agencies, print outlets, and various social media platforms (Mckibbin & Fernando, 2020). The WHO aids countries to strengthen regulations including post-marketing surveillance that enables it to eliminate substandard falsified medicines (Fliers, 2020). It also develops international norms and standards so that countries worldwide can regulate health products and technologies consistently. This means that the organization is largely in charge of health issues, and what they would have passed, regardless of being biased or being produced with some strings attached, will be received by the majority (Da Silver, 1999).

From this scenario, it is crystal clear that the World Health Organization, as a health body, polices the news and health information around the world, thereby making it easier to impose vaccines, especially to countries in the Global South, leading to global storms. Globalization spews problems to some sections of humanity, while it yields benefits to the other sections of humanity which thrive on cannibalizing others. Nhemachena et al. (2021) aptly argue that Africans are dying physically, socially, and culturally due to direct and indirect effects of neocolonialism. Fletcher (2020) notes that Johnson and Johnson once charged South Africans about 15% more for the same vaccine dose that it charged in Europe, despite having conducted its clinical trials there. In light of such egregiously unbalanced and unfair corporate behaviors by the West, one can easily see the skewed nature of the relationship between the West and the Global South. At the same time, Russia and China will be waiting to benefit from Africa's misery by presenting themselves to Africans as the lesser evil though their vaccines have insufficient clinical trial data which was released (Allison, 2020).

Incidentally, the WHO has also been accused of stonewalling the inception of vaccines that have been developed in Africa. Andry Nirina Rajoelina of the Republic of Madagascar quit the World Health Organization and claimed that he was offered 20 million dollars by the WHO to kill their COVID organic cure. Madagascar had made headlines with the introduction and launch of their locally manufactured herbal drink of COVID-19 (Maluleke, 2021). Even as the Westerners urge the world to accept their fast-tracked COVID-19 vaccine, they ironically demonized Madagascar's herbal cure for COVID-19 which was produced much earlier than the Western nanovaccines. Agyemany (2020) notes that such behavior by Western states and their international institutions constitute evidence of neo-imperial Western fundamentalism wherein everything African is demonized and dismissed as substandard, dangerous, risky, untested, savage, barbaric, and unsafe. Ultimately, COVID-19 became a source of divisiveness and exclusion and a symbol of power with those able to manufacture and produce the vaccine being more powerful than those who cannot produce and procure it.

To alter this dominant discourse, Nhemachena and Mawere (2017) advocate a concerted push by the Africans for a political and epistemic distance from the Western colonial and neocolonial forms of knowledge as well as the political and economic ideologies that they promote. He refers to the adoption of a stance of epistemic disobedience, where the state and scholars from Africa are free to reject Western-based forms of knowledge in favor of indigenous knowledge systems that are more appropriate and effectively identify and address issues of importance to them. Indigenous knowledge (IK) systems are continually constructed with positivist sciences—this is implicated in the Madagascan issue where her COVID-19 organic remedy was dismissed as lacking scientific tests. Why would they not conduct those tests to equally prove that it does not work remains a big question.

Africa's Response to COVID-19

In many African countries, the challenge is often compounded by a struggling health infrastructure, the shortage of health workers, overdependence on traditional healers, and high population mobility across porous borders (Mckibbin & Fernando, 2020). However, despite these challenges, the continent managed to address the impacts of the pandemic. The governments of several African countries including Uganda, Kenya, Malawi, and Ghana implemented a series of vulnerability reduction and containment measures to curtail the transmission of COVID-19, and these include closure of international airports, closure of schools and other high congregation points, and freezing public and private transport.

A number of measures were put in place in most African countries. There was a swift response to the pandemic. Most countries leveraged continental and regional collaboration. The regional block, the Africa Centres for Disease Control and Preventions, established the Africa Task Force for Novel Coronavirus to coordinate the response to the pandemic across the continent. Furthermore, in many countries, there was fast implementation of lockdown measures. For instance, South Africa implemented one of the strictest lockdowns worldwide which contributed to the decrease of the rate of infection from 42% to 4% (Allison, 2020). There was also quick adoption of public measures, for example, handwashing, mask wearing, and closing of schools, among others.

African countries have experience in dealing with viral diseases outbreak, for instance, Ebola, tuberculosis, cholera, and malaria. This will help them in establishing innovative strategies for training, isolation, and caring of COVID-19 patients. Consequently, many African nations managed to successfully roll out COVID-19 preparedness plans as well as engage with communities in high risk border areas, crowded urban slums, and informal settlements (Fletcher, 2020). Western African countries, for example, were able to apply insights from addressing the 2015–2016 outbreak (Galatas, 2017). A number of African countries have learned that there is need for countries to decentralize the response to the community level and increase the capacity to identify and diagnose cases. This ultimately helps a number of African countries to fight against COVID-19.

Looking Ahead

Africa should have its manufacturing industries, and its governments should prioritize the health sector. A financing mechanism that is aimed at creating a sustainable vaccine manufacturing industry in Africa should be well supported in order to curb the proliferation of poor health facilities. Collaboration with different stakeholders and African countries should be prioritized so as to help each other in times of crisis. The regional block should also play its role in ensuring that its mandate is met. This includes the reorganization of the healthcare system, public health and biomedicine. Regional powerhouses such as South Africa, Nigeria, Egypt, and Kenya should lead the efforts to produce the vaccines in Africa. As a regional organization, the African Union should work to get rid of the continent's vestiges of colonization and apartheid. The African Union's mandate should be anchored on the determination of Africans to extricate themselves from mental servitude and the continent from the malaise of underdevelopment and exclusion in a global world. Most importantly, African businesses, universities, entrepreneurs, intellectuals, and scientists should work together on developmental projects in the continent.

Progenitors argue that the work around surveillance and accessing the patterns of illness must start at the individual level and then slowly reach the community level. African countries have been better able to work with community groups to disseminate information about infectious diseases. The Ebola experience highlighted the importance of reading and engaging with people (Harari, 2018). It is vital to not only disseminate information but also value the feedback from locals and incorporate that information into response strategies. Incorrect and false information should be done away with.

There should be the restrengthening of an uncompromised healthcare system in order to make it effective and efficient for both rural and urban areas. Additionally, African governments should revamp the institutions that train healthcare service providers to make the system more responsive to the real health needs of the people and not just the wealthy ones that compensate physicians handsomely. African states should also align their education systems with targeted and expected outcomes.

The aftermath of recent epidemics and pandemics like Ebola and COVID-19 have highlighted the need to reinforce national public health capabilities and infrastructure, including disease surveillance systems and laboratory networks as well as human capacity training (Fletcher, 2020). National public health capabilities and infrastructure development remain at the core of global health security because they are the first line of defense in infectious disease emergencies (Da Silver, 1999). Additionally, crisis management plans should be ready in each African country, and the involvement of the international community should catalyze such preparedness and response in specific African countries found to be at moderate to high risk of importation of COVID-19 and with a relatively low capacity to manage health emergencies.

Conclusion

It is imperative to note that the exploitative transnational corporations are the same ones producing vaccines, supposedly to save the Africans from COVID-19, hence their desire to experiment on the African populace. While the Western and Eastern world are producing COVID-19 vaccines, the Africans are patiently and flatly waiting to be penetrated and corporeally invaded with the nanovaccines from the West. From the above expose, it may be duly noted that the inequalities which exist between the Global South and the West are rooted in the colonial period where Africans were relegated to the periphery of the global sphere in all areas. This situation has also been largely realized in vaccine distribution in the fight against the corona virus leading to the global storms.

References

Agyemany, E. K. (2020). *Decoding 2019 Novel coronavirus outbreak: Conspiracies: Impact*. Blue Rose Publishers.

Allison, S. (2020). Bill Gates, Big Pharma and entrenching the vaccine Apartheid. *The Mail and Guardian*. 30 January 2021. https://mg.co.za/coronavirus-accesentials/2021-01-30-bill-gates-pharma-and-entretching-the-vaccine-apartheid

Ashcroft, B., Griffiths, G., & Tiffin, H. (2007). *Post-colonial studies. The key concepts* (2nd ed.). Routledge.

Bagdikian, B. H. (2004). *The new media monopoly*. Beacon Press.

Bajaj, S., Maki, L., & Stanford, C. F. (2022). Vaccine apartheid: global cooperation and equity. *The Lancet, 399*(10334), 1452–1453. Retrieved July 1, 2023, from 10.1016/S0140-6736(22)00328-2.

Bernnett, S. (2009). *Journalism, democracy and the public interest: Rethinking media pluralism for Digital age, working paper.* Oxford Reuters Institute for Study of Journalism.

Blank, S. (2020, December 21). Debunking the myth about COVID-19 vaccine. https://www.uab.edu/news/youcanuse/item/11771-debunking

Coronavirus Disease (COVID-2019) Situation Reports. (n.d.). Accessed March 22, 2020, from https://www.who.inty/emergencies/disease/novel-coronavirus-2019/situatio-reports

Da Silver, E. J. (1999). Biological warfare, bioterrorism, biodefence and the biological and toxin weapons convention EJB. *Electronic Journal of Biotechnology, 2*(3), 109–139.

Dubois, W. E. B. (2008). The souls of Black Folk. Retrieved from www.

Fanon, F. (1963). *The wretched of the Earth.* Grove Press.

Fanon, F. (2008). *Black skin white masks.* Pluto Press.

Fletcher, E. R. (2020, September 15). World Bank unleashes US12 billion in fast track finance for COVID 19 vaccines purchases by low and middle income countries. Healthy Policy watch. https://healthypolicy-watch.News/77209-2

Galatas, I. (2017). *The misuse and malicious uses of new biotechnologies* (pp. 103–108). Fiverr.

Gill, P. (2013). Nano carriers, nonvaccines and nonbacterial as Nano biological concerns in modern vaccines. *Scientia Iranian, 20,* 1003–1013.

Harari, Y. N. (2018). *21 lessons for 21th century.* Penguin Random House.

Laumas, A. (2020). Moving the needle: The politics of the Corona virus Vaccine in the Harvard International Review. Accessed June 30, 2023.

Maluleke, T. (2021, March 13). Opinion: The social and cultural implications of covid 19. News24.

Mckibbin, W. J., & Fernando, R. (2020). The global Macroeconomic impacts of Covid 19, Seven Scenario. *SSRN Electronic Journal.*

Mugabe, R. (2001). *Inside the third Chimurenga: Our land is our prosperity.* Department of Information and Publicity, Office of the President and Cabinet.

Mutambara, A. (2021, January 31). Confronting COVID, the personal strategy and inexcusable collective Africa ineptitude: Znews. https://znews.com/arthur-mutambara-talks-tough-confronting-covid-the-persona-startegy-and-inexcusable-collective-african-ineptitude

Nhemachena, A. (2021). *kusinaamaihakuendwe*: Diasporan Zimbabweans, COVID 19 and nomadic global citizenship. In M. Endo (Ed.), *African potentials for world making.* Bamenda Laanga RPCIG.

Nhemachena, A., Makamani, R., & Mukesu, M. (2021). Patrolling epistemic boarders in a world of borderless pandemics. Epistemological policemen in COVID 19. Affiliated 21th century Africa Bamenda Laanga RPCIG.

Nhemachena, A., & Mawere, M. (Eds.). (2017). *GMO, consumerism and the global politics of Biotechnology: Rethinking food, bodies and identities in Africa's 21th century.* Bamenda Laanga RPCIG.

Quijano, F. R. (2019). Vaccination, most deceptive tool of imperialism. in Bullbat.com. Accessed June 25, 2023, from https://www.bulatlat.com/2019/10/12/vaccination

Santos, B. S. (2016). Epistemologies of the South and the future. *From the European South, 1,* 17–29.

Sardar, Z. (2008). Foreword to the 2008 edition. In F. Fanon (Ed.), *Black skin white masks.* Pluto Press.

Singer, J. A. (2020, November 6). Fast vaccines and drugs not only during the pandemics. https://www.cato.org/publications/commentary/fast-trackvaccines

United Nations Development Program, Human Development Report. (n.d.). *Globalisation with a human face.* Oxford University Press.

WA Thiongo, N. (1994). *Decolonising the mind. The politics of language in African Literature.* ZPH.

Chambiwa Elijah is a holder of a Diploma in Education from the University of Zimbabwe (Dip Ed), Bachelor of Education Degree from Midlands state University (BEd), Master of Education Degree (MEd), and a PhD candidate at Catholic University in Zimbabwe. He is an academician and a curricularist with a wide range of educational experience. Elijah has published a number of articles and book chapters. His research interests include pan-anthropological studies, issues in development, and human rights.

Sakirai Gift is a holder of a Master's degree. He is a poet, writer, and academic whose poems and short stories have been featured in both print and electronic media such as The Standard, Newsday, Newshawks among others. Sakirai is presently teaching English at a teacher training college in Mutare Zimbabwe

Chapter 12
External Funding for Small and Medium-Sized Enterprises in Post-COVID Africa

Wehnam Peter Dabale

Abstract The COVID-19 pandemic has significantly impacted the Global South's small and medium-sized enterprises (SMEs). This chapter focuses on the factors that affect external funding and how they correlate with the success of SMEs in the aftermath of the pandemic. The pandemic has hit Africa particularly hard, causing a drop of 8% in the continent's largest economy's gross domestic product (GDP) between 2020 and 2022. Nigeria, one of the continent's economic powerhouses, has been significantly affected, highlighting the urgent need for external funding. SMEs in the Global South face several challenges, including high interest rates, collateral requirements from financiers, and a need for more awareness of funding options. These options are essential for SMEs to recover from the COVID-19 pandemic and promote their growth. This chapter contributes to understanding business financing and provides valuable insights to policymakers, financial institutions, and business owners.

Introduction

The year 2020 was a challenging year for businesses globally due to the COVID-19 pandemic. Small and medium-sized enterprises (SMEs) faced significant difficulties, particularly in the Global South, where economic and political challenges were exacerbated. The adverse effects of the pandemic on SMEs included reduced market demand, disrupted supply chains, and limited access to financing resources. As a result, understanding the factors affecting SMEs' ability to obtain external funding is crucial in developing effective post-pandemic recovery and growth strategies.

External funding refers to financial resources SMEs can obtain from external sources, such as loans, investments, and grants. Policymakers, business support

W. P. Dabale (✉)
Africa University, Mutare, Zimbabwe
e-mail: Dabalew@africau.edu

G. Moyo, S. J. Ndlovu-Gatsheni (eds.), *Global Storms and Africa in World Politics*, Global Power Shift, https://doi.org/10.1007/978-3-031-83868-2_12

groups, and entrepreneurs must comprehend the various elements that impact SMEs' capacity to obtain external funding. This understanding is critical to developing effective strategies for post-pandemic recovery and growth.

This chapter examines the relationship between factors influencing external funding and the success of SMEs in the Global South following the COVID-19 pandemic. The chapter begins with an introductory analysis of the current condition of SMEs in the Global South, focusing on the particular case of Nigeria. The discourse emphasizes the importance of external investment as a crucial source of support for SMEs in maintaining their operations, fostering innovation, and capitalizing on expansion opportunities.

In addition, the chapter analyzes the distinct factors that impact the availability and accessibility of external funding for SMEs in the Global South, considering the unique characteristics of the business landscape in this region. The chapter also reviews the current body of literature, empirical research, and statistics on SME financing in the Global South. These insights are integrated with perspectives from interviews or surveys administered to SME owners, financial institutions, and subject matter experts, providing a robust and comprehensive understanding of the topic.

The primary objective of this chapter is to provide a better understanding of SME finance in the Global South. Notably, based on the research findings, it offers practical suggestions for policymakers, financial institutions, and SME proprietors. The chapter underscores the importance of external funding for SMEs during and after the COVID-19 pandemic and explores the factors that affect SMEs' ability to obtain such funding. It also examines the correlation between external funding and SMEs' performance, providing a comprehensive view of the topic.

Life Cycle Theory of the Firm

The Berger and Udell life cycle theory is a framework that explains how firms' financial needs and preferences change as they progress through different stages of development. This theory is commonly used to understand the financing behaviors and challenges of small and medium-sized enterprises (Berger & Udell, 2018). When applied to global storms and external funding of SMEs in the Global South, it highlights the difficulties SMEs face in accessing external funding during economic uncertainty. Resolving these challenges requires a multifaceted approach that involves both public and private sector stakeholders working together to create a more resilient and supportive financing environment for SMEs in the region.

SMEs in the Global South need external financial resources to expand, diversify, upgrade equipment, and invest in new business ventures. Adequate financing is necessary for them to meet their financial commitments and achieve satisfactory levels of profitability. Robust financing alternatives play a significant role in fostering economic expansion by enhancing SME activities. Berger and Udell proposed the financial growth cycle hypothesis, which explains how a successful firm goes through various stages of growth. The theory posits that the financial requirements of a firm transform as the organization progresses along its life cycle.

When considering the life cycle theory of firms in the context of post-COVID-19 and external funding of SMEs in the Global South, as mentioned earlier, these SMEs require external financial resources for their expansion, diversification, equipment upgrades, and investments in new business ventures. Enhanced efficiency through adequate finance is necessary for SMEs in developing countries to meet or enhance their financial commitments. Robust financing alternatives play a significant role in fostering economic expansion by enhancing SME activities.

According to the World Bank (2017), younger SMEs need help obtaining external financing. As a result, these enterprises often rely on internal resources or financial support from acquaintances and family members to initiate and sustain their operations, mainly when limited information about the firm is available. SMEs that are smaller and younger and have lower transparency levels are on the left side of the financing continuum. These businesses rely on internal funding from owners, trade creditors, or angel investors.

The financial growth paradigm is a critical factor in explaining the financial needs of SMEs in the Global South, as the model considers the cyclical nature of financial growth and the various financial options available to companies during the initial, expansion, and maturation phases. By adopting this theory, the examination of external financial options can be assessed based on the various growth stages of the organization. Although the concept has faced criticism regarding the criteria used to link financial alternatives with a company's distinct growth stages, lenders consider factors such as the organization's size, age, and long-term viability when assessing loan applications. Therefore, well-established companies with a reputable track record of expansion often receive more opportunities for external financing.

Global South and the Heterogeneity of SMEs

The term "heterogeneity of SMEs" refers to the fact that small and medium-sized enterprises differ in many ways, such as their size, industry, location, management, and structure. Policymakers, stakeholders, and SMEs need to understand and appreciate this diversity to create specific strategies and support systems to help SMEs overcome economic challenges and succeed in a global market. The heterogeneity of SMEs makes them a fascinating aspect of the business world.

SMEs in the Global South come in different sizes, operate in different industries, are in different geographic regions, and have different management styles and organizational structures. This diversity is critical in determining how SMEs respond to global economic storms like financial crises, trade wars, and pandemics such as COVID-19. One key aspect of SME heterogeneity is their size. SMEs can range from microenterprises with just a few employees to small or medium-sized companies with hundreds of employees. This size heterogeneity directly influences the ability of SMEs to weather global economic storms. Smaller SMEs may struggle to obtain capital or have limited resources to cope with economic downturns. In contrast, larger SMEs may have more robust financial structures and diverse revenue streams, making them more resilient.

In the Global South nations, the SMEs have unique characteristics. The owners are involved in management and ownership functions and rely on internal funds and loans. According to Adegboye and Iweriebor (2018), SMEs are more uncertain but have a greater capacity for operational flexibility. There are also more significant knowledge disparities between internal and external stakeholders. The size of SMEs varies, ranging from microenterprises with only a few employees to small or medium-sized companies with hundreds. The size difference affects their resilience during economic downturns. Smaller SMEs often need more resources and may need help accessing capital during such times. Larger SMEs have more robust financial structures and diverse revenue streams, making them more resilient. Furthermore, Fisher and Reuber (2010) identified several critical attributes of small firms in the Global South, categorizing them under four overarching themes: labor characteristics, sectors of operation, owner gender, and efficiency. Since individual entrepreneurs own the majority of SMEs, the working proprietorship category accounts for the most significant portion of employment.

In most countries in the Global South, over 50% of the workforce comprises employees of SMEs. These workers often require direct compensation for their work, as their enterprise involvement is usually related to their home responsibilities. Nevertheless, their active participation accounts for approximately 25% of the workforce. The remaining 25% is reserved for employees and individuals undergoing vocational training in a specific business domain. SMEs tend to have more operational workers than larger organizations. Consequently, there is a reduction in the capital cost base associated with creating employment (Liedholm & Mead, 2013; Schaper, 2012).

The SMEs' business operations in the Global South nations primarily encompass retail and manufacturing sectors (Fisher & Reuber, 2010). They widely recognize that many small and medium-sized enterprises (SMEs) operate mainly in retail. The retail sector's SME activity exhibits significant variations among countries and regions in the respective operation nations, including rural and urban areas. Retail enterprises are commonly situated in metropolitan locations, whereas manufacturing operations have the potential to start in both rural and urban regions. The degree of manufacturing activity within a nation is subject to various determinants, including the accessibility of essential raw materials for production, the preferences and consumption patterns of domestic consumers, and the comparative export proficiency of the country concerning other nations.

The Global South's SMEs are divided into urban and rural enterprises. Urban enterprises are two, namely, "organized" and "unorganized" (Awuah & Addaney, 2016; Amewuda & Ackah, 2021). Structured organizations generally have salaried employees, operate from a registered office space, and comply with local regulations. On the other hand, unstructured organizations usually consist of artisans working in open areas, temporary structures, or their own homes (Amewuda & Ackah, 2021). Kayanula and Quartey (2010) state that small and medium-sized enterprises (SMEs) without organization often have only a few salaried employees. Apprentices and family members are typically the primary sources of labor used to run the business. The industry in which the SME operates considerably influences its response to global economic storms and politics. For example, a technology-focused SME may have more flexibility to adapt to remote work during a pandemic. At the same time, a manufacturing-based SME could face supply chain disruptions due to trade wars or geopolitical tensions. The geographical location of an SME also plays a crucial role, as regional economic disparities and varying regulatory environments can significantly impact how SMEs navigate global storms and politics. Moreover, SMEs' management style and organizational structure contribute to their heterogeneity. Entrepreneurial SMEs led by innovative and adaptive leaders may be more agile in responding to global economic storms and politics, while family-owned SMEs prioritize stability and long-term sustainability.

Determinants of External Funding

Global storms and politics can significantly impact the business environment and financing. They can cause a decrease in consumer demand, disrupt supply chains, increase operating costs, and create uncertainty in financial markets. Such factors can directly impact SMEs as they often require more resources and flexibility to weather such challenges. During an economic downturn, consumer spending and investments usually decrease, leading to declining revenues and profitability for SMEs. Similarly, natural disasters and pandemics can disrupt operations and cause financial strain on SMEs. Researchers such as Anheier et al. (1997), Steel and Webster (2011), Aryeetey et al. (2014), and Gockel and Akoena (2012) have highlighted these challenges.

Parker et al. (2015) highlighted the financial difficulties small enterprises operating in the Malawian market face. These challenges stem from the higher costs of acquiring domestic inputs caused by the firms' limited cash flows. According to Aryeetey et al. (2014), a study conducted on a sample population revealed that 5% of participants identified the element of production constraint as a significant challenge. In contrast, Daniels and Ngwira (2013) emphasized that approximately 33% of small enterprises in Malawi reported encountering challenges related to inputs. This study found that input constraints vary depending on the firm's size. For instance, business promoters are present in 8.2% of companies in Botswana, 7.5% of companies in Swaziland, and 6.3% of companies in Lesotho. Access to finance is a significant challenge for small and medium-sized enterprises (SMEs) in Nigeria and Malawi. Studies have found that many SMEs require more credit to meet their working capital and raw materials needs, with 24–52% of respondents reporting this deficit.

Many SMEs in the Global South, precisely 38% in Africa, need help accessing finance due to limited availability in domestic and international finance markets—various factors, such as high perceived risk, limited access to information, and increased expenses. SMEs require assistance in obtaining long-term funding through debt or equity mechanisms. While SMEs in developing nations may consider the lack of access to finance insignificant, it can still impact labor specialization and hinder operational flexibility within these businesses. Additionally, locating qualified and unskilled workers can challenge these SMEs.

The input constraints, which are the limitations or restrictions placed on the input data or variables in a given problem or system to the Global South nations, are also factors in determining external funding. These constraints define the conditions within SMEs that face numerous problems in input markets. According to Levy (2013), small firms often have two primary limitations: the cost of inputs and the availability of these inputs for manufacturing. The challenges faced by different nations vary in nature, with the primary differentiating factor being the apparent access or lack of access to inputs, cost, or availability. This issue is particularly significant in determining whether the challenges are because of foreign or local inputs (World Bank, 2017; Parker et al., 2015).

Another significant barrier to SMEs in the Global South is the restricted accessibility of enhanced techniques and technology, which diminishes their competitive advantage and innovative capabilities. Outdated tools are also a challenge for SMEs, with 18% of enterprises identifying it as one of four problems that hinder their expansion. Many SMEs are now facing competition from overseas markets. These organizations need to adapt and address this challenge in their local markets. The main difficulty faced by medium-sized firms in Nigeria, as a study conducted by Aryeetey et al. in 2014, found that 12.5% of these enterprises need help with this issue. In order to improve the ability of local firms to compete in the global market and political climate, it is vital to remove impediments to trade, decrease import taxes, and eliminate quotas and restrictions on imports while increasing the availability of raw materials and intermediate goods for manufacturing and facilitate access to new technologies to support smaller businesses.

The World Investment Report 2014 suggests that a more lenient approach toward direct foreign investment will promote subcontracting arrangements involving SMEs. Create opportunities for local workers to improve their skills and knowledge, leading to the transition into local entrepreneurs. The expectation is that liberalization will enhance the competitiveness of domestic enterprises and foster the entry of new firms, aided by the reduced costs of imported inputs that were previously inaccessible. It is essential to note that AlQershi (2021) have documented a different perspective. They observed that tailors in Nigeria, who previously produced many pairs of trousers in a given month, experienced prolonged periods of no orders following the implementation of the liberalized trade regime. Expanding overseas markets was hindered by limited worldwide market exposure, inadequate quality control standards, and standardized products. Only 1.7% of enterprises export their output, according to available data.

Despite structural reforms in many Global South nations, issues must be addressed at the company level to facilitate growth. Although regulatory restrictions have led to some improvements, they still hinder small businesses' growth. The significant costs associated with setting up new businesses, including obtaining licenses and meeting registration requirements, continue to impede the operations of small and medium-sized enterprises (SMEs). Legal claims can also be expensive to settle, and prolonged court proceedings can harm SMEs. In Nigeria, for instance, registering and starting a business is a significant challenge, with 16 procedural steps and an average of 127 days required to obtain licenses for a new firm, according to the World Bank's Doing Business Report (2016). In South Africa, the process takes even longer, with an average of 176 days to obtain a license and 18 distinct stages that must be completed. The absence of antitrust regulation benefits larger firms, allowing them to maintain a dominant position in the market. Limited protection for intellectual property rights also hampers SMEs' access to foreign innovations (Kayanula & Quartey, 2010).

Furthermore, SMEs face a significant challenge due to a need for more entrepreneurial and business management skills in the Global South. Management education and experience are necessary for the growth and advancement of SMEs. Compared to corporations, SMEs often need help attracting highly skilled individuals. The need for more skilled management personnel in most countries within the area intensifies the impact on SMEs. The limited availability of support services and the associated high costs significantly challenge SMEs in enhancing their management capabilities, primarily due to the need for consulting companies equipped with appropriate and cost-efficient management solutions tailored specifically for SMEs, as well as the need for more information or the limited time to use current services, which results in a vulnerable demand for training requirements.

Despite multiple organizations offering skills enhancement and consulting services, there still needs to be a noticeable skills gap within the SME sector. According to the findings of Daniels and Ngwira (2013), a significant proportion of SMEs in Malawi, approximately 88 out of 100, expressed the need for training across several skill areas. However, as of 2012, the study revealed that only a meager 6% of the identified firms requiring training could access such opportunities. The case study conducted in Nigeria has shown significant progress in this regard. Nevertheless, many nations of the Global South required significant enhancements in this particular domain.

Politics of External Funding

Global storms and political events can significantly impact small and medium-sized enterprises (SMEs), particularly in terms of their need for external funding sources. For instance, financial crises or natural disasters can disrupt supply chains, reduce consumer demand, and create financial uncertainty, which can negatively impact SMEs. In such situations, SMEs may need external funding to weather the storm, maintain operations, and seize growth opportunities. Several factors can affect the availability and accessibility of external funding for SMEs during global storms and political events, and much research has been done on this subject.

Finance is crucial for most small and medium-sized enterprises (SMEs) that support economic development in the Global South, especially in the current global political climate. It enables businesses to acquire seed capital and fund their operating expenses. Various scholars have conducted finance studies, emphasizing that debt capital is the primary external source of funding for most businesses (Abbasi et al., 2017; Longenecker et al., 2014). Debt refers to the monetary resources a business borrows and must repay within a specific timeframe, typically with interest (Hisrich & Peters, 2015; Anderson & Dunkelberg, 2013).

SMEs choose these funding options to retain complete autonomy and control over their business operations. The company obtains a loan and must repay the loan amount with interest at specific periods. The distinguishing features of this type of financing are the strict terms of the financing and the use of collateral to guarantee loan repayment. The firm retains full ownership without relinquishing any portion of this financing arrangement. SMEs often opt for this method of financing instead of equity finance due to its inherent advantage in granting them complete autonomy and control over their business operations. However, whether this type of financing is suitable for nascent and fast-expanding enterprises with a high risk-return profile remains to be determined. According to the OECD (2010), these enterprises require assistance obtaining debt financing due to the uncertainties associated with their start-up phase.

Trade credit is a form of external financing that can help small businesses with their financial needs. This is relevant when a company purchases products or services with a deferred payment arrangement. The credit provided is a short-term loan that lasts 30–60 days. During this period, interest accrues, and payment is due at the end of the credit term. Nonbank financing is a popular method for obtaining external finance, second only to bank lending. Financial instruments, such as invoice discounting, factoring, and leasing, can also help businesses obtain external funding.

Factoring and invoice discounting are particularly useful for small and medium-sized enterprises (SMEs) as they can help these businesses achieve rapid growth, improve productivity, and overcome cash flow constraints. These financing methods are critical in economies where SMEs face significant financing constraints and during financial crises when banks reduce their support for SMEs. Leasing is another form of finance based on assets that allows SMEs to obtain funding for a limited time, typically medium or short term. In a lease agreement, one party transfers possession of an asset to another party for a specific duration. The lessee is obligated to make regular payments as stipulated in the contract, and at the end of the lease term, the lessee can choose to purchase the equipment.

Venture capitalists and funders can also provide nonbanking financing to SMEs and entrepreneurs. Venture capital financing involves mobilizing funds from investors and allocating them to high-risk, relatively unknown enterprises, typically those in the early stages of development. Venture capitalists can provide financial support and valuable assistance in addressing various organizational challenges and making strategic decisions that impact the growth of SMEs, especially in the Global South.

Providing government aid for these financing mechanisms can mitigate market vulnerabilities and improve finance accessibility for SMEs. Small businesses typically need more collateral or a limited financial history to obtain bank loans, making these alternative financing options even more important.

External Funding and Performance of SMEs

In recent years, there has been an increasing interest in the performance of small and medium-sized enterprises (SMEs) in the Global South. Several studies have identified various factors that contribute to the success of SMEs, including their attributes, strategy, ability to innovate, willingness to take risks, proactive approach, knowledge management, and entrepreneurial mindset. These factors are crucial for accurately evaluating or managing the performance of SMEs. However, despite the growing number of studies on SMEs, further research is still needed to measure their performance in various business contexts. Earlier studies examining how factors affect the performance of SMEs used different sample groups from businesses that varied in size, age, ownership structure, industry, and environment.

In addressing this gap, a recent study analyzed the factors impacting financial performance in developing economies, specifically Ghanaian SMEs. The study found a strong correlation between a company's ownership structure and financial performance. Additionally, the results suggest a direct association between a company's age and size and financial performance. However, the influence of company-specific characteristics and industries varies across different dimensions of financial performance and between the industrial and service sectors. While larger companies generally perform better than smaller ones due to economies of scale, a broader range of commercial activities, more significant influence in negotiations with customers and suppliers, and better access to financial resources, there is conflicting empirical evidence about the correlation between size and performance.

A study investigating the moderating role of company size on the relationship between innovation and company performance of SMEs in 29 countries in Eastern Europe and Central Asia found conflicting results regarding the influence of company size. The results suggest that a firm's size and financial resources play a dual role in determining the effect of innovation on the company's performance, whether the effect is beneficial or detrimental. It is empirically proven that most of the research on ownership structure and financial performance was carried out in the countries of the Global North. At the same time, multiple studies have investigated the relationship between ownership structure and financial performance to enhance understanding of SME performance in the Global South.

Conclusion

Small and medium-sized enterprises (SMEs) in Global South countries face numerous challenges due to the pandemic, economic difficulties, and political complexities. To help these SMEs rebuild, innovate, and expand, they need external funding, which can be obtained through international aid, foreign investment, multilateral financial assistance, or debt or equity financing. However, to attract and optimize external funding, it is essential to create a supportive environment by addressing systemic challenges and promoting sustainable growth. This can be achieved by implementing supportive policies, enhancing regulatory frameworks, and strengthening institutional capacities to allocate and utilize external funding effectively. Promoting transparency, accountability, and good governance is crucial to building trust among international financiers and investors.

The relationship between external funding and SME performance in the Global South after COVID-19 is complex due to various challenges and political dynamics. Access to financial support is essential to help SMEs expand and become more resilient. Ultimately, it demands a forward-thinking approach that aligns economic recovery efforts with long-term development objectives. By harnessing external funding responsibly and strategically, Global South SMEs can weather the storm of global uncertainties and emerge as drivers of sustainable economic progress, promoting innovation, job creation, and inclusive prosperity for their nations.

It is also crucial for stakeholders, including governments, international organizations, and financial institutions, to recognize the importance of providing targeted financial support to SMEs in the Global South. This support would strengthen their capacity to withstand the effects of global storms and facilitate their post-disaster recovery. Initiatives such as concessional loans, grants, and insurance schemes tailored to the specific needs of SMEs can play a pivotal role in enhancing their resilience and sustainability amid global storms and politics.

References

Abbasi, W. A., Wang, Z., & Abbasi, D. A. (2017). Potential sources of financing for small and medium enterprises (SMEs) and role of government in supporting SMEs. *Journal of Small Business and Entrepreneurship Development, 5*(2), 39–47.

Adegboye, A. C., & Iweriebor, S. (2018). Does access to finance enhance SME innovation and productivity in Nigeria? Evidence from the World Bank Enterprise survey. *African Development Review, 30*(4), 449–461.

AlQershi, N. (2021). Strategic thinking strategic planning strategic innovation and the performance of SMEs: The mediating role of human capital Management Science Letters 1003–1012. https://doi.org/10.5267/j.msl.2020.9.042

Amewuda, A., & Ackah, D. (2021). Relationship between tax and SMEs sustainability. *Finance & Management Engineering Journal of Africa, 3*(06), 27–39.

Anderson, R. L., & Dunkelberg, J. S. (2013). *Managing small businesses*. West Group.

Anheier, H. K., Priller, E., & Seibel, W. (1997). *The Third Sector: Comparative studies of nonprofit organizations* (pp. 2014–2017).

Aryeetey, E., Baah-Nuakoh, A., Duggleby, T., Hettige, H., & Steel, W. F. (2014). *Supply and demand for finance of small enterprises in Nigeria*. The World Bank.
Awuah, S. B., & Addaney, M. (2016). The interactions between microfinance institutions and small and medium-scale enterprises in the Sunyani municipality of Ghana. *Asian Development Policy Review, 4*(2), 51–64.
Baeck, P., Collins, L., & Zhang, B. (2014). Understanding alternative finance. *The U.K. alternative finance industry report.*
Berger, A. N., & Udell, G. F. (2018). The economics of small business finance: The roles of private equity and debt markets in the financial growth cycle. *Journal of Banking & Finance, 22*(6–8), 613–673.
Daniels, L., & Ngwira, A. (2013). *Results of a nationwide survey on micro, small, and medium enterprises in Malawi*. Growth and Equity Through Microenterprise Investments and Institutions Project.
Fisher, E., & Reuber R. (2010). Industrial clusters and SME promotion in developing countries. Commonwealth Trade and Enterprise Paper No. 3.
Gockel, A. F., & Akoena, S. K. (2012). *Financial intermediation for the poor: Credit demand by micro small and medium scale enterprises in Nigeria: A further assignment for financial sector policy?* ILO.
Hisrich, R. D., & Peters, M. P. (2015). *Entrepreneurship: Starting, developing and managing a new Enterprise* (3rd ed.). Irwin.
Kayanula, D., & Quartey, P. (2010). *The policy environment for promoting small and medium-sized enterprises in Nigeria and Malawi, Finance and development research Programme, working paper series, paper no 15*. IDPM, University of Manchester.
Levy, B. (2013). Obstacles to developing indigenous small and medium enterprises: An empirical assessment. *The World Bank Economic Review, 7*(1), 65–83.
Liedholm, C. E., & Mead, D. C. (2013). *Small enterprises and economic development: The dynamics of micro and small enterprises*. Routledge.
Longenecker, J. G., Moore, C. W., & Petty, J. W. (2014). *Small business management: An entrepreneurial emphasis* (9th ed.). Publishing Co.
OECD. (2010, June). Small & medium-sized enterprises. Local Strength, global reach. OECD policy brief.
Parker, R., Riopelle, R., & Steel, W. F. (2015). *Small enterprises are adjusting to liberalization in five African countries*. The World Bank.
Schaper, M. (2012). Introduction: The essence of eco-entrepreneurship. *Greener Management International, 38*, 529–566.
Steel, W. F., & Webster, L. M. (2011). *Small Enterprises in Nigeria: Responses to adjustment industry*. The World Bank Industry and Energy Department.
World Bank. 2017. SMEs country indicators data sources.

Wehnam Peter Dabale is an experienced administrator, academic, and entrepreneur with over two decades of experience. He is the Alumni Relations, Internationalization, and Church Relations Director at Africa University in Zimbabwe. Dabale's passion for research is evident in his role as a doctoral candidate at the University of South Africa (UNISA), where he is exploring areas such as human resource management, macroeconomics, business leadership and management, entrepreneurship, and financing in Africa.

Chapter 13
COVID-19 and the Global South: An Integrative Review

Idah Moyo and Benny Moyo

Abstract COVID-19 first broke out in China in 2019 but by March 2020 had assumed pandemic proportions on a global scale. Both the Global North and Global South put in place measures to contain the pandemic. Yawning gaps emerged in the fragile healthcare systems in the Global South. The socioeconomic inequalities globally were exacerbated. Vaccine imperialism manifested itself in the form of pharmaceutical companies in the North producing and distributing vaccines in the North. The ratio of vaccination was higher in the Global North. While the World Health Organization (WHO) had come up with COVAX, a global initiative aimed at achieving justice and equity in the distribution of the vaccines, many countries in the Global North breached this. Lessons learned from COVID-19 by the Global South ranged from the need to build robust and resilient healthcare systems to being in a state of preparedness for any epidemic.

Introduction

First perceived as a local epidemic, COVID-19 first broke out in Wuhan in China in 2019. It had, however, assumed pandemic proportions by March 2020, as it had spread globally. Both the Global South and North put in place innovative pandemic containment measures. COVID-19 strained the fragile economies of the Global South and their equally fragile healthcare systems. It exacerbated the healthcare system manpower constraints in the Global South. It has had a massive impact on the Global South from which it will take decades to recover. This has been aggravated by the fact that this is a region that has been historically underdeveloped, characterized by fragile health systems and socioeconomic inequality. This chapter

I. Moyo (✉)
Health Studies, University of South Africa, Pretoria, South Africa

B. Moyo
Bulawayo Progressive Residents Association, Bulawayo, Zimbabwe

G. Moyo, S. J. Ndlovu-Gatsheni (eds.), *Global Storms and Africa in World Politics*, Global Power Shift, https://doi.org/10.1007/978-3-031-83868-2_13

will explore the ravages of COVID-19 in different regions, the mitigation measures by different countries, and vaccine imperialism and its impact.

Contextual Background

The global spread of COVID-19 saw governments adopt mitigation measures to contain the pathogen: lockdowns, closure of learning institutions, and restrictions on movements, among others. According to McCann and Matenga (2020:166), these containment measures brought into focus systemic faulty lines in the global socioeconomic system. The Human Rights Watch (2020:1) notes how the devastating impact of the virus manifested itself in various ways: the scramble for basic medical supplies, transnational market competition, the neglect of the disadvantaged societies, fear of the virus being used as a scapegoat for human rights abuse, and withdrawal of aid by humanitarian organizations from the neediest regions. There was a shocking display of what McCann and Matenga (2020:162) call the "economy of privilege": governments protecting vested internal interests and selective policies of cooperation with least developed countries. COVID-19 saw food shortages and a severe impact of conflicts in countries like Lydia, Ukraine, Yemen, Sudan, and Syria. In its report of the World Economic Situation and Prospects of 2020, the United Nations (2020:127–128) paints a gloomy picture of the economic, health, and social crisis occasioned by the pandemic.

COVID-19 and Its Devastating Trail

An integrative review of the literature on COVID-19, the Global South versus the Global North, was done. Literature search was conducted using the following databases: Medline, PubMed, EBSCOhost: Africa-wide information, Science Direct, Health Source: Google Scholar and Academia Edition for articles on COVID-19 published between 2019 and 2023. Innovations and lessons learned during the pandemic were captured. The studies that were included for the review process were mostly qualitative ones focusing on experiences of COVID-19 and reports by global bodies like the World Health Organization and the United Nations.

The Global South is characterized by fragile economies and equally fragile healthcare systems. The challenges faced by the Global South countries are formidable, making them vulnerable to pandemics like COVID-19 according to the World Health Organization (2020a:15). The World Bank (2020:12) states that only four African countries had reached and maintained the 15% minimum threshold of their national budgets for the healthcare systems as per the Abuja Declaration. Scholars like Kieny (2017:537) posit that strengthening healthcare systems would contribute to the attainment of the Sustainable Development Goal 3 by reducing poverty and providing equitable health outcomes and improving well-being.

According to Muswere (2020:61) and the United Nations (2023:1), significant progress toward the attainment of the SDGs has been made. However, for the Global South, HIV/AIDS and tuberculosis pose a serious threat toward the attainment of the SDGs by 2030. Yet, as argued by Kieny et al. (2017:537), resilient healthcare systems contribute to the attainment of the SDGs as they reduce poverty, improve general well-being, and provide equitable health outcomes. The situation was further exacerbated by the ravages of COVID-19.

Evidence from The Lancet (2020:1) and Sun et al. (2021:1–2) has highlighted the fact that healthcare workers have a unique and critical role to play in the fight against pandemics like COVID-19. In the Global South and elsewhere, Cohen et al. (2020:1) and Shanafelt et al. (2020:2134) argue that the people are faced with the risk of exposure, high workloads, and moral dilemma in a rapidly changing work environment. During COVID-19, the resilience of the healthcare systems was stretched to the limit as they were overwhelmed with a serious shortage of personal protective equipment, high workloads, and shortage of drugs.

Jaca et al. (2022:587) posit that in the Global South, universal health coverage, that is, access to quality services (treatment, palliative care, and rehabilitation) irrespective of one's financial status, is a big challenge. In low- and middle-income countries in the Global South, most of the people do not have access to quality healthcare services. Quality, according to Fadlallah et al. (2018:6–7) and Friebel et al. (2018:3), means access to timely, affordable, effective, and safe treatment regardless of one's socioeconomic status.

In many parts of the Global South, there are challenges of access and coverage of healthcare services. According to Hodes et al. (2017:738–740), there is a shortage and inequitable distribution of healthcare providers and service capacity characterized by inadequate number of healthcare personnel and stock-outs of medicine and equipment. This, the authors argue, is further compounded by poor and late remuneration of personnel, inaccessibility of primary health centers, population growth, and poorly developed health information systems. It is a combination of some or all these challenges that according to Hodes et al. (2017:740) leads to demotivation of staff and a flight of skills and poor patient care. For example, the Global South has a low number of healthcare professionals (1:30 per 1000 population). The shortage is projected to be 6.1 million by 2030, according to the Sustainable Development Goals Centre and Sustainable Goal Network.

Jaca et al. (2022:587) posit that the fragile nature of the health infrastructure in many countries in the Global South casts doubt on whether it can deliver equitable healthcare to their communities, let alone the marginalized ones. The authors further argue that to attain universal health coverage, infrastructure can help play an important role. Patients in respiratory distress require oxygen, but a study by Mangipudi et al. (2020: e1124) found that there is shortage of oxygen in the Global South. This is also corroborated by Ross and Wendel (2023:3–4), whose study found a lack of continuous oxygen supply in Ethiopia, Nigeria, Kenya, and Democratic Republic of the Congo. A study by Rajbhandari et al. (2020:397) found a gap in the capacity of healthcare systems to deliver care to patients with respiratory conditions due to the lack of pulse oximeters and oxygen tanks. A healthcare system needs to have potable and safe water for patients; however, one study by Yiek et al. (2021:5–6) found evidence of infections linked to water containing hospital equipment.

Many countries implemented lockdown measures in a bid to contain the pandemic. According to Hale et al. (2021:529), these entailed, among others, restrictions in internal movements, travel restriction to and out of the country, restrictions on public transport, bans on public gatherings, imposition of curfews, and social distancing. Hale et al. (2021:533) further indicate that for measurement of the stringent index, prevention measures were compiled. These included COVID-19 messages encouraging the following: social distancing, wearing of masks, and handwashing. In addition, the World Health Organization (2022:3–4) states that service industries like saloons, schools, and restaurants were closed. Hospitality industry operations were also closed.

Some governments put in place safety nets and public distribution of food for residents. However, according to the USAID, PEPFAR (2020:1–2), none of these mitigatory measures were tailor made for key populations like sex workers. In line with the World Health Organization (2020b:4–5) COVID-19 protocols and guidelines, governments set up quarantine and isolation centers for COVID-19 positive patients.

The downside of these measures was an economic meltdown and financial losses that affected many in different ways. For example, evidence from studies by Gichuna et al. (2020:1433) and the Global Network of Sex Work Projects (2021:1) shows that the stigma society attached to sex workers meant that sex workers were more vulnerable to harassment by law enforcement agents trying to enforce COVID-19 restrictions and containment measures.

The disproportionate impact of the COVID-19 induced economic meltdown and government-imposed restrictions on sex workers as reflected in study findings in Zimbabwe, Kenya, and Uganda by Moyo et al. (2022:190), FHI360 (2020:2–3), and Kawala et al. (2020:1–2), respectively. The findings of these studies were that the lockdown measures saw sex workers losing their income resulting in their having challenges getting money for transport to access HIV care services.

While the state has an obligation to provide healthcare, the COVID-19 pandemic exposed yawning gaps in the system. Studies by Moyo et al. (2021:7–8) in South Africa and Bajaria et al. (2021:1) in Tanzania showed how governments were found unprepared for the pandemic as some public healthcare facilities had a shortage of such critical COVID-19 precautionary products such as access to running water, disinfectants, hand sanitizers, and personal protective equipment. This was also the case in Ethiopia as highlighted by Deressa et al. (2021:1).

The state has an obligation to provide psychosocial support to healthcare providers in its employee. Studies by Liu et al. (2020: e17) and Adams and Walls (2020:1439) demonstrate how frontline healthcare providers suffered from anxiety and fear of transmitting the COVID-19 virus to their families and get no support. Yet, on the other hand, positive examples from China show that the provision of psychological support to frontline healthcare providers played a critical role during emergencies in positive mental health outcomes as noted by Chen et al. (2021:1175–1176), Wang et al. (2020:400), and Zaka et al. (2020:884–885).

Vaccine Imperialism

Burki (2021:922) note how Margaret Harris made a prophetic observation to the effect that high-income countries must open the floodgates to allow low- and middle-income countries access to the COVID-19 vaccines. This is a point that is further amplified by Chifamba in Chap. 10 of this book on apartheid vaccines. The global distribution of the COVID-19 vaccines follows the global socioeconomic order. To mitigate the challenges posed by the differences between the Global South and North, the world community came up with COVID-19 vaccines. Global access facility to coordinate the vaccine distribution. This is a multistakeholder initiative convened by the World Health Organization and the coalition of epidemic preparedness innovations. This is a global initiative that brings together governments and manufacturers to ensure equitable access to the COVID-19 vaccines to countries with high, middle, and low incomes. Its underlying philosophy according to the WHO and Sharma et al. (2022:434) is to reduce the dangers of vaccine nationalism and allow countries without economic or political leverage to establish bilateral/multilateral vaccine agreements to access vaccines. Through this facility, it was expected to vaccinate 20% of the population of all its members by 2021 as indicated by the World Health Organization. According to Sharma et al. (2022:434), one of the advantages of this initiative was the organization of an advance commitment to support the manufacture and distribution of vaccines for the Global South by the provision of financial support from overseas development assistance and private foundations.

This circumvents vaccine imperialism, according to Emanuel et al. (2021:371–372), who had come up with a proportional allocation system. According to this system, there would be tier-by-tier distribution of equal proportion to member countries in a graduated manner till 20% of the top population is reached. While the distribution kicked off with promises of solidarity and equity, it was overtaken by the emergency of bilateral agreements. According to Usher (2021:2322), by August 2020, the United Kingdom had signed five such deals while the United States had seven. Scholars like Eccleston-Turner and Upton (2021:427) have expressed the fear that while COVAX had the potential to improve the development of COVID-19, the advantages were being eroded by vaccine imperialism. This resulted in low COVID-19 vaccination rates in the Global South, as noted by Chifamba in Chap. 10 of this book. One challenge about COVAX was its inability to respond to new COVID-19 outbreaks in the Global South. Wise (2021:1) posits that while G7 nations had pledged 870 million vaccine doses for the Global South, the World Health Organization had estimated that 11 billion would be required.

Another facet of vaccine imperialism is the Intellectual Property Rights Law. Durell (2016:791) indicated that it is about patents, trademarks, and trade secrets as they apply to COVID-19 vaccines. Members of the World Trade Organization are obliged by the Trade Related Aspects of Intellectual Property Rights to protect the patent owned rights over production including medicines. This implies that the manufacturer is guaranteed a market monopoly. South Africa and India made an application to the World Trade Organization for a waiver of the Intellectual Property Rights Law over the COVID-19 vaccine—a point highlighted by Okereke (2021:1). This would have allowed member states to engage in COVID-19 vaccine research, manufacture, and distribution, as postulated by Erfani et al. (2021:2). Opponents of the waiver were from the high-income countries including the United Kingdom, Germany, and Japan. They argued that obstacles to the mass production of the vaccine were not intellectual property rights but the inability of the Global South to make vaccines. This was also ably argued by Chambiwa and Sakirai in Chap. 11 on vaccine imperialism. They posit that the African is an observer and not a participant in vaccine development. This is despite the fact that India and China are currently producing hepatitis B vaccines, according to Erfani et al. (2021:2–3). Countries like Cuba, China, and Brazil have demonstrated their ability to produce low-cost vaccines that more than meet the stringent international quality criteria as indicated by Padmanabhan et al. (2010:672). Perhaps liberalizing the patent laws and removing barriers to technology transfer would be a positive step toward vaccine justice as argued by Asundi et al. (2021:1038).

Innovations and Creativities from the Global South

One of the response pillars by the World Health Organization Africa was coordination, planning, financial, and monitoring during COVID-19. The Global South responded to the pandemic in innovative ways. Temporary isolation and treatment centers were set up in schools and tents. Healthcare facilities were equipped with ventilators and cloth face masks were produced. Leading in technology and innovation was Rwanda: using advanced technology for patient examination and good recordkeeping, using drones to reach remote areas according to the World Health Organization (2022:9).

Aharon et al. (2021:4–5) indicate that the outbreak of COVID-19 saw innovations like the use of hotels as quarantine centers. COVID-19 also resulted in a shift to online sales. It boosted e-commerce as a platform for business between consumers, retailers, and enterprises as noted by Myovella et al. (2020:1). Unable to leave their homes to go shopping due to restrictive measures, people did online shopping as posited by Yuan et al. (2021:9). Tuti (2021:298) notes how sites that previously sold nonessentials began selling food, sanitizers, and masks. In addition, Alwan et al. (2023:47331) also highlighted how online sales of medical goods grew phenomenal.

Response to COVID-19

Hale et al. (2021:738–740) stated that many countries implemented lockdown measures in a bid to contain the pandemic. These entailed, among others, restrictions in internal movements, travel restrictions in and out of the country, restrictions on public transport, ban on public gatherings, imposition of curfews, and social distancing. These authors further state that measures were compiled for stringent index prevention. These included COVID-19 prevention messages encouraging the following: social distancing, wearing of masks, and handwashing. Some governments even passed laws penalizing nonadherence to these protocols.

In addition, according to the World Health Organization (2022:7), service industries like gyms, hair salons, schools, and restaurants were closed. Hospitality industry operations were closed. Other governments put in place safety nets and public distribution of foods for residents. However, none of these mitigatory measures were tailor made for key populations like sex workers, as posited in FHI360 (2020:1–2).

In line with the World Health Organization (2022:7) COVID-19 protocols and guidelines, governments set up quarantine and isolation centers for COVID-19 patients. The downside of these measures was an economic meltdown and financial losses that affected many in different ways. For example, the stigma society attached to sex workers meant that they were more harassed trying to enforce COVID-19 restrictive and containment measures as noted by Gichuna et al. (2020:1433) and Global Network of Sex Work Projects (2021:1). The disproportionate impact of the COVID-19 induced economic meltdown and government-imposed restrictions on sex workers is reflected in study findings in Kenya and Uganda by FHI360 and Kawala et al. (2020:2). The findings of these studies were that the lockdown measures saw sex workers losing their income, resulting in their having challenges getting money for transport to access HIV services.

Governments have an obligation to provide psychosocial support to healthcare providers they employ. Studies by Liu et al. (2020: e17) and Adams and Walls (2020:1439) demonstrate how frontline healthcare providers suffered from anxiety and fear of transmitting the COVID-19 virus to their families but got no support. Yet, on the other hand, positive examples from China show that the provision of psychological support to frontline healthcare providers plays a critical role during emergencies and pandemics in promoting positive mental health outcomes as noted by Chen et al. (2021:1175), Wang et al. (2020:400), and Zaka et al. (2020:884–885). Tessema et al. (2021:1) posit that due to the fragile nature of healthcare systems in Africa, the response to the COVID-19 pandemic was slow and inadequate.

Lessons Learned

The following are some of the key lessons learned from the COVID-19 pandemic:

- Continuous multipronged messaging is needed to reinforce containment measures so that pandemic fatigue does not set in. This will increase vaccine uptake and risk awareness.
- Individual countries have the capacity of innovation and manufacturing. Country appropriate solutions can be found.
- There is need for emergency response funds to meet any epidemic. Many countries did not have this, and yet citizens need cushioning against loss of income due to restrictive measures. Economic mitigation measures need to be put in place in the event of epidemic induced economic measures.
- Gaps, challenges, and limitations emerged: low COVID-19 testing capacity, limitations in sustained surveillance mechanisms, untapped research potential in COVID-19 case management and response, as well as weak emergency supply chain systems. These gaps need to be attended to so as to build resilient healthcare systems.
- Globalization and ease of connectivity facilitate disease spread.
- While each epidemic has its own attributes that call for new strategies for containment, it is critical to leverage on experiences of previous outbreaks. Documenting and using these lessons is a must in order to initiate a rapid emergency response. Also required is the ability to learn about the virus.
- Even with limited resources, the Global South was able to respond quickly to the pandemic. Countries activated a multi-sectoral response, enabling the marshaling of resources coordinated by ministries of health. Thus, countries were able to garner public support in enforcing lockdowns.
- Key in containing pandemics is the willingness of the community to take responsibility to contain the spread. If the community's risk perception is high, containing the pandemic becomes easier.

Looking Ahead

Governments must weigh the advantages and long-term benefits of having emergency response plans and resources to address emergencies such as COVID-19 and their subsequent shocks. In that respect, self-sustaining relief mechanisms are critical. It is in the interest of the Global South to consider putting in place measures to build robust and resilient healthcare systems to ensure treatment continuity of other diseases even in the face of the pandemic, especially noncommunicable ones like diabetes mellitus, hypertension, and cardiac conditions, for example. Because the risk of the disease spreading is high due to the nature of international travel, a coordinated global response to contain the disease and obtain the vaccine is crucial. COVID-19 responses showed that the Global South has the potential to produce country specific solutions. Therefore, countries may consider scaling-up funding for research and strengthening of healthcare systems.

Conclusion

Key among lessons learned from COVID-19 is the need for the Global South to build resilient healthcare systems. The gaps, limitations, and challenges talk to the need to build robust emergency healthcare systems. This can be achieved by leveraging on our experiences of COVID-19 and its containment. This in turn calls for documentation and research as each epidemic/pandemic unfolds to tap on lessons learned. Instead of relying solely on the Global North for vaccines and other medications, the Global South has the potential to manufacture its own vaccines and medicines as India and Cuba have amply demonstrated. This is because given the current socioeconomic dispensation, equitable access to medicines manufactured in the Global North is very challenging. One of the lessons learned from the restrictive measures to contain the pandemic is that whatever restrictive measures are in place, they must be accompanied by economic mitigation measures to support citizens. This is with reference to vulnerable population groups. In addition, the Global South needs to put in place epidemic awareness measures to raise citizens' risk perception of epidemics so that the communities can take responsibility when the need arises.

References

Adams, J. G., & Walls, R. M. (2020). Supporting the health care workforce during the COVID-19 global epidemic. *JAMA, 323*(15), 1439–1440.

Aharon, D. Y., Jacobi, A., Cohen, E., Tzur, J., & Qadan, M. (2021). COVID-19, government measures and hospitality industry performance. *PLoS One, 16*(8), e0255819.

Alwan, S. Y., Hu, Y., Al Asbahi, A. A. M. H., Al Harazi, Y. K., & Al Harazi, A. K. (2023). Sustainable and resilient e-commerce under COVID-19 pandemic: A hybrid grey decision-making approach. *Environmental Science and Pollution Research, 30*(16), 47328–47348.

Asundi, A., O'Leary, C., & Bhadelia, N. (2021). Global COVID-19 vaccine inequity: The scope, the impact, and the challenges. *Cell Host & Microbe, 29*(7), 1036–1039.

Bajaria, S., Exavery, A., Toroka, N., & Abdul, R. (2021). Poor linkage to care for HIV-positive OVC with disabled caregivers: A longitudinal study in Tanzania. *BMC Public Health, 21*, 1–9.

Burki, T. (2021). Global COVID-19 vaccine inequity. *The Lancet Infectious Diseases, 21*(7), 922–923.

Chen, S. H., Liu, J. E., Bai, X. Y., Yue, P., & Luo, S. X. (2021). Providing targeted psychological support to frontline nurses involved in the management of COVID-19: An action research. *Journal of Nursing Management, 29*(5), 1169–1179.

Cohen, I. G., Crespo, A. M., & White, D. B. (2020). Potential legal liability for withdrawing or withholding ventilators during COVID-19: Assessing the risks and identifying needed reforms. *JAMA, 323*(19), 1901–1902.

Deressa, W., Worku, A., Abebe, W., Gizaw, M., & Amogne, W. (2021). Availability and use of personal protective equipment and satisfaction of healthcare professionals during COVID-19 pandemic in Addis Ababa, Ethiopia. *Archives of Public Health, 79*, 1–14.

Durell, K. (2016). Vaccines and IP rights: A multifaceted relationship. In *Vaccine design: Methods and protocols, volume 2: Vaccines for veterinary diseases* (pp. 791–811).

Eccleston-Turner, M., & Upton, H. (2021). International collaboration to ensure equitable access to vaccines for COVID-19: The ACT-accelerator and the COVAX facility. *The Milbank Quarterly, 99*(2), 426–449.

Emanuel, E. J., Luna, F., Schaefer, G. O., Tan, K. C., & Wolff, J. (2021). Enhancing the WHO's proposed framework for distributing COVID-19 vaccines among countries. *American Journal of Public Health, 111*(3), 371–373.

Erfani, P., Binagwaho, A., Jalloh, M. J., Yunus, M., Farmer, P., & Kerry, V. (2021). Intellectual property waiver for covid-19 vaccines will advance global health equity. *BMJ, 374*, n1837.

Fadlallah, R., El-Jardali, F., Hemadi, N., Morsi, R. Z., Abou Samra, C. A., Ahmad, A., Arif, K., Hishi, L., Honein-AbouHaidar, G., & Akl, E. A. (2018). Barriers and facilitators to implementation, uptake and sustainability of community-based health insurance schemes in low-and middle-income countries: A systematic review. *International Journal for Equity in Health, 17*, 1–18.

FHI360. (2020). Meeting targets and maintaining epidemic control (EpiC). Strategic considerations for mitigating the impact of COVID-19 on key-population-focused HIV programs. https://www.fhi360.org/wp-content/uploads/drupal/documents/epic-kp-strategic-considerations-covid-19.pdf

Friebel, R., Molloy, A., Leatherman, S., Dixon, J., Bauhoff, S., & Chalkidou, K. (2018). Achieving high-quality universal health coverage: A perspective from the National Health Service in England. *BMJ Global Health, 3*(6), e000944.

Gichuna, S., Hassan, R., Sanders, T., Campbell, R., Mutonyi, M., & Mwangi, P. (2020). Access to healthcare in a time of COVID-19: Sex workers in crisis in Nairobi, Kenya. *Global Public Health, 15*(10), 1430–1442.

Global Network of Sex Work Projects. (2021). Sex worker-led organisations in DRC issue statement in the wake of escalating violence against sex workers. https://www.nswp.org/fr/news/archive/202105

Hale, T., Angrist, N., Goldszmidt, R., Kira, B., Petherick, A., Phillips, T., Webster, S., Cameron-Blake, E., Hallas, L., Majumdar, S., & Tatlow, H. (2021). A global panel database of pandemic policies (Oxford COVID-19 government response tracker). *Nature Human Behaviour, 5*(4), 529–538.

Hodes, R., Price, I., Bungane, N., Toska, E., & Cluver, L. (2017). How front-line healthcare workers respond to stock-outs of essential medicines in the Eastern Cape Province of South Africa. *South African Medical Journal, 107*(9), 738–740.

Human Rights Watch (HRW). (2020, May 20). Yemen: Displaced at heightened COVID-19 risk. www.hrw.org/news/2020/05/22/yemen-displaced-heightened-covid-19-risk

Jaca, A., Malinga, T., Iwu-Jaja, C. J., Nnaji, C. A., Okeibunor, J. C., Kamuya, D., & Wiysonge, C. S. (2022). Strengthening the health system as a strategy to achieving a universal health coverage in underprivileged communities in Africa: A scoping review. *International Journal of Environmental Research and Public Health, 19*(1), 587.

Kawala, B. A., Kirui, B. K., & Cumber, S. N. (2020). Why policy action should focus on the vulnerable commercial sex workers in Uganda during COVID-19 fight. *The Pan African Medical Journal, 35*, 102.

Kieny, M. P., Bekedam, H., Dovlo, D., Fitzgerald, J., Habicht, J., Harrison, G., Kluge, H., Lin, V., Menabde, N., Mirza, Z., & Siddiqi, S. (2017). Strengthening health systems for universal health coverage and sustainable development. *Bulletin of the World Health Organization, 95*(7), 537.

Lancet, T. (2020). Maintaining the HIV response in a world shaped by COVID-19. *Lancet, 396*(1703), 32526-5.

Liu, S., Yang, L., Zhang, C., Xiang, Y. T., Liu, Z., Hu, S., & Zhang, B. (2020). Online mental health services in China during the COVID-19 outbreak. *The Lancet Psychiatry, 7*(4), e17–e18.

Mangipudi, S., Leather, A., Seedat, A., & Davies, J. (2020). Oxygen availability in sub-Saharan African countries: A call for data to inform service delivery. *The Lancet Global Health, 8*(9), e1123–e1124.

McCann, G., & Matenga, C. (2020). COVID-19 and global inequality. In *COVID-19 in the global south* (pp. 161–172). Bristol University Press.
Moyo, I., Mgolozeli, S. E., Risenga, P. R., Mboweni, S. H., Tshivhase, L., Mudau, T. S., Ndou, N. D., & Mavhandu-Mudzusi, A. H. (2021, December). Experiences of nurse managers during the COVID-19 outbreak in a selected district hospital in Limpopo province, South Africa. In *Healthcare* (Vol. 10, No. 1, p. 76). MDPI.
Moyo, I., Tshivhase, L., & Mavhandu-Mudzusi, A. H. (2022). Utilisation of HIV services by female sex workers in Zimbabwe during the COVID-19 pandemic: A descriptive phenomenological study. *African Journal of AIDS Research, 21*(2), 183–193.
Muswere, A. (2020). Is Africa capable of achieving the sustainable development goals in the 2020–2030 decade of programming. *Journal of Public Administration and Governance, 10*(4), 5372–5372.
Myovella, G., Karacuka, M., & Haucap, J. (2020). Digitalization and economic growth: A comparative analysis of sub-Saharan Africa and OECD economies. *Telecommunications Policy, 44*(2), 101856.
Okereke, M. (2021). Towards vaccine equity: Should big pharma waive intellectual property rights for COVID-19 vaccines? *Public Health in Practice, 2*, 100165.
Padmanabhan, S., Amin, T., Sampat, B., Cook-Deegan, R., & Chandrasekharan, S. (2010). Intellectual property, technology transfer and manufacture of low-cost HPV vaccines in India. *Nature Biotechnology, 28*(7), 671–678.
Rajbhandari, R., McMahon, D. E., Rhatigan, J. J., & Farmer, P. E. (2020). The neglected hospital-the district hospital's central role in global health care delivery. *The New England Journal of Medicine, 382*(5), 397–400.
Ross, M., & Wendel, S. K. (2023). Oxygen inequity in the COVID-19 pandemic and beyond. *Global Health: Science and Practice, 11*(1), e2200360.
Shanafelt, T., Ripp, J., & Trockel, M. (2020). Understanding and addressing sources of anxiety among health care professionals during the COVID-19 pandemic. *JAMA, 323*(21), 2133–2134.
Sharma, S., Kawa, N., & Gomber, A. (2022). WHO's allocation framework for COVAX: Is it fair? *Journal of Medical Ethics, 48*(7), 434–438.
Sun, S., Xie, Z., Yu, K., Jiang, B., Zheng, S., & Pan, X. (2021). COVID-19 and healthcare system in China: Challenges and progression for a sustainable future. *Globalization and Health, 17*, 1–8.
Tessema, G. A., Kinfu, Y., Dachew, B. A., Tesema, A. G., Assefa, Y., Alene, K. A., Aregay, A. F., Ayalew, M. B., Bezabhe, W. M., Bali, A. G., & Dadi, A. F. (2021). The COVID-19 pandemic and healthcare systems in Africa: A scoping review of preparedness, impact and response. *BMJ Global Health, 6*(12), e007179.
Tuti, M. (2021, July). Maintaining sustainability competitiveness in food entrepreneurship during COVID-19 pandemic. In Proceeding international conference on economics, business and https://pdf.usaid.gov/pdf_docs/PA00Z3VT.pdfUnitedNations,2020. World economic situation and prospects 2020. https://www.un.org/development/desa/dpad/publication/world-economic-situation-and-prospects-2020/
United Nations Office for the Coordination of Humanitarian Affairs (OCHA). (2023). Global humanitarian response plan: COVID-19. United Nations Coordinated Appeal. United Nations. https://www.unodc.org/unodc/en/press/releases/2020/March/covid-19-global-humanitarian-response-plan.html
USAID, PEPFAR. (2020). Strategic considerations for mitigating the impact of COVID-19 on key-population-focused HIV programs. https://pdf.usaid.gov/pdf_docs/PA00Z3VT.pdf
Usher, A. D. (2021). A beautiful idea: How COVAX has fallen short. *The Lancet, 397*(10292), 2322–2325.
Wang, C., Pan, R., Wan, X., Tan, Y., Xu, L., McIntyre, R. S., Choo, F. N., Tran, B., Ho, R., Sharma, V. K., & Ho, C. (2020). A longitudinal study on the mental health of general population during the COVID-19 epidemic in China. *Brain, Behavior, and Immunity, 87*, 40–48.

Wise, J. (2021). Covid-19: G7 vaccine promises fail to meet scale of challenge, say critics. *BMJ, 373*, n1520.
World Bank. (2020). *Public expenditure and financial accountability assessment: Federal Democratic Republic of Ethiopia (Southern nations, nationalities and peoples region)*. World Bank.
World Health Organization. (2020a). *Pulse survey on continuity of essential health services during the COVID-19 pandemic: Interim report, 27 August 2020 (No. WHO/2019-nCoV/EHS_continuity/survey/2020.1)*. World Health Organization.
World Health Organization. (2020b). *Maintaining essential health services: Operational guidance for the COVID-19 context: Interim guidance, 1 June 2020 (No. WHO/2019-nCoV/essential_health_services/2020.2)*. World Health Organization.
World Health Organization. (2022). Africa's response to the COVID-19 pandemic: A summary of country reports–January 2020 to December 2021. In Africa's response to the COVID-19 pandemic: A summary of country reports–January 2020 to December 2021.
Yiek, W. K., Coenen, O., Nillesen, M., van Ingen, J., Bowles, E., & Tostmann, A. (2021). Outbreaks of healthcare-associated infections linked to water-containing hospital equipment: A literature review. *Antimicrobial Resistance & Infection Control, 10*, 1–19.
Yuan, J., Zou, H., Xie, K., & Dulebenets, M. A. (2021). An assessment of social distancing obedience behavior during the COVID-19 post-epidemic period in China: A cross-sectional survey. *Sustainability, 13*(14), 8091.
Zaka, A., Shamloo, S. E., Fiorente, P., & Tafuri, A. (2020). COVID-19 pandemic as a watershed moment: A call for systematic psychological health care for frontline medical staff. *Journal of Health Psychology, 25*(7), 883–887.

Idah Moyo is currently a Clinical Services Specialist for Populations Solution for Health in Zimbabwe. She is a Public Health Specialist with focus on integrated HIV programming. Dr. Moyo holds a PhD in Health Studies from the University of South Africa. She is also a holder of several diplomas, a BA, and Master's in Nursing Science. She is also a research fellow at the Department of Health Studies, University of South Africa. Her research focus is on HIV, Key populations, Maternal and Child Health and Public Health. Dr. Moyo has over 25 peer-reviewed publications and three book chapters.

Benny Moyo is currently the secretary for education in Bulawayo progressive residents' association (BPRA). He has over four decades of experience as an educator and high school principal. He is a lecturer at the Catholic University of Zimbabwe (CUZ). He holds a Master's Degree in Education from Solusi University and a Bachelor's Degree in Education from the University of Zimbabwe. His research interests include language and education, communication and development, language policy and language planning, as well as language and ethnicity.

Chapter 14
Emergency Humanitarian Commodity Management Conundrum During the COVID-19 Pandemic Era: A Zimbabwean Experience

Shepherd Gudyani

Introduction

The place of the Global South in world politics must be reevaluated in light of three global storms. The first is the global financial crisis of 2008, which had a negative impact on the capitalist economies all over the world. The COVID-19 pandemic outbreak in 2020 is the second example, which exposed both the shortcomings of the health system and the inequalities in the current international system (Laborde & Vos, 2020). The third event, which will have major effect on the Global South, is Russia's invasion of Ukraine by force in February 2022. These global storms have also exposed the systemic (McKeon, 2015), structural, institutional, epistemological, ethical, and leadership weaknesses of the existing world order. The COVID-19 outbreak in November 2019 and its rapid spread from China to all countries across the world challenged preconceived beliefs about the vulnerability of populations, the tenacity of international institutions, and even the durability of globalization. According to the World Health Organization (2020), COVID-19, a contagious illness brought on by the SARS-CoV-2 virus, spread viciously across the world with the majority of the virus-infected individuals experiencing a mild to severe respiratory disease and recovering without the need for special care. However, some people got serious illnesses and needed medical assistance.

Developing countries in the Global South face issues from this epidemic that are at least as onerous as those faced by developed countries in the Global North. Inadequate public health systems, subpar living conditions, and a lack of services in rural locations with dispersed people or metropolitan areas with high population density are some of the challenges (McLaren et al., 2020). The national accounts of

S. Gudyani (✉)
Heritage, Historical and Sustainable Development, Great Zimbabwe University, Masvingo, Zimbabwe

G. Moyo, S. J. Ndlovu-Gatsheni (eds.), *Global Storms and Africa in World Politics*, Global Power Shift, https://doi.org/10.1007/978-3-031-83868-2_14

middle-income countries, whose economies are usually export-oriented and dependent on commodities, are severely strained by the decline in global demand. Some nations rely substantially on international remittances and tourism; thus, any fall in these sectors exacerbates unemployment and income losses. The regional organizations' reactions to this widespread threat to people's lives and livelihoods revealed the diversity within the Global South.

Collective responses were required to address the social and economic repercussions of the COVID-19 outbreak in Zimbabwe and throughout Africa. Zimbabwe and the African continent, who already have serious problems with food security, were seriously threatened by the quick spread of the epidemic and the shutting of borders as a result of COVID-19 lockdown restrictions. For the past 20 years, Zimbabwe and the majority of African countries have relied on external actors and humanitarian assistance. Millions of people cross Africa and other continents in search of a better life in nearby nations, which is a serious scenario. These populations in Zimbabwe and the rest of Africa mostly rely on unofficial humanitarian supply chains (HSCs) to provide for and send money to family members in their home nations as well as food and other necessities. The catastrophic Coronavirus in 2019 (COVID-19 pandemic) worsened the socioeconomic and political conditions over the whole African continent.

Global and African logistics and supply chain management as well as Zimbabwean humanitarian efforts were impacted by the COVID-19 pandemic catastrophe. In order to shield more vulnerable areas from sudden-onset disasters, supply networks must respond swiftly and nimbly when a crisis arises (Mbohwa, 2020). Emergency response is practically impossible when logistical resources are limited. The absence of storage facilities is a major issue in handling logistics and humanitarian relief. Both the administration and its humanitarian issues are extremely concerned about this. Disaster response teams or organizations must look into ways of increasing their logistical and management capacities in order to address global challenges (United Nations World Food Programme (UNWFP), 2020). According to UNWFP (2020), using mobile storage units (MSUs), which are used by major humanitarian organizations like UNWFP worldwide as temporary warehouses for the food that the organization procures and distributes to vulnerable food insecure households around the world, is one such solution that can be achieved. MSUs are used by state governments and humanitarian actors to increase storage capacities in dealing with threats to their socioeconomic and political stability.

The importance of having appropriate logistics management systems has been demonstrated by the Haiti example, even when mirrored against global storms such as the COVID-19. The effective distribution of humanitarian relief depends on adequate logistical planning and storage, as demonstrated by examples from Haiti. The execution of development and humanitarian relief projects in Haiti is made even more difficult by a lack of acceptable and sufficient logistical infrastructure, according to the DCLA Haiti Storage Assessment (DCLA) (2015). Even before the 2010 earthquake, Haiti's storage infrastructure was insufficient to completely satisfy the requirements of the humanitarian community (DCLA, 2015). According to UNWFP

(2020), this had a considerable effect on the UN Agency's attempts to respond to the earthquake.

The logistics and organizational issues related to humanitarian aid took on a new dimension as a result of the COVID-19 epidemic. Working staff were compelled to leave their regular work locations, including the majority of the enormous nod warehouses, when lockdown began and offices were closed. The humanitarian assistance initiatives in Zimbabwe that were based on an in-kind (commodity-based, food and nonfood products) model and where all deliveries were made from a single central warehouse, such as the Manica warehouse in Harare or another outside the country, were put under some strain as a result (UNWFP, 2021).

Before the COVID-19 epidemic, the UN World Food Programme relied on Manica warehouse in Harare for the storage and handling of large amounts of its food and nonfood commodities for various response programs. This would also imply that there were numerous activities and social interactions taking place during the time before COVID-19 arrived. This demonstrates how challenging it can be to react to global storms, hazards, or calamities. Humanitarian emergency logistics, according to Mbohwa (2020), often concentrate on the response phase of disaster management with an emphasis on search and rescue, sustaining or saving life, and reestablishing self-sufficiency. In the face of the COVID-19 pandemic, the position of Africa in dealing with disasters was exposed. The fragility of the continent was revealed in the way it responded to the pandemic, the challenges it faced, and the strategies employed to counter those challenges.

As the COVID-19 spread across the world, it affected vulnerable people, particularly in underdeveloped nations, and calls for increased humanitarian assistance increased (Wilkins Hospital, 2021). However, as already been indicated, operational hurdles include logistical concerns, organizational issues with emergency response (which impact decision-making and coordination), and issues with disaster management policy (mitigation, prevention, and preparedness). The social and economic circumstances of the disaster area, the overstretching of financial resources (due to the multiplicity of responding actors, the marginalization of local actors by international actors, and assistance without a needs assessment), and ineffective coordination all have an impact on humanitarian assistance in times of need (Thevenaz & Resodihardjo, 2010).

Locating Africa in Global Politics Through COVID-19 Lenses

The sustainable humanitarian supply chain management model by Kunz and Gold (2015), which contends that disaster response operations should primarily aim to provide aid to as many victims as they can in the shortest amount of time, with little regard for the socioeconomic environment and challenges, served as the foundation for locating of the African continent against global storms such as the COVID-19 pandemic. The COVID-19 pandemic severely weakened the African region's socio-eco-political capacity to address its own problems due to the fragile nature of the

African continent. The COVID-19 scenario significantly weakened the continent's capacity, but it was still necessary to use the right strategies to overcome logistical and commodity management challenges in order to successfully distribute humanitarian help to those in need. However, according to the Sustainable Humanitarian Supply Chain disposition, disasters are not a means to an end; rather, they are an opportunity to review the context of the current issue, and the perspective needs to be broadened and thoroughly take into account the local environment as well as opportunities to introduce new strategies that help with the operations (Kunz & Gold, 2015).

According to the framework, supply chain architecture for humanitarian situations like the COVID-19 needs to be in line with the enablers of disaster response for relief organizations as well as adaptable and suitable for the current circumstances, the long-term needs of the afflicted people, and any socioeconomic and political threats. In this regard, the COVID-19 pandemic probed further the capacity of Africa to stand against threats to its socioeconomic and political stamina. When specific conditions and goals are met, the administration and distribution of humanitarian aid run more smoothly. The use of mobile storage units would become a part of the various strategies to distribute humanitarian aid and manage humanitarian logistics, even in difficult situations, like as during the COVID-19 pandemic era, but also indicated the position of Africa in terms of its political economy and readiness to deal with its own challenges. According to Clapp and Moseley (2020), humanitarian assistance is generally understood to refer to aid and action intended to save lives, relieve suffering, uphold and protect human dignity throughout the course of and after man-made crises and natural disasters, as well as prevent and improve preparedness for the occurrence of such situations.

Movable Storage Units and Logistics Management

Movable storage units are characterized as solitary storage units that are portable and can be moved to different locations with ease as needed in an effort to examine the impact of movable storage units in the reaction against COVID-19. An MSU, similar to a scientific warehouse, may be constructed on level or firm ground or at a greater elevation in 2–3 days, according to Clapp and Moseley (2020). Its dimensions are 24 meters by 10 meters by 5.5 meters, and it can store around 450 metric tons. It is comprised of a waterproof material that also allows for airflow. A movable storage unit is a building, similar to a scientific warehouse that may be easily constructed on level and hard ground or on a raised elevation with little material required, according to the United Nations World Food Programme (UNWFP, 2020). This type of storage facility's adaptability is more adapted to the conditions of disaster response, especially in a world that continues to be ravaged by global storms.

It can be built in a variety of sizes, but it must be large enough to assist in handling massive commodity programs for both food and nonfood items. UNWFP (2020) states that the MSU has dimensions of 24 meters by 10 meters by 5.5 meters and a storage capacity of over 450 metric tons. It is made of a material that is waterproof while yet allowing for airflow. Additionally, the NRS Relief (2021) recently discussed the adaptability of mobile storage units, adding that they can also be referred to as such. In reality, the mobile storage unit is a very modular structure that can be transformed into a variety of other solutions, including hospital wards and even fully functional field hospitals or emergency rooms for teams responding to a situation like the COVID-19, according to the NRS Relief (2021) and Mbohwa (2006).

The term "logistics management" describes the process of purchasing, storing, and moving products from one location to another. According to Schmidhuber et al. (2020), it entails maintaining the inventory, resources, and relevant information as well as delivering the products to the appropriate location at the appropriate time and to the appropriate client. According to Mbohwa (2020), logistics is the process of effectively managing the procurement, movement, and storage of materials and goods for a particular operation, as well as the related information flow. In order to complete tasks outlined for an event, such as responding to humanitarian needs through an organization and its teams on the ground, logistics is used. The management also emphasizes the need to complete duties in the least expensive way possible. According to Mbohwa (2020), humanitarian emergency logistics call for the delivery of the necessary goods in good condition, when and where they are needed, a variety of conveyance, frequently improvised at the local level, and restricted, quick, and focused deliveries from outside the region.

Additionally, it necessitates the coordination and prioritization of the use of scarce and shared transport resources, as well as the storage, staging, and movement of bulk commodities, as well as the safety of those receiving assistance and those providing it. Due to the modifications and restrictions brought about by the requirement to halt the spread of the disease and safeguard the vulnerable groups, several logistical variables were in action with the COVID-19. Nevertheless, Mbohwa (2020) noted that despite the COVID-19's complications, the primary operational factors that influence a disaster response remain: the infrastructure's capacity, the quantity and availability of transportation resources in the nation or region, the politics of the situation, and civil unrest in the operational area. The UNDAC (2006) states that the supply chain serves as the foundation for the construction and management of emergency logistics.

Compounded Food Security Crisis

Food security and nutrition have been significantly impacted by the COVID-19 pandemic, which began spreading quickly and widely in late 2019 (Micha et al., 2020). Through a number of factors, the crisis has impacted food systems and put people's access to food in peril. As a result of lockdowns brought on by the global health crisis, there was a substantial disruption in the food supply chains. However, there was also a significant worldwide economic slowdown and a very unequal recovery as new virus types circulated, posing additional hazards to public health and food security. These crises have led to lower wages and higher, more volatile food costs, which have made food unaffordable for many people, undermined their right to food, and slowed progress toward achieving the SDGs. According to the UNWFP (2020), even developed nations were massively affected by the COVID-19 as food insecurity statistics soured high because of the pandemic.

Zimbabwe's and many other African economies experienced recessions, making them susceptible to COVID-19 shock-induced food shortages. Zimbabwe's economy is more diversified (UNWFP, 2015), and because it is a part of international supply networks, trade interruptions also had a wider and more lasting effect. Zimbabwe experienced more challenging humanitarian situations including food crisis and stress. This is explained by the considerably higher vulnerability to losing jobs in the formal sector and the closure of the many value chains that were sources of income for the people, limited use of agricultural land, and others. The signs of the global and Zimbabwean food security problem brought on by the COVID-19 epidemic included food supply chain disruptions, disruptions to social protection programs and altered food environments, and global economic recession and associated income losses.

Following the implementation of lockdown measures, there have been significant disruptions to the food supply chains, which have had an impact on the availability, cost, and quality of food in Zimbabwe. When the epidemic first began, the closing of restaurants and other food service establishments caused a substantial decline in demand for specialty commodities like chocolate and some expensive cuts of meat as well as perishable foods like dairy products, potatoes, and fresh fruits. According to Terazono and Munshi (2020), food products were being abandoned or plowed back into the fields as the first pandemic-related lockdowns got underway because of either fallen demand or challenges delivering these foods to markets. Farmers who lacked sufficient cold storage facilities were left with food they couldn't sell.

In Zimbabwe, lockdown measures during the first several months of the pandemic were particularly detrimental to food transit through international commerce routes. Food producers who depended on selling their crops through far-off export markets were particularly susceptible as borders closed and demand for some food items decreased, especially those who were focused on perishable food and agricultural products like fresh fruits and vegetables. Clapp and Moseley (2020) drew attention to the fact that, during the COVID-19 outbreak, some food exporting countries also imposed export restrictions on significant staple foods like rice and wheat, which resulted in some disruptions in the global movement of these foods as well as higher prices for these crops in comparison with others. Some countries, such as those where food insecurity is a serious problem, like Zimbabwe, rely substantially on the import and export of commodities, rendering them particularly vulnerable to supply chain interruptions of this kind.

The COVID-19 pandemic has had a significant and negative economic impact on global income and livelihoods (UNWFP, 2021). The loss of purchasing power among individuals who lost their employment has considerably harmed food security and nutrition, especially for those that were already at risk. In particular, those who work in the informal economy have been affected. According to the World Bank, between 119 and 124 million more people were believed to be living in abject poverty. Six months into the pandemic, according to Torero (2020), the lives of food producers and system employees were further harmed as food demand fell as a result of dropping salaries. At the start of the pandemic, the United Nations (UN) calculated that almost one-third of livelihoods in the food chain were under danger (UNWFP, 2021). The pandemic in Zimbabwe has had a particularly significant impact on the employment in the food and accommodation industries, with a decrease in employment notably hurting micro and small firms. In low-income countries, COVID-19 has led to bigger reductions in labor income than job losses, notably in the agriculture industry and other sectors where informal and self-employment are common (Gwarisa, 2020).

In Zimbabwe and other nations across the Africa and the world at large, social protection systems have been affected by the epidemic, which has had an impact on nutrition and food security. The loss of household, community, and school lunch programs occurred in both high- and low-income countries because the majority of food systems and environments were shuttered when the lockdowns started. Children were denied access to school meals as a result of school closings following the epidemic, according to the UNWFP (UNWFP, 2020). In certain nations, governments and the WFP worked together to create alternate strategies for providing food aid to school-aged children, such as take-home rations, vouchers, and cash transfers (UNWFP, 2020).

The pandemic has significantly changed the food ecosystems (Makoni, 2021). The context and, consequently, how individuals engage and interact with the food system to get, prepare, and consume food have changed as a result of the lockdown measures and supply chain disruptions mentioned above. People who had been eating at restaurants and food stands suddenly found themselves cooking at home as a result of the closure of these establishments. Foods that were previously produced and packaged specifically for food service, however, were unable to be easily repackaged for retail sales and home use due to supply chain rigidities. The connection that used to be there between smallholder farmers and markets (Kay et al., 2014) had been disrupted by the COVID-19 pandemic. According to the UNWFP (2020), as the COVID-19 pandemic spread, many nations moved to close informal food markets because they were seen as potential sites for the spread of disease. This action was a reflection of a "formality" bias in public health and food policy. In developing nations, informal markets play a crucial role as sources of food and income (Makoni, 2021). In Zimbabwe, formal grocery stores that sell packaged and processed foods were permitted to continue operating.

Emergency Humanitarian Commodity Management

This chapter established the role of MSUs and other logistical procedures during the COVID-19 epidemic in Zimbabwe and the Southern African region with the participation of mostly external actors, however with also a wide range of regional and local participants, including those who benefited from humanitarian interventions in Zimbabwe. This chapter benefited greatly from contributions made by stakeholders to the Lean Season Assistance (LSA) program, a World Food Programme initiative that was implemented in rural Zimbabwe in response to the COVID-19 epidemic. The program was created as a reaction to the state of food insecurity, which was principally caused by the COVID-19 outbreak and the related economic hardships and which greatly benefitted from the usage of MSUs. The usage of mobile storage units (MSUs) to combat the COVID-19 outbreak in Zimbabwe has greatly aided in protecting the socioeconomic position of the country and continent at large in the event of calamities rather than only aiding Africa's ability to handle the COVID-19 crisis. Further, discussions that cut across Africa's experience with COVID-19 helped to shape the position of Africa against global storms in this chapter. Mobile storage units were crucial in storing humanitarian goods during the COVID-19 pandemic. Many external actors and organizations struggled with a lack of storage space for medical equipment and supplies, humanitarian goods, and other types of relief as demand for these items skyrocketed.

In order to deal with the COVID-19 challenges, organizations such as the UNWFP deployed mobile storage units in their operational areas where programs such as the Lean Season Assistance program were being implemented. MSUs were distributed to districts in needy and local areas where programs were being implemented by the UNWFP Supply Chain Unit in collaboration with the Food Security and Livelihood cluster, Social Welfare, and the Logistics and Preparedness cluster and other sectors. In order to provide a flexible covered storage area that may be used and deployed in accordance with each district's needs (according to its tonnage requirements), the MSUs became a plan. The MSUs also served as transactional warehouses, where food items such grains, pulses, vegetable oil, nutritive food products, COVID-19 protective gear, and other supplies were kept until they were sent to distribution centers.

As goods were now being shipped directly from various suppliers to the district MSUs (from as far away as the entire Southern African region), the UNWFP and other partners were able to reduce the number of employees working in the main warehouses in this case. This reduced the number of times people would mix as well as the transactional costs associated with warehousing and logistics, delays, and pressure to deliver goods once field distribution plans were shared. To ensure that part of the supplies would be prepositioned for later months, the UNWFP and World Vision Zimbabwe ensured that the capacity of each district MSU covered the requirements and demands for a complete cycle of distribution or beyond.

All regions in Africa and within countries followed roughly the same COVID-19 preventive methods; if an organization discovers positive cases among its staff, the organization was compelled to place the remaining personnel in quarantine. In this instance, work was suspended in order to give worker safety high priority. However, work went on as long as the cooperating partner (both international and local NGOs) rigorously followed the preventative rules in areas where commodities could have already been prepositioned and took advantage of the safety that was provided by the mobile storage units to quick change plans and position supportive teams to distribute humanitarian and health assistance. The presence of mobile storage units ensured that teams using the facilities always had access to clearly marked water points, handwashing points, and clearly marked instructions for various purposes, such as safe water for drinking, water for handwashing stations, water for cleaning and disinfecting surfaces, and water in sufficient quantities and temperature checking screening points. In order to ensure that sanitation facilities were routinely maintained and disinfected, as well as that prevention supplies were replenished to meet the needs of the staff running the MSU and those bringing in goods from various distant suppliers, the UNWFP and partners had the COVID-19 focal persons. These individuals would work together with everyone intending to benefit from the use of the movable storage units.

With the MSUs allowing weekly shifts of small groups to ensure proper social distance during the operations as well as proper management of spaces for commodities and people, the availability of multiple solutions to stop the COVID-19 helped to facilitate ongoing processes of receiving and dispatching commodities to the distribution points. It was also about enabling people and commodities to coexist peacefully and safely so that disaster response efforts may continue. This is what logistics management (see Mbohwa, 2006) has been all about during the COVID-19 pandemic. This chapter noted that maintaining a clean workplace was a top priority and that frequent cleaning of the floors, surfaces, and any other contact points as well as the linen was one of the most important lessons learned from using MSUs. This also included disinfecting and cleaning the actual MSU building, which was made possible by the way they were constructed.

Aprons, boots, waste containers, and water containers, all of which needed to be cleaned and disinfected, were available in adequate quantities. To disinfect surfaces, sodium hypochlorite (chlorine) at 0.1% (equal 1000 ppm) was also available. Frequently touched items were cleaned and disinfected using common household cleaning sprays or wipes. Cleaning workers (hygienist) got training on decontamination techniques as well as the World Health Organization-recommended donning/doffing personal protective equipment (PPE) procedures. Also, organizations trained sanitation workers and waste handlers on PPE donning and doffing, decontamination, and IPC (infection prevention and control) procedures. Every day before they enter the MSUs, all staff had their temperatures taken. Designated MSU or warehouse supervisors were keeping an eye on compliance with COVID-19 protocols (such as mask use, physical separation, and hand hygiene).

Utilizing hydrogen peroxide, sodium hypochlorite (chlorine), or chloride of lime helped to keep surfaces cleaned every day after work. Through the Ministry of Health and Child Care, field staff and loaders at the MSUs received regular training. The organization of commodities in the MSUs was in such a way that when working in groups, the loaders avoided working excessive hours. Also, to prevent heavy concentration of loaders at one truck, the MSUs contained more than one bay for offloading and dispatching, which was key on avoiding receiving and dispatching at the same time, thus preventing the congregation of drivers from various locations. To prevent loaders from spending a lot of time in the MSUs, daily dispatch tonnage wasn't too high—this was done to also prevent unneeded pressure that results in the breakdown of stated measures, providing sufficient time for receiving and for dispatches. By lowering the tonnage per day and lengthening the number of days, fewer loaders are required.

Some traditional storage facilities were instantly overflowing as a result of the COVID-19 crisis because of the sudden increase in demand for medical supplies, personal protective equipment (PPE), and other essential items. Makoni (2021) claims that mobile storage containers provided additional space for the short-term storage of these goods, relieving pressure on storage facilities. Since they are designed to protect items from weather and pests, mobile storage containers are a safe and secure option for the storage of humanitarian goods throughout the pandemic. To safeguard the kept items from theft and damage, many units have high-tech security features including locks and alarms. Participants in the field research stated that the MSUs offered immediate safe and secure storage, which aided in the efforts for humanitarian aid. In accordance with the tonnages that were anticipated to be transported throughout the districts, the storage facilities would be built rapidly and in sufficient numbers. Regions in Manicaland such Buhera and Chipinge districts of Zimbabwe, were able to construct more than four MSUs, which were used to store and tranship goods like grains, vegetable oil, pulses, corn-soya blend porridge (CSB+), mealie meal, and other COVID-19 machinery. Some participants claimed that the MSUs lessened pressure on all sides, even those who were receiving and distributing humanitarian aid. Storage that was safe and secure was one of the primary goals to sustain communities from the COVID-19 scourge.

Customized mobile storage units were available to satisfy the unique requirements of various programs and the modalities that were being used to implement the response programs. They were available in a range of sizes and in some instances include shelves, lighting, and climate control to keep the food commodities and COVID-19 equipment stored in good condition. This adaptability has proved especially helpful during the pandemic when humanitarian programs needed to store many kinds of food, nonfood, and medical goods. Deliveries of mobile storage units were made promptly and frequently in only a few days. This prompt delivery has been essential during the epidemic, particularly in places where there has been an increase in cases and where medical supplies, food assistance, and equipment were urgently needed. The COVID-19 epidemic has shown that movable storage units are a dependable and effective way to store humanitarian aid. According to Khorsandi (2020), they have helped organizations to satisfy the urgent demand for healthcare supplies and equipment by offering more storage capacity, safe and secure storage alternatives, flexibility, and quick delivery.

Because MSUs can be situated close to the recipients for their services, and truck turnaround times were also reduced. This also made it easier to hire secondary transporters, which minimized the likelihood that recipients would encounter transporters coming from high-risk areas. It allowed for simple alterations in accordance with field team recommendations, new COVID-19 regulations, or level of restriction. Commodities didn't need to be prepositioned because MSUs and food distribution points (FDPs) were in close proximity. Having MSUs in the various districts enabled transporters to get at the FDPs earlier, which reduced recipient wait times and facilitated that communities uphold COVID-19 standards. Dispatches were also made based on situational analysis; for example, it was simple to halt dispatches in risky areas or areas where COVID-19 was common. Dispatches were simple to modify in order to meet the altered FDPs with a minimal number of beneficiaries, i.e., dispatches were completed to suit any changes or new developments, particularly when a new FDP was created in an effort to lower the overall number of recipients at an FDP.

Movable Storage Units

Despite the global storms and in the context of COVID-19, businesses and organizations needed more storage space due to the rapid increase in demand for basic products, humanitarian aid, and medical supplies. According to Murewanhema and Makurumidze (2020), mobile storage units provide an effective temporary storage solution for the surplus of commodities. During the COVID-19 period, the MSUs provided both temporary storage and also safer spaces to allow humanitarian assistance to be channeled to the communities in need. Movable storage units have been modified into quarantine facilities, providing isolation and stay away spaces for individuals who needed to be separated from the general population. They have been used to set up temporary quarantine centers in villages, wards, airports, military bases, and other locations to prevent the spread of the virus. Movable storage units have given inventory management of humanitarian aid more room, hence maintaining the stability of the supply chain. The UNWFP (2021) claimed that these units have provided businesses with a tactical way to hold their goods until they can be delivered or dispersed, given the interruptions in transportation and distribution brought on by quarantines and lockdowns. Because they provide temporary storage, flexibility, and valuable uses like quarantine facilities and drive-through testing locations, mobile storage units have proven effective in the COVID-19 environment. They have aided in overcoming logistical difficulties and offering crucial support in the face of the pandemic.

Despite obstacles, Zimbabwe has managed to make creative use of mobile storage units during the COVID-19 pandemic. Zimbabwe used portable storage units for short-term storage. According to Klassen and Murphy (2022), movable storage units have been employed in various nations to provide short-term storage for necessary supplies and items during the COVID era. To meet the increased demand for storage space during the epidemic, these units have been placed in close proximity to hospitals, distribution facilities, and other crucial areas in Zimbabwe. Furthermore, portable storage units were used to provide mobile testing and medical services. According to Laborde and Vos (2021), mobile testing and medical facilities have been made out of portable storage solutions in African nations. These units had the beds, medical equipment, and other materials required to set up testing facilities, temporary clinics, and isolation wards. In areas with limited resources, they have proved essential in enhancing the healthcare and other humanitarian infrastructure.

Zimbabwe was able to manage humanitarian supplies with the help of mobile storage units by collaborating with UN and international organizations like the WFP. This indicates that the distribution and logistics support were better. Distribution and logistics activities were made easier and more effective, thanks to mobile storage units. These storage units have made it possible to stage, sort, and manage commodities properly in remote locations or close to transportation hubs, improving the supply chain in Zimbabwe's difficult conditions. Since the COVID era was generating a food crisis, these mobile storage units were employed as community outreach spaces and helped in terms of food storages. In Zimbabwe, the majority of these locations had food shortages; as a result, the government of Zimbabwe, in collaboration with the World Food Programme and other partners such as World Vision Zimbabwe, Care International, and others, deployed mobile storage for community outreach programs. According to Makoni (2021), Zimbabwe was able to give food, hygiene kits, and other necessities to vulnerable populations during the COVID-19 crisis by transforming these units into mobile food banks or community commodity centers.

Overall, despite its difficulties, Zimbabwe has shown resilience and ingenuity by using mobile storage units to meet its particular needs and restrictions throughout the COVID-19 pandemic. These units have been useful resources for assuring the supply of goods, assisting with healthcare services, and resolving logistical issues in settings with low resources (Murewanhema & Makurumidze, 2020). Zimbabwe has recognized and demonstrated its adaptability and flexibility through the use of movable storage units. The epidemic brought to light the value of adaptability and flexibility in handling quickly changing circumstances. Zimbabwe discovered that mobile storage units could be quickly set up and used for a variety of purposes, including storage, testing, medical facilities, or quarantine facilities. This adaptability enabled a more effective and efficient response to the crisis's changing needs.

The healthcare infrastructure was strengthened. The need for a robust and flexible healthcare infrastructure has been highlighted by the usage of mobile storage facilities. Having portable medical facilities that can be swiftly put up to augment capacity during a healthcare crisis is important, as recognized also by many other nations. As part of emergency preparedness plans, this lesson has led initiatives to fund and build mobile healthcare infrastructure in Zimbabwe. According to Sharma and Gupta (2020), the pandemic emphasized the crucial role that supply chain management and logistics play in maintaining the effective flow of necessities like food and medicine during crisis period. Zimbabwe discovered the value of mobile storage facilities for managing excess inventory, improving inventory control, and addressing brief supply chain disruptions. The significance of efficient logistics planning and coordination has been highlighted by this.

Zimbabwe has learned a vital lesson about crisis readiness from the COVID-19 pandemic. The country came to understand the importance of making proactive investments in and building out portable storage options, healthcare infrastructure, and emergency response capabilities. The need of being well-prepared to react quickly and successfully to emergencies in the future is emphasized in this lesson. The significance of resource optimization and maximizing the usefulness of existing infrastructure has been brought to light by mobile storage facilities. Zimbabwe discovered that reusing existing mobile storage units can help deal with resource shortages and offer quick and affordable solutions during emergencies. Overall, the COVID-19 pandemic's utilization of mobile storage facilities has taught nations the value of adaptability, flexibility, cooperation, and preparedness. Future strategic planning and response initiatives to improve emergency preparedness and response skills will be informed by these lessons.

Challenges in the Usage of Movable Storage Units

There may have been shortages and delays in acquiring moveable storage facilities as a result of rising demand. This challenge has also been confirmed by Gwarisa (2020). It may have been difficult to get these units right away due to supply chain problems, such as low shipping capacity or limitations on manufacture and delivery, which was further made complex by the COVID-19 crisis. Despite their most welcome advantages, there were some difficulties in some instances to keep mobile storage units secure and tidy. To stop the COVID-19 virus from spreading, these units needed to undergo comprehensive sanitization procedures. According to Ondoa (2020), maintaining adequate hygiene inside the units and executing strict cleaning procedures can take a lot of time and resources. This caused bit of a holdup in the units' quick adoption in Zimbabwe.

The need to move or repurpose these units can become necessary if the circumstance changes. Large-scale storage unit relocation and repurposing has been logistically challenging and demanded careful planning to ensure minimal interference with continuing activities. Security measures had to be put in place to stop theft and unauthorized access depending on the contents of the units. To further protect the safety of anybody working in or accessing these units, safety procedures like fire safety measures and structural stability assessments had to be taken into account. According to Dzinamarira (2020), maintaining the security of mobile storage units can be difficult, especially in areas where theft and unlawful entry are common. Since theft is a common thing in most societies, Zimbabwe cannot be spared—it has been difficult to put in place the necessary security measures, which could result in loss or damage to the stored products in some instances.

To protect the safety and well-being of inhabitants, movable storage units used for quarantine or medical purposes must adhere to particular rules and regulations. It might have been difficult and time-consuming to meet these compliance criteria and finish the appropriate certification in the shortest possible time required to respond to the COVID-19 pandemic. Due to a lack of funding or suitable infrastructure, Zimbabwe had trouble accessing mobile storage units. It has been difficult to obtain these units in sufficient numbers because the cost of purchasing and shipping them was prohibitive. There may not have been adequate infrastructure in some remote districts to facilitate the deployment of mobile storage units. These units needed enough acreage, the ability to move things, and facilities for loading and unloading. Inadequate infrastructure made it difficult to deploy these units successfully in some instances.

Mobile storage units come in a wide range of shapes and sizes. It could have been challenging to work with fewer units and less storage space in Zimbabwe. This limitation may have made it challenging to accommodate the surge in storage demand brought on by the pandemic. Mobile storage units can be modified for other COVID-19-related purposes including setting up quarantine facilities or medical facilities. Zimbabwe, however, was one of the countries whose resources would not have been sufficient to adequately convert or repurpose these units, which constrained their ability to meet some pandemic response needs.

Toward Sustainable Solutions

Africa needs to reassert itself to be able to face global storms head on and respond adequately. In the case of global storms like COVID-19, global wars, climate change, and others, the utilization of mobile storage units offered a rationale and a lesson for creativity. Due to the MSUs' importance in improving humanitarian assistance in the African setting, Africa must increase its storm preparation, socio-economic preparedness, and political preparedness in order to adopt and implement these innovations and respond to global storms. Due to the COVID-19 pandemic's exposures of Africa's limits, the use of MSUs necessitates the need for outside humanitarian assistance as a temporary fix, allowing the continent to develop its own plans and solutions. Disaster risk reduction and responding to global storms are closely related, which is why readiness is also emphasized. Prioritizing prepositioning and training related to MSU usage, deployment, and administration is recommended. Policies pertaining to borders that provide simple access and the flow of response supplies must be given top priority throughout Africa. MSUs needed to transfer commodities over international borders, and with the right rules and policies in place, delays and other constraints cannot impede storm response efforts. Even in situations where accessibility issues are common, planning with the poorest groups in mind facilitates prompt and efficient responses. Lastly, the place of the Global South in world politics must be reevaluated in light of many global storms that are ravaging the world. With the early warnings from the Russia-Ukraine war, Africa has to step up, plan, and be ready to respond to these storms. The involvement of other parties is necessary to bolster the handmade African solutions and their organic content.

Conclusion

Globally, COVID-19 has had a major impact—it has left vulnerable communities and individuals facing serious health problems as well as the need for humanitarian aid. The COVID-19 management and logistics support provided Zimbabwe and Africa with invaluable knowledge as efforts to cope with global storms continue to accumulate. The chapter illustrated that Zimbabwe benefited from mobile storage units in conjunction with external actors to work towards a response to COVID-19. After the COVID-19 outbreak, Zimbabwe was faced with logistical and operational issues that could only be resolved with the flexibility and scalability that MSUs offered. During the crisis, MSUs allowed for the rapid and flexible scaling up of storage capacity or repurposing. This flexibility made it possible to respond to the storm's shifting requirements more deftly, deploying MSUs quickly and easily to locations where storage, medical facilities, and quarantine centers were critically required. This quick deployment made it possible to respond more quickly and decreased the pressure on the infrastructure. Another advantage was resource optimization, which made greater use of the existing infrastructure, and mobility, which made it possible to relocate storage units in line with demands and increase accessibility to essential supplies or medical services. The most difficult issue to be addressed was the deployment and management of MSUs, which included setup, travel, and maintenance and necessitated meticulous logistical planning and coordination. The main challenges were water and power because they also came with costs. Relocating storage facilities necessitated costly specific setup, shipment, and ongoing maintenance. Ample planning was insufficient, with utilizing MSUs effectively also required prior preparation, training, and coordination. In order to use MSUs in future storms, several issues must be resolved and especially considerations around preparedness and logistical planning. These concerns mostly center on logistical planning and readiness. MSUs did not only increased humanitarian assistance in Zimbabwe but also in many other developing nations, enabling Africa to weather global storms with strength and resilience. This indicates that Africa must not only rely on outside actors but also adequately prepare for these storms.

References

Clapp, J., & Moseley, W. (2020). This food crisis is different COVID 19 and the fragility of the neoliberal food security order. *Journal of Peasant Studies, 47*(7), 1393–1417. https://doi.org/10.1080/03066150.2020.1823838

Development Coordination and Logics (DCLA), (2015). *United Nations Development Programme (UNDP)*, UNDP 2015.

Dzinamarira, T. (2020). Coronavirus disease 2019 (COVID-19) response in Zimbabwe: A call for urgent scale-up of testing to meet national capacity. *Clinical Infectious Diseases, 72*, ciaa130.

Gwarisa, M. (2020). *Blood shortages hit Zimbabwe*. Health Times. https://healthtimes.co.zw/2020/06/01/justin-blood-shortages-hit-zim/

Kay, A. S., et al. (2014). *Connecting smallholders to markets: Analytical guide. Civil Society Mechanism (CSM).* http://www.csm4cfs.org/wpcontent/uploads/2016/10/ENG-ConnectingSmallholdersToMarkets_web.pdf).
Khorsandi, P. (2020). *WFP chief warns of 'hunger pandemic' as global food crises report launched. World Food Programme Insight.* https://insight.wfp.org/wfp-chief-warns-of-hunger-pandemic-as-global-food-crises-reportlaunched-3ee3edb38e47
Klassen, S., & Murphy, S. (2022). Equity as both a means and an end: Lessons for resilient food systems from COVID-19. *World Development, 136*, 105104.
Kunz, N., & Gold, S. (2015). *Sustainable humanitarian supply chain management—exploring new theory*. Coggin College of Business, University of North Florida.
Laborde, D., & Vos, R. (2020). COVID-19 risks to global food security. *Science, 369*(6503), 500–502. https://science.sciencemag.org/content/369/6503/500
Laborde, D., & Vos, R. (2021). *Estimating the poverty impact of COVID-19: The MIRAGRODEP and POVANA frameworks.* IFPRI Technical Note, IFPRI. https://tinyurl.com/y9fazbzf
Lal, R. (2020). Home gardening and urban agriculture for advancing food and nutritional security in response to the COVID-19 pandemic. *Food Security, 12*(4), 871–876.
Makoni, M. (2021). COVID-19 worsens Zimbabwe's health crisis. *The Lancet, 396*(10249), 457.
Mbohwa, C. (2006). *Identifying challenges and collaboration areas in humanitarian logistics: A Southern African perspective ER*. Department of Quality and Operations Management University of Johannesburg South Africa.
Mbohwa, C. (2020). *Humanitarian logistics: Review and case study of Zimbabwean experiences.* Department of Quality and Operations Management University of Johannesburg South Africa.
McKeon, N. (2015). *Food security governance: Empowering communities, regulating corporations*. Routledge.
McLaren, H. J., Wongc, K., Rosalind, N. K., & Mahamadachchi, K. N. D. (2020). Covid-19 and women's triple burden: Vignettes from Sri Lanka, Malaysia. *Vietnam and Australia. Social Sciences, 9*(5), 87.
Micha, R., et al. (2020). *Global nutrition report: Action on equity to end malnutrition.* https://globalnutritionreport.org/reports/2020-globalnutrition-report/
Murewanhema, G., & Makurumidze, R. (2020). Essential health services delivery in Zimbabwe during the COVID-19 pandemic: Perspectives and recommendations. *Pan African Journal, 35*, 143. https://www.panafrican-med-journal.com/content/series/35/2/143/full/
NRS Relief. (2021). *COVID-19 emergency response solution.*
Ondoa, P. (2020). COVID-19 testing in Africa: Lessons learnt. *The Lancet Microbe, 1*(3), 103.
Schmidhuber, J., Pound, J., & Qiao, B. (2020). *COVID-19: Channels of transmission to food and agriculture.*
Sharma, A., & Gupta, P. (2020). Covid-19: Impact on health supply chain and lessons to be learnt. *Journal of Health Management, 22*(2), 248–261.
Terazono, E., & Munshi, N. (2020, July 30). Choc waves: How coronavirus shook the cocoa market. *Financial Times.*
Thevenaz, P., & Resodihardjo, S. L. (2010). All the best laid plans … conditions impeding proper emergency response. *International Journal of Production Economics, 126*, 7–21.
Torero, M. (2020). *Prepare food systems for a longhaul fight against COVID-19. COVID-19 and global food security.* https://doi.org/10.2499/p15738coll2.133762_27.
United Nations Disaster Assessment and Coordination (UNDAC) Assessment. (2006). https://efaidnbmnnnibpcajpcglclefindmkaj/, https://preparecenter.org/wp
United Nations World Food Programme (UNWFP). (2015). *Haiti digital logistics capacity assessments*. Storage Assessment, Haiti Logistics Cluster.
United Nations World Food Programme (UNWFP). (2020). *Overview of mobile storage units alternate mechanisms for grain storage.*
United Nations World Food Programme (UNWFP). (2021). *End-of-season update for 2020/21 and overview of the food security situation in 2020/21.*

Wilkins Hospital. (2021). *Zimbabwe COVID-19 isolation and treatment reports*. http://www.xinhuanet.com/english/2020-04/10/c_138963696.htm

World Health Organization. (2020). *Coronavirus disease (COVID-19):* Situation Report, 185. https://apps.who.int/iris/handle/10665/333573

Shepherd Gudyani is a food security and Disaster Risk Reduction Specialist at World Vision Zimbabwe. He holds a Bachelor of Science Honors Degree in Local Governance Studies, Master of Science in International Affairs, and Master of Arts in Development Studies, all from Midlands State University in Zimbabwe. He also holds a Master of Science Degree in Disaster Risk and Livelihoods Management from Women University in Africa. He is currently studying towards a PhD in Development Studies at Great Zimbabwe University. His research interests are within human security, community development, food security, poverty reduction, and disaster management. Shepherd is a trained Cash and Voucher transfer expert.

Part IV
Russo-Ukraine War, Coups in Africa and African Agency

Chapter 15
The Impact of the Russia-Ukraine War on the Global South: The Case of Africa

Charles Mutasa

Abstract Russia, Africa, and the Global South need each other. Russia remains an ally of the Global South, especially Africa against Western countries' extremism and bully political tactics and shenanigans. Without the likes of Russia and China, an unpleasant unipolar world which drives the Global South into further poverty, exploitation, lack of self-determination, and misery is likely to emanate. Russia's presence has helped several African countries to strengthen their negotiating powers vis-a-vis Western powers, defend their national sovereignty, and strengthen world multipolarity. Russia's relations with the Global South, especially Africa, can be strengthened by boosting intergovernmental commissions, business councils, sports commissions, and cultural centers between Russia and Africa and countries in the Global South.

Introduction

The term "Global South," just like the term "Third World," is controversial and brings along lots of historic, analytical, intellectual, ideological, and political debates. Alfred Sauvy coined the term in 1952, alluding to a part of the world which was not identified with the capitalist or communist proposition toward modernity—despite the influence of the socialist bloc on different liberation movements. The Third World tradition is associated with the leftist agenda in the search for autonomy, independence, and self-determination (Ballestrin, 2020). Nonetheless, put simply, the term carries connotations that speak—in post colonialism and Cold War episodes—to fundamental political and economic developments in poor and developing countries in contrast to the richest and developed ones in the North (Bourguignon, 2016:11–15). However, as Arif Dirlik (2007) notes, several

C. Mutasa (✉)
Independent Consultant, Harare, Zimbabwe

G. Moyo, S. J. Ndlovu-Gatsheni (eds.), *Global Storms and Africa in World Politics*, Global Power Shift, https://doi.org/10.1007/978-3-031-83868-2_15

developed and powerful countries seem to align themselves to the Global South, that is, Brazil, Russia, China and India, and South Africa.

Sajed (2020) argues that given the current global integration and modernization processes, the term Global South is not just a replacement of the term "Third World." It now includes countries in the North that are easily linked with oppression, exploitation, and neocolonial relations, including ambiguous political and economic spaces inhabited by immigrant communities in Western societies, especially the indigenous and black communities. Ballestrin (2020) argues that although Southeast Europe and the Balkans were politically integrated into the European Union, they only have limited access to Northern political and economic structures, but in terms of their socioeconomic and cultural terms, they are still part of the Global South (Ballestrin, 2020). Capitalist expansion at different historical junctures and in different ways is responsible for the conceptualization and reconceptualization of these two terms, "Third World" and "Global South" (Randall, 2004:41).

The dependency theory argued that Third World countries are not "behind" or in need of "catching up" to the richer countries of the world. Ghosh (2001) argues that Third World countries are poor because they were coercively integrated into the European economic system only as producers of raw materials or to serve as repositories of cheap labor and were thus denied the opportunity to market their resources in any way that competed. For Kay (2011:523), Gunder Frank identified underdevelopment as a conscious political action by the colonial metropole whereby resources belonging to the colonial society/periphery are being extracted and used but used in a way which benefits dominant states and not the poorer states in which their sources are found with dominant states. On the other hand, Rodney argued that underdevelopment is not a product of colonial conquest but also a capitalist world system, which ensured that the metropole exclusively benefited from wealth extraction in the periphery (poor countries) through a form of consistent supply of raw materials (see Matunhu, 2011:66).

In the context of the Russia-Ukraine war, the Global South has several challenges to maintain itself as an indispensable political project toward a fairer and equal world. Interestingly, at the UN debates, the Western countries are busy pledging military support for Ukraine, while those from the Global South are calling for a negotiated peace settlement (see McCarthy, 2023). Interestingly, as Sajed (2020) notes, the place of the Global South in internationalism and international relations largely seems to be defined and determined with what happens between Russia and the United States.

Russia-Global South Relations

As Petras and Veltmeyer (2013) note, due to the fact that Russia did not colonize any country but rather supported and assisted liberation movements against colonialism, Moscow's relations with many countries in the Global South (especially in sub-Saharan Africa, Latin America, and Asia) are well-established giving the country credibility as a reliable partner. Russia is a major nuclear power, the world's largest natural gas exporter, the 2015 largest oil exporter (BP, n.d.), and one of the five nations with veto power on the UN Security Council. In the Middle East, the war in Ukraine is seen not the way the West would want to have it "as good guys in the West versus bad guys in Russia." Anti-Americanism emanates from past military interventions by the United States and its allies, which created a cynical mood toward the West's actions in Ukraine. However, as Askew (2023) notes, this hate for America and NATO does not necessarily translate into the love for Russia.

Russo-Africa relations have been key to the rejection of a "unipolar world," with one dominating power or a group of powers. Russia has emerged as a balancing force in international affairs, especially regarding US policies which are designed to have a US-dominated world. To Russia, Africa with its 1.2 billion people (Tatiana, 2017) play a geopolitical and economic role in furthering Moscow's interest. Africa has remained Russia's support base at the UN. Putin summarized it by saying, "there is still sincere goodwill in Africa towards Russia" (Foreign Policy, 2022a). The Russia-Africa Forum is a convenient platform for discussion of new joint projects and development programs between the African Union (AU) and Russia. AU member states have provided a political support base for Russian-led initiatives at the United Nations, especially around issues of recognition of national sovereignty of states and the principle of noninterference by the UN Security Council. For example, Russia and China have stood against sanctions and arms embargos against Zimbabwe following the June 2008 postelection violence resisting Western countries' attempt to politicize international law. In turn, African leaders like Mugabe have stood in support of Russian positions, including its stance against the invasion of Iraq by the United States in 2003 (Shubin, 2004).

Effects of the War on Africa

Both Africa and Asia are bothered by the allocation of huge sums of aid to Ukraine by Europe and America, while they experience a large decline of aid since the onset of the Russia-Ukraine war. As OECD (2023) reports, the large supply of weapons and the provision of financial support to Ukraine have resulted a decrease in aid flows to Africa and Asia. As Bill Gates notes, many charitable foundations within the European Union have abandoned the Global South, which is in dire need of humanitarian assistance, especially food aid, in preference of Ukraine (Business Times, 2023). The International Monetary Fund (IMF)'s multimillion dollar tranche allocation run counter to its 80 years' tradition of not lending funds to countries at war. By allocating 15.6 billion to Kiev over 4 years as part of an emergency program without spending restrictions and fiscal reforms demanded, the IMF exhibited blatant favoritism, thereby angering countries in the Global South (Business Times, 2023). The Deen (2023) reported the United Nations warned that the Russian invasion of Ukraine will drive about 1.7 billion people into poverty, destitution, and hunger as the 2 countries provided about 30% of the world's wheat and barley, one-fifth of its maize, and over half of its sunflower oil.

As United Nations Assistant Secretary-General, Ahunna Eziakonwa, notes, Russia's war in Ukraine has disrupted Africa's promising recovery from the COVID-19 pandemic by raising food and fuel prices, disrupting trade of goods and services, tightening the fiscal space, constraining green transitions, and reducing the flow of development finance in the continent (see Sen Ashish, 2022). The war has put several households and communities in a precarious position. The AfDB (2022) notes that six African countries (Eritrea, Egypt, Benin, Sudan, Djibouti, and Tanzania) imported over 70% of their wheat from Ukraine and Russia, and the war has caused shortages and sharp price increases of the commodity. The AfDB notes that the Russian invasion of Ukraine triggered a shortage of about 30 million tons of grains on the continent, along with a sharp increase in cost. One case of a directly affected African country is that of Kenya, which relied heavily on Russia and Ukraine for oil, wheat, fertilizers, iron, and steel as critical imports for their sustenance and development. Kiptoo (2022) notes that in Kenya, 67% of the wheat consumption is from Russia, 22% from Ukraine, and 11% from the rest of the world. As a net importer of wheat, without imports from Ukraine and Russia, it is difficult for Kenya to meet its consumption of about 900,000 tons per year, with only an annual national wheat production of approximately 350,000 tons (KIPPRA, 2022). Climate change induced erratic and unreliable weather patterns have exacerbated the situation. A disruption in these critical trading areas is adversely impacting these African countries.

The sanctions against Russia directly impact Kenya. In the face of depressed demand, some Kenyan farmers have reduced production of commodities that solely targeted the Russian market in the past. According to Kiptoo (2022), in 2021, Kenyan exports to Russia were worth 83 USD million (KES 10.47 billion), while its imports from Russia were worth 310 USD million (KES 37.66 billion). Since the Russia-Africa Summit held in Sochi in 2019, Kenya and Russia were partnering in the higher education sector, with Russia providing both undergraduate and post-graduate scholarship opportunities to Kenyans for human resources development. Beyond these, several development and technical cooperation partnerships were being explored, which included other forms of investments, one of which is energy. The cost of oil products has increased in line with price hikes in production and transport costs. According to MoALF (2022), a spike in fertilizer prices in Kenya due to the Russia-Ukraine war forced the Minister of Agriculture to introduce a fertilizer subsidy program, which is proving to be difficult in terms of management. The NTEP (2023) claims that trading statistics indicate that in 2021, Kenya imported almost 30% of its wheat from Russia and Ukraine. Kenya's exports to Ukraine mainly consisting of tea, coffee, cut flowers, and vegetables have decreased, as these exports are adversely affected by the war. Wheat is used to produce bread, which is one of the most consumed food commodities in Kenya. Kiptoo (2022) argues that since Kenya is a commodity market, a country that generates most of its revenue through commodity exports, the war means considerable loses of trade with both Ukraine and Russia. Given the imposition of sanctions on Russia, shipping companies have stopped taking orders associated with Russia, while the banks have excluded Russian banks in the SWIFT payment system, making the payment of commodities impossible. Kenya is currently diversifying its commodity sources through engaging countries like India and Australia to bridge its wheat and other commodity deficits caused by the Russia-Ukraine war.

Politically, the United States is not comfortable with Africa's neutral stance on the Russia-Ukraine war, and more so, it seems offended with African Russian relations that seem to implicitly condone than condemn Russian invasion of Ukraine. Thus, instead of promoting global democracy, the war in Ukraine has created divisions. The Washington Press Secretary has indicated that the United States is contemplating on introducing a bill [Countering Malign Russian Activities in Africa Act] that would oblige the United States "to punish African countries who aid and abet what it sees as Russian "malign" activities on the continent" (Muronzi, 2023). What is clear is that the United States is offended by Russian influence in the continent and its warming diplomatic ties with countries like South Africa, Egypt, Ethiopia, and Uganda, among many others. In Uganda, President Yoweri Museveni was blatant and did not mince his words when he said:

> We don't believe in being enemies of somebody's enemy… We have forgiven our former enemies: the colonialists that did bad things to us, how can we be against somebody who never harmed us but instead helped us…we want to trade with Russia. … I am pro-myself and I deal with all the other people according to how they relate with my own interests. (Monitor, 2022)

Museveni reminded the West of Africa's historical ties with Moscow and the longtime relationship between Africa and Russia, which spans to more than 100 years at a time the United States expected African countries to isolate Russia. Russia and Uganda agreed to cooperate in the areas of cybersecurity, space technology, and pathogen technology, among many others. Overall, a diplomatic rift is unfolding between the United States and several African countries who have a cynical view of a global order that is more often dictated to them by the West. A resentment of Western domination in global affairs based on a self-centered approach is being resisted by the Global South. As Handy and Djilo (2022) note, the United States expected African countries to join it in condemning Russian invasion of Ukraine, but on the contrary, several African countries are cementing their relations with Russia, snubbing the US "big brother expectation," which is aimed at whipping them into effecting NATO sanctions on Russia. Ukrainian President Volodymyr Zelensky received a lukewarm reception when he addressed the African Union's heads of states, as most African leaders appeared to be indifferent to Ukraine's occupation. Some African countries, especially the fragile states, are caught in between, having to choose between the Western aid they get to function and the historical and ideological ties they have with Russia, which they also rely on for grain and fertilizer.

The Business Day (2022) notes that African countries that have been heavily affected by the Russia-Ukraine war are those that rely heavily on food and energy imports. For instance, Benin and Somalia get all their wheat from Ukraine and

Russia. In 2019 and 2020, Egypt, Sudan, Kongo, Senegal, and Tanzania were 82%, 75%, 69%, 66%, and 64% dependent on Russian and Ukrainian wheat imports, respectively (Business Day, 2022). The level of Algeria's vulnerability to the war is that, for its coal needs, it is 94% dependent on Russia. Besides high commodity prices straining most households, particularly the poorest, increased crop and energy costs have exacerbated their plight. The Business Day (2022) further notes that because of the war, crude oil prices have risen to more than $100 per barrel, while gasoline prices have become exorbitant. Consequently, Africa is paying a higher price for energy imports, which results in high local pump price and expensive merchandise imports at a time incomes are stagnant.

Russian View of Africa

Russia perceives Africa as an area where it can diminish Western influence by leveraging historical ties and fostering alliances with African nations. Nonetheless, with the fighting in Ukraine, Africa can be another battlefield for the superpowers. On the other hand, Africa's vast natural resources, including minerals, oil, and gas reserves, undoubtedly provide attractive economic opportunities for Russia. For instance, the Russia-Ukraine war has considerable effects on the West Africa region's political stability and economic post-COVID recovery, threatening political order and upsetting the supply and pricing of energy, oil, wheat, and corn (Geopolitical Mirror, 2023). Both Ukraine and Russia are key exporters of agricultural products, food grains, and critical minerals to the region. According to the Monitor (2022), the 2022–2023 political upheavals and protests in Mali, Burkina Faso, and Niger can be mostly interpreted as Africans revolt against Europe and United States' influence, with ardent calls for the establishment of pro-Russian and anti-Western governments. For instance, Seddon (2023) argues that Niger's coup has shown some alignment with Russia as protesters openly displayed the Russian flag in a context of the growing influence of Russia's Wagner Group in these territories. By solidifying partnerships with countries like Niger, Russia is likely to undermine Western-backed initiatives and projects, such as economic aid and military cooperation.

Onuah (2023) observes that Russian influence in West Africa has grown while the West has waned since a string of coups began. Niger's takeover is the seventh in West and Central Africa in 3 years. Military leaders in Mali and Burkina Faso have kicked out troops from former colonial power France and strengthened ties with Moscow. There are fears in some Western circles that Russia is likely to use its influence in Africa to crowd out Western influence in the region. For example, Seddon (2023) further argues that Niger military's suspension of uranium exports to France is likely to affect France's electricity generation. Similarly, since the January 2022 coup, the Burkina Faso military asked France to fully withdraw its troops in the country while hailing Russia as a strategic ally. The Wagner Group has a strong foothold in Mali, Central Africa Republic, Sudan, and Libya. Seddon (2023) also claims that the coups in the West Africa Sahel region seem to be well coordinated and involving Russia. Mali has voiced its support for Niger's military leaders, while Putin is reported to have spoken to Mali coup leader regarding the Niger coup. Ironically and economically, there are reports that some African countries are considering seizing trade opportunities emanating from the European Union's decision to phase out dependence on Russian oil and gas. Nigeria, Tanzania, Senegal, Niger, and Algeria are contemplating establishing a trans-Saharan gas pipeline aimed at increasing exports of natural gas to European markets (see Adibe, 2022). Only time will tell where things are headed regarding the international relations between Africa and Europe.

Africa's Mediation Efforts

Efforts to mediate in the Russia-Ukraine conflict by the Global South have not been successful. The Global South avoided taking sides in the Ukraine war given the catastrophic disruptions and hikes in commodity and food prices being experienced in their countries. Brazil, India, Indonesia, and South Africa refused to join sanctions on Russia (Kundnani, 2023).

Attempts by African leaders—individually and collectively—to be mediators between Moscow and Kyiv were crucial but marred by several hurdles, including member states' divergent views and interests when it comes to their relations with Russia. South African President Cyril Ramaphosa argued that there are benefits in Africa not taking sides in the Russia-Ukrainian war as that facilitated mediation with easy access for Africans to both warring sides. He thus said in an interview with Bloomberg: "The position of neutrality can cost. The benefit in all this is that we can talk to both sides" (Muronzi, 2023). However, South Africa's naval drills with Russia in February 2023 raised concerns among Western countries who thought that South Africa was partisan though it was refusing to publicly declare such a position. Several African countries, especially Zimbabwe, have seen it fit to foster relations with Moscow as part of dealing with its frosty relations with Western countries over property and human rights issues especially the redistribution of land.

The Russia-Ukraine war adds complexity to Africa global relations. Stephen Chan, a UK-based political science professor, notes that in the absence of a unipolar world (US dominated) and a bipolar world (where both Russia and the United States dominate), Africa will find it difficult to navigate through unfamiliar political order, especially having to choose between three powers: the United States, Russia, and China (Muronzi, 2023).

The African Union Delegation's mediation efforts [the ten-point plan] to end the Russia-Ukraine war saw them visiting the two warring countries in June 2023. The mediation was strategic and important in that it demonstrated Africa's geopolitical role in global politics and international affairs. Besides this, it was vital for the AU to take this important step given the war's impact on its population's food, fuel, and fertilizer. However, the move by a few Africa leaders to represent the AU was not sanctioned by all member states. Just like the first African initiative that was represented by the AU Chair and President of Senegal Macky Sall, with AU Commission Chairperson Moussa Faki Mahamat, was not sanctioned by the whole African Union membership, though it included a visit to Russia, but not Ukraine. The Institute of Security Studies (ISS, 2023a, b) argues that despite Africa's non-aligned stance, four of the nations involved (Egypt, South Africa, Republic of the Congo, and Uganda) supported Russia. In contrast, Zambia and Comoros are more aligned to the West. African states' voting on UN General Assembly resolutions has shown that the continent remains divided on the Ukraine issue, exposing member states' divergent views and interests when it comes to their relations with Russia. Nonetheless, the African peace initiative demonstrates the willingness and ability of African states to contribute to global crisis management through diplomacy rather than as regular recipients of the world's support.

Despite the spirited efforts by African leaders to mediate and end the war between Moscow and Kyiv, it is very clear that all mediation has failed because it's all about Russia and West relations. Ukraine is just but a proxy and a playing ground for the superpowers. As Macron recognized following his latest talks with Putin, "the geopolitical objective of Russia today is clearly not Ukraine but to clarify the rules of cohabitation with NATO and the EU" (Foreign Policy, 2022b).

Significance of the Russia-Africa Summit Amid War

The second Russia-Africa Summit, originally slated for October 2022 in Addis Ababa, Ethiopia, took place in July 2023 in St Petersburg due to the war in Ukraine and Western sanctions imposed on Russia. The Summit was significant for the increasingly isolated Russia to bolster its relations and support from African states. Russia needs the continent's continued support at the United Nations General Assembly and to be assured of the same as it endeavors to expand its geostrategic influence. The Summit also allowed Moscow to demonstrate its capability to circumvent Western efforts to isolate it over the war in Ukraine. According to ISS (2023b), the Summit was significant for Africa following the disruption to grain exports and the effects of Western sanctions on Russian oil and gas exports. For some African countries, the worsening food crisis in their countries as Ukraine failed to export grain across the Black Sea needed to be resolved sooner than later. Bonnell (2023) argues that for others, the continent's failure to get Russian military support necessitated the need for such Summit to dialog along related pertinent issues. Overall, many African countries did not want to jeopardize their relations with both the West and Russia; thus, they wanted to demonstrate their neutrality by either attending or absenting themselves.

ISS (2023a, b) notes that apart from the fact that too much pressure was exerted on African countries to isolate Russia, there are other interpretations as to why the second Russia-Africa Summit had a low turnout. One reason given is the fact that not much resulted from the 2019 Sochi Summit. Folashadé (2022:633) argues that, "the other reason, especially for the lower turnout of heads of state could also be attributed to the growing fatigue of African states in participating in the growing club of Africa+1 summits, which often do not yield many benefits to their individual countries." These include, among others, US-Africa Summit, UK-Africa Summit, Middle East-Africa Summit, Sino-Africa Summits, and Tokyo International Conference on African Development (TICAD). Nonetheless, African leaders through the African Union underlined the depth of African concern at the war's consequences, particularly energy and grain supply disruptions. Reuters (2023) reports that Moscow's partial response was an offer to send 25,000–50,000 tons of cost-free grain to Burkina Faso, Zimbabwe, Mali, Somalia, Central African Republic (CAR), and Eritrea within 3–4 months. However, this offer communicates a contradictory approach given Moscow's continued attacks on Ukraine's ports by Russia, which destroyed tons of grain destined for African countries. Consequently, Africa will continue to suffer the effect of interferences in the Black Sea Initiative through soaring food prices with dire implications on the stability of many states.

Lesson Learned

- The West should change its attitude and stop lecturing and treating African countries' leaders as babies that need to be told what to do and when to do it. The West must respect the Global South partners as equals who are entitled to their positions when it comes to the war in Ukraine and how to deal with Russia. The West must cease using threats to hoodwink the Global South into their ideological positions. The same occurred with the [9/11] September 11, 2001, attacks, when President George W. Bush declared, "You are either with us, or you are with the terrorists" (Voice of America, 2009). In another bizarre and counterproductive situation, some US lawmakers want the Biden administration to punish South Africa for its alleged support for Russia's invasion of Ukraine, because it had abstained in a UN vote on the Russian invasion (see Imray, 2023). If the law of the powerful nations reasserts itself above international law—beating the same drum—the Global South is likely not to cooperate in international affairs.
- For several citizens in Africa, the war in Ukraine has been viewed as a distant conflict, except for the direct effects on food and basic commodities.
- The war in Ukraine has led to a reduction in international import and export flows to several African countries that relied heavily on commodities from both Russia and Ukraine, especially wheat, oil, gas, and many others. The sanctions imposed on Russia are disrupting its trade with Global South countries, thereby causing unnecessary hunger, poverty, and suffering in the Global South.
- The invasion of Ukraine has affected the Global North and Global South relations and exposed the hypocrisy hidden in internationalism among countries, with the North emphasizing largely punishing and holding Russia accountable while the Global South calling for an end to the war through a negotiated peace deal. The Western countries have concentrated on supplying military support to

Ukraine, while most countries in Africa and from the Global South have focused on peace-brokering and refusing to condemn Russia for her actions.
- The Ukraine war's consequences on the continent make it no longer a "non-African conflict." Food price shocks could fuel public discontent and exacerbate state-society tensions, adding to complex threats to peace and security in Africa.
- The war in Ukraine has disturbed the recovery from COVID-19 for most countries in the Global South. The war came at a point they thought they were doing well on their path to recovery from the effects of the COVID-19 pandemic, only to be thrown back into poverty and hunger as relations and supplies from Russia were cut or disrupted through sanctions.
- Most Global South countries have found it extremely difficult to condemn Russia when they fully know that in the last 100 years or so they depended on it for decolonization and support within the UN Security Council. Russia has aligned itself to the Global South, and its influence with the grouping cannot be easily stopped by Western sanctions and aggression.

Conclusions

Russia, Africa, and the Global South need each other. Russia remains an ally of the Global South, especially Africa against Western countries' extremism and bull political tactics and shenanigans. Without the likes of Russia and China, an unpleasant unipolar world which drives the Global South into further poverty, exploitation, lack of self-determination, and misery is likely to emanate. Russia's presence has helped several African countries to strengthen their negotiating powers vis-a-vis Western powers, defend their national sovereignty, and strengthen world multipolarity. Russia's relations with the Global South, especially Africa, can be strengthened by improving Russia's image through broad information aimed at getting Russia well-known in the continent and vice versa. In the spirit of strengthening Russia-African relations, and other countries in the Global South, efforts must be made to boost cooperation of intergovernmental commissions, business councils, sports commissions, cultural centers.

References

Adibe, J. (2022). The Russo-Ukrainian War's Impact: Africa and a 'Neo-Cold War. *E-International Relations*. https://www.e-ir.info/2022/12/20/the-russo-ukrainian-wars-impact-africa-and-a-neo-cold-war/.

AfDB. (2022). Ukraine war threatens food crisis and political upheaval across Africa, warns top economist. *AfDB*. https://www.afdb.org/en/news-and-events/ukraine-war-threatens-food-crisis-and-political-upheaval-across-africa-warns-top-economist-50269

Askew, J. (2023). Why does so much of the Global South support Russia, not Ukraine?. *Euronews*, 31 March 2023. https://www.euronews.com/my-europe/2023/03/29/why-does-so-much-of-the-global-south-support-russia-not-ukraine.

Ballestrin, L. (2020). The Global South as a political Project. *E-International Relations*. https://www.e-ir.info/2020/07/03/the-global-south-as-a-political-project/#_ftn3.
Bonnell, C. (2023). Russia halts landmark deal that allowed Ukraine to export grain at time of growing hunger. *AP*. https://apnews.com/article/russia-ukraine-war-grain-food-security-ba7f9146b745337a1948a 964cb30331c.
Bourguignon, F. (2016). Inequality and globalization: How the rich get richer as the poor catch up. Princeton: Princeton University Press. *Foreign Affairs, 95*(1), 11–15.
BP. (n.d.). Russia. *British Petroleum*. http://www.bp.com/en/global/corporate/energy-economics/statistical-review-of-world-energy/country-and-regional-insights/russia.html
Business day. (2022). What is the impact of the Russia-Ukraine crisis on Africa's trade and economy? Businessday. Available from https://businessday.ng/sponsored/article/what-is-the-impact-of-the-russia-ukraine-crisis-on-africas-trade-and-economy/
Business Times. (2023). Africa and Asia are dissatisfied with the allocation of loans to Ukraine. *Business Times*. https://businesstimes.co.zw/africa-and-asia-are-dissatisfied-with-the-allocation-of-loans-to-ukraine/
Deen, T. (2023). The War in Ukraine triggers a record increase in world military spending. *Interpress Services News Agency*. https://www.ipsnews.net/2023/04/war-ukraine-triggers-record-increase-world-military-spending/
Dirlik, A. (2007). Global south: Predicament and promise. *The Global South, 1*(1), 12–23.
Folashadé, S. (2022). Africa+1' summit diplomacy and the 'new scramble' narrative: Recentering African agency. *African Affairs, 119/477*, 633–646.
Foreign Policy. (2022a). What the west (still) gets wrong about Putin. *Foreign Policy*. https://foreignpolicy.com/2022/06/01/putin-warukraine-west-misconception
Foreign Policy. (2022b). Why mediation around Ukraine keeps failing. *Foreign Policy*. https://foreignpolicy.com/2022/02/10/mediation-ukraine-russia-2014-war-west/
Geopolitical Mirror. (2023). The geopolitics of Russia's Foray into West Africa, situation reports. *Geopolitical Mirror*. https://www.geopoliticalmonitor.com/the-geopolitics-of-russias-foray-into-west-africa/
Ghosh, B. M. (2001). *Dependency theory revisited*. Routledge Revivals.
Handy, P.-S., & Djilo, F. (2022). Unpacking Africa's divided stance on the Ukraine war. *Institute of Security Studies* [ISS]. Available from https://issafrica.org/iss-today/unpacking-africas-divided-stance-on-the-ukraine-war
Imray, G. (2023). *US lawmakers ask Biden administration to punish South Africa for alleged support for Russia*. https://apnews.com/article/united-states-south-africa-weapons-russia-ukraine-17e8a32a592e9372463c9e037496da0e
ISS. (2023a). Africa's Ukraine-Russia mediation needed a clearer AU footprint. *ISS*. Available from https://issafrica.org/iss-today/africas-ukraine-russia-mediation-needed-a-clearer-au-footprint
ISS. (2023b). Russia-Africa summit: What was in it for Africa? Petersburg. *ISS*. https://issafrica.org/pscreport/psc-insights/russia-africa-summit-what-was-in-it-for-africa#:~:text=The%20summit%20was%20significant%20forof%20state%20at%20St%20.
Kay, C. (2011). Andre Gunder Frank: 'Unity in Diversity' from the development of underdevelopment to the world system. *New Political Economy, 16*(4), 523–538.
KIPPRA. (2022). Russia-Ukraine conflict and wheat supply in Kenya. *KIPPRA*. https://kippra.or.ke/russia-ukraine-conflict-and-wheat-supply-in-kenya/
Kiptoo, E. (2022). *What does the Ukraine-Russia War mean for Kenya*? https://southernvoice.org/what-does-the-ukraine-russia-war-mean-for-kenya/
Kundnani, H. (2023). The War in Ukraine, Democracy, and the Global South. *RKK International Centre for Defence and Security*. https://icds.ee/en/the-war-in-ukraine-democracy-and-the-global-south-we-have-a-problem/
Matunhu, J. (2011). A critique of modernization and dependency theories in Africa: Critical assessment. *African Journal of History and Culture, 5*(3), 65–72.
McCarthy, M. (2023). UN Calls for Russia to Leave Ukraine. *Politico.*. https://www.politico.com/news/2023/02/23/un-resolution-condemning-russia-ukraine-invasion-00084234

MoALF. (2022). Fertilizer subsidy 2022. *Ministry of Agriculture, Livestock and Fisheries*. https://www.planning.go.ke/launch-of-fertilizer-subsidy-programmefsp/

Monitor. (2022). We don't believe in being enemies of somebody's enemy, Museveni tells Russia's Foreign Minister. *Monitor*, Tuesday. https://www.monitor.co.ug/uganda/news/national/we-don-t-believe-in-being-enemies-of-somebody-s-enemy-museveni-tells-russia-s-foreign-minister-3892970

Muronzi, C. (2023). Is Africa still 'neutral' a year into the Ukraine war? *Aljazeera*, 26 February 2023. https://www.aljazeera.com/features/2023/2/26/is-africa-still-neutral-a-year-into-the-ukraine-war

NTEP. (2023). *Kenya imports from Ukraine, The National Treasury and Economic Planning*. https://tradingeconomics.com/kenya/imports/ukraine

OECD. (2023). Foreign aid surges due to spending on refugees and aid for Ukraine. *OECD*. https://www.oecd.org/newsroom/foreign-aid-surges-due-to-spending-on-refugees-and-aid-for-ukraine.htm

Onuah, F. (2023). Niger junta says open to talks as Putin, US stress peace. *Reuters*, 16 August 2023. https://www.reuters.com/world/africa/malis-president-says-he-had-call-with-putin-about-niger-coup-2023-08-15/

Petras, J., & Veltmeyer, H. (2013). *Imperialism and capitalism in the twenty-first century: A system in crisis*. Ashgate.

Randall Vicky (2004). Using and abusing the concept of the Third World: Geopolitics and the comparative political study of development and underdevelopment, in Taylor & Francis (Eds) *Third World Quarterly - Journal of Emerging Areas 25*(1):41–53. https://www.jstor.org/stable/3993776

Reuters. (2023). Zimbabwean President says country has food, but grateful to Putin grain offer. *Reuters*, 27 July 2023. https://www.reuters.com/world/africa/zimbabwean-president-says-country-has-food-grateful-putin-grain-offer-2023-07-27/

Sajed, A. (2020). From the third world to the global south. *E-International Relations*, July 27, 2020. https://www.e-ir.info/2020/07/27/from-the-third-world-to-the-global-south/

Seddon, S. (2023). Niger coup: Russia warns Ecowas not to take military action. *BBC News*, 11 August 2023. https://www.bbc.com/news/world-africa-66478430

Sen Ashish, K. (2022). *Russia's War in Ukraine is taking a toll on Africa*. Wednesday, June 15, 2022, https://www.usip.org/publications/2022/06/russias-war-ukraine-taking-toll-africa

Shubin, V. (2004). Russia and Africa: Moving in the right direction? In I. Taylor & P. Williams (Eds.), *Africa in international politics: External involvement on the continent* (p. 113). Routledge.

Tatiana, S. (2017). *Africa Population 2017*. http://worldpopulationreview.com/continents/africa-population/.

Voice of America. (2009). *Bush, 'You are either with us, or with the terrorists,'* 27 October. https://www.voanews.com/a/a-13-a-2001-09-21-14-bush-66411197/549664.html

Charles Mutasa, PhD, is an expert in international relations, civil society, development policy, human rights, and governance issues. He is the Country Director for Diakonia Zimbabwe since June 2022, and a part-time Lecturer for postgraduate Development Studies at the Zimbabwe Open University (ZOU) since mid-2017. He is the editor of the book: *Africa and the Millennium Development Goals: Progress, Problems, and Prospects*; and a co-editor of the book: *Africa and the World: Bilateral and Multilateral International Diplomacy*. Charles has worked for various INGOs (Christian Aid, Dan ChurchAid, and Trocaire) as a Programs Adviser/Manager and as an Executive Director for two African Regional Networks: African Forum and Network on Debt and Development (AFRODAD), and Mwelekeo waNGO (MWENGO), and the Poverty Reduction Forum in Zimbabwe. Prior to joining the civil society sector in 1999, he worked in the Zimbabwe public service as a Health Statistician/Demographer and Senior Policy Analyst.

Chapter 16
Russia's Search for International Recognition and Ontological Security in the Global South Post the Ukraine Conflict

Dylan Yanano Mangani and Ntsikelelo Benjamin Breakfast

Abstract In 2022, drawing from its essential and historical affinities with the Global South, in the wake of its "military operation" in Ukraine, Russia began to repackage and propagate its foreign policy within a new post-Cold War thinking. Suffice it to say, its conceptual dimension suggested international practices of searching for recognition and ontological security in spatial "imaginaries" such as Africa. What is noticeable about Russia's politics of recognition in Africa is a departure from the traditional constructions of foreign policy toolkits—the deployment of national militaries and economic incentives—to a new form of engagement that utilizes non-state actors and soft power tools such as information, multilateralism, and security diplomacy. Russia is depicted as a global power utilizing its security toolkits, coalescing with beleaguered incumbents to stifle meaningful political transitions in specific African states begging the question of whether Africa is an ontological security and self-identity reservoir for a post-Cold War Russia.

Introduction

Since it invaded Ukraine in February 2022, Russia's international behavior has been analyzed in the West through the "statism" international relations theory focused on statehood *gosudarstvennost* and great power status *derzhavnost*. Consequently, within Western media and academic circles, there is an emphasis on Russia's growing expansionist influence as a critical variable. Russia has been accused of attempting to erect an "Iron Curtain" between NATO member states and itself, an imperialist interpretation of international relations and creating a European security complex.

D. Y. Mangani (✉) · N. B. Breakfast
Department of History and Political Studies, Nelson Mandela University,
Port Elizabeth, South Africa
e-mail: Dylan.Mangani@mandela.ac.za; Ntsikelelo.breakfast@mandela.ac.za

G. Moyo, S. J. Ndlovu-Gatsheni (eds.), *Global Storms and Africa in World Politics*, Global Power Shift, https://doi.org/10.1007/978-3-031-83868-2_16

Such depictions are couched in Cold War geopolitical rivalry language, suggesting a new wave of great power competition (Davis & Slobodchikoff, 2022). Elsewhere in the Global South, Russia's post-Ukraine invasion posture is ambiguous and complex, veering between a developmental trajectory and a tactical alliances posture. For example, Russia's presence in Africa can be traced to the inaugural 2019 Russia-Africa Summit in Sochi, which signaled Russia's attempt to inculcate soft power tools in its reengagement efforts with Africa. Russia has yet to match its global hegemony status with advanced economic capabilities as a fully fledged strategic competitor. This is based on the observation that sub-Saharan-Russian trade amounts to US$ 3 billion compared to China and the United States, estimated at US$ 56 billion and US $27 billion. Despite its limited economic capacity, Russia's exponential presence in Africa demonstrates a significant trajectory in its foreign policy spatial "imaginaries." Several factors can explain this. Lewis (2018) conceptualizes spatial imaginaries as:

> cognitive frames that filter information and provide meaning for events while legitimising particular policy decisions. They play an important role in asserting boundaries between "them" and "us," and thus constructing and shaping national identities constituted by differences.

This is to say, the mental maps Russia has toward Africa are presented in a "developmental" trajectory underpinned by "anti-imperial," "anti-colonial," anti-West, and sovereignty themes. In Africa, Russia strives to attain (a) a strategic-independent actor status in the international community and (b) a historical great power identity through repertoires of engagements in African hot spots, reinforcing the role of a "power broker," "mediator," and "stabilizer." These objectives fall into the Gramscian hegemony theoretical understanding of international relations. In this regard, the neo-Marxist scholar Antonio Gramsci utilizes the concept of hegemony to illustrate power dynamics in international relations. Gramsci's notion of hegemony is based on his critique of some of Marxism's partial analysis of international relations based on economic determinism, which considers economic factors as the primary determinant of state relations (Gill, 1993). The concept of hegemony in the Realist conception of international relations speaks to a single dimension of dominance based on states' economic and military capability. However, Joseph (2000) broadens our conception of hegemony, invoking the idea that a state may not be hegemonic based on traditional economic and military rubrics but must also possess the political, cultural, and economic conditions that justify its claims as a leader of society. This reasoning follows and shares comparable justifications with Nye's concept of soft power. The central argument for the soft power concept is the premium placed on a country's cultural values, ideology, and institutions as power maximizers. This is further elaborated by Hobden and Wyn Jones (2008), who opined that successive powers have managed to shape a world order that suits their interests [...] because they have managed to generate broad consent for that order even among those who are disadvantaged by it. Hegemony filters through structures of culture, ideology, political values, and other consortiums of consent that may deem a state attractive to other states enough to follow it. Gramscian's notion of hegemony is consensual in understanding the acceptability of Russia's image in the Global South in the post-2022 Ukrainian war dispensation.

On the other hand, Siegle (2022) gives credence to the Global South regions, such as Latin America, Asia, and Africa, as instrumental "theaters" through which Russia pursues a realist "zero-sum" game of economic and political opportunism in the world's underdeveloped regions. There is an emphasis on Russia's lack of investments in traditional statecraft trade, economic investments, and security assistance. In Africa, Russia is often depicted as deploying a new form of engagement that utilizes non-state actors and soft power tools such as media and information. Russia's deployment of the Wagner Group, a Russian private military contract company, and its usage of the Internet Research Agency proffer new interpretations of its security and arbitration architectures. This has generated debates and speculations within specific Western media circles concerned about Wagner's "asymmetrical" and "transactional" political-military activities. Russia has taken advantage of anti-US and anti-Western sentiments in Latin America and Asia, establishing allies with states such as Venezuela, Nicaragua, Thailand, and Myanmar.

The case studies of Venezuela and Nicaragua demonstrate Russia's readiness to establish a foothold in the Western hemisphere—the US neighborhood. These examples help to amplify and reproduce some of the long-standing analysis of the Marxist Gramscian conception of hegemony that it filters through structures of culture, ideology, political values, and other consortiums of consent that may deem a state attractive to other states enough to follow it. Gramscian's notion of hegemony is consensual in understanding the acceptability of Russia's image among these regimes, especially after it invaded Ukraine. The United States and the West view these countries as lacking democracy and good governance as critical variables. Therefore, Russia is depicted as a global power utilizing its security toolkits, coalescing with beleaguered incumbents to stifle meaningful political transitions in the Global South. However, the deployment of Wagner is low-cost effective and calculative of the pitfalls of direct involvement of a foreign military that resonate across the African continent. In this instance, Russia serves as Africa's security and sovereignty provider. This position is buttressed by Russia's significant inroads as Africa's largest arms supplier.

Crisis of the Liberal International Order

Much ink has been spilt on the controversies emanating from the Ukrainian crisis, which, according to Ghincea (2022a, b), depicted a deterioration in the flagship of the liberal international order led by the United States and the North Atlantic Treaty Organization (NATO). Similarly, Mearsheimer (2019), in *Bound to Fail: The Rise and Fall of the Liberal International Order*, identifies the onset of the Ukrainian crisis in 2014 as an extension of great power politics that can be traced to a new post-Cold War dispensation in which the United States emerged as a sole global leader, while Russia emerged as a "regional power in structural decline." The implications were that at the turn of the late 1990s, the United States, uncontested, was at liberty to "shape a political context that is congenial to Russia's assimilation into a larger framework of European cooperation while fostering the independence of its newly sovereign neighbours" (Brzezinski, 1997:52). This view shares commonalities with the neorealist perspective that places blame on NATO's unmitigated expansion in Eastern Europe, former Soviet Union backyard, and the political implications which gave rise to Russia's ontological security concerns.

The concept of ontological security dates to the phenomenal works of psychologist R. D. Laing titled *The Divided Self*. The argument posited here is that ontological security is a condition in which an individual's continual mental state is derived from a sense of continuity regarding events in their life (Ferguson, 2021). An individual's identity needs to be secure and harmonious with itself. Therefore, uncertainty can potentially threaten one's identity. Mitzen (2006) furthers that when an individual does not know what to expect, it becomes unclear how to meet their ends. Ends are synonymous with identities, consequently suggesting uncertainty breeds an opaque identity. Politically, identity is a critical aspect of collective ontological security. Stable recognition of the self-image of states derived from historical facts and interactions with other states (Narozha, 2021). Russia's self-identity depends on how different world regions viewed Moscow in the post-Cold War period. Consequently, Tsygankov (2016) buttresses Brzezinski's argument written earlier that in the post-Cold War, the United States and NATO countries sought to democratize Russia in a way that it would pursue a "common European home" shaped by a natural affinity with the Western hemisphere in shared values such as a free market economy, democracy, and human rights. In 1994, US President Bill Clinton reinforced this view by stating that:

> Our national security strategy is based on enlarging the community of market democracies while deterring and containing a range of threats to our nation, our allies, and our interests. The more that democracy and political and economic liberalisation take hold in the world, particularly in countries of geo-strategic importance to us, the safer our nation is likely to be and the more our people are likely to prosper. (Goldgeier & McFaul, 2003:11)

Observers marveled at the supposed "enlarging the community of market democracies" because it assumed attempts at socializing Russia into the European community of states, promoting human rights and democracy. This misreading of a post-Cold War and liberal international order was because observers were uninformed about how reconstructing and resocializing Russia into a Western democratic clientele state was meant to curtail Moscow as a great superpower and thus compromise her ontological security. Russia's ontological security depended on how it safeguarded its historical status as a great power. Clinton's observations about enlarging market democracies were synonymous with NATO's expansion into Eastern Europe. NATO's conduct in post-Cold War Eastern Europe was that of a protagonist rooted in the futility of the Fukuyamian perspective's "end of history" and its proclivity to usher a dismissive, intolerant, and insensitive international security architecture void of Russia's contribution. This is qualified by Brzezinski (1997:55), who said:

> By 1999, the first three Central European members will have been admitted into NATO, although their inclusion in the EU will probably not take place before 2002 or 2003; by 2003, the EU is likely to have initiated accession talks with all three Baltic republics, and NATO will likewise have moved forward on their membership as well as that of Romania and Bulgaria, with their accession likely to be completed before 2005; between 2005 and 2010, Ukraine prodded it has made significant domestic reforms and has become identified as a Central European country, should also be ready for initial negotiations with the EU and NATO.

Brzezinski's geostrategic sketch of a post-Cold War Europe involving NATO's rapid expansion into Russia's backyard corresponds with Narozha's (2021) analysis of the nexus between the West's admonition of Russia and the consequential international security framework that resulted in Moscow's invasion of Georgia, Crimea, and Ukraine in later years to come.

Conversely, liberal views depict the Russo-Ukraine war as an "invasion" that falls in the Westphalian settled norms of state sovereignty and territorial integrity. The often-cited arguments are that Russia's fear of Ukraine's steady gravitation toward a functioning Western-oriented democracy threatened the future of Moscow's internal politics. Fears that a reformed Ukraine would serve as a source of political mobilization and activism that would eventually threaten kleptocratic and elite rule in Russia are a basic tenet of the liberal arguments surrounding the Ukrainian crisis (Ghincea, 2022a, b). Contested understandings of the Russian invasion of Georgia in 2008, Crimea in 2014, and Ukraine in 2022 are part of the lingering narratives of Moscow's realist preferences underpinned by foreign policy expansionism. By annexing Crimea in 2014, observers conclude that Russia solidified its control of the Black Sea, thereby providing a chokehold over NATO's military interests in the Mediterranean, Middle East, and North Africa, where Moscow previously had no influence (Masters, 2023). This is to suggest that the "Russian Empire" idea is integral to Russian leaders' foreign policy objectives from Lenin to Putin and is geographically defined.

Russia's Global South Relations in the Post-2022 Ukrainian Invasion

In 2022, drawing from its essential and historical affinities with the Global South, Russia began repackaging and propagating its foreign policy within a new post-Cold War thinking in the wake of its military operation in Ukraine. This led to its first official foreign policy document, dubbed 2023 "Foreign Policy Concept," which was couched in aggressive, ideological, and propagandistic language. According to Seungsoo (2023), the use of colorful and often at times nationalist terms such as the Russian world, Russophobia, traditional values, neocolonialism, Western hegemony, a multipolar world, and Anglo-Saxon was aimed at reinventing Russia's acceptability in the non-Western Global South. In his conception of hegemony in international relations, the neo-Marxist Antonio Gramsci argues that a state may not be hegemonic based on traditional economic and military rubrics but must possess the political, cultural, and economic conditions that justify its claims as a leader of society. This reasoning follows and shares comparable justifications with Nye's concept of soft power. The central argument for the soft power concept is that the premium is placed on a country's cultural values, ideology, and institutions as power maximizers (Gill, 1993). Russia's deliberate use of terms such as "neocolonialism," "traditional values," and "multipolar world" suggested a deeper understanding of the priorities of the Global South and projected herself as an honest broker and ally fighting against the US unipolar world order. This rhetoric has found purchase among Global South states that have cultivated anti-US and anti-Western attitudinal sentiments since the end of the Cold War and the rise of a unipolar dispensation. Its classification of the United States, Britain, and Western Europe as "the Anglo-Saxon" axis maintained a combative stance aimed at caricaturing the West's neocolonial agenda in Ukraine. The "Foreign Policy" document analyzes the nexus between the West's admonition of Russia and the consequential international security framework depicted in Moscow's invasion of Ukraine. This is to say that the United States, NATO in particular, forced Russia's military operation in Ukraine.

Leadership response to Russia's invasion of Ukraine largely fell on Europe and the United States. The response was coercive measures, including economic sanctions, isolating Russia diplomatically, and information diplomacy, which led to restricting the Russian state-owned television Russia Today to its global audience. Herman and Chomsky, cited in Mangani (2019), opine that media and information are ways societies are manipulated and that consent for socioeconomic and political issues is generated in the public mind through controlled propaganda. In other words, the media's role is to interpret society and its needs by defining and shaping what is deemed appropriate and necessary to both the state and private and public life. Thus, by restricting Russia Today's viewership globally, the United States and its Western allies sought to define and shape the Ukraine crisis from a singular and dominated Western narrative that caricatured Russia as an invader losing the war against Ukraine. As the Ukrainian crisis unfolded, Russia was isolated diplomatically and, therefore, pivoted toward the Global South in search of allies, security, and leadership.

In the post-Ukrainian crisis, Russia has built on its strategic priorities in the Asian region: to profit from the lucrative Asian market, its economic integration framework, and Moscow's role as a stabilizer for peace and security in that region. Accordingly, Russia's foreign policy is a hybrid of internal considerations—developing its Far East frontiers and external realities—the end of a unipolar system, and the subsequent emergence of a multipolar system in which the Asian region is a focal point of expanding global power (Peace Nexus Foundation, 2022). Russia has benefitted from momentous political changes in Asia, such as the 2021 military takeover in Myanmar, as the region's leading arms supplier. The Russian military factor underpinning its relations with Asian countries, particularly in Southeast Asia, helps to curtail the United States' ambitions as the region's security guarantor. This has been demonstrated by the Association of Southeast Asian Nations (ASEAN) divided opinion on the crisis in Ukraine. Though the ASEAN has always maintained a united approach to international relations, the Ukrainian crisis suggested differences in opinion among the bloc. Most ASEAN voted in favor of the United Nations General Assembly (UNGA) Resolution on March 2, 2022. However, the bloc did not take sides by naming or blaming Russia or Ukraine as the instigator of the conflict, suggesting its preference for neutrality. These variances may be explained by internal political contradictions in some of these states. It would appear Russia has strategically aligned with regimes often seen as either military or authoritarian by the West, such as Cambodia, Vietnam, and Myanmar. These regimes have volatile internal politics, creating a vacuum through which Russia reinforces itself as a "power broker," "mediator," and "stabilizer." These attractive themes can be analyzed from the soft power and hegemonic lens advanced by the Gramscian conception of international relations, emphasizing nonmilitary and noneconomic means that make states attractive to other states. Russia's anti-US ideology and political values may help to explain its affinities among some of the Asian military regimes. In Myanmar, the junta-led government, which took power in 2021, supported Russia's war with Ukraine. A penetrative analysis suggests that Myanmar's position signaled a strategic military-security relationship with Russia. Before the Ukraine crisis, Russia used its veto power in the United Nations Security Council (UNSC) to defend and protect the Tatmadaw's State Administration Council, a military junta in Myanmar (Sriyai & Khemanitthathai, 2022). In doing so, the junta in Myanmar became a recipient and client of Russian arms; this relationship allowed the junta to support Moscow's war in Ukraine.

Myanmar has also utilized media constructions and information narratives to caricature Ukraine while justifying Russian actions. Following Russia's invasion of Ukraine, the Tatmadaw's regime began an information and media offensive to demonize Ukraine's leader, Volodymyr Zelensky. In a commentary titled "Past Lessons from Wars of Aggression (The Fifth): A Lesson from Ukraine with an Unsatisfactory Past" in the "Myanma Alin," the junta drew parallels between Zelensky's inept leadership and the ousted Burmese Aung San Suu Kyi. The commentary accused both leaders of being too Western: the hallmarks of nationalist discourses in anti-Western societies. Therefore, Suu Kyi's ouster and Ukraine's invasion were justified in the eyes of anti-Western audiences (Storey, 2022). The idea was to draw sympathy and legitimacy internally and internationally from Russian supporters and those of Suu Kyi who may have been dissatisfied with the 2021 military coup.

While Myanmar openly supported Russia, Thailand opted for a "bamboo diplomacy." This type of diplomacy allows a state to bend to international events, a pragmatic approach that has seen Thailand historically managing security threats: colonialism, Japanese aggression during World War II, and the Cold War. While appearing benevolent by voting in favor of the UNGA resolution that condemned the Russian invasion of Ukraine, Thailand did not mention Russia as an aggressor in its explanation of the vote statement in the UNGA. Bangkok reiterated its commitment to the principles of the UN Charter. Economic pragmatism may help explain this. According to Sriyai (2022), Thailand's economic and trade relations with Russia are much stronger than Ukraine, accounting for US$ 2.7 billion and

US$ 386. 47 million, respectively, in favor of Moscow. Furthermore, internal political contradictions such as Bangkok's less commitment to democracy and human rights may have given Thailand a pretext to support Russia in fear of the backlash on its internal human rights record.

Like some Asian countries, India has chosen a nonaligned response to the war in Ukraine. Compelling reasons can be found in India's quest for Asian regional leadership, reforming the global governance structure and institutions such as the UNSC and, most pertinently, the unipolar system. Unsurprisingly, India is part of Brazil, Russia, India, China, and South Africa (BRICS), a rising multilateral institution whose capacity and mandate seek to provide alternative international public goods for the Global South. In this context of ideological affinities, Russia is regarded as a "friend of India" within New Delhi's public discourse (TI Observer, 2022). Pertinently, in the quest for regional dominance, India has been faced with a mosaic of security challenges such as unmitigated inflows of migrants from Sri Lankan, Bangladesh, and Myanmar, cross-border terrorism, maritime security, communalism, human trafficking, resource distribution, and so forth. India relies on Russia's military diplomacy to manage these threats and modernize its military. Additionally, the post-Ukrainian crisis period has been earmarked by the exponential rise in India's demand for Russian energy to feed its enormous population. As Russia became diplomatically isolated internationally following the Ukrainian crisis, Moscow took advantage of India being the world's sixth largest energy consumer. At the same time, India benefitted from Western nations' cuts on Russian oil imports. An exponential rise in Russian oil going to India from 2% in 2021 to 20% in the post-Ukrainian crisis demonstrates how Moscow has been able to counter its global diplomatic isolation with natural resources at its disposal (Masters, 2023).

Notwithstanding the onset of criticism about the Sino-Russia alliance's lack of historic global governance leadership in a liberal international order, therefore indicting the axis as a fully fledged alternative and strategic competitor, its reformist agenda has renewed debates about its potential alternative to the Western world. China's response to the Ukrainian conflict mirrors pragmatism that calculated the complexities of providing military assistance to Russia, which may have had a bearing on Beijing's relations with the West while economically supporting Moscow (Duben, 2022). Its response also mirrors a search for ontological security in which Russia became a strategic partner and actor in its efforts to recalibrate international relations. How China responds to international events such as the Ukrainian crisis has a bearing on her search for identity and security. China's choices can also be summed up as "benevolent neutrality." While projecting itself as a neutral actor in the conflict, Beijing has deliberately chosen to describe the conflict in Ukraine as a "war" and not a Russian invasion. To understand China's position, an ideological-political context is important. A decisive phase in Sino-Russia relations was earmarked by the "no limits friendship" pact forged during Russian President Vladimir Putin's attendance at the 2022 Beijing XXIV Winter Olympics Games. At this historic event, other world leaders diplomatically isolated China following its opaque handling of the coronavirus (COVID-19) pandemic. Therefore, President Putin's visit gave credence to Beijing's international optics. Additionally, the Russian state visit solidified an ideological commitment toward recalibrating the global governance framework in pursuit of "international equity and justice" arising from a "failed" US unilateral framework. Consequently, a clarion call was made for a bilateral response to "external interference and regional security threat" (Pant, 2023: 21).

The view that the global governance structure needs reform is often drawn from the argument that though a US-led international order ushered in democracy, good governance, and human rights, a more compelling consequence of this unilateralism found expression in the form of global terrorism, financial crises, and anti-US sentiments in the Global South. These countervailing developments to US unilateralism demonstrated the need for concerted collective action encapsulated in multilateralism. To China, Russia's war with Ukraine is an attempt to contain NATO aggression and contest the liberal international order. This containment is key to Russia's search for ontological security and identity. Commonalities are found in Russia's historic claim over Ukraine and China's historic claims over Taiwan. Since immemorial, China has often recognized Taiwan as a province that should be integrated into mainland China. Its foreign policy has often exported the notion of a "One China" policy. The West has responded to China's claims as violating Taiwanese sovereignty and territorial integrity (Duben, 2022). It is plausible that China's support of Russia's claims over Ukraine laid a basis for Moscow's future support for Beijing over Taiwan.

Furthermore, from this Russia-China Summit, the latter emphasized key critical moments in history, such as the unmitigated expansion of NATO eastward in Europe that forced Russia into a corner and the futility of economic sanctions imposed on Moscow. Contested understandings of China's support of Russia have been drawn from different perspectives, which include a deliberate attempt by Beijing and Moscow to recalibrate and reform the global governance structure to solidify national security threats. Other less optimistic perspectives suggest China intends to support Russia in the war to distract the United States' attention from the Indo-Pacific and Southeast Asian region. The more the United States focused on the Ukrainian crisis, the easier it was for China to establish its foothold as a regional hegemony in Southeast Asia unmitigated. The Russia-China Summit also spoke to bilateral economic diplomacy between the two countries. In line with a US$ 400 billion deal to export Russian gas to China signed in 2014 (Gabuev, 2015), both countries agreed on an additional gas supply to China, which would be settled in euros instead of the traditional US dollar. This historic agreement has formed the basis of China's economic diplomacy as a counterweight to the Western economic sanctions as the Ukrainian crisis unfolded. Sino-China relations also demonstrate the recalibration of Moscow's economic direction toward Asia as it reduces its dependency on the European market.

It was not until Chinese President Xi Jinping's official visit to Russia in March 2023 that Beijing's support for Russia in the Ukrainian crisis became apparent. Before the visit, China pursued a "benevolent neutrality," which may have been informed by balancing her global economic and political strategic ambitions. This may predispose Beijing's call for a multilateral peace approach to the conflict, underscored by a 12-point peace plan that sought to satisfy Russia's historical claims to the conflict and international community expectations. Consequently, the peace plan contained elements of respecting Westphalian settled norms of sovereignty, peace, and ending coercive economic sanctions on Russia (Pant, 2023). A carrot-and-stick approach is evident in China's conduct of the Ukrainian crisis. While advocating for an inclusive peace solution to the Ukraine crisis, China signed a joint statement, "Deepening the Russian-Chinese Comprehensive Partnership and Strategic Cooperation for a New Era and Plan to Promote the Key Elements of Russian-Chinese Economic Cooperation." These bilateral agreements signaled an economic intervention to counterweight further sanctions imposed on Russia, which included negotiations about the new Power of Siberia-2 gas pipeline across Mongolia (Fraioli, 2023).

Speaking before the US Senate Armed Service Committee, as the Head of the US Southern Command, in March 2015, then Chief of Staff John Kelly warned of an exponential growth of Russian presence in Latin America, which had the hallmarks of Cold War politics aimed at stifling and containing the US presence in the region (Ellis, 2022). This growth combines soft and hard power diplomacy, supposedly using anti-US propaganda, trade, military arms, and counter-drug agreements (Gurganus, 2018). The entry point here is that Russia has strived to attain a strategic-independent actor status in the international community by establishing good offices among Latin American friends and retaining her historically great power identity by establishing a foothold in the United States' backyard. The argument about Russia striving to attain its historical great power status *derzhavnost* has been echoed by Ellis (2015), who argues that Russia's exponential presence in Latin America is focused on building political and military alliances with the region in the US "sphere of influence." This could potentially threaten the US ontological security in her immediate neighborhood. In the long term, this forces the United States to divert its attention and resources to the new threats closer to home while retreating from Eurasia. A vacuum created by the US departure from Eurasia allows Russia to reassert itself in Eurasia uninterrupted. The United States has caricatured Russian activities in Latin America in the post-Ukrainian crisis as:

> Primarily designed to intimidate the U.S. and to offset Russia's international political and economic isolation brought about by its unprovoked invasion of the Ukraine, including reactions to its associated brutality in Russia's targeting of civilian populations in the Ukraine and its likely human rights violations against the Ukrainian people. (Ellis, 2022:5)

The idea inculcated is that the crisis in Ukraine has rendered Russia a pariah state and, therefore, diplomatic isolation. The observations by the United States also fit into the neoliberal narrative that seeks to project Russia in foreign policy expansionism. In the wake of international condemnation of its actions and isolation, Russia has sought the Latin American region as a haven for image and power retention. Thus, Ellis (2022:6) says:

> The examples that I have just provided show how Russia's projection of threats leverages these regimes. They thus highlight how malign actors such as Nicholas Maduro, the Ortegas, and Miguel Diaz-Canel do not simply deprive their own people of democracy, prosperity, and basic individual freedoms and protections. Rather, their efforts to spread their authoritarian, often corrupt form of government and work against U.S. interests pose

> a risk that is magnified exponentially by their willingness to serve as a port of entry for Russia, a nuclear-armed U.S. rival, actively engaged in threatening the U.S. in its own near abroad.

Ellis's views form part of the liberal arguments in the West, portraying Russian interests in Latin America as propping up malign regimes as image and power retention mechanisms resulting from the crisis in Ukraine. Chaguaceda and Herrera (2022) build on this by conceptualizing Russia's relations with specific Latin American regimes as autocratic cooperation and illiberal confluence, in which Moscow deliberately cooperates and rewards Bolivarian regimes across Latin America, with commercial opportunities and military protection, who are anti-Western and antidemocratic. Another explanation is that Russia aims to garner as much support as possible from the region's hegemonic players, such as Mexico, Brazil and Argentina, who are also members of the Group of 20 (G20) bloc. The G20 is a premier forum for international economic cooperation, and therefore, Russia seeks alliances to subvert diplomatic isolation.

However, simply casting Russian interests in the most unfavorable light falls into Cold War entrapments. It is important to note that Chomsky and Herman (2008) argue that narrative agendas are depicted by five key filters, including ownership, advertising, sourcing, flak communism, and fear. The last filter characterizes the long-standing animosity between the United States and Russia in their global dominance competition. Mangani (2019) builds on this idea, suggesting that communism and fear were generated in the United States during the Cold War and were designed specifically to manufacture propaganda narratives against the Soviet Union and communism as enemies of the American people. Some characteristics of this filter involve generating fear in the public by demonizing one's opponent. These narratives bear a resemblance to the post-Cold War, expressing the view that Russia seeks to curtail international liberalism by supporting authoritarian regimes across the Latin American continent. Such depictions of Russia help psyche the world to rally behind the United States as a bastion of the free world while curtailing Russian interests in the Global South. Conversely, the Venezuelan, Cuban, and Nicaraguan examples mentioned by Ellis have demonstrated Russia's brand of politics that understands the priorities of Latin American states, including anti-US sentiments in the region. Therefore, Russia has also deployed information and media tools, such as RT and Sputnik news agencies, as platforms to question the US-led democratic project in Latin America while insisting on traditional values such as sovereignty, territorial integrity, and noninterference, the hallmarks of nationalist discourses in Bolivarian regimes. The premium on military agreements is also noticeable in Russia's engagement with Latin America. Having built on its Cold War interactions, Russia has an expansive military cache in Latin America, supplying 25% of the region's military fleet (Chaguaceda & Herrera, 2022). These have been in the form of aircraft, ammunition, and army vehicles.

Africa in Perspective

Russia's growing influence in Africa has been interpreted as a significant pivot from Western markets, actors, and institutions while courting Africa as an integral part of its global agenda. Within civil society, media, and academic circles, there is an emphasis on Russia's growing influence in Africa, suggesting a new wave of great power competition—a critical variable of realism theory. Although limited in economic scope, Russia's interests in Africa are evidently concentrated in infrastructure construction, military hardware, nuclear technology, hydropower, and natural resources. Russia has yet to prove itself to be a strategic economic competitor in Africa. Vuksanović (2023) says that as of 2021, Russia's trade with Africa stood at US$ 17 billion, while African exports to Russia were a mere US$ 1.9 billion. This starkly contrasts with China's exports to Africa, which amounted to US$190 billion in the same year. Its inaugural 2019 Russia-Africa Summit in Sochi signaled Russia's attempt to inculcate soft power tools in its reengagement efforts with Africa. However, Russia's invasion of Ukraine in 2022 forced a recalibration of its African interests that coincided with anti-Western sentiments on the continent (African Centre for Strategic Studies, 2022). Suffice it to say that its conceptual dimension suggested international practices of searching for recognition and ontological security in spatial "imaginaries" such as Africa. Spatial imaginaries are strategic geographies whose significance influences political decision-making, provides meaning for political events, and legitimizes political actions.

Since the Ukraine war, Russia has strived to attain a strategic independent actor status in the international community by establishing good offices among African friends. The liberalist perception in the West is that Moscow's security posture in Africa is opportunistic and calculative. It is opportunistic in its departure from the traditional deployment of national militaries to a new form of engagement that utilizes non-state actors and private military entities—the Wagner Group. It is rendered calculative in that Russia has exploited long-standing and growing seething sentiments over the futility of Western neoliberal and global governance architecture. In some African circles, particularly in the military regimes in Mali, Burkina Faso, Sudan, Niger, and Libya, and former liberation movement governments in Zimbabwe, South Africa, Angola, and Mozambique, the Ukrainian crisis forms part of the long-standing global efforts by Russia to provide an alternative multipolar global governance architecture. The continued marginalization of Africa in the global governance architecture has had consequential African international relations depicted in anti-French sentiments in formerly Francophone states and a significant pivoting of the continent toward Moscow for ideological and military technological cooperation. Though Russia has yet to establish itself as a fully fledged economic competitor, its noneconomic diplomatic tools have critiqued some partial analysis of economic determinism as a decisive factor in interstate relations. The attacks on the French embassy in Ouagadougou, Mali, in 2022; the ransacking of French businesses in Darkar, Senegal; and the sporadic demonstrations across Francophone Africa, which have led to the exit of French military cooperation in Burkina Faso, Niger, and Mali, demonstrated Russia's brand of politics that understands the priorities of African states: noninterference, state sovereignty, and a commitment to multilateralism in resolving political issues and conflicts. In these countries, Russia has avoided the deployment of national militaries to a new form of engagement that utilizes non-state actors and soft power tools such as media and information. Regarding media and information, Russia has deployed propaganda narratives to prop up anti-Western, particularly anti-French, sentiments in the CAR, Niger, and Burkina Faso (African Centre for Strategic Studies, 2022).

Another important element in the recalibration of Russia's foreign policy toward Africa is its security-military framework, which has grown exponentially following its war in Ukraine. Russia's security-military framework can be traced to its 1993 military doctrine encapsulated in the Military Technological Cooperation (MTC). Russia defined this as the importation and exportation of military hardware, including weapons, military technologies, and extensive scientific and military research and projects (Basu, 2001). Apart from further providing military advisors and specialists in Russia's sphere of influence, the military doctrine provides services rendered by private military companies in Moscow's near and further abroad in regions such as Africa. Since 2015, Africa has recorded 49% of its military equipment from Russia, with Rosoboronexport, the official Russian Defense Industry exporting agency, African contracts amounting to at least US$ 21 billion of its total US$56 billion in 2016. In his report titled "Russia's Private Military Diplomacy in Africa: High Risk, Low Reward, Limited Impact," Ovigwe Eguegu opines that Russia has signed military-technical agreements with at least 20 African states, indicating an increased military-security diplomacy frequency compared with its yesteryear engagements on the continent.

Russia's deployment of Wagner in African hot spots in the last few years proffers new interpretations of its security and arbitration architectures. This has generated debates and speculations within specific Western media circles concerned about Wagner's "asymmetrical" and "transactional" political-military activities. Therefore, Russia is depicted as a global power utilizing its security toolkits, coalescing with beleaguered incumbents to stifle meaningful political transitions in specific African states. However, the deployment of Wagner is low-cost effective and calculative of the pitfalls of direct involvement of a foreign military that resonate across the African continent (Parens, 2022). In this instance, Russia serves as Africa's security and sovereignty provider. Furthermore, Wagner can be read from the Gramscian template of hegemony couched in attractive soft power. A penetrative analysis of Wagner's objectives is to proffer assistance to African regimes under political isolation and economic sanctions from Western countries. Russia is depicted as a responsible global hegemony by aligning itself with these states while providing security guarantees through Wagner. Examples are seen in the Malian and Mozambican case studies where Wagner was deployed post-2019 to fight Islamic terrorism linked to the Islamic State of Iraq and Syria (ISIS) in Cabo Delgado province in northern Mozambique. This may reinforce the argument that Russia has exploited long-standing and growing seething sentiments over the futility of Western neoliberal and global governance architecture. It is not far-fetched that Russia's presence in the Cabo Delgado provides a chokehold over the French's Total LNG project. Russian interests in the Maghreb and the Horn of Africa following its invasion of Ukraine are complex, veering between a political noninterference agenda and a calculative geopolitical strategy framework that provides chokeholds over NATO in the Middle East and the Mediterranean. To achieve this, Russia has significantly supported Libyan General Khalifa Haftar's Libyan National Army (LNA) in the country's civil war with military resources.

Conclusion

This chapter set out to dissect Russia's international choices toward the Global South after its war in Ukraine. It deployed the ontological security framework, a condition in which an individual's constant mental state is derived from a sense of continuity regarding events in their life (Ferguson, 2021). An individual's identity needs to be secure within the self; therefore, uncertainty can potentially threaten one's identity. Mitzen (2006) furthers that when an individual does not know what to expect, it becomes unclear how to meet their ends. Ends are synonymous with identities, consequently suggesting uncertainty breeds an opaque identity. Politically, identity is a critical aspect of collective ontological security, stable recognition of the self-image of states derived from historical facts and interactions with other states (Narozha, 2021). Russia's self-identity depends on how different world regions viewed Moscow in the post-Cold War period. The chapter argued that various interpretations surround Russia's invasion of Ukraine, including NATO's unmitigated expansion toward Eastern Europe and the subsequent security dilemma this posed for Russia. Other arguments associate Russia's invasion of Ukraine with Moscow's never-ending pursuit of stifling democratic projects across Europe. Consequently, Russia sought to stifle Ukraine from becoming a democracy. These arguments often find expression in the Westphalian settled norms of territorial and sovereignty rights that Russia violated through its invasion of Ukraine, leading to Moscow's diplomatic isolation globally. Therefore, this chapter contributes insights into Russia's recalibration of her foreign policy in the Global South in search of allies, hegemonic status, and ontological security by taking advantage of resources at her disposal, such as military and natural resources.

References

African Centre for Strategic Studies. (2022). *Mapping disinformation in Africa*. African Centre for Strategic Studies.

Basu, B. B. (2001). Russian military-technical cooperation: Structures and processes. *Strategic Analysis, 25*(3), 437–450. https://doi.org/10.1080/09700160108458967

Brzezinski, Z. (1997). A geostrategy for Eurasia. *Foreign Affairs, 76*(5), 50–64.

Chaguaceda, A., & Herrera, A. D. (2022). *Russia in Latin America: The illiberal confluence.* Accessed August 30, 2023. https://blogs.lse.ac.uk/latamcaribbean/2022/07/28/russia-in-latin-america-the-illiberal-confluence/

Chomsky, N., & Herman, E. (2008). *La fabrique du consentement.* Marseille, Agone.

Davis, D., & Slobodchikoff, M. O. (2022). Great-power competition and the Russian invasion of Ukraine. *Journal of Indo-Pacific Affairs*, 215–226. https://media.defense.gov/2022/Jul/31/2003046336/-1/-1/1/14%20SLOBOHICKOFF_COMMENTARY.PDF

Duben, B. A. (2022). *What Putin's war in Ukraine means for the future of China-Russia relations.* LSE IDEAS.

Ellis, E. R. (2015). *The New Russian engagement with Latin America: Strategic position, commerce, and dreams of the past.* Strategic Studies Institute.

Ellis, E. (2022). *Russia in the Western Hemisphere: Assessing Putin's Malign influence in Latin America and the Caribbean.* Centre for Strategic and International Studies.

Ferguson, I. (2021). R.D. Laing's The Divided Self: An Existential Study of Sanity and Madness (1965). *Aotearoa New Zealand Social Work, 33*(2), 56–60.

Fraioli, P. (2023). The state of China–Russia cooperation over natural gas. *The International Institute for Strategic Studies, 29*(4), 1–4.

Gabuev, A. (2015). *A "Soft Alliance"? Russia-China relations after the Ukraine crisis.* European Council on Foreign Relations.

Ghincea, M. (2022a). Afterword: The Russo-Ukrainian war and great power competition. In *Great powers' foreign policy* (pp. 472–492). Brill Publishers.

Ghincea, M. (2022b). Afterword: The Russo-Ukrainian war and the great power competition. *Foreign Policy*, 472–492.

Gill, S. (Ed.). (1993). *Gramsci, historical materialism, and international relations.* Cambridge University Press.

Goldgeier, N., & McFaul, M. (2003). *Power and purpose: U.S. Policy toward Russia after the Cold War.* Brookings.

Gurganus, J. (2018). *Russia: Playing a geopolitical game in Latin America.* Carnegie Endowment for International Peace.

Hobden, S., & Wyn Jones, R. (2008). Marxist theories of international relations. In J. Baylis, S. Smith, & P. Owens (Eds.), *The globalization of world politics. An introduction to international relations* (4th ed.). Oxford University Press.

Joseph, J. (2000). A realist theory of hegemony. *Journal for the Theory of Social Behaviour.* [e-journal] 30(2). Available through SAGE Publications.

Lewis, D. G. (2018). Geopolitical imaginaries in Russian foreign policy: The evolution of 'Greater Eurasia'. *Europe-Asia Studies, 70*(10), 1612–1637.

Mangani, D. Y. (2019). *Changes in the conception of nationalism in Zimbabwe: A comparative analysis of ZAPU and ZANU liberation movements 1977–1990.* PhD thesis.

Masters, J. (2023). *Ukraine: Conflict at the crossroads of Europe and Russia.* Accessed August 28, 2023. https://www.cfr.org/backgrounder/ukraine-conflict-crossroads-europe-and-russia

Mearsheimer, J. (2019). Bound to fail: The rise and fall of the liberal international order. *International Security, 43*(4), 7–50.

Mitzen, J. (2006). Ontological security in world politics: State identity and the security dilemma. *European Journal of International Relations, 12*(3), 341–370.

Narozha, T. (2021). Revisiting the causes of Russian foreign policy changes: Incoherent biographical narrative, recognition and Russia's ontological security-seeking. *Central European Journal of International & Security Studies, 15*(2), 56–81.

Pant, H. (2023). *Russia-China relations and a changing world order.* Indian Council of World Affairs.

Parens, R. (2022). *The Wagner Group's Playbook in Africa.* Foreign Policy Research Institute.

Peace Nexus Foundation. (2022). *Russia's policy in Myanmar and Southeast Asia.* PeaceNexus Foundation.

Seungsoo, H. (2023). *Key characteristics of Russia's 2023 'foreign policy concept' and its implications*. Korea Institute for National Unification.

Siegle, J. (2022). *The future of Russia-Africa relations*. Accessed June 19, 2023. https://www.brookings.edu/blog/africa-in-focus/2022/02/02/the-future-of-russia-africa-relations/

Sriyai, S. (2022). Thailand's perspectives on the Russian invasion of Ukraine. In D. Malitz & S. Sriyayi (Eds.), *Civil societies' reactions of East- and Southeast Asian countries to the Russian war on Ukraine: Preliminary observations* (pp. 57–61). Institute of East Asian Studies.

Sriyai, S., & Khemanitthathai, S. (2022). Different reactions in Myanmar toward the Russia-Ukraine war. In D. M. Malitz & S. Sriyai (Eds.), *Civil societies' reactions of East- and Southeast Asian countries to the Russian war on Ukraine: Preliminary* (pp. 45–50). Institute of East Asian Studies/Institut für Ostasienwissenschaften.

Storey, I. (2022). The Russia-Ukraine war and its potential impact on Russia. *ISEAS: Yusof Shak Institute, 2022*(47), 1–11.

TI Observer. (2022). "Non Alignment 2.0." *TI Observer*, *21*, 1–51.

Tsygankov, A. P. (2016). *Russia's foreign policy: Change and continuity* (4th ed.). Rowman & Littlefield.

Vuksanović, V. (2023). *Moscow's continent: The principles of Russia's Africa policy engagement*. SAIIA.

Dylan Yanano Mangani is a Research Fellow at Nelson Mandela University. He holds a PhD in Political Science from the University of Venda. He has ten years of research experience in African nationalist politics, focusing on Russia's African security foreign policy, elections and electoral systems in Africa, nationalist politics, African organic crises, and the BRICS. He is a member of the South African Association of Political Studies (SAAPS), the Institute for Local Government Management of South Africa (ILGMS), the South African BRICS Youth Association (SABYA), and the CoP BRICS Research Forum for 2023–2024. He has published research articles in accredited academic journals and presented papers at local and international conferences. Most recently, Dr. Mangani contributed a chapter titled Praetorianism and Political Transitions in Lesotho: A Critique of the Lesotho Military.

Ntsikelelo Benjamin Breakfast is an Associate Professor, Head of the Department of History and Political Studies, and Acting Director of the Centre for Security Peace and Conflict Resolution at Nelson Mandela University. He is the former Head of the School for Security and Africa Studies at Stellenbosch University (SU). While he held the Headship position of the School for Security and Africa Studies, he was responsible for the management of three Departments and supervising Heads of Departments, including senior academics at the Professoriate level. Prof Breakfast has held the position of Chair of the Department of Political Science in the Faculty of Military Science at SU and has published locally and internationally in accredited journals.

Chapter 17
Resurgence of Coups and Anti-French Sentiments in West Africa: A Review of the "Unconstitutional" Change of Governments in Burkina Faso and Niger

Divane Nzima, Mubarak Aliyu, Herbert Mba Aki, and Gorden Moyo

Abstract Unconstitutional changes of government through military coups have been frequent in postcolonial Africa, especially in West Africa. The Sahel region, including Mali, Burkina Faso, Niger, and Gabon, has seen a recent surge in military coups since 2020, termed "the coup contagion." This chapter examines the coups in Burkina Faso and Niger between 2022 and 2023, highlighting common themes. These include growing insecurity from armed terrorist insurgents, which destabilized national security and created divisions within the military. Anti-French sentiments have also risen due to France's strong influence, including military presence and questionable mining practices. The chapter contextualizes these coups in the global geopolitical landscape amid the Russia-Ukraine war, noting the acceptance of Russian private military groups and calls for France's expulsion. Despite uncertainties, the coups reflect a growing anti-imperial stance, suggesting a trend toward revolutionary change against neocolonial forces in the Sahel.

Introduction

This chapter contributes on the review of recent global storms by focusing on the wave of unconstitutional change of governments that has engulfed the Sahel region. Particular attention will be on Burkina Faso and Niger where the most recent coups occurred between 2022 and 2023. In doing so, the chapter also gives an assessment of the heightening anti-French sentiments that are believed to be at the center of

D. Nzima
Department of Sociology, University of the Free State, Phuthaditjhaba, South Africa
e-mail: NzimaD@ufs.ac.za; MoyoG@ufs.ac.za

M. Aliyu
Abuja, Nigeria

G. Moyo, S. J. Ndlovu-Gatsheni (eds.), *Global Storms and Africa in World Politics*, Global Power Shift, https://doi.org/10.1007/978-3-031-83868-2_17

discontentment leading to the coups and later expulsion of the French ambassador in Niger and French military in various former French colonies in West Africa. These coups are without doubts actions that can arguably be said to be contributing anti-global imperialism driven by the failure of Western civilization. The chapter starts by giving an overview of unconstitutional change of governments in Africa with particular attention on West Africa that has experienced the most coups. Thereafter, the chapter looks at common themes leading to and in the aftermath of the coups in the two selected countries. In this regard, there is a focus on growing insecurity that was highlighted as the major cause of the coups in both countries. Furthermore, the chapter focuses on the role of political ideologies and the shifting alliances that might have led to the coups in respective countries of focus. Additionally, the chapter explores the overbearing influence of France in its former colonies and how this might explain the heightened anti-French sentiments which were common across the countries such as Mali, Burkina Faso, and Niger. Before the conclusion, the chapter ends by assessing the coups in the context of the global geopolitics as well as how regional bodies such as ECOWAS acted in response to the coup contagion in the region and particularly in Niger.

Overview of Undemocratic Change of Government

Scholarly investigations into "undemocratic" change of governments in the form of military coups in the African continent have revealed compelling insights. Within the time frame spanning 1956–2001, a total of 80 successful coups occurred, with a peak of 99 attempted coups observed between 1970 and 1989 (Barka & Mthuli, 2012; McGowan, 2003; Young, 2012). While subsequent years witnessed a decline in attempted coups to 67 between 1990 and 2012, military coups continue to sporadically manifest, characterized by varying causative factors and motivations (Souaré, 2014). Early research on military coups identified several root causes for their proliferation, emphasizing the role of weak state institutions, economic hardships, deep-seated social divisions, and repressive governmental policies (Day et al., 2020).

Atta-Asamoah (2023) delineates three distinct waves of coups in postindependence Africa, each marked by recurring causal patterns and operational modes. The first wave, spanning the 1960s to the 1970s, primarily targeted liberation leaders whose political objectives clashed with the interests of dominant colonial powers. These coups were often violent and resulted in the demise of the deposed leaders, accompanied by extrajudicial executions and human rights violations. The second wave, covering the period from 1990 to 2001, was chiefly motivated by the failure to embrace democratic governance and address the needs of citizens. Finally, the third

H. Mba Aki (✉)
Political Science, Université Omar Bongo, Libreville, Gabon

G. Moyo
Faculty of Humanities, University of the Free State, Qwaqwa, South Africa

wave, which commenced in 2021, appears to be a response to multiple constitutional amendments aimed at extending term limits, manipulated elections, deteriorating security conditions, and a resurgence of anti-colonial sentiments. Notably, in contrast to previous coup waves, the recent coups have been relatively bloodless in nature.

An examination of the recent surge in coup occurrences reveals the presence of recurring patterns of both commonality and divergence within these cases. First and foremost, the upswing in coup activities has predominantly manifested in Western African nations, with particular emphasis on the Sahel region. It is noteworthy that Gabon represents a noteworthy exception to this trend, while francophone countries have played a pivotal role as the principal arena for these coup occurrences.

Second, the dynamics of coup attempts display considerable variability across distinct nations. For instance, the coup plotters in Niger in June 2023 articulated their motivations as a response to the strategic tool to garner public support on the ongoing deterioration of the security landscape and deficiencies in social and economic governance. In Guinea, the junta cited mismanagement, corruption, and poor governance under Alpha Condé as justifications for their actions. It is important to acknowledge that, even though certain coups, such as those in Guinea and Gabon, were framed as endeavors to restore democratic order, the underlying drivers are characterized by multifaceted and diverse factors.

Lastly, these takeovers have exhibited a palpable undercurrent of anti-imperialist sentiment, particularly directed against France. This sentiment was exemplified by the expulsion of French troops from Mali and the emergence of analogous expressions of dissent in Niger including the forced departure of the French ambassador. Concurrently, foreign military elements, such as the Wagner Group, were deployed to ensure stability in the aftermath of coups in Mali and Burkina Faso, with comparable expectations pertaining to Niger's future stability.

Hence, the recent upswing in military coups gives rise to apprehensions concerning democratic transition, the role of armed forces, and anti-French sentiment in francophone Africa. Firstly, there is a notable concern regarding the trajectory of democracy and political transition. Are these coups indicative of a response to ongoing political transitions, a process traditionally overseen by democratic institutions with the authority to impeach leaders engaged in corruption and poor governance? In Chap. 19 of this book, Aaron Rwodzi critiques the future of democracy in Africa in view of what he calls "the legitimation of coups" which he sees as a direct failure of democracy.

Secondly, while the military has historically served as a pivotal force in sustaining authoritarian regimes through coercive means in certain regional countries, the surge in coups prompts inquiry into whether we are witnessing the emergence of republican armies with the intent of reinstating democratic order. Alternatively, as observed (Day et al., 2020), are these coups indicative of the involvement of politicized armies seeking to redefine their relationships with the civilian populace and authorities? Lastly, in the postcoup period in the Sahel region, the presence of an anti-imperialist sentiment raises questions about whether these coups are directed against neocolonialism or if it is an expression of anti-imperialism and the failure of the Western civilization or as argued in Chap. 19. In the following section, we examine some of the common themes in Burkina Faso and Niger. These are some of the countries that recently experienced "undemocratic" change of government through military coups where anti-French sentiments dominated the political discourse.

Common Themes in Recent Military Coups

Burkina Faso and Niger are neighboring countries, and they share a border that stretches 622 km in the upper volta region of West Africa. Between these two neighbors, there has been three military coups between 2022 and 2023. Two of the military coups happened in Burkina Faso where President Roch Marc Christian Kaboré was ousted in January 2023 and replaced by Paul-Henri Sandaogo Damiba as Interim President, who was later ousted in September 2022 and replaced by Ibrahim Traore who currently leads the transitional government. In the neighboring Niger, President Mohamed Bazoum was overthrown in July 2023 and replaced by the military leader General Abdourahamane Tchiani who currently heads the transitional government. There are several reasons that have been cited for these unconstitutional changes in government in both these countries. Among the reasons for the coups, security concerns have been highlighted as one of the core contributors that are common in both these countries. There have been surging security threats from terrorist armed groups that include Jama'at Nusrat al-Islam wal Muslimin (JNIM) and the Islamic State Greater Sahara (ISGS) who operate along the shared borders of Burkina Faso and Niger. In addition, both countries have had challenges with governance issues manifesting in poor development outcomes marred by allegation of corruption and mismanagement. However, the most pronounced theme in these two countries and other francophone countries in West Africa has been the heightening anti-French sentiments. This anti-colonial stance has shaped and fueled popular support for victors in the unconstitutional change of governments, as has been the trend in Mali, Burkina Faso, and Niger recently. In the following subsections, we will take a closer look at these common themes leading up to and in the post math of the wave of coups in the Sahel with a special focus on Burkina Faso and Niger.

Rising Insecurity and Armed Conflict

The growing concerns on insecurity in the Sahel region continue to be a threat to peace and security in countries such as Burkina Faso and Niger. This has also negatively impacted democratic transitions of power as it has been cited as one of the reasons for instituting coups. In Burkina Faso, jihadist attacks have caused over 7569 deaths, while over two million have been displaced since 2015 (Moderan & Koné, 2022). The country has experienced deadly attacks by jihadist insurgents who have largely targeted civilians, government officials, and army personnel. Given that the attacks often target civil servants, this has had a negative impact on public services which often get suspended owing to these security disturbances. The security threats intensified in 2021 under the administration of President Kaboré when the country experienced several violent incidences with 2294 casualties. In the same year, one of the most fatal attacks happened in Solhan, a village close to the Niger border where 132 people were killed by armed militants (Moderan & Koné, 2022). This caused countrywide alarm and could arguably be cited as the beginning of heightened discontent with the way the president and his government were handling the security matters in Burkina Faso. However, it was the death of 53 police officers who were stationed at the Inata military post in November 2021 in the hands of jihadist militants that sparked calls for President Kaboré's resignation (Moderan & Koné, 2022). The growing security crisis and general lack of confidence by the defense and security cluster as well as by civilians on President Kaboré ability to defuse the situation culminated in a coup in January 2022.

When Paul-Henri Sandaogo Damiba took over as the Interim President, he was expected to decisively deal with the growing insecurity. However, his rule was short-lived as he was deposed in September 2022 and replaced by the young leader Ibrahim Troaoré. Notably, worsening insecurity was highlighted as the primary reason for the coup. The military government led by Paul-Henri Damiba was castigated for its failure to effectively fight armed terrorist groups that continue to exacerbate the security crisis. Acled (2023) confirms that the problem of insecurity worsened under the Damiba administration. While Damiba cited the need for the security sector reform as the key reason for the coup, this stalled during his administration. Attacks by armed militants increased by 23% under Damiba's watch, while internal displacement among civilians worsened (Acled, 2023). Given that the Kaboré administration had increased the defense and security budget by over 270% from 2016 to 2021 and established the *Volontaires pour la défense de la patrie*, a corps of civilian auxiliaries aimed at providing support to the military in dealing with security threats and still failed to gain the confidence of the army and civilians, the failure by the Damiba administration was inexcusable (Moderan & Koné, 2022).

While the Damiba administration maintained counterterrorism cooperation with France, this cooperation failed to deliver the desired outcomes. In addition, cooperation with the French military became one of the fault lines as much of the population disapproved the presence of these foreign forces in Burkina Faso. The motives of the French military were held with great suspicion among the ordinary citizens. For the average Burkinabé, the failure of the French military in tackling terrorism in the region was beginning to spark allegations of ulterior motives by the French government, and conversations on the impact of counterterrorism on national sovereignty were becoming commonplace (Acled, 2023). As a result, events in Mali, where a military coup driven by anti-French sentiments had led to the withdrawal of the French military, were seen by many as a victory against imperialism. Similarly, since taking over the country in September 2022, the Interim President Ibrahim Troaoré has remained resolute in his anti-imperialist stance pivoted on commonly held anti-French sentiments in Burkina Faso and the Sahel region.

In 2021, for the first time since independence in 1960, Niger experienced the transfer of power from a democratically elected government to another. However, before this auspicious occasion, some elements within the military tried to carry out a coup before President Bazoum was inaugurated (Ajala, 2021). While this turned out to be a failed attempt, it was nonetheless a sign of the continued existence of problems within the security sector which suggested that a reluctance toward embracing democratic transitions in Niger remained in place (Ajala, 2021). The history of Niger is awash with constant threats of military coups. To date, there has been at least five successful military coups and several failed attempts since the country gained independence from France in 1960 (Ajala, 2023). Changes of government through unconstitutional means have become too much of a common practice such that the hope for a return to democracy continues to fade especially in the aftermath of a peaceful transition in 2021 and a return to a military coup in 2023 (Ajala, 2023; Center for Preventive Action, 2023).

Like other countries in the Sahel, Niger faces the growing security threat from armed insurgents from groups such as the Islamic State affiliates, Boko Haram and Al Qaeda in the Islamic Maghreb, that operate within the country. The failure of the government to effectively deal with these armed insurgents was highlighted as one of the major reasons for the coup (Aksa & Balima, 2023). Niger has been a strong ally of Western governments in the fights against growing terrorist activities in the Sahel through military assistance (Bisong et al., 2023). The United States has invested resources such as money and military assistance including troops stationed in Niger to help the government fight armed insurgents (Ajala, 2023). In addition, France also has military presence in Niger, of which some of the troops were accommodated after being forced out of Mali in 2022 following the coup in 2020. Despite the growing presence of foreign military forces in Niger, the state of security in the country did not improve, and this led to discontent in the security sector, thereby justifying the coup against President Bazoum (Ajala, 2023; Aliyev, 2023). A noticeable theme across the Sahel is the growing suspicion of the activities of Western military forces and their commitment to curbing insecurity through counterterrorism. It is important to note that the growing presence of Western military forces in Niger (and arguably in the Sahel) coincided with the increase in the activities of armed insurgents targeting civilians and military personnel (Center for Preventive Action, 2023). A similar trend was highlighted in the neighboring countries such as Mali and Burkina Faso where the discontent with worsening insecurity culminated in the military coups. It is thus not surprising that upon taking power, the new military government in Niger suspended all relations with France and requested the French army to leave the Niger territory (Aliyev, 2023).

In retrospect, the gesture by Niger to accommodate French troops who were expelled from Mali coupled with the presence of foreign troops from the United States might have positioned Niger against its neighboring countries who felt threatened by Western hegemony that is inherently opposed to military coups. This view is further strengthened by the support that the Niger military government received from neighboring countries such as Mali, Burkina Faso, and Chad when threatened by military intervention by the regional body ECOWAS. All the recent coups, including that in Niger, have a strong position against Western imperialism as shown by the unbridled resistance to continued French military influence (Ajala, 2023;

Aliyev, 2023). However, while security matters outside the state and local military architecture were pivotal in the emergence of the coups in both Burkina Faso and Niger, the fault lines may have been exacerbated by the antagonism in political ideologies and shifting alliances. In the next section, we examine how differing ideologies in Burkina Faso and shifting alliances in Niger influenced the recent coups in the Sahel.

The Role of Political Ideology and Shifting Alliances

Although the September 2022 coup in Burkina Faso was largely motivated by insecurity, ideological differences also played a major role in the deposal of Damiba by Traoré. Captain Traoré raised concerns over how ousted Interim President Damiba handled internal politics. It was believed that this mishandling of internal politics was one of the factors that negatively impacted the handling of security operations against terrorism in the country. A key internal political event cited by Captain Traoré was the decision by Colonel Damiba to invite ousted President Blaise Compaoré to a meeting in Ouagadougou. In contextualizing this concern, it is important to highlight the role played by former President Compaoré after the assassination of Thomas Sankara who remains greatly admired by Captain Traoré and many people in Burkina Faso who subscribe to Pan-Africanism.

Blaise Compaoré has been a key figure in Burkinabé politics, serving as president of Burkina Faso from 1987 to 2014. He came into power following the assassination of the Pan-Africanist revolutionary leader Thomas Sankara, who renamed the country Burkina Faso (Land of the Upright People), from the colonial name of Upper Volta. Thomas Sankara is famous for carrying out sweeping socialist reforms during his administration—notably equal rights for women, mass vaccination programs, agrarian reforms, and anti-corruption initiatives. Sankara sought to reduce the influence of traditional rulers and break free from conservative and authoritarian governance. On the contrary, Compaoré took an opposing approach, aligning himself with the conservative segments of society and safeguarding their privileges, which in turn became the foundation of his authority. Despite his decades in power, the memory of Sankara's assassination remained fresh in the mind of the average Burkinabé citizen. This event, coupled with the elitist rule of Compaoré, culminated into a popular uprising which removed him from power in 2014.

Interestingly, many of the activist groups involved in the mass protests against Compaoré's regime were the so-called Sankarists who were heavily driven by the Pan-Africanist and anti-imperialist ideologies of Thomas Sankara. Following his ousting, Compaoré went into self-exile in Cote d'Ivoire, giving way for another revision of politics in Burkina Faso. The political instability which ensued after Compaoré's exit would reflect the struggles between Sankarists and Compaoré loyalists, or "Compaorists." Unfortunately, the act of inviting the ousted President Blaise Compaoré to a meeting in Ouagadougou by Colonel Damiba was interpreted as an act of betrayal to the people's revolution. On the security front, it did not help

Damiba's cause that he continued cooperation with the French army much against the approval of the masses. This must also be viewed against the background that suspicions of the involvement of France in the assassination of Thomas Sankara still linger on. The masses and indeed some within the military ranks had not forgiven Compaoré for his role in the assassination of Thomas Sankara and thus the reversal of the people's revolution. Therefore, the coming in of Captain Traoré as the Interim President of Burkina Faso through a military coup can also be explained as an act of settling historical scores between the Sankarists and the Compaorists in the politics of Burkina Faso.

In Niger, many experts on the ground saw the coup as the endpoint of an extended period of discord between President Mohamed Bazoum and his top security official, General Abdourahmane Tchiani (Anna & Petesch, 2023). Apart from the growing insecurity caused by terrorist armed groups and the loss of confidence in the French military counterterrorism support activities, in Niger the coup was also motivated by power struggles between President Bazoum and General Tchiani loyalists. General Tchiani had led the presidential guard for 10 years under President Issoufou, commanding the most formidable and well-equipped force stationed in the capital Niamey. He played a crucial role in preventing a coup attempt in March 2021, 2 days before President Bazoum assumed office, and continued in his position under the new president. However, President Bazoum's anti-corruption reforms targeted the presidential guard, initiating a closer examination of its budget and seeking to reduce its manpower. This obviously worsened the General's mistrust in the President who also preferred having foreign military forces despite the military feeling undermined by the act. By the time the coup happened, it had become apparent that President Bazoum was preparing to replace General Tchiani as head of the presidential guard. This is despite his proven loyalty and role in ensuring that the President assumed office in 2021 when he thwarted a coup attempt.

The developments leading to the coup in 2023 demonstrated how power struggles between loyalists of President Bazoum and General Tchiani rather than fundamental ideological differences were at the center of the fallout. This battle was further made apparent when an attempted escape by ousted President Bazoum was foiled in Niamey on October 19, 2023. Bazoum, who was held by the military junta since the coup, had reportedly tried to flee with the help of collaborators within the security forces. These further highlighted the fractures that existed in the military and the enduring influence that the ousted president continued to wield within the country's armed forces despite his detention. The ideology and political direction of the military junta in Niger remains hard to define since the coup in July 2023. However, what is certain is that the interim leaders are popular with the masses for their bold stance against continued French influence aligning with the growing trend in former French colonies in Africa. In the next section, we explore France's overbearing influences that have culminated in the coup contagion in the Sahel.

Growing Anti-French Sentiments

The recent wave of coups in West Africa have renewed the concerns around France's overbearing influence on the policies and affairs of its former colonies. Among all the countries that recently had unconstitutional change of government, including Mali, Burkina Faso, and Niger, there has been discontentment with the activities of France and its influence on state affairs. To that end, some of these coups have been supported by the masses who have demonstrated clear public disapproval of France to the extent of seeing the recent developments in the Sahel as a triumph of the people's revolution against imperial France. The question is, "How did we get to this point where anti-French sentiments have reached these heights leading to what others have termed *the coup contagion*?" Well, the term *Françafrique* is commonly used to refer to France's sphere of economic, political, and military influence in its former colonies across the continent. Sörenson (2008) categorizes the French-African relationship into four historical phases since independence, namely, the French Empire, the French Union, the French Community, and today's network structure which encompasses French and African political leaders, civil servants, officers, and businessmen. The common theme in all these categories has always remained France's undue influence and a tight grip over its former colonies. *Françafrique* has defined the monetary policy in the former colonies with the CFA franc since 1945 when the franc—an official colonial currency—was officially created based on France's objective to promote economic integration within its colonies. The franc later became the CFA and has since then served to exercise control over the resources and economic and political frameworks of the former colonies (Kirwin et al., 2022). France's use of the CFA currency to maintain its hold on former colonies has been lamented as one of the worst forms of neocolonialism (Kirwin et al., 2022). The continued economic stagnation in countries such as Burkina Faso and Niger which manifest in growing poverty and poor access to resources and high cost of living has cast suspicions on the role of France in actively influencing underdevelopment. France's continued exploitative relations with these countries such as the mining interests in uranium that disproportionately benefit France have been used as an example of how France has been sabotaging the economies of its former colonies (Aliyev, 2023). This and France's colonial past have been some of the leading causes of heightened anti-French sentiments that came into the spotlight during and after the coups in countries such as Burkina Faso and Niger, as many in the Sahel believe that the leading source of their problems is France (Kirwin et al., 2022; Aliyev, 2023).

France has also consistently maintained a military presence in its former colonies in the Sahel region of West Africa. This has emerged as one of the causes of the fissures that led to the recent coups in countries such as Mali, Burkina Faso, and Niger due to public discontentment. The French counterterrorism efforts in West Africa have provoked questions over the sovereignty of former colonies (Bisong et al., 2023). There were concerns that the increasing security pressures from Paris were taking precedence over domestic policy priorities particularly in a country like

Niger that had been positioned as a strategic partner in fighting illegal immigration from sub-Saharan Africa and in dealing with armed insurgents in the Sahel (Bisong et al., 2023). Despite the presence of the French military in the region, violent attacks by militant groups consistently increased, spreading from Mali to Burkina Faso, Niger, and Chad over time (Kirwin et al., 2022; Aliyev, 2023; Bisong et al., 2023). The worsening insecurity was seen by many through a colonial lens, especially with French forces on the ground and the mining operations by French corporations in Niger that carried unsettling neocolonial overtures (Kirwin et al., 2022; Aliyev, 2023). This has further led to concerns that France's military presence only serves to protect French mining investments by having an influence over the political and military complex as opposed to the purported counterterrorism efforts. As captured by Aliyev (2023:356), below:

> It is seen that France is trying to maintain political and military activity in its former colonies, especially in Niger, through economic support and humanitarian aid programs. In this sense, France endeavours to strengthen its sphere of influence in other former colonies such as Niger by activating political economy.

To make matters worse, reports that civilians were killed during an airstrike by French forces in Mali were confirmed by the United Nations in 2021 (United Nations, 2021). Thus, it is not surprising that the political concerns over sovereignty, coupled with economic concerns over unethical resource extraction, and security concerns over the killing of innocent civilians manifested into strong anti-French sentiments. These started in Mali and then spread to other countries in the Sahel such as Burkina Faso and Niger. These sentiments became a major factor in the military coups in the latter two countries, which are discussed in this chapter. In the next section, we discuss these recent coups in the context of global politics and how the regional body ECOWAS positioned itself in the face of the coup contagion in the Sahel.

ECOWAS' Response to the Coup Contagion

Amoateng (2022) suggests that in the initial four decades postindependence, coups in Africa and particularly in West Africa occurred against the backdrop of Cold War politics, where the West led by United States and the East led by the Soviet Union were vying for consolidating their spheres of influence on the continent. Recent demonstrations in support of the coups in countries such as Burkina Faso and Niger brought to the fore emerging fissures in geopolitics that have been developing considering the Ukraine-Russia war. In Chap. 15 of this book, Charles Mutasa explores in detail how the Russia-Ukraine war is causing fissures in global geopolitics and the steps that can be taken to secure global unity.

Nonetheless, during the demonstrations in the aftermath of the coups, the masses where brazenly clear on their stand against the influence of France in West Africa and their preference for Russian military support. This was made clear because in calling for the expulsion of France, the Russian flag was waved as confirmation of their preference in the current global geopolitical standoff between the West and the East. According to Issaev et al. (2022), a survey of the perceptions of Russia's "return" to Africa has shown that Russian engagement in West Africa is welcome among the young people. Therefore, given that the coups were led by young military generals, it is not surprising that in the aftermath of the coups, governments in Mali, Burkina Faso, and Niger formally cut ties with Paris and moved toward closer alliances with Moscow. It could thus be argued that these developments are a preview of the resurgence of Cold War politics and spheres of influence. It is important to emphasize that the recent coups have been modeled as a triumph against French neocolonialism and once again Moscow has become a trusted ally. During the struggle for independence, Moscow was a trusted ally to deliver independence from Western colonizers, and this might be what is influencing the shift of the gaze toward Moscow as an old-time trusted ally. In Chap. 16 of this book, Dylan Mangani and Ntsikelelo Breakfast go deeper into Russia's recalibration of foreign policy that suggests a drive toward establishing new allies in the Global South such as maintaining a presence in the Sahel region.

Recent research on the impact of the Russia-Ukraine war on Africa also indicates that the war has exacerbated rifts among African political leaders, negatively impacting the continent's collective foreign policy on the international stage (Niyitunga & Adunimay, 2023). The lack of a cohesive political outlook for the continent has made it vulnerable to international influences by major world powers, mainly Russia, China, and the West. Due to the history of close ties between the Soviet Union and independence movement leaders in Africa, many Africans within the civil society, labor unions, and even intellectuals believe that modern-day Russia is an ally with the continent's interests in mind. In the recent coups, the Wagner Group—a private military company with close ties to the Russian government—has been favored as an alternative to the French military for fighting insurgency in the Sahel. In Mali, Wagner fighters were first deployed in December 2021, drawing condemnation from Europe and the United States who already had military presence in the region.

Today, more than 1000 Wagner forces operate in Mali, carrying out counterterrorism efforts and helping to fight the Tuareg rebellion in the north of the country. The Russian government has since tried to position itself as a socioeconomic partner, in addition to counterinsurgency operations for countries in the region. In October 2023, it signed a memorandum of understanding with the government of Burkina Faso to help build a nuclear power plant that will deliver on the latter's energy needs. However, Soviet-era support for the African continent is different from the modern support being received from Russia. Despite the sentiments being driven by resistance to neocolonialism and general elements of coloniality from the West, these elements can be found with the Russian counterparts as well. Security-for-minerals contracts have raised concerns about Russian desires to exploit anti-French sentiments as a way of furthering its own economic interests. Furthermore, the presence of Wagner forces in Mali has proven ineffective in fighting terrorism, raising questions about the impact of Russian private military contractors on the security landscape in the Sahel. Although Russian and Wagner's presence in Burkina Faso is yet to be seen, the example of Mali calls into question the dynamics of today's international politics as compared to the Cold War of the 1960s and if the modern Russian state is truly ideologically aligned with African countries. Most importantly, this begs the question, "Why must Africa always need external allies when it has regional bodies?"

During the early 2000s, the African Union demonstrated a stringent opposition to unconstitutional changes through initiatives like the Algiers decision, prohibiting coup perpetrators from attending summits, and the 2000 Lomé Declaration, which underscored a zero-tolerance approach to coups (Elamin, 2023). This stance found general support within subregional entities like the Economic Community of West African States (ECOWAS) (Elamin, 2023). However, practical responses to coups within ECOWAS have been heavily influenced by contextual factors surrounding each coup incident.

Officially, ECOWAS's reaction to coups is expected to align with the mechanisms outlined by the ECOWAS Monitoring Group, designed to address extra-constitutional changes within member states. This framework includes strategies such as imposing sanctions, suspending membership, and deploying peacekeeping forces to respond to such occurrences (Elamin, 2023). However, implementing these measures encounters challenges within ECOWAS due to its decision-making reliance on consensus. Consensus building, particularly concerning the imposition of sanctions and the deployment of military forces across borders, proves to be an arduous task.

The effectiveness of economic sanctions imposed by countries facing their own economic constraints often lacks the necessary sway to dissuade a leader pursuing power for reasons unrelated to economic gain. Furthermore, the success of deterrence strategies relies on the consistent and predictable application of these tools. Despite recurring instances of instability and insecurity, ECOWAS has dispatched a peacekeeping force on only seven occasions since its establishment. Even amidst recent coup occurrences, the most recent instance of ECOWAS deploying a security or peacekeeping force was observed in 2017. After the coup in Niger in 2023, ECOWAS threatened military invasion to force the reinstatement of President Bazoum (Moses & Ige, 2023). However, this threat was thwarted by a counterthreat from Mali, Burkina Faso, and Guinea who all indicated that they would join forces with Niger to fight any military intervention. It is important to note that all these countries are former French colonies who believe that the recent coups are justified as they are a great step toward freedom from the overbearing neocolonial influence of France. Therefore, the action of ECOWAS was arguably seen as aligning with colonial and imperialist interests instead of being in solidarity in the fight against neocolonialism as the anti-French sentiments continue to heighten in all former French colonies in West Africa.

In the future, we are faced with the prospects of an ECOWAS without Mali, Burkina Faso, and Niger. This follows a withdrawal announcement made by the three countries in January 2024 following their disgruntlement over ECOWAS's response to the military coups in the Sahel region. While the process for withdrawal from the reginal block normally takes a year, the three countries that have entered a defense pact called the "Alliance of Sahel States" are proposing an immediate departure. We are yet to see how ECOWAS will handle this current impasse in the region. These countries that all have experienced the global storms through the recent wave of coups accuse ECOWAS of aiding the imperialist agenda by imposing unfair sanctions. There is a strong belief that the coup action in the Sahel was orchestrated as part of the anti-global imperialism fight. In addition, these coups are a sign of the failure of the Western civilization agenda which in the case of the Sahel has continually pushed for unequal economic benefits through exploitative mineral extraction. Most of the recent coup leaders have emphasized common themes such as rising insecurity and economic stagnation with emphasis on the need to rid their countries of imperial domination from France. In the future, we are likely to see minimal activity from the former colonial power following the expulsion of the French military from the region and the formation of the Alliance of Sahel States to counter the French influence through ECOWAS.

Burkina Faso and Niger have consistently been affected by rising insecurity from armed insurgents whose operations have heightened since the fall of Gaddafi's Libya. The whole regions of West Africa and the Sahel have been experiencing terrorist attacks from jihadist armed insurgents, affiliates of the Islamic State, Boko Haram, and Al Qaeda in the Islamic Maghreb, among many others. This has put too much pressure on the countries' militaries to provide security to the civilians and ensure conditions that allow the public service to function. On this front, we are likely to see two outcomes in the future:

1. The insecurity is likely to increase given the departure of the Frech army that was helping in fighting these armed insurgents. The disgruntled former colonial power might create some destabilization through economic sanctions which might create a resource strain for these countries leading to minimal resources available to fight the insurgents. Already the military governments in the Sahel States are feeling the ECOWAS sanctions which they have accused of forwarding the imperial agenda of France.
2. The fight against the armed insurgents may be better organized now that there will be no foreign interference. In the past, there were concerns that the presence of the French military undermined the efforts of the army personnel. Now that they decide the methods of confronting the armed insurgents, their strategies are likely to yield better outcomes. In addition, the concerted effort in ensuring greater security through the Alliance of Sahel States might yield positive results leading to better security in the region.

Conclusion

This chapter has focused on the wave of unconstitutional change of governments as some of the global storms that have engulfed the Sahel region with particular attention on Burkina Faso and Niger where the most recent coups occurred between 2022 and 2023. As a starting point, an overview of coups in Africa was given, highlighting the prevalence of successful and attempted coups since the dawn of independence. While coups have been spread across the breath and length of the continent of Africa, the incidence of successful and attempted coups has been more prevalent in West Africa where most of the countries previously fell under French colonial rule. Insecurity in the region largely from armed insurgents was one of the reasons for the coups. The continued collaboration with foreign military forces in fighting insurgents created fissures within the local military personnel who often felt undermined as the interests of France seemed to override local priorities. These concerns arguably heightened discontentment particularly given the unethical mining activities of France who disproportionately benefited from Niger's uranium while Niger continued to experience economic stagnation. Therefore, on a more structural level, while economic stagnation was blamed on poor governance, corruption, and nepotism, there was growing consensus that linked it to neocolonial exploitation by France through resource extraction with little benefit to the local economy. Indeed, most of the people in countries such as Burkina Faso and Niger believed that France was the main source of their suffering, thus justifying coups that sought to expel the former colonial master.

Mostly importantly, this chapter has acknowledged that the recent coups in the Sahel have occurred during a period where there is a major shift in geopolitics given the war between Russia and Ukraine. While the French military operations and ambassadors were being requested to leave in countries such as Burkina Faso and Niger, the masses in their demonstrations were embracing the Russian private military group—Wagner which has played a notable role in the Russia-Ukraine war. Russian flags were being waved in celebration of the coups by masses who saw the success of the coups as a triumph against neocolonialism. The reemergence of Russia in West African affairs is quite nostalgic given the role played by the Soviet Union in the struggle for liberation, yet it is also held with skepticism given its economic interests in Africa. Nonetheless, the masses through demonstration have clearly made known their preference of Russia over Western countries such as France. In all this, the influence of regional bodies such as ECOWAS has been found to be underwhelming and less inspiring. When the coup in Niger happened, ECOWAS's threat of military intervention was met by a counterthreat of war by Mali, Burkina Faso, and Guinea who pledged to stand with Niger. It appears all these former colonies of France are ready to stand in solidarity against neocolonialism as anti-French sentiments gain traction in the region. Therefore, the position taken by ECOWAS proved to be less effective against the solidarity and determination to cut ties with France even if this is done through unconstitutional change of governments. Given the foregoing, it is highly likely that we are yet to experience more coups in the future as fissures continue to emerge. Until a lasting homegrown solution is found, democratic transitions of government will remain an elusive dream.

References

Acled, C. (2023). How Burkina Faso became the epicentre of conflict in the Sahel. *Al Jazeera* (July 11). https://acleddata.com/2022/03/11/how-burkina-faso-became-the-epicenter-of-conflict-in-the-sahel-al-jazeera/

Ajala, O. (2021). Botched coup in Niger points to deep fissures in the country. *The conversation*. https://theconversation.com/botched-coup-in-niger-points-to-deep-fissures-in-the-country-158330

Ajala, O. (2023). What caused the coup in Niger? An expert outlines three driving factors. *The conversation*. https://theconversation.com/what-caused-the-coup-in-niger-an-expert-outlines-three-driving-factors-210721 on 04/12/2023

Aksa, M., & Balima, B. (2023). Niger soldiers say President Bazoum's government has been removed. *Reuters*. https://www.reuters.com/world/africa/soldiers-nigers-presidential-guard-blockade-presidents-office-security-sources-2023-07-26/

Aliyev, A. (2023). A new battleground between the west alliance and Russia? In the context of Niger. *Journal of Namibian Studies: History Politics Culture, 36*, 337–366.

Amoateng, A. (2022). *Military coups in Africa: A continuation of politics by other means?* ACCORD: Governance and Leadership. https://www.accord.org.za/conflicttrends/military-coups-in-africa-a-continuation-of-politics-by-other-means/

Anna, C., & Petesch, C. (2023). Two rivals claim to be in charge in Niger. One is detained and has been publicly silent for days | AP News. *AP News*. https://apnews.com/article/niger-coupwest-africa-military-president-eab748ddfcc6de40f7e0fe967accb6da

Atta-Asamoah, A. (2023). Africa's three waves of coups. *Institute for Security Studies Today*. https://issafrica.org/iss-today/africas-three-waves-of-coups

Barka, H. B., & Mthuli, N. (2012). *Political fragility in Africa: Are military coups d'Etat aNever-Ending Phenomenon?* https://www.afdb.org/en/documents/document/economic-brief-political-fragility-in-africa-are-military-coups-detat-a-never-ending-phenomenon-29430

Bisong, A., Jegen, L., & Mounkaila, H. (2023). *What does the regime change in Niger mean for migration cooperation with the EU?* Briefing note 168. 11 September 2023. Maastricht: ECDPM.

Center for Preventive Action. (2023). Violent extremism in the Sahel. *Global conflict tracker*. https://www.cfr.org/global-conflict-tracker/conflict/violent-extremism-sahel on 04/12/2023.

Day, C., Khisa, M., & Reno, W. (2020). Revisiting the civil-military conundrum in Africa. *Civil Wars, 22*(2–3), 156–173. https://doi.org/10.1080/13698249.2020.1736808

Elamin, M. O. I. (2023). Navigating complexities: African Union's peace and security strategy challenges after Niger and Gabon Coups. *International Journal, 10*(3), 2070–2081.

Issaev, L., Shishkina, A., & Liokumovich, Y. (2022). Perceptions of Russia's 'return' to Africa: Views from West Africa. *South African Journal of International Affairs, 29*(4), 425–444.

Kirwin, M., Ouedraogo, L., & Warner, J. (2022). Fake news in the Sahel: "Afrancaux News," French counterterrorism, and the logics of user-generated media. *African Studies Review, 65*(4), 911–938.

McGowan, P. J. (2003). African military coups d'état, 1956–2001: Frequency, trends and distribution. *The Journal of Modern African Studies, 41*(3), 339–370.

Moderan, O., & Koné, F. R. (2022). What caused the coup in Burkina Faso? *Institute for Security Studies*. https://issafrica.org/iss-today/what-caused-the-coup-in-burkina-faso on 04/12/2023.

Moses, I. K., & Ige, T. S. (2023). Political instability in Africa; An account of the 2023 Niger Coup. *Best Journal of Innovation in Science, Research, and Development, 2*(8), 109–111.

Niyitunga, E. B., & Adunimay, A. W. (2023). A convoluted post-cold war world: Effects of Russo-Ukrainian War on Africa's international relations. *Journal of African Foreign Affairs, 10*(2), 61.
Sörenson, K. (2008). *Beyond Francafrique: The foundation, reorientation, and reorganisation of France's Africa politics*. https://urn.kb.se/resolve?urn=urn:nbn:se:fhs:diva-2416
Souaré, I. K. (2014). The African Union as a norm entrepreneur on military coups d'état in Africa (1952–2012): An empirical assessment. *The Journal of Modern African Studies, 52*(1), 69–94.
United Nations. (2021). UN investigation concludes French military airstrike killed Mali civilians (2021, April 1). *UN News*. https://news.un.org/en/story/2021/03/1088722
Young, C. (2012). *The postcolonial state in Africa: Fifty years of independence, 1960–2010*. University of Wisconsin Press.

Divane Nzima, PhD, is a Senior Lecturer and Subject Head in the University of the Free State, Department of Sociology. He is an NRF-rated researcher who holds a Y2 rating. His research and teaching interests cut across various disciplines such as Sociology, Demography, and Development Studies. He has published research on the intersection of migration and development, family dynamics and parenting, the wellbeing of the elderly in resource-constrained countries as well as artisanal mining and agricultural value chains. He has also taken an interest in political sociology with a keen interest on the nature and methods of political contestations to wield political power.

Mubarak Aliyu is an independent Political Analyst specializing in the West Africa and Sahel Region. His research interests cut across political, social, and economic development in Africa. He holds an MSc in Development Studies from the London School of Economics and Political Science, where he specialized in African Development. He is also an alumnus of the LSE Programme for African Leadership.

Herbert Mba Aki serves as an Assistant Professor of Political Science at Université Omar Bongo in Libreville, Gabon. He earned his PhD in Political Science and International Studies from Hanyang University in Seoul, South Korea, in 2021. His research interests include environmental policy, governance and sustainability. Herbert takes an active role in academic networks, serving as the Coordinator of the Africa Working Group (2020-2023) within the Young Scholars Initiative (YSI) and as the Representative for Low- and Middle-Income Countries (LMIC) at the Future Earth Assembly. He is also a fervent advocate for good governance in Africa through his active participation in initiatives such as the Now Generation Network (NGN) with the Mo Ibrahim Foundation and as a founding member of Democratic Solidarity Africa (DSA), an initiative of the Forum 2000 Foundation.

Gorden Moyo (PhD) is currently the Senior Research Fellow in the Department of Sociology, Faculty of Humanities at the University of the Free State (UFS) in South Africa; Senior Lecturer in the Faculty of Social Sciences and Humanities at Lupane State University (LSU) in Zimbabwe; Member of the Editorial Board of the Sabella Abidde Publishing House, University of Alabama (USA); Director of the Public Policy and Research Institute of Zimbabwe (PPRIZ); Associate Member of the International Society for Development and Sustainability (ISDS) in Japan; the President of the Development Studies Association of Zimbabwe (DeSAZ); Member of the Southern African Development Parliamentary Forum Technical Group on Public Financial Management; ex-Minister of State in the Prime Minister's Office, ex-Minister of State Enterprises and Parastatals, and ex-Member of Parliament of Zimbabwe (2009–2013); ex-British Council Facilitator of the Pan-African Leadership Interaction Programme in 19 countries across Africa including Botswana, Cameroon, Eritrea, Ethiopia, Eswatini, Ghana, Kenya, Lesotho, Liberia, Malawi, Mauritius, Namibia, Nigeria, South Africa, Tanzania, Uganda, Zambia, and Zimbabwe. He is a Chevening Scholar whose primary research interests are in global finance, international economic relations, developmental states, public leadership, military commercialism, Africa-China relations, and African Agency among others. He has published several articles in peer-reviewed journals and several book chapters. His most recent books include *African Agency, Finance, and Developmental States* (Palgrave McMillan, 2021); *Making Politics in Zimbabwe's Second Republic: The Formative Project by Emmerson Mnangagwa* (Springer, 2023) co-edited with Prof Kirk Helliker; and *Africa in the Global Economy: Capital Outflows, Enablers and Decolonial Responses* (Springer, 2024).

Chapter 18
Global Politics and Recent Political Changes in West and Central Africa: A Decolonial Analysis

Funa Moyo and Sihlanganiso Khumalo

Abstract Coloniality of governance is our intervention for analyzing the nexus between the modern world system and political changes in West and Central Africa. Arguably, the idea of a state is weaved in the Euro-modern epistemology and implanted through the post-1945 juridical decolonization, which created diverse states clamoring for complete decolonization, proxies for USA/Communists or former colonialists, deploying different aspects of coloniality of governance which tend to be the major factor behind violent political changes. The chapter questions the naturalization of frowned upon Euro-modern coup d'état. This library study examines the reasons behind the coups and their impact. The main finding is that, although the main causes of coups are painted local, they have qualities of a global war.

Introduction

Notwithstanding lexical innovations such as control of authority, colonial governmentality, coloniality of power in postcolonial Africa, and various elements that constitute the colonial matrices of power, we use coloniality of governance to denote a rallying point of the lens that we use to analyze a possible nexus between global politics and political changes in West and Central Africa. We argue that global coloniality of governance forms the center of the problem of political changes in West and Central Africa. Notwithstanding that the military in the postcolonial era protects the states against possible threats to peace and order, the military institutions

F. Moyo (✉)
Institute of Development Sciences (IDS-NUST), National University of Science and Technology, Bulawayo, Zimbabwe
e-mail: funa.moyo@nust.ac.zw

S. Khumalo
Department of Development Studies, Lupane State University, Lupane, Zimbabwe

G. Moyo, S. J. Ndlovu-Gatsheni (eds.), *Global Storms and Africa in World Politics*, Global Power Shift, https://doi.org/10.1007/978-3-031-83868-2_18

have also posed security risks to civilian governments. Literature opines that military institutions use coercive force against the very regimes that constituted them. Thus, the African continent has been a center of political turmoil for decades, with coups being a common occurrence. In recent times, West and Central Africa have witnessed a surge in coups, which have had significant impacts on the stability of the region. This point is also discussed by Nzima, Aliyu, Aki, and Moyo in Chap. 16 and Rwodzi in Chap. 18 of this book. This chapter uses decolonial analysis to explore the recent coups in West and Central Africa and their implications.

Explaining Decolonial Analysis

Different theorists, scholars, peace mission diplomats, and activists have used different analytical projects to analyze political changes in West and Central Africa. This chapter uses decolonial analysis. Escobar (2002) gives Anibal Quijano, Enrique Dussel, and Mignolo as the main resources of the modernity/coloniality research group that laid conceptual foundations of the decolonial analysis. Grosfoguel, Nelson Maldonado-Torres, and Boaventura des Santos are also leading decolonial theorists. Mignolo had a discussion with Mr Sihlanganiso Khumalo after a decoloniality symposium in South Africa in August 2018 and the Afterword in Walsh and Mignolo (2018: 249), Walter D. Mignolo asserts that Sabelo Gatsheni-Ndlovu is a leading decolonial theorist in Africa who uses "…local Histories of Africa in dialogue with Coloniality and Decoloniality." Decoloniality is relevant to the analysis of global politics and political changes in West and Central Africa because it has a unique entry point from the epistemic dimension since epistemology is constitutive of ontology.

In keeping with the view that knowledge produces reality (Walsh & Mignolo, 2018; Ndlovu-Gatsheni, 2018a, b), this chapter intervenes at the epistemic level of the question of political changes in West and Central Africa. Such an entry point unmasks what Dussel (1998) accurately framed as the Eurocentric modernity paradigm of knowing or knowledge that was inaugurated by Western civilizations (Mignolo, 2000) that produces and names political changes in West and Central Africa and then goes on to show that other theories of knowledge that flow from a planetary modernity paradigm of knowing (Dussel, 1998) or modern world systems (Mignolo, 2000), which inspire and embrace disobedient pluriversal futures, exist. Decolonial analyses provide for that space and effort.

The essence of decoloniality is to simultaneously reduce provincial coloniality and modernity/rationality which pretends to be a universal epistemology to size while valorizing and using colonized and silenced indigenous epistemologies to think and solve existential problems constituting daily lived experiences of the majority in the South long after the end of juridical colonialism (Quijano, 2007; Grosfoguel, 2007; Walsh & Mignolo, 2018). Coloniality and modernity/rationality is an Anibal Quijano short notation for the idea that the world order of control, domination, racism, and exploitation of the colonized subjects and their lands that was inaugurated in 1492 by colonizers is constitutive of the arrogant and proud Western systems of knowledge production that nullified other planetary epistemologies. Decolonial analysis is liberatory in attitude and praxis.

Escobar gives an instructive description of the decolonial perspectives:

> …decolonial thought or perspective has been under construction since the late 1990s. It is a compelling framework that has articulated a complex lexicon, proposing that eurocentrism is the knowledge form of the modern/colonial world system since 1492. This perspective develops a decided critique of modernity, proposing the need for epistemic decolonization as a crucial domain of struggle towards transmodernity or alternatives to modernity. In other words, decolonial thought aims to go beyond intra- European or intra-modern perspectives on modernity to establish other grounds for thought and action. (Escobar, 2015: 8)

While the above citation corroborates the view that decolonizing knowledge is the main task toward solving the existential questions of our times, it ignores the idea that decoloniality is not a single perspective. Decoloniality is sponsored by the critique of Eurocentric modernity as a project of territorial and epistemic expansion (Andreotti, 2011) that is rolled over by its darker side, the logic of coloniality, to rule over planetary modernity (Escobar, 2002; Mignolo, 2011b). While Escobar and others view decoloniality as an alternative to coloniality and modernity/rationality, Mignolo (2011a) prefers to frame it in non-global designs terms as just an option from a list of epistemic projects options like rewesternization, dewesternization, and spirituality. Gordon (2011) added that decolonizing knowledge demands a shift in the geography of reason, a call for knowledge production away from white male philosophies. Maldonado-Torres (2004) comprehensively submits that decoloniality is a family of analytical approaches that view coloniality as the fulcrum of our contemporary problems. This chapter views decoloniality as a conglomerate of non-compliant analytic and praxis tools.

The delves into decolonial conceptual tools. These are new world order, epistemic racism, epistemic restitution and ecologies of knowledges (Quijano, 2007; Santos, 2007; Maldonado-Torres, 2007), Coloniality (Quijano, 2007), Myth of the twenty-first century and epistemic situatedness (Grosfoguel, 2007), knowledge is constitutive of ontology (Walsh & Mignolo, 2018), coloniality of peace (Maldonado-Torres, 2020) and the innovation of this chapter, coloniality of governance.

The first tool is about relations of Western domination after 1519 and 1532 conquests and colonialism of the Latin America that had started with the voyages of 1492. Quijano (2007) notes that colonization started unequal relations between the colonizers and the colonized based on modernity/rationality. Maldonado-Torres (2007) refers to the arrogance and the attitude of self-sufficiency of coloniality and modernity/rationality as epistemic racism because it infantilizes and folklorizes theories of knowledges of the South. Being conscious of long-term epistemic colonization remnant in the postcoloniality, Quijano (2007) calls for epistemic restitution which can lead to ecologies of knowledges (Santos, 2007) as the main intervention.

Coloniality is a concept that was coined by Anibal Quijano (Arias, 2013). Coloniality is the hidden negative and violent constitutive side of Euro-modernity which is concealed by the elusive magnanimity of the rhetoric of Eurocentric modernity. Coloniality, due to its logic of violent exploitation and multipronged social domination of the South by Western Europe and North America, is the energy that produces decoloniality (Mignolo, 2011b), and coloniality/modernity/decoloniality is the decolonial triad framed by Mignolo (Walsh & Mignolo, 2018) to signify that coloniality is constitutive of modernity and coloniality and modernity give rise to the need for decoloniality. Decoloniality denotes multi- and pluriversal yet situated efforts to disentangle from the logic of coloniality. Coloniality refers to invisible structures of power which continue as ghosts (Ndlovu-Gatsheni 2021 key note address) to impact living in the South long after juridical independence.

The third tool is the myth of the twenty-first century and epistemic South (Grosfoguel, 2007). Grosfoguel (2007) aptly observes that coloniality did not evaporate with administrative independence in the 1950s but continues to disable imagining futures in the South. Curating the pedigree of his decolonial scholarship in the preface of the second edition of his 2013 book, Ndlovu-Gatsheni (2022) notes that his entry point is that decolonization is an incomplete project, thus reiterating that there are remnants of coloniality in the postcoloniality (Ndlovu-Gatsheni, 2013).

Epistemology is constitutive of ontology (Walsh & Mignolo, 2018). For instance, the state as reality was curated by Western European-North American epistemology of universal structures of governance, thereby folklorizing indigenous systems and subsuming the nonaligned existence of colonial subjects. Another captured concept is that of coup d'etat. Coup d'etat has French origins and it denotes a sudden, violent, and unlawful seizure of power from a legitimate government. The concept universalizes government that is weaved in Euro-modern epistemology and imposes elected leaders as uncontested ontology, hence persuading all across space and time to frown at political changes that do not comply with the Western notion of allowable political change without asking if there are other options or at least coup from whose perspective and why coup?

Maldonado-Torres (2020) protests peace that comes in the terms of the West, after a war that is sanitized as inevitable for progress, reason, and civilization, and in the terms of the victor, to be an allusion. He notes that such peace, which is conceptualized as harmony within a given order, is a potent tool in the arsenal of colonialism and racism. The idea of coup as a frowned upon political change engine has some linkages with the peace that Maldonado-Torres debunks:

> Peace is not quietness. Peace does not have to do with using violence or nonviolence in opposition to an unjust state of affairs either. Peace, is above all, an outcome of decolonial maturity: of a firm and wise opposition against war where our relationships with others announce and anticipate the formation of radically different, and truly peaceful, communities and societies. In this moment we are in peace with ourselves because we have become those who we need to be in order to work with others in the effort to end war. We also develop capacity to be in peace with others with whom we struggle in the effort to build, as Fratz Fanon put it, 'the world of you.' Only such a world, a world of you, can be a world of peace. (Maldonado-Torres, 2020)

The notion of decolonial maturity denotes a situation where those with different views and interests from those leading state or government, although decoloniality prefers delinking with the government, resolutely oppose war and relate with those leading in a manner that anticipates a governance that sets afoot different but truly peaceful communities. The coup leaders, in their own right or as proxies, have to develop capacity to be in peace with themselves and those they are persuaded to replace, in an effort to build their worlds of choice. Such convivial collaboration has a potential to achieve a world of peace.

This chapter innovated coloniality of governance. In keeping with the invention of tradition (Ranger, 1983), which submits that colonialism changed the traditions in colonies since the 1870s, this chapter asserts that the government in postcolonial republics is an ontology that reflects altered traditions. The structure of the government flows from Euro Renaissance and Enlightenment formulations which disfigured traditions of governance of the South. Those governance systems that were constituted by epistemologies of belonging, dignity, communication, and communality were replaced with systems constituted through charisma, compliance, vote, and violence. The second face of this coloniality is that leaders must comply with the dictates of standards weaved in templates which are constituted by the Euro-modern epistemology, which, though not trying to throw away the baby with bathwater, are standards that set leaders in the South for double failure, failure to meet expectations by citizens and expectations by global power structure. The third is a rigid system of political transitioning that names free and fair elections, penalizing other transitionings as coups. The last shade of this coloniality is control and subsumption of individual existence. Coloniality of governance views individuals as onerous bunch of life that has no interest in decolonial self-determination but that has to put up with a government that is put in place through predetermined processes. In a fascist/Stalinist arrogance, the state or nation state matters more than human lives. In keeping with delinking with the state and private sector, Mignolo in (Walsh & Mignolo, 2018) and in the Foreword to the book *Constructing the Pluriverse* (Reiter, 2018) suggests emergent global political societies as pluriversal methods of flexible decolonial self-determination by individuals who self-organize around objectives that meet their immediate needs directly and in a durable fashion and re-exist apart from the state/government.

On the other hand, academic ethics demand that theorization goes beyond commitment to a framework. In view of the academic ethics, the weaknesses of decolonial analyse are presented. Pappas (2017: 4) raises four fundamental rebuttals on decolonial philosophies. These are "(1) starting with a theoretical global standpoint and a grand historical metanarrative about injustice, (2) an inflated notion of what counts as ideology and theoretical barometers of good and evil, (3) centering the project of liberation on shared beliefs or ideas, and (4) adopting or 'using' indigenous thought and 'speaking for' the oppressed." These rebuttals sensitize decolonial analyses to the possible pitfalls. The rebuttals are predicated on a faulty conflation of decoloniality with the leftist liberation movements. They also collapse into ad hominem criticism because they dismiss most of the decoloniality theorists as non-natives who have appropriate indigenous knowledge and claim to represent indigenous peoples.

Historical Context: Understanding Coups in West and Central Africa

Scholars attribute coups to a combination of historical, economic, political, and external factors, with colonialism and neocolonial influences playing significant roles. It is this weight apportioned to colonialism and neocolonialism that corroborates the view that coloniality is the central problem. Coloniality of governance explains the weight of colonialism and neocolonialism as key cause of the phenomenon even better. Colonialism had far-reaching consequences in Africa. The exploitative nature of colonial rule often led to economic exploitation, political marginalization, and social unrest. Although colonialism had dangled the rhetoric of Euro-modernity as civilization, its darker side, the logic of coloniality, manifested painful destructions. Colonial powers sought to exploit Africa's natural resources, hence the establishment of large plantations for export crops and the establishment of extractive industries. Economic exploitation created disparities in wealth, with a minority of European colonial administrators and local collaborators enjoying immense wealth, while the majority of Africans remaining impoverished. Colonial powers imposed their own political systems on Africa, often dividing the continent into colonies and protectorates. These political systems, designed to serve the interests of the colonial powers, marginalized African leaders and hindered the development of indigenous institutions. Colonial rule disrupted traditional social systems and created tensions between different ethnic groups. The imposition of Western education and Christian values, combined with forced assimilation policies, led to resistance and uprisings by indigenous populations. These social tensions often erupted into violent conflicts, laying the foundation for future conflicts.

Some scholars aver that after gaining independence, many African countries faced the challenge of unfinished decolonization (Ndlovu-Gatsheni, 2013). Neocolonialism continued the practice of economic exploitation, with Western countries and international financial institutions imposing policies whose rhetoric was promotion of economic growth and trickling down development in the South while their darker side, as epitomized by structural adjustment programs, meant to destabilize the grip on economic control by the postcolonial state and privilege the interests of global capitalism. These policies hindered the development of indigenous industries. Neocolonial powers often interfered in the internal affairs of African states, supporting compliant regimes and undermining democratically elected governments. This interference, combined with corruption within African governments, contributed to the political instability that destabilized many postcolonial states. Neocolonialism further exacerbated existing social tensions, as former colonial powers supported autocratic leaders or exploited ethnic divisions to maintain control of authority. This has contributed to a cycle of conflict, as marginalized groups sought to assert their grievances through armed resistance. Coloniality of governance perpetuates these conflicts, hindering the development of democratic systems and perpetuating social and economic inequality.

This section provides an in-depth analysis of the so-called coups in Guinea, Mali, and Chad, focusing on the underlying factors that have promoted these so-called coups. The analysis focuses on the intricacies of the causes, consequences, and patterns of coups, as well as the impact on governance, stability, and development in West and Central Africa. It also explores the impact of coups on the political and economic development of the region and beyond. By understanding the historical, social, and political contexts, political analysts and policymakers can gain valuable insights into the dynamics of coups and their implications for governance and stability.

It is argued that the US Central Intelligence Agency (CIA) was assisted by Britain to mastermind the overthrow of Kwame Nkrumah in 1966 because they considered him the greatest threat to their interests (Quist-Adade, 2016; Chiwanza, 2019; Langani, 2018). To add onto the thesis of the globality of local violent political changes in West and Central Africa, Nana (2022) argues that colonial heritage and the Cold War between the Capitalists and the Communists are part of the causes of military coups in Africa. The legacy of colonization, the struggle for independence, and the subsequent challenges of postcolonial governance have all played a significant role in shaping the region's political landscape. For instance, Kemence (2013) argues that the abrupt departure of colonial military powers is the major cause of the military coups in West Africa. The observation by Kemence is predicated on self-blame or what Kapoor (2023) calls imperial amnesia. The analysis can get deeper and aver that the replacement of direct colonialism with neocolonialism (Nkrumah, 1965) seems to be at the center of violent political changes in West and Central Africa.

Case Analysis of Coups

Recent coups in Mali, Chad, Burkina Faso, and Guinea have sparked international scrutiny of the underlying motivations for these noncompliant political changes. One common characteristic in the manifestation of coups in the West and Central Africa is the involvement of foreign powers and dissatisfaction of the military with autocratic rule, extreme poverty, cultural pluralism, poor governance, corruption, exclusionary development, and suppression of dissent and ethnic minorities (Patomaki, 2008; Cawthra, 2010; Barka & Ncube, 2012; Kemence, 2013; Fosu, 2018; Brooke-Holland, 2023; UNDP, 2023).

Mali's noncompliant political change occurred in March 2012. It is alleged that a group of soldiers led by Captain Amadou Sanogo seized power in Mali, ousting President Amadou Toumani Touré. Literature suggests the coup was precipitated by widespread dissatisfaction with the government's handling of a Tuareg rebellion in the north of the country. Sanogo's junta, the National Movement for the Liberation of the Azawad (MNLA), sought to restore order and defend Mali's territorial integrity. This brief review of events shows that peace in the terms of Captain Amadou Sanogo displays a deficiency of decolonial maturity on the party of all involved.

Peace that follows violence is colonized peace. The intervention of President Francois Hollande in the security interest of France and labeling the new government of Mali terrorist and the approval of French intervention in Mali by Prime Minister Benjamin Netanyahu who presides of a state that was formed in 1948 for ideological reasons are gems of the existence of coloniality of power. Colonial structures of power were put on Mali as French Sudan since 1892 did not disappear with juridical colonialism in 1960, hence naming 2012 political changes in Mali in disapproving terms such as a coup and participants as a military junta and the new government as terrorist and intervening in a sovereign state to control its affairs.

The coup had far-reaching consequences for Mali, as well as the broader West Africa. It exacerbated the security crisis in the north, leading to the outbreak of a jihadist insurgency. The MNLA's control over the north was quickly seized by jihadist groups, including Al-Qaeda in the Islamic Maghreb (AQIM) and Ansar Dine. The instability caused by the coup allowed these groups to expand their operations and threaten neighboring countries. Ordinary people are subsumed into athletics of power.

The coup also strained relations between Mali and its international interests. France, which had been providing military assistance to Mali's government, suspended its operations and imposed economic sanctions on the new government. The coup also weakened the country's democratic governance and hindered its efforts to address its economic challenges. The extant analysis has a net effect of subsumption existence of ordinary human being under a so-called democratic nation state or government. Nuanced analyses of the 2012 political changes in Mali that are predicated on decolonially pluriversal and pluriversally decolonial emergent global political societies (EGPSs) and their epistemologies of decolonial governance and re-existence as units of analysis still beckon our gazes.

The other coup in Mali occurred on August 18, 2020, when a group of Malian soldiers led by Colonel Assimi Goita ousted President Ibrahim Boubacar Keita. The coup was a response to widespread discontent in the country, demanding for Keita's resignation. Mali was facing an Islamist insurgency in the north, which had spread to the central regions. This instability undermined the legitimacy of Keita's government, as he failed to effectively combat the insurgency. Secondly, accusations of corruption and mismanagement plagued the Keita administration. The growing discontent among Malians, particularly within the military, fueled the perception that the leaders had failed to deliver on their promises of development and improved governance. Mali's constitutional court, tasked with resolving disputes within the government, had emerged as a point of contention. The court's decision to invalidate the results of a parliamentary election, prompting Keita to dissolve parliament and appoint new leaders, aggravated the existing political tensions. These factors combined to lead to the military coup and the installation of a military junta led by Goita. The coup aimed to restore stability and address Mali's pressing security issues, but it also raised concerns about the potential erosion of democracy. Colonel Goita declared himself as the interim president and formed a transitional government. The coup was welcomed by some Malians, who saw it as an opportunity for change and promise to address the needs of the people. However, it faced international condemnation, with the African Union suspending Mali's membership. The construction of coups and resolutions thereof seems to be based on the rampant practice of inverting majority rule to rule majority which is one of the pillars of coloniality of governance.

The coup in Chad on April 20, 2021, followed a similar pattern. President Idriss Déby Itno, who had ruled the country for more than three decades, was killed during fighting against rebels in the north. His son, Mahamat Idriss Déby Itno, was immediately declared interim president by the military. The coup in Chad was primarily motivated by a desire to maintain stability and preserve the country's unity in the face of a rebellion. The Chadian military expressed concerns about corruption within the government. President Idriss Déby had faced growing opposition from various rebel groups, particularly rebels loyal to the slain rebel leader, Mahamat Nouri. The deteriorating security situation, coupled with economic challenges and the aging leadership of Idriss Déby, contributed to a sense of discontent among the military. These factors, combined with a desire to secure a stable transfer of power, ultimately led to the coup and the installation of Mahamat Idriss Déby as interim president. The junta, known as the Patriotic Salvation Movement (MPS), justified its actions by citing the need to stabilize the country and ensure its territorial integrity. However, the coup also raised concerns that it could further destabilize the region, particularly regarding the ongoing fight against terrorism in the Sahel. The coup also strained Chad's relations with its international controlling interests, especially France, which provided military support to Deby's regime. The mention of the involvement of France in coups implies its hold onto its former colonies long after juridical independence.

The coup in Burkina Faso on January 24, 2022, was caused by escalating political tensions within the government. President Roch Marc Christian Kaboré who had ruled Burkina Faso for 10 years faced growing discontent among his opponents, particularly within the military, over his failure to address security concerns and tackle corruption. The coup leaders, led by Lieutenant Colonel Paul-Henri Sandaogo Damiba, claimed the move was necessary to protect the state and restore stability. They accused Kaboré's government of ineptitude, citing widespread insecurity and escalating jihadist violence in the country. The coup in Burkina Faso was welcomed by some citizens, who saw it as an opportunity for change. The armed forces promised to restore stability and address the needs of the people. However, it faced international condemnation, with the African Union suspending Burkina Faso's membership and imposing sanctions. The coup in Burkina Faso highlighted the ongoing challenges posed by Islamist militancy in the region. The growing insecurity, coupled with dissatisfaction with Kaboré's leadership, prompted the military to intervene. The coup leaders vowed to tackle security threats and restore democracy, but concerns remain about the potential erosion of democracy.

The coup in Guinea occurred on September 5, 2021, when the military seized power and ousted President Alpha Condé. The factors contributing to this coup can be traced back to the growing dissatisfaction with Condé's rule, including allegations of corruption and human rights abuses (Kemence, 2013; Fosu, 2018; Nana, 2022). President Condé's controversial decision to amend the constitution and secure a third term in office fueled resentment and widespread protests (Kemence, 2013; Fosu, 2018; Brooke-Holland, 2023; UNDP, 2023). This discontent, coupled with allegations of corruption and a deteriorating economy, caused a military takeover (UNDP, 2023). The military, led by Colonel Mamady Doumbouya, formed a transitional government and promised to hold elections within a reasonable timeframe. The coup in Guinea has raised concerns among regional and international actors (Kemence, 2013; Quist-Adade, 2016; Chiwanza, 2019; Suleiman & Onapajo, 2022). It has created political instability in the country and raised questions about the prospects for democratic governance. The African Union and the Economic Community of West African States condemned the coup and called for a return to constitutional order.

Political dynamics in West and Central Africa are contributing to the occurrence of violent political changes. The problem with this kind of power captured knowledge production is that it constrains its gaze of analysis on those who are powerful and negates the weak but who form the majority. This analysis renders ordinary citizens as both people without agency and numbers that neither matter. Major narratives in these analyses explain the causes in different structural theories: political development, military centrality, ethnic antagonism, as well as world system/dependency theory (Hiroi & Omori, 2013; Suleiman & Onapajo, 2022). While all these theories give indicators of governmental instability and military coups in West Africa, this chapter widens the scope to a more prominent factor that contributed to this situation. A close analysis of political dynamics reveals that political instability, weak democratic institutions, and power struggles among political elites are some of the key drivers behind coups (Hiroi & Omori, 2013; Suleiman & Onapajo, 2022; Pryce & Time, 2023). It is imperative to examine how factors such as ethnic tensions, economic disparities, and external influences have contributed to the vulnerability of the region to coup attempts.

Literature raises issues such as corruption, economic mismanagement, social unrest, and the erosion of democratic norms as significant triggers for coup attempts (Collier, 1978; Jackson & Roseberg, 1982; Patomaki, 2008; Cawthra, 2010; Barka & Ncube, 2012; Kemence, 2013; Fosu, 2018; Brooke-Holland, 2023; UNDP, 2023). By examining these causes, one can gain a deeper understanding of the underlying issues that contribute to political instability in the region (Hiroi & Omori, 2013; Kemence, 2013; Suleiman & Onapajo, 2022; Pryce & Time, 2023). Additionally, Mishra and Toprak (2022) contend that the proliferation of insurgents and extremist violence coupled with weak, fledging, and transitional democracies has provided fertile grounds for military intervention in civilian and political matters across Africa.

Impact of Coups

The coups have led to political instability, economic disruptions, and social unrest (Hiroi & Omori, 2013; Kemence, 2013; Suleiman & Onapajo, 2022; Pryce & Time, 2023). Coups in Africa also result in negative consequences such as disregard for respect of human rights, lack of rule of law, and autocratic system of governance. The recent coups in West and Central Africa, particularly in Guinea, Mali, and Chad, have had significant ramifications for both regional and global politics. They have raised concerns about democratic governance, political stability, and international partnerships in the affected countries. The impact of these coups extends beyond the borders of these nations, affecting regional security and global efforts to combat terrorism.

Some analysts come from the state fragility theory. This theory suggests that decolonization and state formation in Africa were often accompanied by high levels of political, economic, and social instability. The transition from colonial rule to new state structures created opportunities for individuals or groups to seize power and manipulate institutions for personal gain. State capture was seen as a way to maintain control and stability in these fragile states (Hiroi & Omori, 2013; Kemence, 2013; Suleiman & Onapajo, 2022).

Others pin explanations on the colonial legacy theory. This theory highlights the aftereffects of colonial structures, institutions, and practices after decolonization. The legacy of colonial rule, such as the unequal distribution of resources, clientelism, and weak governance, created ideal conditions for state capture (Pryce & Time, 2023; Mishra & Toprak, 2022; UNDP, 2023). Individuals or groups with connections to the previous colonial regime were able to leverage their power to retain control over postindependence institutions.

Astute capitalists use the resource curse theory. It suggests that natural resources, such as oil, minerals, or agricultural products, have the potential to hinder economic growth and political stability. The concentration of wealth generated from these resources can lead to state capture, as elites and interest groups exploit the resources for personal gain (Patomaki, 2008; Cawthra, 2010; Barka & Ncube, 2012; Kemence, 2013; Fosu, 2018). In Africa, this is particularly relevant, as many countries have experienced significant natural resource wealth alongside widespread corruption and state capture.

Neopatrimonialism theory emphasizes the intimate relationship between political elites and institutions. It suggests that decolonization in Africa was often accompanied by the formation of clientelistic networks, where political elites rewarded their supporters with positions of power and access to resources (Suleiman & Onapajo, 2022; Pryce & Time, 2023; Nana, 2022; UNDP, 2023). This patronage system facilitated state capture and perpetuated corruption.

Those in pursuit of peace at all costs prefer the conflict theory. Conflict theory suggests that disputes over power and resources can drive a state capture dynamic. Decolonization in Africa was often accompanied by conflicts, both between indigenous groups vying for independence and between the former colonial powers and newly independent states (Collier, 1978; Jackson & Roseberg, 1982; Patomaki, 2008). These conflicts provided opportunities for individuals or groups to seize power and manipulate institutions for their own gain.

While the above theories explain possible causes of coups because there is no self-sufficient theory, they however tend to assume that coloniality is over, shift the blame to purely domestic causes, and project the ordinary majority as a by the way function of the elite. Coloniality of governance in our view gives a plausible explanation of the phenomenon.

The Role of External Actors in the Current Coups

While coups have been blamed on internal factors such as political instability, corruption, and ethnic tensions by the Euro-modern epistemology, the involvement of external actors (France and the United States as rewesternization and coloniality of power and Russia and China as dewesternization) has been hidden by such constructions. This section exposes the dark side of domestic coups in West and Central Africa. France, as a former colonial power in many West and Central African countries, has historically maintained strong ties with its former colonies. France has been accused of being linked to the killing of at least 22 African presidents since 1963, including Burkina Faso's Thomas Sankara (Kemence, 2013; Fosu, 2018; Nana, 2022). Thus, in several coup attempts, France has been accused of either supporting or opposing the overthrow of governments. Thus, the French military presence has enhanced the power of government being friendly to it (Jackson & Roseberg, 1982; Nana, 2022). For example, in the case of the 1987 coup in Burkina Faso, France was accused of supporting the incumbent president, while in the 2009 coup in Madagascar, France condemned the coup leaders and supported international sanctions against them (Brooke-Holland, 2023; UNDP, 2023). The US involvement in coup attempts has often overtly sought to maintain stability and promote democratic governance in the region (Patomaki, 2008; Cawthra, 2010) while covertly pushing personal interests. The United States has been accused of supporting or turning a blind eye to coup attempts that align with its geopolitical interests (Fosu, 2018; Rodney, 2018; Handy et al., 2020; Arrief et al., 2022; Camara, 2023). For example, in the 2005 coup in Togo, the United States was criticized for not condemning the coup and instead engaging with the new government. These instances highlight coloniality of power as the darker side of domestic coups.

Inversely, coups are struggles to vanquish coloniality of power evidenced by growing demand for the expulsion of French troops from West and Central African countries affected by the ongoing coups. This demand arises from historical grievances, concerns of neocolonialism, and allegations of French interference in local affairs (MTAC, 2023; Demuynck & Bohm, 2023; Centre for Democracy and Development (CDD), 2023). The presence of French troops perpetuates a cycle of dependency and hinders the development of independent military and security apparatus within these countries. French military interventions often prioritize

French interests over the long-term stability and sovereignty of the affected nations (Kemence, 2013; Fosu, 2018; Nana, 2022). The demand for the expulsion of French troops stems from a desire for self-determination and the right to shape domestic political destinies without external interference (Brooke-Holland, 2023; UNDP, 2023; Nana, 2022). Some view the continued presence of French troops as a remnant of colonialism, questioning the extent to which these countries have truly achieved independence.

China's increasing economic presence in Africa promotes speculations about her role in coup attempts. While China officially maintains a policy of noninterference in the internal affairs of other countries, its economic investments and military cooperation agreements have raised concerns (Siegle, 2012; Sakane, 2023; Kurlantzick, 2023). In recent years, China has become a major player in the infrastructure development of many African countries, including those affected by coup attempts (Kemence, 2013; Fosu, 2018; Sakane, 2023). The extent to which China's economic influence translates into political power and potential involvement in coups is an area that requires further study. Mignolo (2011a) described China's involvement in global politics as dewesternization and quest for multiversity, a situation where the world has many state led centers of power. Decoloniality decenters the state and seeks to establish self-governing pluriverses. The presence of China could be a push for dewesternization.

Russia's involvement in coup attempts in West and Central Africa has been relatively limited compared to other external actors. However, there have been instances where Russia's interests intersected with political developments in the region (Handy et al., 2020; Suleiman & Onapajo, 2022). In the case of the 2013 coup in the Central African Republic, Russia supported the government of President François Bozizé, who was later overthrown. Russia and the Wagner military corporation are believed to be heavily involved in the Niger, Mali, Burkina Faso, Chad, and Sudan coups (Suleiman & Onapajo, 2022; Blank, 2023; Sakane, 2023). Russia's involvement in this case was primarily driven by its desire to protect its economic interests in the country, particularly in the mining sector. Additionally, Moscow clearly exploits regional, tribal, ethnic, and religious conflicts for its strategic interests. The waving of the Russian flag during the current coups in West and Central Africa can be seen as a symbolic gesture of solidarity or soliciting support from certain Russia (MTAC, 2023; Demuynck & Bohm, 2023). The flag might imply association of Russia with dewesternization and disenchantment with the West, particularly France, by anti-West coup leaders.

Implications for the Future of West and Central Africa

These events disrupt the stability and trust in democratic institutions, often leading to social unrest. Citizens may lose faith in the ability of their governments to provide security, justice, and basic services, resulting in increased frustration, hence civil unrest (Collier, 1978; Jackson & Roseberg, 1982; Patomaki, 2008; Cawthra,

2010; Barka & Ncube, 2012). Similarly, Kemence (2013) and Fosu (2018) argue that coups can exacerbate existing ethnic, religious, and regional divides, as different factions vie for power. Ethnic tensions may lead to violence and displacement of vulnerable populations (Brooke-Holland, 2023; UNDP, 2023). This can create a breeding ground for radicalization and the spread of extremist ideologies, posing a threat to the region and global security.

Political instability deter foreign investment, which is crucial for economic growth and development (Collier, 1978; Jackson & Roseberg, 1982; Patomaki, 2008; Cawthra, 2010; Barka & Ncube, 2012). The interruption of trade and commerce can lead to economic recession, high unemployment rates, and increased poverty levels. Corruption often thrives in the aftermath of coups, as new regimes may prioritize personal gain over public welfare. Mismanagement of resources, embezzlement, and lack of transparency hinder economic progress and further marginalize vulnerable communities (Brooke-Holland, 2023; UNDP, 2023). The resulting economic downturns can have ripple effects, impacting neighboring countries and global economic stability.

Coups have both domestic and international implications. Domestically, they disrupt the democratic process and undermine the rule of law (Collier, 1978; Jackson & Roseberg, 1982; Patomaki, 2008; Cawthra, 2010; Barka & Ncube, 2012; Kemence, 2013; Fosu, 2018). This erosion of democratic norms weakens governance and undermines the progress made in building accountable and transparent institutions. Internationally, coups in West and Central Africa can impact global politics too. They may alter existing alliances and partnerships, as new regimes may seek support from different actors (Kemence, 2013; Brooke-Holland, 2023; UNDP, 2023). This realignment of alliances can have consequences for regional security dynamics and global power balances. The international community's response to coups sets a precedent for future interventions, influencing norms and practices in global politics.

They have implications for global politics. They highlight the fragility of democracy and the challenges faced by emerging democracies (Collier, 1978; Jackson & Roseberg, 1982; Patomaki, 2008; Cawthra, 2010; Barka & Ncube, 2012; Kemence, 2013; Fosu, 2018). This serves as a reminder to the international community to prioritize democratic governance and support democratic transitions in order to prevent future coups. Coups can affect the balance of power among global actors (Collier, 1978; Jackson & Roseberg, 1982; Patomaki, 2008; Cawthra, 2010; Barka & Ncube, 2012; Kemence, 2013; Fosu, 2018). They may lead to shifts in alliances, as countries recalibrate their foreign policies in response to changing political landscapes. This can impact geopolitical strategies and alter the dynamics of regional and global power structures (Brooke-Holland, 2023; UNDP, 2023).

Decolonial analyses help us to understand how both foreign and local actors come together to fuel military coups in Africa. The foreign influences during postcoloniality and Cold War and post-Cold War era have played a great role in fueling conflicts and coups in Africa (Barka & Ncube, 2012; Kemence, 2013; Fosu, 2018). Most sub-Saharan African states can still be classified as neocolonial since they continue to depend heavily on external support, including military and economic aid, for their survival. Against this backdrop, foreign powers find it easy to fuel political and socioeconomic problems, including coups in sub-Saharan Africa, whenever this will help advance their interests (Patomaki, 2008; Cawthra, 2010).

Coups have also created opportunities for non-state actors, such as extremist groups, to exploit the power vacuum and further destabilize the region (Nana, 2022; Brooke-Holland, 2023; UNDP, 2023). This has implications for global security, particularly in the fight against terrorism and the management of migration. The coups in Guinea, Mali, and Chad have strained relations between these countries and their international interests. They have prompted condemnations and calls for a return to constitutional order from regional organizations such as the African Union and ECOWAS. They have led to the suspension of financial assistance and military cooperation from some countries. Recent coups have highlighted the challenges of democratic governance and political stability in the region (Brooke-Holland, 2023; UNDP, 2023). The coups have drawn international attention and raised questions about the effectiveness of regional and international mechanisms to address political crises.

Decolonization of governance is the first area that requires unmasking and showing that other options exist. Resurgent and insurgent knowledges must be surveyed for knowledges of governance predicated on humanity, belonging, dignity, and open ended being. Open ended governance allows for the world of decoloniality pluriversal and pluriversally decolonial Emergent Global Political Societies which ordinary citizens free self-organization for liberated genial re-existence. These two pillars anchor on the foundational decoloniality of power which unshackles Western European-North American-Chinese violence and show that other epistemologies of relationships predicated on humane epistemologies of copresence and decolonial maturity.

Conclusion

We thought coloniality of governance as a four pronged addition to the colonial matrices of power. Political transitioning predicated on charm and that complied with Western European-North American standards of governance, majority vote, and violence must be exposed and governance houses of belonging, dignity, communication, and communality be raised as options. The Foucaultian panoptical gaze of global structures of power must be provincialized (Quijano, 2007) and free situated governance action and learning spaces. Debunk 5-year multiparty elections as an option, and excavate other situated options of political transitioning. Unmask the control and subsumption of individuals under governance structure hidden in the rhetoric of serving communities, and allow hamlets for EGPS. Liberating governance from all other matrices of power and constructing many options of re-existence will drain domestic and global coloniality of power and obviate the need for violent anti-people political transitioning. Decolonial maturity as an attitude of the mind is a precondition for the decoloniality of governance. Decoloniality of governance is an option for the copresence of states with many worlds in a world with many worlds.

References

Andreotti, V. (2011). (Towards) decoloniality and diversality in global citizenship education, Globalisation. *Societies and Education, 9*(3–4), 381–397.

Arias, S. (2013). Coloniality and its preoccupations. *Latin American Research Review, 48*(3), 214–220.

Arrief, A., Blanchard, L., & Plock. (2022). *"An Epidemic of Coups" in Africa?* Issues for Congress. Congressional Research Service.

Barka, H. B., & Ncube, M. (2012). *Political fragility in Africa; Are Military Coups d'état a never–ending phenomenon*. African Development Bank.

Blank, S. (2023). *The niger coup exposes Russia's grand strategy for Africa*. Nexstar Medical.

Brooke-Holland, L. (2023). *Coups and political stability in West Africa*. Number 9861. Political Map of West Africa-Nations Online commons library.parliament.uk.

Camara, K. (2023). *A coup in Niger: What it means for Africa, US and Partners*. United States Institute of Peace.

Cawthra G. (2010). *The role of SADC in managing political crisis and conflicts*. The Cases of Madagascar and Zimbabwe. Maputo, Friedrich Ebert Stiftung (Mozambique).

Centre for Democracy and Development (CDD). (2023). *Prigozhin's Death and Wagner's Future in Africa*. CDD.

Chiwanza, T. (2019). 'France has Assassinated 22 African Presidents Since 1963', *the African Exponent*. https://www.africanexponent.com/post.

Collier, R. B. 1978. Parties, coups and authoritarian rule. Patterns of political change in tropical Africa. *Comparative Political Studies, 11*(1).

Demuynck, M., & Bohm, M. (2023). *Unravelling the Niger Coup and its implication for Violent extremism in the Sahel*. https://www.cct.nl/publication

Dussel, E. (1998). Beyond eurocentrism: The world-system and the limits of modernity. In F. Jameson & M. Miyoshi (Eds.), *Thecultures of globalization* (pp. 3–31). Duke University Press.

Escobar, A. (2002). The Latín American modernity/coloniality. *Review of International Studies, 49*(3), 346–335.

Escobar, A. (2015). Degrowth, post development, and transitions: A preliminary conversation. *Sustainability Science, 10*, 451–462. https://doi.org/10.1007/s11625-015-0297-5

Fosu, A. K. (2018). Governance and Development in Africa. A review essay. *Working Paper Serious* No. 298. African Development Bank, Abidjan, Cote de 'Ivor.

Gordon, L. (2011). *Shifting the geography of reason in an age of disciplinary decadence*. Temple University.

Grosfoguel, R. (2007). The epistemic decolonial turn: Beyond political-economy paradigms. *Cultural Studies, 21*(2/3), 203–246.

Handy, P., Akum, F., & Djilo, F. (2020). *Censuring Coups isn't enough – African and International actors should tackle the poor quality of democracy and governance*. Daily Maverick, South Africa.

Hiroi, T., & Omori, S. (2013). Causes and Triggers of Coups d'état: An even history analysis. *Politics & Policy, 41*, 36–64. https://doi.org/10.1111/polp.12001

Jackson, R. H., & Roseberg, C. G. (1982). Why Africa's weak states persists. The empirical and the juridical in statehoods. *World Politics, 35*(1), 1–24.

Kapoor, I. (2023). Decolonising development studies. *Review of International Studies, 49*(3), 346–355.

Kemence, K. O. (2013). *Understanding the root causes of military coups and governmental instability in West Africa*. A thesis presented to the Faculty of US Army Command and General Staff College. Military Art Science. General Studies. Fort Leaven worth, Kansas.
Kurlantzick, J. (2023). *How China and Russia have helped foment coups and the growing militarisation of politics*. Council of Foreign Relations.
Langani, M. (2018). Neo-colonialism and the poverry of 'development' in Africa. Palgrave Macmillan.
Maldonado-Torres, N. (2004). The topology of being and the geopolitics of knowledge: Modernity, empire, and the colonial difference. *City, 8*(1), 29–56.
Maldonado-Torres, N. (2007, March/May). On the coloniality of being: Contributions to the development of a concept. *Cultural Studies, 21*(2–3), 240–270.
Maldonado-Torres, N. (2020). *Notes on the coloniality of peace*. Frantz Fanon Foundation. Foundation-frantzfanon.com.
Mignolo, W. D. (2000). *Local histories/global designs: Essays on the coloniality of power, subaltern knowledges and border thinking*. Princeton University Press.
Mignolo, W. D. (2011a). *The Darker side of western modernity: Global futures, decolonial options*. Duke University Press.
Mignolo, W. D. (2011b). Epistemic disobedience and the decolonial option: A manifesto. *Transmodernity* (Fall 2011), 44–66.
Mignolo, W. D. (2018). Foreword. In B. Reiter (Ed.), *The geopolitics of knowledge: Constructing the Pluriverse*. Duke University Press.
Mishra, A., & Toprak, K. (2022). *Africa's Coup contagion: Factors driving an upsurge in military intervention*. https://www.orfonline.org/contributors.
MTAC Report. (2023). *Russia's influence networks in Sahel activated after coups*. Microsoft Threat Analysis Centre.
Nana, A. E. (2022). *Military Coups in Africa. L A continuation of politics by other means?* Legon Centre for International Affairs and Diplomacy, University of Ghana.
Ndlovu-Gatsheni, S. J. (2013). *Coloniality of power in post-colonial Africa: Myths of decolonization*. Council for Development of Social Science Research in Africa.
Ndlovu-Gatsheni, S. J. (2018a). *Epistemic freedom in Africa: Deprovincialisation and decoloniality*. Routledge.
Ndlovu-Gatsheni, S. J. (2018b). *The African idea of development*. Handbook of African.
Ndlovu-Gatsheni, S. (2021). Decoloniality and African thought: A new paradigm for African studies. Routledge.
Ndlovu-Gatsheni, S. J. (2022). Preface to the second edition to *Coloniality of Power in Postcolonial Africa*.
Nkrumah, K. (1965). Neo-colonialism.The last stage of imperialism. Thomas Nelson & Sons.
Pappas, G. F. (2017). The limitations and dangers of decolonial philosophies: Lessons from Zapatista: Villoro. *Radical Philosophy Review*. https://doi.org/10.5840/radphilrev201732768
Patomaki, H. (2008). *The political economy of global security. War, future crises and changes in global governance*. Routledge.
Pryce, D. K., & Time, V. M. (2023). The role of coups d'état in Africa: Why Coups occur and their effects on the populace. *International Social Sciences Journal, 73*, 1019–1034. https://doi.org/10.1111/isssj.122428
Quijano, A. (2007). Coloniality and modernity/rationality. *Cultural Studies, 21*(2–3), 168–178.
Quist-Adade, C. (2016). The Coup that Set Ghana and Africa 50 Years Back. *Pambazuka News*, 2 March.
Ranger, T. S. (1983). *The invention of tradition in colonial Africa*. Cambridge University Press. https://www.pambazuka.org/governance/coup-set-ghana-and-africa-50-years-back
Reiter, A. (2018). Dictators, Democrats,and Development in Southern Asia: Explaining Divergent Paths.Plagrave Macmillan.
Rodney, W. (2018). *How Europe underdeveloped Africa* (p. xiii). Verso.

Sakane, K. (2023). *International network analysis* "Era of Coups", in Africa (Part 1). *The emergence of Russia and China amid the decline of the west.* Japan International Cooperation Agency. The Sasakawa Peace Foundation.
Santos, B. S. (2007). Beyond abyssal thinking: From global lines to ecologies of knowledges. *Revista Critica de Ciencias Sociais, 80.*
Siegle, J. (2012). *Africa's Coup and the role of external actors*. Africa Centre for Strategic Studies.
Suleiman, M. D., & Onapajo, H. (2022). *Why West Africa has had so many Coups and has had so many coups and how to prevent more*. International Relations, Curtin University, Department of Political Science and International Relations, Nile University of Nigeria.
United Nations Development Programme (UNDP). (2023). *Soldiers and citizens. Military coups and the need for democratic renewal in Africa*, UNDP. www.undp.org/africa. www.soldiers and citizens.org.
Walsh, C., & Mignolo, W. D. (2018). *On decoloniality: Concepts, analytics and praxis*. Duke University.

Funa Moyo holds a PhD in Public and Development Management from the University of Witwatersrand, Masters of Science in Development Studies from the National University of Science and Technology and a Master of Education in Educational Administration, Planning and Policy Studies from Zimbabwe Open University. He is senior lecturer and researcher at the Institute of Development Studies, Faculty of Commerce at NUST. He is interested in natural resource governance, environmental management and development, social capital, sustainable livelihoods and rural development, risk reduction, resilience building and disaster management. He has published in number of refereed and peer-reviewed journals. He is involved in the World Food Programme (WFP) and NUST partnership through the Sustainable Livelihood Programming (SLP) project focused on empowering local authorities on community-based planning, resilience building, and food security enhancement.

Sihlanganiso Khumalo is a Development Studies academic. He is lecturing Development Studies at Lupane State University. He has lectured both undergraduate and postgraduate Development Studies modules at the Catholic University of Zimbabwe and the National University of Science and Technology. His research interests are inspired by the desire to privilege debates and praxis that enhance decolonially pluriversal struggles that seek to transform the painful lived experiences of the marginalized communities and key populations in developing nation states. His focus areas include rural development, human rights and development, and coloniality of power in the idea and praxis of development.

Chapter 19
Coups d'etat and Democratic Backsliding in Africa: Legitimizing Unconstitutional Power Grabs and Implications for Continental Political Stability

Aaron Rwodzi

Abstract This chapter examines the sudden allure of a coup in twenty-first-century Africa resulting from external interference in the continent's economic affairs. Benefits accruing from coups include power and unbridled access to state resources, whereas the downsides such as failure and ultimate imprisonment are less likely particularly if the incumbent administration is civilian. The plethora of coups in Africa comes against the backdrop of the Organization of African Union's policy of noninterference, which makes coup plotters forget about external costs to be incurred. This chapter, through discourse analysis and related literature, underscores the central role foreign-trained officers play in the successful execution of coups and how the institutionalization of Western-style democracy is stifled as citizens conceptualize coups as a liberating force from civilian bondage. Through discourse analysis and available literature on the coup phenomenon in Africa, this chapter critiques the role of international players in sustaining coup plots that stand to undermine the democratic gains of yesteryears and recommends that people should shift from their outright condemnation to taking bold and proactive political measures that are in synch with African political and economic realities in order to curb their recurrence.

Introduction

By treating coups as unfortunate phenomena but normal means of transferring power in Africa, particularly in states where elections are rigged and have become ritual exercises in time wasting, the chapter critiques local conditions in Africa vis-a

A. Rwodzi (✉)
Department of Humanities, Business Development and Arts Education,
Midlands State University, Gweru, Zimbabwe
e-mail: rwodzia@staff.msu.ac.zw

G. Moyo, S. J. Ndlovu-Gatsheni (eds.), *Global Storms and Africa in World Politics*, Global Power Shift, https://doi.org/10.1007/978-3-031-83868-2_19

viz. the incessant role of Western and Eastern international actors in inadvertently providing coup leaders and their executers a helping hand toward the finish line to consolidate putschists' power. This chapter is conceptually grounded within the coup-proofing and legitimacy frameworks whose key elements entail the deliberate creation of institutional redundancy so as to limit interbranch communication by promoting military personnel on loyalty as opposed to human expertise and legitimizing military takeovers as a new form of democracy. As such, it focuses on the broad externally motivated causes of the spate of coups that have rocked Africa in recent years. The sudden demise of democratic tenets as originally clearly ingrained in African constitutions when there was a dramatic shift toward constitutionalism and observance of the rule of law in the 1980s is closely associated with ambitious military men usurping power with the kind of popular support unprecedented in African power politics.

The four research questions addressed in this study are as follows: (1) What explains the sudden plethora of coups in Africa? (2) Why have coups been sanitized as if they represent basic characteristics of goodwill toward the collective good of the nations where they take place? (3) Can soldiers who successfully organize the putsch be regarded as saviors of the people against recalcitrant regimes that do not yield to election results? (4) What is the future of democracy amidst recurrent externally backed coups in Africa? In a bid to answer these questions, this study made use of published and unpublished material, key informant interviews, and interviews by various regional and international news channels such as Al Jazeera. The chapter begins with a historiography of African coups and progressively analyzes recent coups in their different contexts. The author concludes that continental and international legitimation of coups in Africa points to the failure of Western democracy and heralds new perceptions about the futility of elections particularly when, as is generally the case, they retain unpopular incumbents through chicanery and outside support. It recommends an Afrocentric paradigm that places hope on the purview of African conceptions of political morality, democracy, and social justice.

Historiographical Trends in African Coups

The political history of Africa is incomparably littered with coups that first took center stage after the decolonization process with the first wave of independence in the 1960s. That heralded the European unceremonious and acrimonious departure from Africa, a phenomenon that was greeted with celebratory hype right across the continent. This dramatic shift toward self-determination was influenced by World War II that ended in 1945 and the aftermath of that war that also gave rise to the Cold War between the Western world as dominated by the United States and the Eastern world dominated by the Soviet Union. These two superpowers emphasized that World War II was a war for democracy, an idealism that gained traction by reason of the fact that both of them had no colonies in Africa and so wanted to be seen as championing the cause for democracy throughout the world. In any case, the term "democracy" is very elusive because it means so many things to so many people. A democratic society is one where the members take responsibility to resolve shared problems in the best interest of everyone (Beckman, 2021). This characterization is expressed in the influential work of Dewey (1939/1988, p. 226) who pictured democracy as a "way of life" characterized by mutual respect and a commitment to peaceful cooperation. The French writer and politician Alexis de Tocqueville (2021) applied the term in a similar way, but he evaluated it less favorably by associating it with the ethos prevalent in egalitarian or affluent societies (Berlin, 1965) and therefore unsuited to Africa. In trying to grapple with issues around democracy, Tocqueville (2021) noted:

> It is above all in the present democratic age that the true friends of liberty and human grandeur must remain constantly vigilant and ready to prevent the social power from lightly sacrificing the particular rights of a few individuals to the general execution of its designs. In such times, there is no citizen so obscure that it is not very dangerous to allow him to be oppressed, and there are no individual rights so unimportant that they can be sacrificed to arbitrariness with impunity.

Embodied in all democratic practices, as Tocqueville shows, are societal and individual values, rights, dignity, and freedom that are inalienable and prescriptive and are represented in constitutions that have to be respected. In other words, democracy entails constitutional supremacy which in turn provides the basis for equality before the law, social cohesion, and free will. Jewey's (1859–1952) most quotable quote on democracy states that:

Democracy is a way of life controlled by a working faith in the possibilities of human nature. Belief in the Common Man is a familiar article in the democratic creed. That belief is without basis and significance save as it means faith in the potentialities of human nature as that nature is exhibited in every human being irrespective of race, color, sex, birth and family, of material or cultural wealth. This faith may be enacted in statutes, but it is only on paper unless it is put in force in the attitudes which human beings display to one another in all the incidents and relations of daily life.

Jewey's analysis of what constitutes democracy points to the relativity of its practical application in different political scenarios. Democracy does not have a genetic definition and so means nothing as it can justifiably be abused. There are three turns which separate democracy of Dewey's times and democracy of today—the global, the ecological, and the digital turn (Peters, 2017). These need to be juxtaposed to changing notions of citizenship. The identified turns significantly enhance our understanding of how circumstances under which Dewey produced his conceptualization of democracy have significantly changed. During the Cold War era that ended with the demise of the Soviet Union in 1991, Africa had become an ideological battleground for the capitalist West and the communist East and for the United States and the Soviet Union particularly to size each other up in trying to fill the void that decolonization created by propagating their framed conceptualizations of ideal democracies. That saw Britain and France, the main colonial powers, losing their preeminence.

One of the major challenges that confronted the African elite that assumed power and replaced colonial administrations was that many of these colonial powers had not adequately prepared their former colonies for self-determination. In the absence of an elaborate decolonization and generic blueprint, some of these powers left in much great hurry to the extent of leaving Africans divided within the territorial colonial frameworks they had envisaged. Another area of serious concern was the fact that colonial administrations differed in their approach to Africans. For example, the British relied on direct and indirect rule which were predicated on the divide and rule tactics. The French used assimilation and association informed by the principles of liberty, equality, and fraternity as cornerstones of the French Revolution that began in 1789. The Belgians used paternalism that characteristically rendered Africans rightless people and objects for a great deal of manipulation. This diversity in colonial background, coupled with the lack of a uniform decolonization agenda, provided fertile grounds for postcolonial factional politics which did not shrink from ethnically motivated military coups as each category sought to gain power and control resources at the expense of others. Foreign powers with economic interests in territories that they had departed from took turns to provide the support to the new African ruling elite they deemed more amenable to their cause and to deliberately fuel hostilities under the guise of promoting democracy. The resultant effect of such colonial hangover was the unprecedented coups that frequently toppled legitimate leaders and replaced them with military generals who then suspended constitutions and ruled by decree.

A coup d'état or a putsch is equivalent to the unsanctioned invasion of a town by soldiers, who then suspend the rule of law (Pryce & Time, 2023, p. 3). The phrase "coup d'état" is of French origin, traced back to the eighteenth century when Napoleon Bonaparte overthrew the Revolutionary Directory from power in 1799 (Olafsson, 2020). According to Powell and Thyne (2011), coups are overt attempts by the military or other elites within the state apparatus to unseat a constitutionally elected leader. As argued by Schultes (2022, p. 2), a sitting head of state using unconstitutional means to retain power is susceptible to a coup, which he defines as successful only if the perpetrators seize and hold power for at least 7 days.

The putschists in most cases drag the elected or appointed officials to jail without recourse to a fair hearing, or due process. Successful putschists usually take away the hard work and security of fathers, mothers, and guardians and turn society on its head through coercive means (Pryce & Time, 2023, p. 3). Paradoxically, the use of the gun is used as an instrument of terror that is paid for by the taxpayers (Pryce & Time, 2023, p. 3). In Africa, coups have been an integral part of the continent's sociopolitical landscape for decades. Ghana, for instance, has experienced five successful coups in 1966, 1972, 1978, 1979, and 1981 (Baudais & Chauzal, 2011). When a coup occurs, it indisputably revolutionizes life in any nation by crystalizing into a concoction of consequences, both intended and unintended. Military takeovers, by and large, are bloody and coercive, because a whole nation is obliged to surrender its will and tenets of governance to a parochial yet ambitious unqualified or unsuited group of opportunistic men whose objective for seizing power may be for self-aggrandizement, to punish foes inside or outside the government and military, and to return the country to a civilian rule after years of military dictatorship or because of the failure of the country's civilian regimes (Baudais & Chauzal, 2011). When they want to appeal for popular legitimacy, the new successful coup executioners immediately churn out unrelenting propaganda to justify the necessity and plausibility of their action. Once they are in power, the purported goodwill they would have demonstrated or insinuated as justification for the coup is overshadowed by their idiosyncrasies, self-interest, and lack of political acuity (Pryce & Time, 2023).

Africa experienced 80 successful coups and 108 failed coup attempts between 1956 and 2001, an average of 4 a year (Adekoya, 13 September 2021). This figure declined sharply till 2019 as most African nations turned to democracy before it was on the ascendance again thereafter. The historiographical debates on coups in Africa are pivoted on the same problems that have generated them over different decades. In the early postcolonial decades when coups were rampant, Africa's coup leaders always gave corruption, mismanagement, and poverty as the same reasons for overthrowing governments by military means and successfully managed to conceal the ulterior motives of outside players that gave them the military backing all the way. The 82 coups in Africa that occurred between 1960 and 2000 had a politically, socially, religiously, and economically devastating effect on the continent as instability, corruption, human rights abuses, impunity, and poverty characterized many African countries during that era. Coups, because of their contagious nature, are such that a successful coup significantly increases the probability of subsequent coups both in the country of execution and among its neighbors.

Discourses around reasons for coups have pointed to a litany of real and imagined justifications across Africa, suggesting that there is not a single one-size-fits-all explanation to their occurrence and recurrence. In West Africa, Mali opened the floodgates when the army staged a mutiny and subsequently undertook a coup led by Colonel Assimi Goita who then followed up with another coup against an interim administration in May 2021 (Duzor and Williamson, VOA News, 3 October 2023). The year 2021 marked the full return of military coups to the stage in Africa as evidenced by four successful military takeovers across the continent in Chad, Mali, Guinea, and Sudan. According to Pilster and Böhmelt (2011), military effectiveness entails a national army's leadership qualities, initiative, and the ability to coordinate different military units. It is this military effectiveness that has made coups either possible or impossible. It is also for this reason that the army has taken center stage in all the successful coups in Africa, including those in Gabon (2019), Zimbabwe (2017), Sudan (2021), Mali (2021), Niger (2010), and Central African Republic (CAR) (2020–2021). These power grabs have incessantly threatened an authoritarian reversal of the democratization process in Africa to the extent that a return to the era of coups has become not only the norm but also fashionable. This dramatic reversal of democracy also indicates that Western or alien notions of democracy denominated as they are in the regularity of elections apparently have no genuine takers on the African continent itself as recent events have shown. The ongoing spate of coups on the African continent is not good news. Most of them were either advertent or inadvertent attempts to navigate democratic transitions within the framework of the existing political terrains. The continent, thus, is on the verge of democratic reversal which is synonymous with the bad old days of military misgovernance, and this is a period often remembered for its lost decades.

Depending on context specific situations, each country is unique in terms of its organizational capacity to withstand a coup. Coups are, by nature of their occurrence, ultimately calculations of benefits versus costs whose upsides such as power and unbridled access to state resources can be tremendous. Therefore, what attracts a coup always exists and is omnipresent. On the other hand, the potential downsides such as failure or imprisonment of coup plotters are viewed as very possible to manage, or at least to prevent, for unconstrained military actors under a civilian administration. Based on this analogy, those soldiers who mount coups dare doing so because they believe they can get away with it, with or without minimal costs.

The recent rise in coups in Africa mirrors a decline in regional and international actors' inclination to enforce anti-coup norms. This could be resulting from a confluence of factors, including a regional democratic recession, an inclination by regional bodies to negotiate compromises with coup leaders, reticence to mount military interventions, and distractions of international actors with their own internal crises and the COVID-19 pandemic, among others. Some military actors claim after gaining power that they are the sovereign representatives of that state especially when they were supported by civilians. However, for coups to be sustained, they need to be recognized both internally and externally. This questionable legitimation of coups especially by external players is awesomely perturbing, and that explains why coup leaders always seek international legitimacy for their actions. If international actors refuse to validate the coup, the putschists become politically isolated. To that end, international actors have a critical role in validating coups. This is also the reason why, in order to compensate for their lack of domestic legitimacy, coup makers crave international validation. The involvement of external authoritarian actors provides them with unequivocal leverage to compromise an African state's sovereignty. The coup in Mali, for example, led the junta to consider inviting Russian mercenaries, an action that would dramatically reshape Malian security and foreign policy (Durmaz, 28 December 2021). The effect of such a decision, taken by unelected military officers operating outside a constitutional framework and absent public accountability, was not in the interests of Malian citizens as that would enhance Russian leverage.

Conceptual/Theoretical Framework

The chapter uses coup-proofing and legitimacy as its theoretical frameworks. Social scientists and other scholars have generally argued that governments and leaders should possess legitimacy, because legitimacy translates into citizens' willingness to comply with an authority or its representatives. This legitimacy must meet international standard practice of undertaking election processes that are conducted in a free, fair, transparent, and credible manner. In further refining their legitimacy argument, Bottoms and Tankebe (2012), extrapolating from the work of Raz (2009), argue that power holders can be classified into three categories: those who exert "naked power" such as military regimes, those who rule by "de facto" authority such as the Iranian government, and those whose rule is considered legitimate, for example, democracies like the United Kingdom and the United States. African states with relatively dynamic economies whose societies were not socially mobilized before independence and which have maintained or restored some degree of political participation and political pluralism have experienced fewer military coups, attempted coups, and coup plots than have states with the opposite set of characteristics (Johnson et al., 2006, p. 622). The legitimacy framework also navigates related terrains of democratic and political instability, justice as fairness, rational choice, and deterrence in order to explain why coups occur, their effects on the general population, and how they can be curbed. Powell et al. (2016), for instance, focus on how coups can be limited through sanctions. Miller (2011) places emphasis on fixing the economy and building strong democratic governments, whereas O'Kane (1993) applies a political economy approach to discuss how coups in Africa can be curbed. Additionally, economic hardships within a country may serve as an excuse for soldiers to undertake a coup, even if it is commonly known that military regimes have not done better than their popularly elected counterparts in terms of reversing a country's economic downward spiral (Johnson et al., 1984; Saaka, 1994; Thompson, 1975).

Civilian Governance Deficits, Insecurity, and Popular Quests for Military Saviors

The following discussion starts with the coup in Guinea when, in 2021, Colonel Mamady Doumbouya, a high-ranking officer trained by the United States, overthrew President Alpha Conde who had resolved to cling to power. Doumbouya was 41 years old and a former French legionnaire and commander of the country's elite Special Forces Group who received training from France, Israel, Senegal, and Gabon, as well as participated in at least one US Special Forces exercise (Centre for Strategic and International Studies, 8 September 2021). Condé developed a feeling of indispensability and firmly believed that he had become a critical cog in the politics of Guinea after having been in opposition leadership for a long time before his election in 2010. He intimated that he was the only person capable of ruling Guinea during a private meeting at the Center for Strategic and International Studies (CSIS) in 2019 (Devermont, 2021). Condé proceeded to hold a controversial referendum during the COVID-19 pandemic era to secure a third term in office (Devermont, 2021). His unilateral decision to hold the plebiscite in defiance of the constitution and contrary to COVID-19 protocols backfired as the majority of Guineans favored a two-term limit on presidential mandates.

What inspired Doumbouya to carry out the coup was the glaring inactivity by the West African region and the international community in condemning in strong terms Condé's third term bid. From this weakness, Doumbouya calculated that there would also be little opposition to the coup if he elected to execute one. His accurate judgement was bolstered by the inaction and ham-fisted responses to similar unconstitutional coup maneuvers in Mali and Chad (Devermont, 8 September 2021). The African Union (AU), the Economic Community of West African States (ECOWAS), France, and the United States were hesitant to effect significant penalty to compel Guinea to return to constitutional order (Devermont, 8 September 2021). Put differently, these organizations and big international powers that wield restraining capacities were complicit in the second Guinean coup that saw Doumbouya seize power. Doumbouya proclaimed that the duty of a soldier is to save the country, quoting the former Ghanaian coup leader Jerry Rawlings, who infamously executed several of his military predecessors (Adekoya, 2021). In his 2017 speech, Doumbouya expressed resentment about the US and French influence in Guinea. According to the British Broadcasting Corporation (BBC), Doumbouya was 1 of 25 Guineans that the European Union (EU) members of parliament threatened with sanction for his alleged human rights abuses during Condé's presidency although neither his name nor that of the unit he commanded appeared in international human rights reports about the repression of protests and other abuses (Devermont, 2021). Doumbouya and the ruling junta, the National Rally and Development Committee (CNRD), revealed very little about their transition plans which remained as secretive as to become a troubling sign in a region where young coup leaders have resisted pressure to swiftly hand over power to civilians (Devermont, 2021).

It can therefore be argued that the economy of Guinea was already plummeting before President Condé's amendment of the constitution which allowed him to run for two more terms in 2020. Yet surprisingly, the aggrieved voters, through a manipulated voting system, went ahead to vote in support of the proposal that was inherently unconstitutional. The grievances behind the flawed 2020 presidential elections and President Condé's third mandate bid were among the main motivations behind the 2021 coup in Guinea (Schultes, 2022, p. 6). The CNRD detained Condé and other top officials before dissolving the government and imposing a nightly curfew. It pledged to form a transitional government soon and committed itself in principle to rewriting the constitution anew (Devermont, 2021). Devermont also notes that the Guinean military's overthrow of President Condé which was an outcome of autocratic overreach, economic mismanagement, and eroding democratic norms points to the failure of regional bodies and international partners to anticipate and respond to an evolving coup playbook.

Addressing Guineans after the September coup, Doumbouya was surrounded by soldiers and with Guinea's flag draped around his shoulders, a coup style ostensibly emulated from Zimbabwe's President Emmerson Mnangagwa after the Zimbabwean 2017 coup when he and his henchmen always drape themselves with scarfs around their necks reflecting the Zimbabwean flag. Doumbouya appeared on state television hours after leading a coup and delivered the statement to his compatriots that: "Guinea is beautiful. We no longer need to rape her. We need to make love to her, that's all" (Durmaz, 28 December 2021). He deployed this crude analogy to describe what his vision would be for the future of his country. The Guinean coup against Conde's largely unpopular move to scrap the presidential two-term limit (Durmaz, 28 December 2021) was used as a justificatory myth by Doumbouya to grab power by claiming poverty and endemic corruption as compelling reasons for his special forces to intervene as he announced that the personalization of political life was over and that people would no longer entrust politics to one man, but to the people (*Nation*, 5 September 2021). He further quoted the former Ghanaian, Jerry Rawlings, that if the people are crushed by their elites, it is up to the army to give the people their freedom (Lewis et al., 6 September 2021).

Similarly, in Burkina Faso, the nation turned on the television and collectively switched to the state television channel, where they saw new leaders, wearing berets and fatigues, announcing that the country's constitution had been suspended, national assembly dissolved, and borders closed (Maclean, 31 January 2022). The new military leader, Lieutenant Colonel Paul-Henri Damiba, vehemently informed the nation in his first public address that he would return the country to constitutional order when the conditions were right (Maclean, 31 January 2022). Paradoxically, the weakness of Burkina Faso's armed forces was a major factor in the coup when 49 military police officers and 4 civilians were killed in the northern outpost of Inata, thus outraging both the military and the public who believed that their officers were not well-enough equipped nor trained to withstand such an attack (Maclean, 31 January 2022). It can be argued that this ostensibly set the stage for this military takeover. The populace was inspired by the way the junta in neighboring Mali had solidly stood up to France, their increasingly unpopular former colonial power, and pronounced that whoever took power then needed to follow the example of Mali by rejecting France and starting to take their own independent decisions (Maclean, 31 January 2022). But a military takeover does not necessarily lead to a more effective response against insurgencies as evidenced by continuing attacks in Mali. As in Mali, many people in Burkina Faso lost faith in democracy and argued that if they waited until the next elections in 2025 to change leaders, their country would no longer be existing (Maclean, 31 January 2022).

Gabonese military officers in 2023 overthrew President Ali Bongo who had ruled the country for almost six decades, and many ordinary citizens took to the streets to celebrate his forced departure (Mensah, 22 September 2023). Bongo appealed for the international community to "make noise" against the coup but without success as dancers and content creators ridiculed and mocked him for his insatiable appetite for what was, indeed, dynastic power (Mensah, 22 September 2023). The contagion effect of earlier coups, Bongo's illness due to advanced age, and palace power struggles triggered the coup in Gabon (The Conversation, 6 September 2023). At the same time, President Emmanuel Macron was, and perhaps still is, struggling to maintain the influence his country gained in West Africa particularly through colonization as his policies heightened popular distrust and anger in Gabon (The Conversation, 6 September 2023).

In Mali in August 2020, the military took advantage of public anger at a stolen parliamentary election and the government's failure to protect its people from violent extremists and arrested President Ibrahim Boubacar Keita compelling him to resign on state television (Mclean, 31 January 2022). The two military coups in Mali occurred in rapid succession because of popular nationwide protests against President Keita's corrupt, nepotistic government that had dismally failed to tackle the country's worsening security crisis. In the first coup, the Malian putschists led by Colonel Assimi Goita initially consented to forming a military-civilian mixed transitional council after the first coup in 2020, promising to surrender power to a civilian authority at the end of the transition (Handy, 8 September 2020). This did not happen once Goita tested power. The coup in Mali happened partly because of the government's failure to stem the spread of groups loosely allied to Al-Qaeda and the Islamic State (Maclean, 31 January 2022). The most popular view which Maclean (January 31, 2022) describes as an explosive cocktail is that politicians did not seem to notice nor care and were driving fancy cars and sending their children to expensive foreign schools. The second coup in Mali by the military junta that occurred 9 months after the first in 2021 was against a civilian authority that had been appointed to lead the transition to democratic elections. The military rulers, seen as standing up to self-interested foreigners, gained overwhelming support despite sanctions from ECOWAS (Maclean, 31 January 2022). Instead, Goita went on to imprison and remove the civilian president and prime minister of the experimental transitional council after a cabinet reshuffle calculated to introduce two military members to replace civilian politicians (Duzor & Williamson, 3 October 2023). The military entrenched itself in power positions and made false promises of holding elections as a way of returning the country to civilian rule later.

A coup unfolded in Chad in April 2021 against a president who had ruled for three decades and was killed on the battlefield, to be unconstitutionally replaced by his son who was quickly installed (Maclean, 31 January 2022). Again, in October 2021, Sudan's top generals seized power, tearing up a power-sharing deal that was supposed to lead to the country's first free election in decades. In view of this coup phenomenon, indications are that more than 114 million people in Africa could now be ruled by soldiers who have illegally seized power (Maclean, 31 January 2022) as an indication of neocolonial military support and maneuvers for emerging military and civilian African leaders who have a strong inclination to open up their economies to foreign manipulation.

The reasons why people would get fed up by their governments as to support military seizures of power are varied. They range from major security threats, relentless humanitarian disasters, and millions of young people having no prospects. Above all, Mali, Burkina Faso, and Chad continue to grappling with relentless Islamist insurgencies that keep spreading, capitalizing on local tensions and grievances against political elites. For example, in all successful coup cases discussed so far, people initially greeted the coup leaders as their liberators and celebrated their freedom from democratic pretenders.

After the coup in each of Mali, Guinea, and Sudan, the AU suspended them all except Chad—a double standard that had the potential to cause dire consequences for Africa (Maclean, 31 January 2022). This was evidence that the AU had become little more than a weak and biased dictators' club. This line of thinking precipitated the notion that bad elections are worse than no elections at all. The ambivalence by the AU portrayed elections as no events and convinced people to affirm that they should actually address the political system that was not working. The West's conception of democracy and multiparty politics revolves around sticking to a strict electoral calendar while ignoring or downplaying other elements of democracy such as a free press, freedom from political repression, or human rights (Maclean, 31 January 2022). It, in my view, relates to the equal sovereignty of nations, big or small, rich or poor, with minimal or no interference in the political and economic affairs of other nations. Yet sovereignty is, as it currently stands, assumed by the small nations particularly those in the Global South, only at the United Nations. Interesting to note is the fact that when citizens' expectations of government are not being met by most elected leaders, they become critical of superficial Western-type democracy and look for solace in the military. Once the military assume power, what has become critical about coup governments is their failure to step away from executive power.

In view of the above discussion, soldiers were viewed as saviors in the twentieth century when military coups in Africa were a common means of changing the political order after the decolonization process. Arguably, it was a necessary political aberration at that time for the new black leaders to introduce one party state dictatorships under the nation-building mantra such as that of Kwame Nkrumah in Ghana in order for them to deal with largely irreconcilable ethnic categories institutionalized by the colonial administration. That required leaders' personalization and consolidation of power and the concomitant cronyism tendencies that resulted in the marginalization of some sections of the population. With time, calls for democratic reforms and constitutionalism grew with the twenty-first century as military coups decreased to two per year until 2019 (Durmaz, 28 December 2021). However, the fact that these coups have made a comeback prompted the United Nations Secretary-General, Antonio Guterres, to decry what he dubbed "an epidemic of coups d'etat" (Durmaz, 28 December 2021).

The recent surge in the militarization of politics is predicated on a blend of external factors such as the increasing and diverse number of international stakeholders who are actively prioritizing their interests on the continent. Internally, escalating widespread public frustrations against corruption, insecurity, and poor governance have inevitably contributed to the sporadic outbursts of coups as immediate causes. For Powell, this militarization came amid an increasing crisis of legitimacy for rulers as he notes that when leaders like Alpha Conde, among others, toyed with constitutions, term limits, and the electoral process, that increased public support for the armed forces to "do something." The militaries assume the position of savior and use civic discontent as a means of legitimizing their unconstitutional power grabs (Pryce & Time, 2023).

Toothless responses to coups, both successful and attempted, have been a major bone of contention by regional and continental bodies. For example, the AU and the regional bodies such as ECOWAS in West Africa suspended the countries where coups had taken place in order to push military rulers to the negotiation table with civilian leaders. African and Western institutions appear relatively powerless in their responses to the recent power grabs. This observation is based on the realization that they have generally favored dialog between the military leadership that grabbed power and aggrieved domestic political actors than endorsing castigatory measures against the transgressing leadership (Durmaz, 28 December 2021). If this analysis is anything to go by, then the absence of such punitive measures against the usurpers of power ensures that democratic consolidation in coup-prone countries does not occur naturally within these states. Instead, this condition literally permits the military to exploit these democratic deficits.

Likewise, the Sudanese and Zimbabwean generals who toppled Omar al-Bashir in 2019 and Robert Mugabe in 2017, respectively, deployed similar arguments. The joy that greeted the two coups were short-lived as Joseph Sany, Vice President of the Africa Centre at the US Institute of Peace, noted that the initial reaction of what people saw on the streets would be of joy, but later, the same people would be demanding action, and the military would not be able to deliver on the expectations, basic service delivery, and more freedoms (Mo Ibrahim Foundation, 2022). In the case of Zimbabwe, the coup posed and continues to pose a serious threat to the democratic gains that the country has made in recent decades, however little. The 2017 military coup was sanctified by the High Court of Zimbabwe which ruled that the actions of the military were constitutionally permissible and therefore legal (Greenfield & Wharton, 2019). Christopher Mutsvangwa, a war veteran and Mnangagwa's right-hand man, characterized the military coup as a correction of the state that was careering off the cliff and intimated that it was a very painful chapter in the history of a young nation in which Mugabe through his old age had surrendered his court to a gang of thieves around his wife (Millenium Report, 15 November 2017). SADC countries and the AU endorsed the regime of Mnangagwa calling it a "military assisted transition" (Crisis Group, 2017, p. 2) instead of an outright military coup since calling it by that name would inevitably attract international sanctions. His cabinet was dominated by military careerists such as Perrance Shiri, Costantino Chiwenga, and Engelbert Rugeje, among others, as well as those who affirmed their political correctness to a new version of ZANU-PF in a new political dispensation led by the coup faction under Mnangagwa. Worryingly, a trend in Zimbabwe is the reality that people are increasingly ceasing to believe that elections can deliver the leaders they want. As long as President Mnangagwa is in control of the gun, legal controls on his abuse of power have little or no meaning in Zimbabwe.

In the case of West Africa, military interventions reflect and deepen a trend of democratic backsliding in Africa. In Burkina Faso, Guinea, and Mali, ousted presidents were once popular figures who themselves ended previous periods of military rule, but they failed to curb insurgent and militia violence and spiraling humanitarian crises once in power (Congressional Research Services, 11 February 2022). The coups in Mali and Guinea followed allegations of election fraud; in Guinea, former President Condé was heavily criticized for his highhandedness in his opposition campaign crackdown. Many citizens in these countries overtly welcomed the coups, although majorities reject military rule in principle (Congressional Research Services, 11 February 2022, p. 2). According to President Macron of France, the preponderance of coups in former French colonies in West Africa ending up in strained postcolonial diplomatic relations is not due to France's failure in its foreign policy insofar as it relates to Africa, but to COVID-19 with its concomitant mass migrations, which phenomenon is indicative of failed states and bad governance (Macrome, BBC, 12 November 2023). It is prudent to assert that political instability in West Africa's Sahel region also coincides with growing diplomatic tensions with the former colonial power, France, over the scope of its regional counterterrorism operations (Congressional Research Services, 11 February 2022, p. 2). The east African body to which Sudan belongs, known as IGAD, has not taken punitive action in response to the recent coup there (Congressional Research Services, 11 February 2022, p. 3). This has been made difficult, if not almost impossible to do, because of prior US training of junta leaders in Burkina Faso, Guinea, and Mali although the Congressional Research Services (11 February 2022, p. 3) refutes American complicity in creating strongmen to further its interests in east Africa.

Several factors are at play across cases and exist elsewhere, including tensions within the armed forces, allegations of high-level corruption, and economic pressures worsened by the COVID-19 pandemic. Edi (2006, p. 10) observes:

> Today, a retrospective look at military regimes shows that they ruined democratic values and confiscated the freedom of West Africans. In Togo, Mali, Benin, Ghana, Gambia, Sierra Leone, Nigeria, Burkina Faso, Liberia, Mauritania, Niger, and Guinea, military regimes did not do better than civilian regimes in promoting democracy and good governance. The record of the absence of freedom for the press, the cases of incarceration of journalists and political opponents, corruption, and the wrong managements of international loans, the weak strategies against poverty, and the perpetual call for aid show that West Africa was a powder keg ready to set aflame. Evidently, military regimes were harsher and more destructive of human rights.

The Resource Curse and Greed

Sporadic coups in Africa can be analyzed from a multidimensional perspective. There is need to consider the role of Western powers like Britain, France, and the United States on one hand and that of Russia, China, and, to a lesser extent, India on the other, in terms of their clash in security, ideological, and economic interests as typified by reverberations of the Cold War situation. External involvement in the economic and political affairs in Africa appears to have substantially hindered democratic governance to a large measure. This is coupled with the lack of concrete and unified international condemnation and the growing number of international actors who have shown willingness to work with the military governments. These directly or indirectly encourage more unconstitutional power grabs by military officials who know they will not face severe consequences or regional and global isolation. China, the continent's largest trading partner, has a noninterference policy on the domestic affairs of African countries, as long as they are committed to long-term economic ties (Durmaz, 28 December 2021) which smack of a unique typology of Sinocolonialism. More African leaders have been wooed by China's economic success on the global stage becoming increasingly convinced that their countries should leave Western prescriptions for good governance and economic growth, thereby advancing Chinese economic and ideological ambitions on the African continent.

Political historians must reckon with Russia's increasing role in coup occurrences in Africa. For example, it backed putschist leaders like Mali's Goita and Sudan's al-Burhan and deliberately ran online disinformation campaigns to spread a positive image of the Kremlin in order to capitalize on the upsurge of anti-French sentiments in francophone Africa (Durmaz, 28 December 2021). Durmaz also intimates that the Russian-linked Wagner Group under the late Yevgeny Prigozhin deployed mercenaries in conflict-ridden countries such as the CAR, Mali, and Libya in order to spread the Kremlin's geostrategic interests. It is further noted that both Russia and China have in recent years increased their influence in Africa because to them, relationship with these countries is the priority, not an interest in democracy (Durmaz, 28 December 2021). As these two powers make efforts to increase and assert their influence, the relationship has begun to copycat the Cold War, when a loss of support from the West did not alarm potential coup plotters because they could quickly win support from the former Soviet Union.

Russian and Chinese involvement in African politics is paralleled with the United State's interference as well. The United States reacted in predictable fashion when there was a military coup in Egypt in 2013 that became a precursor of a trail of similar coups in Africa. This Egyptian coup exhibited the first visible fissures in the regional and international stance on the military coup. The Western world, led by the United States, denied calling the military takeover a coup but, in a clear show of double standards, embraced the new General Abdel Fattah el-Sisi of Egypt as the legitimate president of the military government (Durmaz, 28 December 2021). A similar trend was followed with the 2017 Zimbabwean coup that ended former President Robert Mugabe's 37 years of uninterrupted rule. Although debates around Mugabe's ouster from power remain topical in Zimbabwean politics, it still remains unclear whether the military had forced him to resign publicly on the Zimbabwean national television station (ZTV) because his speech was silent on the resignation issue as he admitted to having been presented with a different prepared speech altogether. When, finally, Mugabe resigned amidst calls for impeachment by the Parliament, Western countries with diplomatic standoffs with him did not construe the ouster as a military coup but sanitized the dethronement event. Because they were so trigger-happy to see Mugabe leave office, the United States and European countries downplayed the fact that his resignation had come through the barrel of a gun. It should be noted that the first port of call for President Mnangagwa's so-called Second Republic's Minister of Foreign Affairs, the late General Sibusiso Moyo, was Britain, a clear testimony that the then British Prime Minister, Theresa May and her Conservative-dominated government, gave a tacit approval of the coup. This is also supported by a reflection of the developments that took place in South Africa in 2002 that Mnangagwa attended which suggested that the British preferred Mnangagwa to Mugabe. Mnangagwa was allegedly secretly invited to represent ZANU-PF at an ANC Congress in Stellenbosch with a view to negotiating Mugabe's exit scheme in 2003, brokered by the retired Rhodesian Colonel Lionel Dyck and supported by the United States and the United Kingdom (Adelmann,

2004). Therefore, the big brothers' complicity in the Zimbabwean coup that toppled former President Mugabe can hardly be wished away.

China's strategy insofar as it relates to Africa is a kind of its own. It is concerned more with adapting to political realities on the ground than shaping them. This has given it unqualified leverage in trade partnerships with African states. The Guinea coup can be viewed as being orchestrated by the United States to neutralize China, whose trade with Africa has dramatically increased 40-fold over the past two decades (Suleiman, 24 September 2021). The United States is also circumstantially implicated in the coup as a video showed some American soldiers celebrating the fall of Condé (Suleiman 24 September 2021), and it cannot be doubted that recent coups in Africa have foreign fingerprints.

Russia's active involvement in African politics, particularly its support for coups, has become a key aspect for interrogation. Because of its close ties with the Wagner mercenary group, Moscow, for example, maintained a close relationship with the military throughout Sudan's democratic transition and is said to have agitated for its seizure of power (Durmaz, 28 December 2021). In return, Durmaz further argues that the Sudanese junta granted Russia access to its naval port to Port Sudan, giving Moscow a military foothold in the important Red Sea corridor (Durmaz, 2021). Given this development, Wagner interests are guaranteed in western Sudan in support of gold and other illicit trafficking through the CAR (Durmaz, 2021). Durmaz also intimates that pro-Russian disinformation campaigns belittled Keita's authority who was democratically elected in 2019 before the August 2020 coup and that such kind of messaging underwrote the opposition protests against Keita that people and the army used as a justification for the coup.

Russian, Chinese, British, and US involvement in coup plotting in Africa is reminiscent of a twenty-first-century Cold War revival. This can be traced back to the demise of the Soviet Union in 1991 which drastically affected Western views about the efficacy of promoting democracy in a unipolar world dominated politically and ideologically by the United States. Promoting their version of democracy no longer made much economic sense as the threat of a rival communist state, in principle more than in practice, had disappeared. What the United States deemed fit to vigorously advance its economic and strategic interests was to render support to military leaders in Africa who are/were potentially well disposed toward it and to deploy double standards to gains stakes in unstable countries. The usual culprits would be those coup leaders who fail to pursue supposedly liberalizing trajectories of their countries (Marinov & Goemans, 24 May 2013) as to ignite the wrath of citizens.

France, with a long history of engagement with its former African colonies, has awesomely based its continued influence on military and security considerations and has continued to pursue its traditional strongman-favoring strategy. For example, President Emmanuel Macron endorsed the Chadian coup and called late President Idriss Deby, who led 30 years of repressive rule, a "loyal and courageous friend" (Durmaz, 2021). Idayat Hassan, the director of the Abuja-based think-tank Centre for Democracy and Development, reasoned that even if some countries within and outside Africa celebrated the departure of the unpopular Chadian leader, the coup was not at all good news. In this case, the inability of Western democracy to deliver public goods and security to the people led citizens to embrace the coup in search of hope (Durmaz, 28 December 2021). However, the case of the Zimbabwean coup government aptly demonstrates that the military transition fell far too short of citizens' expectations by not necessarily bringing the hope that they so desired as evidenced by mass migrations for greener pastures. In view of external interference with, and rapacity over, Africa's resources, continental stability has been rendered weak and unsustainable. This is because political succession in African states indicates trends toward illegitimate and unpopular self-succession, hereditary trends, the appointment of proxies, and only a few instances of emerging liberal democratic regimes (Suleiman, 2021). One such outstanding case is that of Zimbabwe's Second Republic in which President Mnangagwa handpicked his two sons as Cabinet Ministers after the 2023 elections, an action pointing to the creation of Mnangagwa's dynasty rule.

Regional and International Coup Drivers

The incessant prevalence of coups appears to have rendered Western democracy on the continent increasingly illegitimate. Three out of every four failures of democracy are consequences of successful coups, and this has made power grabs the largest single hazard to democracy and democratic transitions (Marinov & Goemans, 24 May 2013). There are regular elections as well as democratic rollbacks, democratic institutionalization, as well as endemic corruption, of political parties as well as widespread ethnic voting and violent politics, increased civil societies as well as local realities of outright incivility and violence, and political freedoms and economic growth as well as political controls and inequality (Suleiman, 24 September 2021, p. 2). To begin with, sectarian cleavages remain important in the CAR. The 2013 coup in CAR was unique in that it was the only coup that was triggered by identity politics. The diamond-rich northern part of the CAR has been historically marginalized by the central government because most of the leaders of CAR come from the southern region (Marawako et al., 2022). In Chad, the 37-year-old Mahamat Idriss Déby assumed control following his father's death on the battlefield in April 2020. The United States initially called for a transition process informed by the Chadian constitution but changed this position when France and the AU chose to support the young leader's rule that was borne out of a coup. At the funeral of Deby's father, President Macron vowed that France would not let anybody put into question or threaten Chad's stability and integrity (Devermont, 8 September 2021). Déby, like his counterparts in Mali, promised an 18-month military-led transition, a dialog, and a new constitution which never came as the military entrenched its power.

The promise of 18-month political transition timelines and the pledge to rewrite constitutions to placate the international community have become the norm in African power grabs. The associated democratic regression has set the conditions for soldiers to seize power or at least use it as pretext for military action. Even if penalties are envisaged by Africa's regional bodies and international powers, no sooner are these punitive measures usually lifted quickly than they are implemented either because other priorities are paramount or at the slightest sign of progress (Devermont, 2021). This leniency has enabled coup leaders to make minimal concessions while preparing for longer stays in power.

ECOWAS and the AU went even further with targeted sanctions to coerce the coup plotters out of power in Mali. The attempted coup in Sierra Leone on November 26, 2023, against President Julius Maada Bio involved gunmen attacking Wilberforce Barracks and overrunning detention centers including a major prison (Al Jazeera, 26 November 2023). ECOWAS reiterated its "paper" zero tolerance for unconstitutional change of government, threatened sanctions on perpetrators, and pledged to help Sierra Leone strengthen its democracy and good governance (Anaedo Online, 26 November 2023). This sudden craving for sanctions from African organizations looks very surprising on account of the AU's tendency to criticize foreign acts such as the Zimbabwe Democracy and Economic Recovery Act (ZIDERA) of 2001 passed by the US Congress against Mugabe's human rights violations (Lahiff, 2003). The Lomé Declaration of 2000 and the African Charter on Democracy, Elections, and Governance of 2007 define facets of unconstitutional change of government (Handy, 08 September 2020). Among these are a military coup against a democratically elected government, mercenary intervention to replace a democratically elected government, replacing a democratically elected government by dissident armed groups and rebel movements, or refusal of an outgoing government to relinquish power following defeat in free, fair, transparent, and credible elections (Handy, 08 September 2020). The regular mention of "democratically elected government" demonstrates both the context and spirit behind the Lomé Declaration. When democratic constitutionalism—which by implication refers to upholding of principles enshrined in the constitution—was a relatively new phenomenon in Africa, the major objective initially was to protect the authority of civilian political institutions from the "authoritarianism" of military interventions (Handy, 8 September 2020). Since 2000, and with the evolution of debates by citizens on democracy and governance in Africa, priorities shifted not only to the quality of electoral processes and the value of term limits but also to legitimacy, performance, and accountability in political and economic governance. All these essential deficits within African constitutional processes or environments have triggered coups. Regarding issues of governance, regional organizations have remained silent in spite of the development of an African Governance Architecture (AGA) in 2011. With only 17 countries having signed and 6 ratifying the 2014 African Charter on the values and principles of decentralization, local governance, and local development, only ink-service is paid to core values like responsiveness, transparency, accountability, and civic responsibility (Handy, 8 September 2020).

The AU and regional organizations in practice have reduced democracy to the holding of elections and selective respect for term limits. Yet the quality of electoral processes is a recurring trigger point, as was the case with Mali's delayed and allegedly rigged March 2020 parliamentary elections and Zimbabwe's 2018 harmonized elections that only served to sanitize President Mnangagwa's 2017 ZANU-PF military alliance in a coup government. Reliance on observer missions by the AU and regional organizations has not helped much during elections. Conclusions about these elections seldom challenge official results but rubber-stamp them, even if civil society and judiciaries identify rigging, which they seldom do. The Zimbabwean court system exemplifies this when the verdict on Nelson Chamisa's Movement for Democratic Change Alliance's (MDC-A's) challenge to the presidential outcome merely protected Mnangagwa's incumbency. Above all, both organizations have always been silent about government inertia on glaring inequality, absence of the rule of law, and skewed electoral governance.

Conclusion

Undertaking this study on the backdrop of increasing prevalence of power grabs in Africa is like chasing a moving target as the continent is confronted with a serious democratic backsliding. The spate of coups is indicative of the reality that Western democracy has not made sufficient and meaningful inroads in national power politics so as to prevent a return to authoritarianism on the continent. Foreign interests continue to prey and capitalize, first, on African poverty and, second, on the continent's persistent economic disparities and decline. This has created opportunities by outside forces to finance military interventions with the hope that the strongmen that they create and back by military means would make their newly established governments more amenable to their neocolonial interests. Foreign powers still wield tremendous political and economic influence and derive solace in their destabilization efforts particularly in countries that are weak but well resourced. Their centuries-old tradition of determining and shaking African spaces in their favor is being invigorated under the guise of promoting democratic practices without paying due regard to Africa's potential ethnic volatility. However, coups could be understood as "good" liberatory political events or episodes against dictators or abuses of constitutional power, especially in the face of the functional incapacity of intergovernmental bodies such as ECOWAS, in the case of West Africa, to prevent rampant incumbent abuses. Urgent calls by international parties for elections to restore constitutional order are equally questionable, particularly when constitutions or flawed voting systems are indeed part of the problem.

References

Adekoya, R. CNN. (3 September 2021). *Cable News Network (CNN), Why are coups making a comeback in Africa?*

Adelmann, M. (2004). Quiet diplomacy: The reasons behind Mbeki's Zimbabwe policy. *Africa Spectrum, 39*(2), 249–276.

Al Jazeera. 26 November 2023.

Anaedo Online. 26 November 2023. https://www.anaedoonline.ng/2023/11/26/update-ecowas-reacts-to-coup-attempt-in-sierra-leone/

Baudais, V., & Chauzal, G. (2011). The 2010 coup d'état in Niger: A praetorian regulation of politics? *African Affairs, 110*(439), 295–304.

Beckman, L. (2021). *Democracy*, Oxford Research Encyclopedias Publisher: Oxford University Press. https://doi.org/10.1093/acrefore/9780190228637.013.2001

Berlin, I. (1965). The thought of Alexis de Tocqueville. *History, 50*(169), 199–206.

Bottoms, A., & Tankebe, J. (2012). Beyond procedural justice: A dialogic approach to legitimacy in criminal justice. *Journal of Criminal Law and Criminology, 102*(1), 119–170.

Centre for Strategic and International Studies. (8 September 2021). Guinea: The Causes and Consequences of West Africa's Latest Coup. https://www.csis.org/analysis/guinea-causes-and-consequences-west-africas-latest-coup

Congressional Research Services. (11 February 2022). *Insight, "An Epidemic of Coups" in Africa?* Issues for Congress.

Crisis Group. (20 December 2017). *Zimbabwe's "Military-assisted transition" and prospects for recovery.* https://www.crisisgroup.org/africa/southern-africa/zimbabwe/b134-zimbabwes-military-assisted-transition-and-prospects-recovery

Devermont, J. (8 September 2021). *Centre for strategic and international studies.* Guinea: The Causes and Consequences of West Africa's Latest Coup, Washington DC.

Dewey, J. (1939/1988). Creative democracy – the task before us. In J. O. Bodyston (Ed.), *John Dewey, the later works 1925–1953, volume 14: 1939–1941* (pp. 224–230). Southern Illinois University Press.

Durmaz, M. (28 December 2021). *Al Jazeera Media Network, Colonel Mamady Doumbouya addressing Guineans after the September 5 coup.*

Duzor, M., & Williamson, B. (3 October 2023). *VOA News. By the Numbers: Coups in Africa — VOA Special Report.* Available at: projects.voanews.com › african-coups.

Edi, E. (2006). Pan West Africanism and political instability in West Africa: Perspectives and reflections. *Journal of Pan African Studies, 1*(3), 7–37.

Greenfield, T., & Wharton, D. B. (2019). *Zimbabwe's coup: Net gain or no gain?.* https://www.news24.com/Africa/Zimbabwe/mdc-40will-never-rule-zimbabwe-says-controversial-mnangagwa-minister-20180531.

Handy, P. P. (8 September 2020). Independent analyst, senior regional adviser, ISS Dakar, Fonteh Akum, Programme Head, ISS Lake Chad Basin and FélicitéDjilo.

Johnson, T. H., Slater, R. O., & McGowan, P. (1984). Explaining African Military Coups d'état. *American Political Science Review, 78*(3), 622–640.

Johnson, T. H. et al. (2006). Explaining African Military Coups d'etat, 1960–1982. *The American Political Science Review*, Vol. 78. The Orkand Corporation.

Lahiff, E. (2003). *The politics of land reform in Southern Africa, sustainable livelihoods in Southern Africa: Institutions, Governance and Policy Processes*, Institute of Development Studies, Sussex, Research Paper 19 http://www.ids.ac.uk/slsa (Accessed 16 October 2023).

Lewis, D., Mcallister, E., & Samb, S. (6 September 2021). *Reuters*, 'Unattainable power': The frustrations that drove Guinea's coup leader. www.reuters.com › world › Africa.

Maclean, R. (31 January 2022). *The New York Times*, Five African Countries. Six Coups. Why Now? https://r.search.yahoo.com/

Macrome, E. (12 November 2023). *French President, British Broadcasting Corporation (BBC).*

Marawako, J., et al. (2022). An analysis of the recurrence of Military Coups in Africa. A probe into the experiences of central African Republic in the 21st century. *International Journal of Humanities Social Sciences and Education (IJHSSE), 9*(2), 67–77. https://doi.org/10.20431/2349-0381.0902008

Marinov, N., & Goemans, H. (24 May 2013). *Coups and democracy.* updates@academia-mail.com

Mensah, K. (2023). *Africa's coup epidemic: Has democracy failed the continent?.* https://www.aljazeera.com/features/2023/9/22/africas-coup-epidemic-has-democracy-failed-the-continent.

Millenium Report. (15 November 2017). *Coup in Zimbabwe: The C.I.A. & MI6 Bribe Army to Remove President Robert Mugabe.* https://themillenniumreport.com/2017/11/coup-in-zimbabwe-the-c-i-a-mi6-bribe-army-to-remove-president-robert-mugabe/

Miller, A. C. (2011). Debunking the 'good' coup d'état in Africa. *African Studies Quarterly, 12*(2), 45–70.
O'Kane, R. H. (1993). Coups d'état in Africa: A Political Economy Approach. *Journal of Peace Research, 30*(3), 251–270.
Olafsson, N. (2020). *When Military Coup d'état Become Acts of Social Justice*. https://www.e-ir.info/2020/01/17/when-military-coups-detat-become-acts-of-social-justice/ [Accessed 20 January 2022].
Peters, M. A. (2017). Dewey's Democracy and Education in the age of digital reason: The global, ecological and digital turns. https://doi.org/10.1080/23265507.2017.1395290.
Pilster, U., & Böhmelt, T. (2011). Coup-proofing and military effectiveness in interstate wars, 1967–99. *Conflict Management and Peace Science, 28*(4), 331–350.
Powell, J. M., & Thyne, C. L. (2011). Global instances of coups from 1950 to 2010: A new dataset. *Journal of Peace Research 48*(2):249–259.
Powell, J., Lasley, T., & Schiel, R. (2016). Combating Coups in Africa 1950–2014. *Studies in Comparative International Development, 51*, 482–502.
Pryce, D. K., & Time, V. M. (2023). The role of coups d'état in Africa: Why coups occur and their effects on the populace. *International Social Science Journal*, 1–16.
Raz, J. (2009). *Between authority and interpretation: On the theory of law and practical reason*. Oxford University Press.
Saaka, Y. (1994). Recurrent themes in Ghanaian politics: Kwame Nkrumah's Legacy. *Journal of Black Studies, 24*(3), 263–280.
Schultes, I. (2022). MO Ibrahim Foundation. *Western Africa's recent coups: Highlight the risk of trading off development for security, the rule of law and rights*.
Suleiman, M. D. (24 September 2021). *Towards a better understanding of the underlying conditions of Coups in Africa*. https://www.e-ir.info/2021/09/24/towards-a-better-understanding-of-the-underlying-conditions-of-coups-in-africa/
Thompson, W. R. (1975). Regime vulnerability and the Military Coup. *Comparative Politics, 74*, 459–487.
Tocqueville, A. (2021). *Democracy in America, 1*. https://www.gutenberg.org/ebooks/815

Aaron Rwodzi holds a PhD in History from the University of KwaZulu Natal. He is an ex-Catholic University of Zimbabwe lecturer, ex-University of Zimbabwe, Women's University in Africa and is currently at the Midlands State University. He earned his Master of Arts (MA) Degree in African History at the University of Zimbabwe after obtaining his Special Honours Degree in History at the same university. His Bachelor of Arts (General) Degree in History and African Politics was obtained at the University of South Africa. He also holds a Certificate in Education from Hillside Teachers' College. He has coordinated research activities at various institutions and participated in Quality Assurance issues. Currently, he is the Secretary of the Development Studies Association of Zimbabwe. His areas of research interest include party politics, political and social history, democracy, ethnicity, race, displacement, and culture.

Chapter 20
African Agency in the Context of a New World Dis(Order)

Mbongeni Nhliziyo

Abstract The geopolitical contestations between the United States and China have intensified in recent years, and this has had a significant impact on the global response to developmental challenges such as climate change, peace, security, and health emergencies. This has resulted in Africa being caught in a web of dilemmas with regard to its in(voluntary) participation in the geopolitical games of the United States and China. In this context, I argue in this chapter that Africa must use its strategic position to its advantage and demand a seat at the table when global decisions are being made. To do so, I argue that Africa must develop its own agency, policy maturity, diplomatic adeptness, political leadership, and policy capacity in order to effectively engage with the United States and China and must not be afraid to stand up to the United States and China when necessary.

Introduction

The geopolitical contestations between the United States and China have intensified in recent years, and this has had a significant impact on the global response to developmental challenges such as climate change, peace, security, and health emergencies. Africa has been caught in the middle of this power struggle, which presents both opportunities and challenges for the continent. In particular, the return of the United States and the subsequent increase of the Chinese footprint on the continent present an opportunity for Africa to get access to new development finance and development assistance. The United States's policies toward the continent, however, are not in the continent's best interests because the United States's main objective there is to restrain China's expanding power. Similarly, China's involvement with Africa has also been motivated by its own aspirations for the world. Thus, as explained by Moyo (2024:170), both Washington and Beijing's presence reinforces

M. Nhliziyo (✉)
Department of Development Studies, Lupane State University, Lupane, Zimbabwe

G. Moyo, S. J. Ndlovu-Gatsheni (eds.), *Global Storms and Africa in World Politics*, Global Power Shift, https://doi.org/10.1007/978-3-031-83868-2_20

a vicious cycle of global capital systems that exploit African resources, perpetuate the imperialization of the continent, and further alienate the continent.

Instructively, in his seminal work, Gorden Moyo argues that the Sino-Washington scramble for global goods and control offers Africa a greater space for negotiating better deals. He argues that Africa has come to the forefront of world politics and economy because of its natural resource endowments, market potential, and geostrategic position in the topography of global matrices of power. He, however, cautions that the fragmentation of the continent undermines this position (Moyo, 2021:45 see also Adeoye, 2020:2). Thus, the intensification of geopolitical conflicts strengthens the growing argument that the continent should use its own agency, driven by the experiences, values, histories, resources, and aspirations of the African people themselves, to control its own future (Lala, 2020:1; Chipaike & Mataruse, 2018:1; Muresan, 2022: 5; Moyo, 2021:45; Moyo, 2024:170). Given the foregoing, I argue in this chapter that unless Africa develops policy maturity, diplomatic adeptness, strong political leadership, political will, and policy capacity consistent with the current geopolitical setting, the continent will be further marginalized and will be taken advantage of by both Beijing and Washington.

Soyinka (2014:25), cited in Hodzi (2020:889), echoes the above and argues that Africa has returned to being the warring ground of the world's traditional (and emerging) hegemonists. Thus, Africa has become a site of global competition and global turf wars. Mohan & Lampert, 2013:92) aver that the emergency and re-emergency of old and new development partners is often portrayed as a relationship in which foreign actors, not African political elites, dominate the agenda and act in coordinated ways. Put differently, African actors are treated as passive and lacking in agency. Soyinka's argument, as well as that of Samuel Ojo Oloruntoba and Falola (2020), Giles Mohan and Ben Lampert (2021), Obert Hodzi (2020), Deborah Brautigam (2011), Dambisa Moyo (2009, 2012), Brown and Chun (2009), Ueli Staeger, 2023a, and Gorden Moyo (2020, 2021), of Africa being a site of competition and rivalry, highlights perceptions, especially in the Global North, of passivity, impotency, and lack of agency in African states, which is not always the case, as will be shown anon.

Whereas Africa remains marginalized and on the peripheries of the global governance system, the African Union has recently exhibited agency endorsing African candidates for top posts in multilateral institutions to mobilise unified support for such candidates. Such candidates are expected to add African voices to global governance policy formulation and decision-making (Adeoye, 2020:4). To this end, Africans such as Ngozi Okonjo-Iweala and Tedros Adhanom Ghebreyesus are currently heads of the World Trade Organization and the World Health Organization, respectively. On the other side of the coin, the global turf war on the continent opens avenues for and increases Africa's role in global politics (Lala, 2020:1). The geo-economic contestations could be enviable if the political leadership on the continent is able to effectively balance between the competing powers and extract the benefits, but in order to do that, the leadership must be strong enough that it does not get taken advantage of by one or all of them (Moyo et al., 2020:97). This demands asserting agency, as shown by former and contemporary African leaders, such as

President Paul Kagame (Rwanda), President Julius Maada Bio (Sierra Leone), the late President John Magufuli (Tanzania), and President Hakainde Hichilema (Zambia), who exercised their agency to force global powers such as China to reconsider how it conducts its business and engages with Africa (Hodzi, 2020:899). In particular, Rwanda's Kagame justified his authoritarian leadership as necessary to achieve economic development (Hodzi, 2020:899). Thus, African leaders exercised agency to (re)negotiate Africa's place and role in the world (Staeger, 2023a:7).

Former Presidents Kenneth Kaunda of Zambia, Samora Machel of Mozambique, Olusegun Obasanjo of Nigeria, Thomas Sankara of Burkina Faso, Nelson Mandela and Thabo Mbeki, both from South Africa, and Muammar Gaddafi from Libya (Falola, 2022:1054), working with other African political leaders, coined the African renaissance, foregrounded Africa's solution to Africa's problems, and transformed the Organisation for African Unity into the African Union with more emphasis on accountable governance and protection of human rights (Oloruntoba & Falola, 2020:5). To that end, Fredon Lala also argued that "the African Union has emerged as Africa's preeminent platform to participate internationally, promoting unity among African nations in global negotiations. As the continent's foremost multilateral institution, the African Union is the main organiser, promoter, protector, and defender of the continent's political, socio-economic, and environmental interests" (Lala, 2020:2). However, despite the African Union's rising preeminence, it is important to underscore that Africa remains fragmented and African "union" and integration, according to Bankole Adeoye, the African Union Commissioner, is "convoluted," "politically stressful," and difficult (Adeoye, 2020:2). One cause of this is the continent's fragmentation. As there are 55 members, states are obligated to have divergent views and national geostrategic interests over continental objectives. However challenging the task may be, African unity remains central to advancing Africa's perspectives and interests (Adeoye, 2020:7). The perceptions of African states as 'lacking policy maturity', 'diplomatic adeptness, lacking agency, passive, impotent, ineffectual, fragile, a scar on the conscience of the world, and hopeless (Moyo et al., 2020:97; Blair, 2001: 1; The Economist, 2000:1) are not without form. For instance, the African Union headquarters were constructed and donated by China, and aid is its largest source of funding, with the European Union being the biggest donor (Pharatlhatlhe & Vanheukelom, 2019:5). Africa is riddled with what Ajayi and Oshewolo (2020:503) term developmental disabilities.

Key developmental disabilities emblematic of the continent include pervasive poverty, unemployment, runaway inflation, genocidal conflicts, re-insurgency of coups (for a nuanced analysis on the re-insurgency of coups in Africa, see Divane Nzima, Mubarak Aliyu, Herbert Mba Aki, and Gorden Moyo's analysis in Chap. 17 of this book), rising authoritarianism, and civil wars (Mills, 2021; 14–15, 33–34). These challenges reflect Africa's lack of material capabilities which ostensibly supports the lack-of-agency argument. The lack of material capabilities means that African states are of no major effect in international politics and are marginal in global forums (Ajayi & Oshewolo, 2020:503). The aggregate GDP of sub-Saharan Africa in 2018 was US$1.7 trillion—at par with the GDP of Canada, slightly higher than South Korea's (US$1.6 trillion), and less than Brazil's (US$1.8 trillion) (Hodzi,

2020:889). With such a paltry GDP and under the weight of constant continental and global storms such as the intrastate-armed conflicts, political instability, poverty, unemployment, authoritarian leadership, and food insecurity, Africa is dependent on foreign aid and humanitarian assistance from external donors. To be clear, donors have poured US$1.2 trillion of development assistance into the continent since the end of Cold War (Mills, 2021:1). This cycle of dependence on donor funds and aid from the Global North has continued to undermine the development trajectory of countries in sub-Saharan Africa (Ajayi & Oshewolo, 2020:503).

Interestingly, the African Union has been able to pursue and exercise African agency without allowing donors to shape its agenda (Staeger, 2023b:502). For example, the African Union refused to be co-opted by the North Atlantic Treaty Organization (NATO) alliance countries and Russia in the Ukraine war (for further detail on the Russia-Ukraine war, see Charles Mutasa's analysis in Chap. 15 and Dylan Yanano Mangani and Ntsikelelo Benjamin Breakfast in Chap. 16 of this book). The continent denied to be seen as swing states in the battle for the preservation, or contestation, of the Western-led liberal international order (Carbone, 2023:553). Instead, the Russia-Ukraine war benefitted the African Union's pursuit of African agency in that, despite the continent's fragmentation and disunity, the African Union spoke on behalf of the continent on an urgent global issue outside of the African continent (Staeger, 2023b:502). This reveals that the African Union leadership navigated considerable internal disunity and external pressure from the NATO alliance countries and the Russian Federation and attempted a nonaligned and solution-focused diplomacy policy by placing issues such as food security and humanitarian impacts on the UN's agenda (Staeger, 2023a:2). In light of the aforementioned, I contend in this chapter that Africa must use its agency to take advantage of the current global (dis)order and be prepared to weather its storms. These storms include extreme poverty, debt colonialism, political instability, climate imperialism (for further detail on global climate crisis, see Part II of this book), global health crisis and global security, trade wars between the United States and China, and other global calamities that have kept Africa out of the global governance framework.

This chapter grapples with three interrelated questions: how do African countries find common agency and exercise it when they have been predominantly sidelined in contributing substantively to the discussions about Africa, its people, and global issues, and what are the challenges and opportunities for the African continent in the context of the changing world order? What role can the African continent and respective countries play in shaping a more just and equitable global order?

US-China Cut Throat Rivalry

The contours of great rivalries are shaped by the statements and rhetoric each competing side uses to craft a narrative about the other. The public confrontation in Anchorage between China's top diplomats, Yang Jiechi and Foreign Minister Wang

Yi, and the American officials, Secretary of State Antony Blinken and National Security Adviser Jake Sullivan, essentially captures in 5 min the intensifying great rivalry between the United States and China. "From now on," as Yang Jiechi emphatically put it, "Let me say here that in front of the Chinese side, the United States does not have the qualification to say that it wants to speak to China from a position of strength" (McCurry, 2021:1). To the contrary, as Foreign Minister Wang has repeatedly said, China will now engage the United States on "equal footing" (Allison et al., 2022:3). In large part, this reflects the great rivalry between China and the United States—one that will continue to intensify. Unfortunately, African countries are presented with a choice between these two leading economies in the intensifying geopolitical contestations, which should not be the case. In this case, African countries do not have to choose between Beijing and Washington and what they represent but should maintain good relations with both powers (Moyo et al., 2020:98). The continent ought to use its agency in these attempts of alignment, but with the goal of "renegotiating them towards a pragmatic mindset where having multiple partnerships does not automatically entail competition between poles of power" (Fisher-Onar & Kavalski, 2022:7).

The geopolitical conflicts between the great powers are captured by the Singaporean Prime Minister's observation. According to him, Southeast Asian countries, including Singapore, are especially concerned, as they live at the intersection of the interests of various major powers and must avoid being caught in the middle or forced into invidious choices (Lee Hsien Loong, 2020:10). As a result, areas of the world, particularly Africa, are at the center of a geopolitical conflict that is becoming more intense and will put their ability to influence strategic contestation between the major powers and their diplomatic abilities to the test (Beeson, 2022:2). Africa will undoubtedly be directly impacted and put to the test as a region of the world that once again finds itself in the midst of a quickly shifting geopolitical landscape, given its lack of agency in international relations.

There is no better way to explain the current world order than China's National Defense in the New Era, which states that:

> International strategic competition is on the rise. The US has adjusted its national security and defense strategies, and adopted unilateral policies. It has provoked and intensified competition among major countries, significantly increased its defense expenditure, pushed for additional capacity in nuclear, outer space, cyber and missile defense, and undermined global strategic stability. NATO has continued its enlargement, stepped up military deployment in Central and Eastern Europe, and conducted frequent military exercises. Russia is strengthening its nuclear and non-nuclear capabilities for strategic containment, and striving to safeguard its strategic security space and interests. The European Union (EU) is accelerating its security and defense integration to be more independent in its own security. (The State Council Information Office of the People's Republic of China, 2019:3)

These words are echoed by the United States, which has consistently argued that China "challenges the rules-based international order" and is the "only competitor with both the intent to reshape the international order and, increasingly, the economic, diplomatic, military, and technological power to advance that objective" (The White House, 2022b:8). Further, the United States argues that China sees itself as the leader of the Global South and developing countries and uses these countries "as an important arena to challenge the rules-based international order, advance its own narrow commercial and geopolitical interests, undermine transparency and openness, and weaken U.S. relations with African peoples and governments" (The White House, 2022a:3). On the other hand, the United States is not innocent; its political and economic interference on the continent is well documented and has a destabilizing effect. Its interference in Libya has left the country ungovernable, and it has also been directly or indirectly involved in current conflicts in Niger and Sudan. Additionally, the structural adjustment policies that were instituted at its instigation have had a destabilizing effect on the continent (Mills, 2021:342). Thus, Africa has often found itself at the epicenter of global rivalry and a testing ground for governance models.

The accusations leveled against China are not without foundation either. China is creating alternative institutions and programs that create a safe haven and remain attractive to African authoritarian leaders, who view democracy as an impediment to development (Nhliziyo, 2023:8). For example, China's no strings attached approach to development financing in Africa allows authoritarian regimes to partially and, in some cases, totally circumvent the accountability and governance requirements set by Western countries and financial institutions, which are intended to improve governance, transparency, and openness, all of which are seen as essential for Africa's development (Hodzi, 2020:198; Nhliziyo, 2023:1). For instance, after years of negotiating with the Bretton Woods twins, the World Bank, and the International Monetary Fund, the China Export Import Bank gave financing to Angola without attaching political or economic reforms, enabling President Eduardo dos Santos to escape conditions that had been attached to International Monetary Fund development finance. At the same time, the willingness of Beijing to provide military and economic development assistance and loans to Zimbabwe enabled Mugabe to evade European Union and US economic sanctions.

Even coup leaders in Guinea signed US$7 billion in bauxite mining and oil exploration deals with China, despite being under African Union, Economic Community of West African States, and European Union sanctions (Hodzi, 2020:198) (see also Aaron Rwodzi's analysis on coups d'etat and democratic backsliding in Africa in Chap. 19 of this book). China is also using "palace diplomacy" through the building of parliaments and presidential palaces to lure African leaders into agreeing to the exploitation of natural resources in their own backyards. Most importantly, China using infrastructure, aid, and other instruments is exporting its political system there and leadership style, creating a huge burden where the principles of democracy are now seen as fallacious and anti-progressive in the development of the continent (Batsani-Ncube, 2022:883; Nhliziyo, 2023:1).

Why African Agency Is Important

In a changing global environment where African countries find themselves in a precarious position to choose between competing powers—not themselves—how do African countries find common agency and exercise it when they have been predominantly sidelined in contributing substantively to the discussions about Africa, its people, and the international agenda? In this context, calls to increase African agency in the changing global order have gained prominence. It is a common cause that African voices, perspectives, and goals have been historically marginalized. Against the backdrop of this historic marginalization, African agency is viewed as being part of global conversations and having a "seat at the table" (Staeger, 2023a:4). Thus, African agency will enable the continent to move past relationships shaped by colonialism and imperialism, which it is currently struggling with. African agency will enable postcolonial Africa to make its own free choices on the world stage, which has not been seen before (Staden, 2023:1).

Agency is evaluated as the ability of African political elites, on behalf of their nations, to act in order to change outcomes or rules (Lala, 2020:1). Chipaike and Mataruse (2018:1) define African agency in international relations as African actors' ability to negotiate and bargain with external actors in a manner that benefits Africans themselves. African agency can be further taken to incorporate African initiatives taken by Africans to improve their socioeconomic well-being as well as project a posture of power and self-help in international engagements. Thus, it is a self-reflective and self-benefiting social action (Chipaike & Mataruse, 2018:1). In defining African agency, emphasis is placed on the ability to project and leverage interests in relation to positions; access to bilateral and multilateral platforms that operate based on a Western-centric canon; the historical impact of structural constraints compounding from slavery, colonialism, liberation, and the postcolonial environment; and allowing the core of one's philosophical and practical being to find expression (Muresan, 2022:568).

The preceding literature showing Africa as a site of global competition highlights perceptions, especially in the Global North, of passivity, impotency, and lack of agency in African states, which is not always the case. African political elites have exerted some agency in their engagements with traditional (and emerging) hegemonists (Mohan & Lampert, 2013:92). African nations including Sierra Leone, Tanzania, and Zambia have canceled and renegotiated infrastructure construction contracts; this is an indication of their agency and an effort to redefine their nations' relations with China. Africa gains more clout on the international scene and demonstrates its agency in (re)negotiating its place there, thanks to the African Union's nonalignment stance toward Russia and Ukraine and the solution that was subsequently put forth.

Precisely, President Julius Maada Bio canceled an airport construction deal backed by Chinese loans in Sierra Leone. In the same manner, President John Magufuli of Tanzania suspended and renegotiated the US$10 billion Bagamoyo Port project agreed by his predecessor, Jakaya Kikwete, arguing that conditions set by the investor were tantamount to mortgaging Tanzania to China (Hodzi, 2020:908). President Hakainde Hichilema canceled $1.6 billion in yet-to-be-disbursed Chinese loans from China Exim Bank and Industrial Commercial Bank of China to help manage its debt overhang (Nyathi, 2022:1) and also canceled a building contract given to General Electric Co. and Power Building Corp. of China because the project to build a 2400-megawatt power station on the Zambezi River is too expensive and failed to follow proper procurement procedures (Okafor, 2023:1). Both projects were agreed upon by his predecessor, Edgar Lungu. Through this, President Julius Maada Bio, President John Magufuli, and President Hakainde Hichilema were able to exert agency by challenging what has been regarded as Chinese influence in their countries. Thus, the reassertion of an African agency canceling or renegotiating a deal at a time when competition between the United States and China for influence in Africa is on the increase is not possibly the surest way to gain the support of the United States but is to get the best deal out of China, which does not want to cede its geopolitical footprint to the United States (Hodzi, 2020:908).

As noted above, African agency can be further understood as African initiatives taken by Africans to improve their socioeconomic well-being (Mohan & Lampert, 2013:92). These initiatives are specifically driven by leaders and find official expression in the nascent Agenda 2063, themed The Future We Want for Africa. This is an endogenous, shared strategic framework for inclusive growth and sustainable development for Africa's transformation. It is also a continuation of the Pan-African drive for self-determination, freedom, progress, and collective prosperity (African Union, 2015:1). Agenda 2063 seeks to deliver on a set of seven aspirations, each with its own set of goals, which, if achieved, will move Africa closer to achieving its vision for the year 2063. These seven aspirations reflect Africa's desire for shared prosperity and well-being, for unity and integration, for a continent of free citizens and expanded horizons where the full potential of women and youth is realized, and for freedom from fear, disease, and want (African Union, 2015:25).

The aspirations of Agenda 2063 include a prosperous Africa based on inclusive growth and sustainable development; an integrated continent, politically united and based on the ideals of Pan-Africanism and the vision of Africa's renaissance; an Africa of good governance, democracy, respect for human rights, justice, and the rule of law; a peaceful and secure Africa; an Africa with a strong cultural identity, common heritage, shared values, and ethics; an Africa whose development is people-driven, relying on the potential of African people, especially its women and youth, and caring for children; and Africa as a strong, united, resilient, and influential global player and partner (African Union, 2015:25). The significance of Africa as an interconnected continent freeing itself from its colonially inherited borders, relative material paucity, and economic underdevelopment is reflected in these goals. It is a revolutionary project with an emphasis on African politics and economy (Staeger, 2023b:502).

Despite its lofty aspirations, the regional body has no corresponding leadership to execute the plans. To this end, President William Ruto of Kenya has asked his peers to cede trade and security powers to the African Union as part of the reforms needed to make the body work. President William Ruto has argued that "to ensure that the African Union performs at the level of its aspirations, it will be necessary to make sure that it empowers itself with sufficient capacity. Otherwise, African Solutions, Agenda 2063, the Africa Continental Free Trade Area, and the Young, Clean, Green Continent of the Future will never be a reality" (Mutambo, 2023:1). Ruto's averments can be taken to mean that it is increasingly important for Africa to exercise its agency to drive the vectors of sustainable development on the continent.

Africa finds itself more entrapped between the competing interests of the great powers as international geopolitical competition heats up. As explained by Charles Mutasa in Chap. 15 of this book, one example of this is the continuing conflict in Ukraine. African nations have mostly adopted ambiguous attitudes and have been unwilling to take sides in the crisis. They haven't denounced Russia's actions or given Ukraine any kind of military support. This hesitation makes sense. Great powers have traditionally taken advantage of Africa, and many African nations are reluctant to remain mere props in a bigger geopolitical scheme. Concerns regarding the war's possible effects on their own economies—specifically, the availability of wheat, grains, and fertilizer—also exist. MackySall, the President of Senegal and Chair of the African Union Assembly in 2022, said on behalf of the African Union at the UN General Assembly in September 2022 that Africa "does not want to be the breeding ground of a new Cold War, but rather a pole of stability and opportunity open to all its partners, on a mutually beneficial basis" (African Union, 2022:1). In this context, it is not surprising that the African Union (AU) has sought to play a constructive role in mediating the conflict. The AU has presented a peace plan that calls for a ceasefire, the withdrawal of Russian troops, and the resumption of negotiations. The AU has also called for the lifting of sanctions against Russia.

The AU's peace plan is a significant step forward. It is the first major peace initiative to be put forward by an African organization. The plan is also significant because it reflects the AU's growing desire to play a more active role in global governance. In this context, the UN Office of the Special Adviser on Africa stated that Africa's increasing ability to speak with one voice on global issues is one of the recognized hallmarks of its growing transformation and strengths as a global player. Africa is on an upward trend and seeks mutually beneficial relations with other regions and continents (UN Office of the Special Adviser on Africa, not dated, cited in Adeoye, 2020:5). This also provides momentum to the African Union, which has long advocated for UN Security Council reform, with the peace plan serving as a first step in that direction. It also shows how Africa is becoming more and more significant to the world economy. In addition to being a significant producer of gas and oil, Africa is a market for goods and services that is expanding quickly. African nations are therefore making a greater effort to actively influence the world system. The peace plan of the AU is not without its problems and shortcomings.

The idea has been rejected by Russia thus far, and it is not certain if the other parties involved in the conflict will accept it. Furthermore, the African Union, the champions of the peace plan, has come under fire for its naiveté in not finding a solution to the continent's ongoing security problems. For instance, the governing body has not demonstrated the leadership required—or at least expected of it—to put an end to the violence in the Democratic Republic of the Congo, Sudan, Ethiopia, and other crises sweeping the continent. Therefore, detractors argue that because the continental organization is unable to resolve its immediate internal issues, it is also incapable of resolving global issues. As such, it lacks moral capacity and has no legitimacy to mediate in the Russia-Ukraine war (York, 2023:1; Balogun & Mwaba, 2023:277). However, the AU's initiative is a welcome step, and it is a sign that Africa is determined to play a constructive role in resolving the conflict in Ukraine.

Asserting African Agency

It is becoming increasingly important for Africa to deploy its own agency to shape its own destiny. The rising geopolitical tensions between the United States, China, and the rising powers, otherwise known as the emerging and developing economies, which are gradually increasing their footprints on the continent, put Africa in a precarious position (Mills, 2021:52). As such, the continent should be careful not to become a pawn in the broader geopolitical games of the United States, China, and the emerging powers. Instead, Africa must use its strategic position and its resource endowments to its advantage and demand a seat at the table when global decisions are being made to respond to global storms, including climate imperialism, debt colonialism, the global health crisis (global health crisis is fully discussed in Part III of this book), global security, and the US-China geopolitical wars, that threaten Africa's development aspirations, particularly those contained in the ambitious Agenda 2063 and the goals contained in the global development initiative, otherwise known as Sustainable Development Goals.

This can be done by developing policy maturity punctuated with diplomatic adeptness, political leadership, strong political will, and policy capacity in order to effectively engage with the United States and China. This is a challenging task in which Africa must be prepared to take risks and make difficult choices in order to protect its own interests. The availability of a unified negotiation policy, the common African position, and a strategic focus by analyzing the strategic objectives of China, the United States, and the emerging economies, opportunities, and threats arising from their entry, however, are the ultimate and binding issue to maximize their bargaining power (Moyo et al., 2020:97; Adeoye, 2020:3). But as long as the continent is still so divided, it is very doubtful that Africa will act or speak in unanimity on foreign policy issues; thus, the continent will remain marginalized (Adeoye, 2020:3).

In this context, the Association of Southeast Asian Nations (ASEAN) offers Africa lessons in agency in international relations and in handling US-China relations as well as the developing and emerging economies for the benefit of their economies. It is one region already charting a peaceful and prosperous path through this great competition era, showcasing considerable strategic autonomy and initiative, and exhibiting leadership in the reconstruction of regional order (Mahbubani, 2023:1). Zhang (2023:3) opines that ASEAN has maintained unity and centrality and convinced major powers to adjust their own regional strategies in response to its security and development concerns, highlighting ASEAN's resilience and strategic initiative. This has been absent in Africa, which is fragmented; even regional economic cooperation lacks the policy, institutional, and political capacity to engage with global powers in a manner that can support their development needs and has been left divided rather than unified (Staeger, 2023b:502). On certain global issues, such as Taiwan, the origins of COVID-19, the ongoing Israeli-Palestinian conflict, and the Russia-Ukraine war, it is more difficult for the region to form a unified voice. In contrast, in the face of growing geopolitical contestations, ASEAN has reconstructed strategic confidence and independence (Zhang, 2023:3).

In this chapter, I contend that African nations have a rare chance to advance an agenda that considers the interests of the big powers—the competition between the United States and China. Taking advantage of the opportunity afforded by China, the United States, and emerging powers competing, with each seeking to increase their footprint on the continent, Africa and the African Union in particular can leverage their cooperation with these major competing powers to meet their own development needs, avoiding being used as pawns by either major power (Moyo et al., 2020:97). In clearer terms, Moyo (2020:568) cautions that the continental body must develop stamina and be savvier in its negotiations and interactions with competing global powers. He makes the case that African development actors ought to think about defusing rival powers on the continent. They can, for example, use their relationship with China to persuade Western powers to be more willing to finance riskier infrastructure projects and capitalize on the concerns of traditional development actors on the continent by seeking favorable deals and contracts from them in exchange for contracts in both physical and digital infrastructure development, which is intended to improve the prospects for the continent's development.

In this context, African countries should continue engaging emerging and developing powers on the global sphere, including Turkey, Qatar, Brazil, India, Russia, Saudi Arabia, Japan, the EU member countries, and the United Kingdom, among others. This will boost the continent's prospects of balancing between the United States and China in this era of great competition. These will act as a third hedge against uncertainties brought about by US-China escalating competition (Zhang, 2023:13). For instance, Turkey mimics China in its engagement with Africa. It engages Africa through the Turkish Co-operation Agency (TIKA), which is operational in 54 African countries. TIKA's role on the continent is to offer alternatives to traditional sources of development assistance. Mills (2021:52) rightly puts it that what Africa needs today is not international financial institutions and their conditional credits that produce dependency; instead of this vicious circle, it is necessary to support the African people to establish their own social, economic, and institutional infrastructure that will enable them to use and manage their own resources.

In the context of an unstable geopolitical environment, other leading developing economies, like India, can be a valuable ally for Africa (Ferede, 2019:86). Additionally, African countries should leverage the contemporary global governance landscape that is rapidly changing with the acceleration of South-South cooperation (Ferede, 2019:86). The changing landscape is characterized by organizational pluralism and the proliferation of South-South multilateralism such as BRICS

(Brazil, Russia, India, China, and South Africa), IBSA (India, Brazil, and South Africa), BASIC (Brazil, South Africa, India, and China), NICs (newly industrializing countries), NIEs (newly industrialized economies), LICs (low-income countries), or MICs (middle-income countries) and the formation of institutions such as the New Development Bank (Ferede, 2019:86). Such institutions rival the traditional powerful hegemonic institutions, including the World Bank, the International Monetary Fund, and the groups of 8 and 20. For the avoidance of doubt, these traditional Eurocentric institutions have continually subordinated the role of Africa in global governance and have contributed to its underdevelopment. They create an unfavorable climate for African countries to develop. They control global goods such as development finance and are unwilling to distribute them fairly to developing countries (Moyo, 2020:75).

The proliferation of South-South multilateralism and organizational pluralism reflects a rising spirit of anti-imperialism in Africa that African agency must tap into—particularly in the age of geo-economic confrontations where the United States, China, and emerging powers seek to grow their global strategic footprints. However, African countries must also be cautious not to be taken advantage of and caught in the web of China's economic and global ambitions. China, which is a member of the BRICS countries, is an economic heavyweight that desires to be seen as the leader of the Global South. To achieve this, it creates institutions and processes that circumvent or exclude those created by the United States (Moyo, 2020:75). Therefore, I contend that African nations need to exercise caution and express their agency in order to avoid being taken advantage of by China, the United States, and other expanding economies that have an increasing interest in the continent.

The US National Security Strategy, Sub-Saharan Security Strategy, and China's Africa Strategy, titled China and Africa in the New Era: A Partnership of Equals, make it evident that both China and the United States attach great importance and strategic value to Africa. Therefore, it is the responsibility of African nations to attach this strategic significance to influencing rival powers' perceptions of the continent and obtaining the best results for its security and development needs. Furthermore, how Africa weathers these global storms will likely influence international relations and help to shape a more equitable and just world order.

Conclusion

This chapter discussed the increasing importance of African agency in the context of a changing and complex global order. The conclusion of this chapter is that while Africa has become a site of global competition, African political leaders have exerted some agency in their engagements with traditional (and emerging) hegemonists. The cancellation and renegotiation of infrastructure construction deals by African countries such as Sierra Leone, Tanzania, and Zambia is indicative of their agency and attempt to reshape their countries' relations with global powers. The

African Union's peace plan is significant because it demonstrates the organization's commitment to playing a more active role in global governance. Given the above discussion, to change the new relationship into a win-win partnership, African agency that is integrated into a larger development strategy and institutional and leadership capability for strategic engagement are required.

References

Adeoye, B. (2020). Common African positions on global issues. *ISS Africa Report, 2020*(30), 1–12. http://issafrica.s3.amazonaws.com/site/uploads/ar-30-2.pdf

African Union. (2015). Background note: Agenda 2063. *African Union*. Accessed on July 4, 2023. Available from https://au.int/sites/default/files/documents/33126-doc-01_background_note.pdf

African Union. (2022, September 20). *77th Session of the United Nations General Assembly address by H.E. Macky Sall, President of the Republic of Senegal, current Chairman of the African Union*. https://au.int/en/speeches/20220920/77th-session-united-nations-general-assembly-address-he-macky-sall

Ajayi, R., & Oshewolo, S. (2020). African development strategies: Whither NEPAD?. *The Palgrave handbook of African political economy* (pp. 503–517). https://www.academia.edu/download/64118388/The%20Palgrave%20Handbook%20of%20African%20Political%20Economy-2020.pdf#page=516.

Allison, G., Resar, A., & Barbesino, K. (2022). The great diplomatic rivalry: China vs the U.S. *Belfer center for science and international affairs*. https://www.belfercenter.org/sites/default/files/files/publication/GreatDiplomaticRivalry_ChinavsUS_vF_220801.pdf

Balogun, E., & Mwaba, A. K. (2023). African Union reform: Challenges and opportunities. *The Palgrave handbook of diplomatic reform and innovation* (pp. 277–294). https://link.springer.com/chapter/10.1007/978-3-031-10971-3_13

Batsani-Ncube, I. (2022). Whose building? Tracing the politics of the Chinese government-funded parliament building in Lesotho. *Journal of Southern African Studies, 48*(5), 883–900. Whose Building? Tracing the Politics of the Chinese Government-Funded Parliament Building in Lesotho (tandfonline.com)

Beeson, M. (2022). Decentered? ASEAN's struggle to accommodate great power competition. *Global Studies Quarterly, 2*(1), ksab044. https://academic.oup.com/isagsq/article-pdf/doi/10.1093/isagsq/ksab044/42255755/ksab044.pdf

Blair, T. (2001). Full text: Tony Blair's speech (Part One). *The Guardian*. October 2. Accessed on July 4, 2023. Available from https://www.theguardian.com/politics/2001/oct/02/labourconference.labour6

Brautigam, D. (2011). *The dragon's gift: The real story of China in Africa*. OUP Oxford. https://www.bpastudies.org/index.php/bpastudies/article/download/130/242

Brown, K., & Chun, Z. (2009). *China in Africa-preparing for the next forum for China Africa cooperation*. China in Africa - Preparing for the Next Forum for China Africa Cooperation | Policy Commons

Carbone, M. (2023). When elephants fight, it is the grass that suffers: The Russo-Ukrainian conflict and the decentring-recentring conundrum in EU-Africa relations. *Journal of European Integration, 45*(3), 539–557. https://www.tandfonline.com/doi/pdf/10.1080/07036337.2023.2190108

Chipaike, R., & Mataruse, K. H. (2018). The question of African agency in international relations. *Cogent Social Sciences, 4*(1), 1487257. https://www.tandfonline.com/doi/pdf/10.1080/23311886.2018.1487257

Falola, T. (2022). Diplomacy and politics. *The Palgrave handbook of Africa and the changing global order* (pp. 1049–1064). https://link.springer.com/chapter/10.1007/978-3-030-77481-3_51

Ferede, W. (2019). The reconfiguration of the global political economy and the future of Africa. *Journal of Sustainable Development in Africa, 21*(1), 85–94. https://jsd-africa.com/Jsda/2019%20V21No1%20Spring/PDF/The%20Reconfiguration%20of%20the%20Global%20Political%20Economy_Wuhibegezer%20%20%20Ferede-revised.pdf

Fisher-Onar, N., & Kavalski, E. (2022). From trans-Atlantic order to Afro-Eur-Asian worlds? Reimagining international relations as interlocking regional worlds. *Global Studies Quarterly, 2*(4), ksac080. https://academic.oup.com/isagsq/article-pdf/doi/10.1093/isagsq/ksac080/48478381/ksac080.pdf

Hodzi, O. (2020). African political elites and the making (s) of the China model in Africa. *Politics & Policy, 48*(5), 887–907. https://onlinelibrary.wiley.com/doi/pdfdirect/10.1111/polp.12380

Lala, F. (2020). Africa in the changing global order: Does African agency matter in global politics? *The changing global order: Challenges and prospects* (pp. 127–143). https://link.springer.com/chapter/10.1007/978-3-030-21603-0_7

Loong, L. H. (2020). The endangered Asian Century. *Foreign Aff., 99*, p. 52. June 4. Accessed on July 4, 2023. Available from https://www.foreignaffairs.com/articles/asia/2020-06-04/lee-hsien-loong-endangered-asian-century

Mahbubani, K. (2023). Asia's third way: How ASEAN survives-and thrives-amid great-power competition. *Foreign Affairs, 102*, 130. https://heinonline.org/hol-cgi-bin/get_pdf.cgi?handle=hein.journals/fora102&section=32&casa_token=DBQymLyYLf4AAAAA:sj_jd2MM5mMfsStS-vCHPOl9vD4_jv2YKzLpW4t9ay7NGB31_C43DgT6j6iRna0rEZwkm0wi3vA

McCurry, J. (2021). US and China publicly rebuke each other in first major talks of Biden era. *The Guardian, 19*. March 19. Accessed on June 23, 2023. Available from https://www.theguardian.com/world/2021/mar/19/us-china-talks-alaska-biden-blinken-sullivan-wang

Mills, G. (2021). *Expensive poverty: Why aid fails and how it can work*. Pan Macmillan South Africa.

Mohan, G., & Lampert, B. (2013). Negotiating china: Reinserting African agency into china–Africa relations. *African Affairs, 112*(446), 92–110. https://academic.oup.com/afraf/article-pdf/112/446/92/28985/ads065.pdf

Moyo, D. (2009). *Dead aid: Why aid is not working and how there is a better way for Africa*. Macmillan. https://media-1.carnegiecouncil.org/import/studio/Dead_Aid.pdf

Moyo, D. (2012). *Winner take all: China's race for resources and what it means for the world*. Basic Books (AZ). https://www.bing.com/ck/a?!&&p=1772e7acf138c055JmltdHM9MTcwNjU3MjgwMCZpZ3VpZD0zMjcxNTA1Ny04MTI1LTZiYWYtMjNkZC00MWQ2ODBhZjZhNGEmaW5zaWQ9NTE4OA&ptn=3&ver=2&hsh=3&fclid=32715057-8125-6baf-23dd-41d680af6a4a&psq=Moyo%2c+D.%2c+2012.+Winner+take+all%3a+China%27s+race+for+resources+and+what+it+means+for+the+world.+Basic+Books+(AZ).&u=a1aHR0cHM6Ly9vbmxpbmVsaWJyYXJ5LndpbGV5LmNvbS9kb2kvcGRmLzEwLjEwM-DIvamlkLjI4ODk&ntb=1

Moyo, G. (2020). China's development finance to Africa and the spectre of debt distress. *The Palgrave handbook of African political economy* (pp. 557–572). https://link.springer.com/chapter/10.1007/978-3-030-38922-2_30

Moyo, G. (2021). *African agency, finance and developmental states*. Palgrave Macmillan. https://link.springer.com/content/pdf/10.1007/978-3-030-72412-2.pdf

Moyo, G. (2024). *Africa in the global economy: Capital flight, enablers, and decolonial responses*. Springer Nature. Africa in the Global Economy: Capital Flight, Enablers, and Decolonial Responses | SpringerLink

Moyo, G., Nhliziyo, M., & Fayayo, R. (2020). The entanglement of Zimbabwe in the US-China geoeconomic frictions: Defining winners and losers. *iBusiness, 12*(3), 81–102. https://www.scirp.org/journal/paperinformation.aspx?paperid=102638

Muresan, A. (2022). Seeking African agency in global clubs. *The Palgrave handbook of Africa and the changing global order* (pp. 567–582). https://link.springer.com/book/10.1007/978-3-030-77481-3

Mutambo, A. (2023). Ruto asks peers to 'donate' powers to African Union. *The East African*. June 08. Accessed on July 4, 2023. Available from https://www.theeastafrican.co.ke/tea/news/east-africa/ruto-calls-for-urgent-reforms-in-the-african-union-4262898

Nhliziyo, M. (2023). *The emergence of the Chinese political and economic model: Potential and risks for democracy in Africa*. A paper presented on Africa Drive for Democracy Conference, 19-21 July 2023, MS Training Centre for Development Cooperation Arusha, Tanzania.

Nyathi, K. (2022). Zambia cancels $1.6b loans from Chinese banks. *The East African*. August 09. Accessed on June 23, 2023. Available from https://www.theeastafrican.co.ke/tea/business/zambia-cancels-1-6b-loans-from-chinese-banks%2D%2D3908408

Okafor, C. (2023). Zambia cancels $5 billion project with China, see why. *Business Insider Africa*. June 15. Accessed on July 1, 2023. Available from https://africa.businessinsider.com/local/markets/zambia-cancels-dollar5-billion-project-with-china-see-why/w0ffvyd

Oloruntoba, S. O., & Falola, T. (2020). The political economy of Africa: Connecting the past to the present and future of development in Africa. *The Palgrave handbook of African political economy* (pp. 1–28). https://www.academia.edu/download/64118388/The%20Palgrave%20Handbook%20of%20African%20Political%20Economy-2020.pdf#page=30.

Pharatlhatlhe, K., & Vanheukelom, J. (2019). Financing the African Union: On mindsets and money. *Brussels: European Centre for Development Policy Management (= Discussion Paper 240)*. The European Centre for Development Policy Management. Accessed on July 1, 2023. Available from https://ecdpm.org/application/files/7216/6074/7083/DP240-Financing-the-African-Union-on-mindsets-and-money.pdf

Soyinka, W. (2014) *Of Africa*. New Haven, CT: Yale University Press.

Staden, V. S. (2023, December 2019). *The incredible shrinking Africa-China relationship*. https://chinaglobalsouth.com/analysis/the-incredible-shrinking-africa-china-relationship/

Staeger, U. (2023a). The war in Ukraine, the African Union, and African Agency. *African Affairs, 122*, adad026. https://academic.oup.com/afraf/advance-article-pdf/doi/10.1093/afraf/adad026/52829566/adad026.pdf

Staeger, U. (2023b). Resource mobilization in security partnerships: Explaining cooperation and coercion in the EU's partnership with the African Union. *Cooperation and Conflict, 58*, 00108367221147785. https://journals.sagepub.com/doi/pdf/10.1177/00108367221147785

The Economist. (2000). Hopeless *Africa. The Economist*. May 11. Accessed on July 1, 2023. Available from https://www.economist.com/leaders/2000/05/11/hopeless-africa

The State Council Information Office of the People's Republic of China. (2019). *China's National Defence in the New Era*. Foreign Languages Press. https://www.airuniversity.af.edu/Portals/10/CASI/documents/Translations/2019-07%20PRC%20White%20Paper%20on%20National%20Defense%20in%20the%20New%20Era.pdf?ver=akpbGkO5ogbDPPbflQkb5A%3D%3D

The White House. (2022a). *U.S. strategy toward sub-Saharan Africa*. The White House. https://www.whitehouse.gov/wp-content/uploads/2022/08/U.S.-Strategy-Toward-Sub-Saharan-Africa-FINAL.pdf

The White House. (2022b). *National security strategy*. The White House. https://www.whitehouse.gov/wp-content/uploads/2022/10/Biden-Harris-Administrations-National-Security-Strategy-10.2022.pdf

York, G. (2023). African peace mission flounders in bid for Russian and Ukrainian support. *Globe & Mail (Toronto, Canada)* (pp. A4–A4). https://go.gale.com/ps/i.do?id=GALE%7CA753584250&sid=googleScholar&v=2.1&it=r&linkaccess=abs&issn=03190714&p=AONE&sw=w

Zhang, J. (2023). Rebuilding strategic autonomy: ASEAN's response to US–China strategic competition. *China International Strategy Review, 5*, 73–89. https://link.springer.com/article/10.1007/s42533-023-00128-3

Mbongeni Nhliziyo holds a Master of Science Degree in Public Policy and Development Management from Lupane State University and is currently a lecturer in the Department of

Development Studies at Lupane State University. He has previously lectured at Zimbabwe Open University. Mbongeni is a research fellow at the Public Policy and Research Institute of Zimbabwe, a leading research organisation on democracy, governance, and policy advocacy in Zimbabwe. His research and teaching interests are in China-Africa relations, public policy, development planni g, and Africa's development. Nhliziyo has published peer-reviewed articles in accredited academic journals.

The manufacturer's authorised representative in the EU is Springer Nature Customer Service Centre GmbH, Europaplatz 3, 69115 Heidelberg, Germany. If you have any concerns regarding our products, please contact ProductSafety@springernature.com

Printed and bound by CPI Group (UK) Ltd, Croydon, CR0 4YY
30/09/2026
02225589-0015